Market Economics
and Political Change

To Gerardo,
Looking forward to
learning from each other.
cheers,
Jim
2/06

Market Economics and Political Change

Comparing China and Mexico

edited by
JUAN D. LINDAU
and
TIMOTHY CHEEK

ROWMAN & LITTLEFIELD PUBLISHERS, INC.
Lanham • Boulder • New York • Oxford

ROWMAN & LITTLEFIELD PUBLISHERS, INC.

Published in the United States of America
by Rowman & Littlefield Publishers, Inc.
4720 Boston Way, Lanham, Maryland 20706

12 Hid's Copse Road
Cumnor Hill, Oxford OX2 9JJ, England

British Library Cataloguing in Publication Information Available

Library of Congress Cataloging-in-Publication Data

Market economics and political change : comparing China and Mexico /
    edited by Juan D. Lindau and Timothy Cheek.
        p.   cm.
    Includes bibliographical references and index.
    ISBN 0–8476–8732–5 (alk. paper). — ISBN 0–8476–8733–3 (pbk. :
alk. paper)
      1. China—Economic policy—1976–   2. China—Economic
conditions—1976–   3. Mexico–Economic policy—1970–   4. Mexico—
Economic conditions   1982–   5. Democracy—China.   6. Democracy—
Mexico.   I. Lindau, Juan David.   II. Cheek, Timothy.
HC427.92.M388   1998
338.951—dc21   98–10415
                                                                                 CIP

ISBN 0–8476–8732–5 (cloth : alk. paper)
ISBN 0–8476–8733–3 (pbk. : alk. paper)

Printed in the United States of America

♾ ™ The paper used in this publication meets the minimum requirements of
American National Standard for Information Sciences—Permanence of Paper
for Printed Library Materials, ANSI Z39.48–1984.

Contents

Preface

The project that led to this book stems from our specialist training and a decade of liberal arts teaching. We have learned that the interdisciplinary use of history and political science provides an especially rich analysis of important theoretical and practical questions. This book seeks to apply the approaches of these two disciplines to the cases of Mexico and China and to the theoretical question of democratization. We have benefitted from the contributions of our colleagues—teaching at research universities as well as colleges—who share this view.

This book is a collective effort going back to 1993. Juan Lindau organized a colloquium, "Market Economics and Political Change: Mexico and the People's Republic of China," which was held at The Colorado College in March 1994. Most of the contributors to this book participated in the colloquium, and several faculty from The Colorado College offered valuable and challenging suggestions on the project then and since. In the preparation of the book we have consistently benefitted from the encouragement and editorial strictures of Susan McEachern. We are grateful, too, to those colleagues who took the time to comment on the comparative project, introduction, and other substantial sections of the book: Tim Brook, Timothy Fuller, Mark S. Johnson, Bernardo Mabire, Lorenzo Meyer, David A. Kelly, David Ownby, Patricia Stranahan, Jeffrey N. Wasserstrom, and Mark Selden. We would also like to thank Jane Stark and Jane Newberry, who provided invaluable secretarial support.

Funding for this project, beginning with the 1994 North American Studies Colloquium at Colorado College, was generously provided by the William and Flora Hewlett Foundation, The Colorado College, and the Gaylord Endowment for Pacific Area Studies.

Juan Lindau and Timothy Cheek
Colorado Springs

Part I
THEORETICAL CONTEXT

1

Market Liberalization and Democratization: The Case for Comparative Contextual Analysis

Timothy Cheek and Juan D. Lindau

Does market liberalization promote democracy? Both scholars and pundits have long tended to answer this question affirmatively.[1] It has been the de facto assumption undergirding U.S. foreign policy. A market economy, in this view, disperses power and decisionmaking, reducing the state's power.[2] Scholars of democratization, in their search for democratizing influences and forces, have focused on non-state factors, especially the emergence of a civil society. In the contemporary literature, civil society has been increasingly de-

1. A notable, oft-cited book expounding this view in the modernization literature was W. W. Rostow, *The Stages of Economic Growth: A Non-Communist Manifesto* (Cambridge: Cambridge University Press, 1960). This conception was also ubiquitous during the debate over the North American Free Trade Agreement, although it has also been used as a more general argument for free trade. For example, see William A. Orme, "NAFTA: Myths versus Facts," *Foreign Affairs* 72, no. 5 (Nov./Dec. 1993): 2–12, for a discussion of this conception. Another exposition of this argument can be found in Maria Lorena Cook, Kevin J. Middlebrook, and Juan Molinar Horcasitas, "Introducción," in *Las dimensiones políticas de la reestructuración económica*, ed. Maria Lorena Cook, Kevin J. Middlebrook, and Juan Molinar Horcasitas (México, D.F.: Cal y Arena, 1996), 39–105.

2. For the role of an autonomous bourgeoisie in facilitating the emergence of democracy, see Samuel Huntington, "Will More Countries Become Democratic?" *Political Science Quarterly* 99, no. 2 (Summer 1984): 193–218, esp. 204.

3

fined as the presence of free, autonomous groups and organizations capable of influencing public policy. These associations reclaim public spaces from the state, empowering the society and encouraging participation, and thus liberal democracy.[3] We agree that liberal democracy is characterized by the rule of law, non-electoral mechanisms for influencing government policy, restraints on the extent of state power, a civil society, and a political culture that sustains these elements.

The relationship between market economics and democratization, however, is much more complex and contradictory. The studies in this volume, while not taking a uniform view of the question, are well summarized by David Finley in the final chapter:

> Without market liberalization, no democracy. With market liberalism, *maybe* democracy—depending on three conditions: liberty preserved by constitutional and political culture, prosperity credibly attributable to the market economy, and the absence of powerful social coalitions mobilized to suppress democracy.

These three conditions mediate the relationship between market economics and democratization. Consequently, economic reform can lead, especially over the short term, to several outcomes, including political liberalization, reassertions of authoritarianism, and fluid, disjunctive environments marked by the presence of both elements[4]

---

3. Despite criticisms this view holds, see Evelyne Huber, Dietrich Rueschemeyer, and John D. Stephens, "The Paradoxes of Contemporary Democracy: Formal, Participatory and Social Democracy," *Comparative Politics* 29, no. 3 (1997): 323–42. They directly link democracy to capitalism. A definition that avoids these problems is provided by Joseph Schumpeter, who argues that contestation and participation define democracy. See Joseph Schumpeter, *Capitalism, Socialism, and Democracy*, 2nd ed. (New York: Harper and Bros., 1947), 269. Other working definitions of democracy rely on structuralist elements, such as electoral systems in the European style that presume stable adversarial political institutions (i.e., two or more legal political parties and reliable one-man, one-vote elections). Haggard and Kaufman stress "the establishment of a pluralistic electoral system" for a functional democracy. See their "Economic Adjustments and the Prospects for Democracy," in *The Politics of Economic Adjustment*, ed. Stephan Haggard and Robert R. Kaufman (Princeton: Princeton University Press, 1992), 319. The non-structuralist approach to democracy stresses that it is a political problem susceptible to political solutions. Friedman holds that the struggle for human rights is "a proven pragmatic instrument that can advance the cause of democratization." See Edward Friedman, "Is Democracy a Universal Ethical Standard?" in *National Identity and Democratic Prospects in Socialist China* (Armonk, N.Y.: M. E. Sharpe, 1995), 235; and Edward Friedman, ed., *The Politics of Democratization: Generalizing the East Asian Experience* (Boulder, Colo.: Westview Press, 1994).

4. A good example for Latin America of this uncertainty is Juan Linz, "The

Comparative Contextual Analysis

This book seeks to explain, through comparative contextual analysis of case studies, the various consequences of market liberalization. Comparative contextual analysis seeks to generate theoretical questions that can be empirically tested in different cultures and can shed light on shared processes at work in disparate circumstances. These comparative questions, however, are generated inductively from a detailed study of the cultural context of specific cases. Comparative contextual analysis is not new, but it does seem somewhat in disfavor among political scientists, comparative sociologists, and historians. "Theorists" tend to view area studies as "mere" empirical work. For their part, area studies scholars frequently dismiss what they view as "empty" theorizing of comparativists.[5] However, without the challenge of explicit, intelligent, and rational theory, analysis runs the risk of antiquarianism, unquestioned assumptions, and a lack of comparative value. We have critiqued Habermas's and others' theories of development on the basis of extended contextual analyses of the societies under study. With the historian's injunction to attempt to do justice to the materials at hand, we have recast Habermasian questions in a way to challenge his assumptions and to direct us in new directions that we

---

Future of an Authoritarian Situation or the Institutionalization of an Authoritarian Regime: The Case of Brazil" in *Authoritarian Brazil*, Alfred Stepan ed. (New Haven: Yale University Press, 1973), 233–254. Authoritarian regimes often view themselves as the sole, true reflection of the nation. See Prasenjit Duara, *Rescuing History from the Nation: Questioning Narratives of Modern China* (Chicago: University of Chicago Press, 1995). Richard Joseph traces another false democratization in the example of post–Cold War African states that held Potemkin elections to lure First World donor dollars. See "Democratization in Africa after 1989: Comparative and Theoretical Perspectives," *Comparative Politics* 29, no. 3 (1997), 363–82.

5. For example, this can be seen in the continuing debate of world revolution nicely brought together in a collection of critical essays edited by Nikki R. Keddie: *Debating Revolutions* (New York: New York University Press, 1995). See, in particular, Jeffrey N. Wasserstrom, "Bringing Culture Back In and Other Caveats: A Critique of Jack Goldstone's Recent Essays on Revolution," and Goldstone's "Analyzing Revolutions and Rebellions: A Reply to Critics," in Keddie, *Debating Revolutions*, 155–199. Most China scholars, for instance, simply ignore Theda Skocpol's *Structure of Revolution: A Comparative Analysis of France, Russia, and China* (Cambridge: Cambridge University Press, 1979) and barely take the time to criticize the extension of her work by her student Jack Goldstone in *Revolution and Rebellion in the Early Modern World* (Berkeley: University of California Press, 1991). The application of less grand theory to the study of the Chinese revolution or recent Chinese history has been piecemeal or procrustean in the fixation and fight over the Habermas version of "civil society" to the history of China since 1700 (see Cheek's chapter).

feel help us understand these societies, their present issues, and likely developments more accurately. Comparative contextual analysis should offer *compelling arguments*, interesting questions, and lines of research about the nature of market reform and political change for the case studies given here and should suggest *helpful methodologies* for extending the study of economic and political change to other areas. Using comparative contextual analysis requires that the link between an emerging capitalist market and a liberal democratic polity be spelled out in specific spheres.

In particular we ask: Just how does market liberalization contribute to the creation of an effective independent judiciary? Previous studies have focused on electoral politics (democratic, free, fair, and binding elections) rather than the balance of powers within a regime. The detailed studies by Lorenzo Meyer and Pitman Potter demonstrate that law and an effective independent judiciary are the "rudder of democracy." These are what China and Mexico still lack for developing something akin to Habermas's "civil society," or what we identify as the underlying value in that model—a humane society. Our studies show that market liberalization does not necessarily lead to the all-important development of an effective, independent, and non-corrupt judiciary. The history of non-constitutional politics and the existence of a large, and largely uncontrolled, security apparatus in Mexico and China add to this problem.

Our second key question is: How exactly does market liberalization contribute to increased citizen participation in the political process? Here, too, the experiences of Mexico and China contradict the habitual explanation of the relationship between market and democracy. The key variable confounding the linkage between the market and a democracy-demanding polity is political culture. Indeed, it has been economic problems in both Mexico and China rather than market liberalization that have promoted increased political participation. In both cases, powerful assumptions in political culture operate as independent variables affecting Habermas's equation of market and democracy. These values include a passive conception of citizenship based on strong family values and the assumption (largely confirmed by recent history) that public order is a tenuous and delicate achievement. The reality of powerful political factionalism and weak judiciaries in both countries only reinforces these values. Attention to the rich context of each country's history shows how market liberalization per se has not, in the short run, directly led to democratic changes in Mexico and China.[6]

---

6. Another example of fruitful comparison is the scholarship on Latin America and Eastern Europe. See Adam Przeworski's *Democracy and the Mar-*

China and Mexico

Both China and Mexico carried out market liberalization in the 1980s while trying to preserve authoritarian political systems. Indeed, authoritarian regimes in both countries survived the democratizing trend sweeping the world in the late 1980s and early 1990s. At the same time, both carried out widespread economic liberalization and market reform. The two countries are the most important alternatives to the path followed elsewhere in the world, including the former Soviet Union and eastern Europe, where political change and reform preceded economic transformation.

In most of Latin America, as well, countries during the 1980s and early 1990s effected democratization before enacting economic reform. The only exception to this pattern, along with Mexico, was Chile. However, unlike Mexico, Chile has a long democratic tradition. The depth of this commitment to democracy in Chile's case was amply demonstrated by the 1988 plebiscite that repudiated the Pinochet regime, despite its substantial macroeconomic successes. No similar, clear-cut commitment to democracy initially emerged in Mexico where the desire for political change among substantial portions of the population coexisted with a widespread and profound fear of altering long-established ruling practices and institutional arrangements. This deep ambivalence about change, grounded in the same concerns, can also be found in China, although the pressure for political reform and democratization are much stronger in Mexico. Paradoxically, as Meyer argues in chapter 5, many of those driven to support democratization and political reform on economic grounds have tended to be opposed to market liberalization and to the regime's neoclassical economic policies. At best, then, the market liberalization carried out by the regime has produced a democratic reaction whose thrust is partially the reversal or attenuation of many of these economic policies.

Neither China nor Mexico meets all the criteria of our definition of democracy. Historically, regular, peaceful contestation and participation have not been a salient characteristic of politics in either country. Neither has historically been marked by a stable adversarial political system or widespread electoral participation. Instead, authoritarianism, characterized by the drive to concentrate and centralize power, has been a much more distinctive element of the two polities. Although contestation and electoral participation are now much higher in Mex-

---

ket: *Political and Economic Reforms in Eastern Europe and Latin America* (New York: Cambridge University Press, 1991) and the stimulating forum edited by Melvin Croan, "Is Latin America the Future of Eastern Europe?" *Problems of Communism* 61, no. 3 (May 1992): 44–57.

ico and indeed qualify Mexico as a nascent democracy according to
these two criteria, other elements, which make the operation of democracy possible, are still absent. The rule of law still does not exist in
either country, and a highly centralized, authoritarian ruling style
characterizes governing in both polities. Both associational activity and
the presence of a civil society, although much stronger in Mexico than
in China, are still suspect. Finally, elements of political culture in both
countries, notably fears of political disorder and concomitant concerns
about the disintegrative effects of political competition, have historically attenuated support for democracy. In Mexico this stemmed from
a "vacant public sphere," which Lindau shows in chapter 7 derived
from a variety of social, cultural, and historical factors. Similarly, China
has had a "directed public sphere" under the Leninist party-state, as
Cheek argues in chapter 8. The open space for the public sphere of civil
society assumed in the Habermas model was thus an inertial swamp in
Mexico and a brick wall of the propaganda system in China.

A weak tradition of democracy in both countries, however, is not a
sufficient reason to compare the two cases. Indeed, one might reasonably ask, why not compare China with Taiwan and Korea, fellow East
Asian countries? Or Vietnam, China's reforming socialist neighbor?
Equally, why not compare Mexico to other Latin American countries?
We find a comparison that breaks out of shared regional cultural and
historical experience offers the promise of locating more fundamental
social and political structures that mediate the relationship between
market and democracy.[7] They provide telling insights into non-economic resistances to democracy. These resistances, flowing from culture, society, historical experience, and other factors, are deeply
embedded, existing "under the skin." Moreover, Mexico offers some
telling insights into China's possible political future. The Chinese
Communist Party's (CCP) steady loss of an ideological core turns it
more and more into a ruling party that resembles Mexico's Party of the
Institutionalized Revolution (PRI).

Other similarities characterize the two countries. Historically, authoritarianism in both China and Mexico has been partially justified by
fears of anarchy and dissolution. We shall see this has been due, in
part, to a lack of faith in both countries in what we call the "rudder of

---

7. Alexander Woodside both makes such a comparison of China and Vietnam and demonstrates the valuable insights to be derived in such analysis—in
this case to clarify what is socialist and Confucian heritage and what is Chinese
or Vietnamese per se. See his "The Two Latecomers: Politics and Economic
Development Time in the Chinese and Vietnamese Reforms" (Paper for the
"Transforming Asian Socialism" workshop at the Australian National University, August 1995).

democracy," an independent and effective legal system. This concern about governability has also reflected a common, Hobbesian conception of political man whose violent propensities are only restrained by strong government. Both countries have powerful, internally ordered societies, revolving around strong family structures which have created *orderly societies, but not naturally orderly polities*. This has inhibited the development of a civil society or a participatory political tradition and created an attenuated citizenship that has encouraged paternalism and elitism. Finally, in both countries, an emphasis on form produced legalistic societies which, nonetheless, have not been marked by the rule of law. In the two polities, law has been part of the surface rather than the substance—an artificial and instrumental construction lacking the depth and reach of custom.

In summary, then, the most notable affinities between China and Mexico have been certain elements of political culture, the nature of state-society relations, historical features of attenuated citizenship and limited participation, and dim views of law and the rule of law. These variables have powerfully influenced political behavior, views of the nature of political man, the priority assigned to the resolution and prevention of different political problems, and the preference for certain political forms and arrangements. While scholars have mentioned a number of inhibitors of democracy, the analysis of these particular factors as a commonly linked whole has not been undertaken. All of these elements affect each other, producing a web that touches and bounds political life. The examination of these affinities and of their linkages informs the thematic content of this book.

Accompanying these similarities between China and Mexico are substantial differences. These distinctions include deep ideological and structural variants between the two countries. Since the founding of the People's Republic of China (PRC) under the Chinese Communist Party (CCP) in 1949, China has been a "propaganda state" in which the dominating ideology of Marxism-Leninism has been buttressed by a fantastic nationwide network of institutions and practices to support party domination in the name of Mao Zedong Thought and the utopian goals of "scientific socialism." The public arena—from media, to schools and universities, to think tanks and creative arts—was directly administered by the Propaganda Department of the CCP.[8] This was a

---

8. Peter Kenez, *The Birth of the Propaganda State: Soviet Methods of Mass Mobilization, 1917–1929* (Cambridge: Cambridge University Press, 1985); and Hsia-ching Chang and Timothy Cheek, "Open & Closed Media," and Yan Huai, "The Organization System," in *Decision-Making in Deng's China: Perspectives from Insiders*, ed. Carol Lee Hamrin and Suisheng Zhao (Armonk, N.Y.: M. E. Sharpe, 1995).

powerful system of "directed culture" sustained by considerable popular support in the 1950s but badly abused in the Cultural Revolution.
The reform era since 1978 has seen the fitful decline of the propaganda
state, but has not seen the equivalent rise of liberal democratic politics
or protections. While China's system has been permeated by ideology,
Mexico's has been largely justified by political pragmatism. Indeed,
except for nationalism, Mexico's regime de-emphasized ideology. The
nationalist thrust of the regime was accompanied by substantial cultural efforts, but these paled in comparison to the intrusiveness and
extensiveness of China's propaganda state. The pragmatic grounding
of the regime and its concomitant lack of a messianic drive largely
explain its greater modesty and restraint in this area. Moreover, unlike
China, Mexico never sought to create an entirely socialized, centrally
planned economy, but instead tried to construct a mixed economy in
which a large private sector coexisted with a substantial state-owned
sphere.

Beyond these differences, size, geographic location, and the degree
of exposure to Western ideas, especially nineteenth century liberalism,
distinguish the two countries. Liberalism in China is forever linked
with those who introduced it and the period in which it was used. The
same imperialist powers that humiliated China's governments in the
late nineteenth and early twentieth centuries brought the liberalism of
Herbert Spencer and John Dewey to China. Chinese liberals such as Hu
Shi and James Yen attempted to apply the principles of British and
American political ideals during China's chaotic warlord period. Their
efforts were an abject failure. Liberalism thus has a foreign taint and a
poor reputation in Chinese politics. *Ziyouzhuyi*, the Chinese translation
for "liberalism," sounds morally suspect—bringing to mind the Daoist
retreat from public affairs and antisocial self-interest rather than Western images of personal rights and responsibilities. The term has further
been demonized in Maoist propaganda as essentially an anti-party personality defect in individuals that will lead to social chaos.[9] In Mexico,
on the other hand, liberalism has been a much more powerful political
force and has enjoyed greater and more widespread moral and intellectual prestige. Liberalism was also initially excoriated in Mexico by
the country's conservatives as a foreign, Anglo-Saxon doctrine, which

---

9. The most literate survey of recent Chinese history is Jonathan Spence's *In
Search of Modern China* (New York: Norton, 1990). On the suspect status of
"liberalism" in CCP ideology, see Yang Shangkun's 1942 speech in Dai Qing,
Wang Shiwei and Wild Lilies: Rectification and Purges in the CCP (New York: M.
E. Sharpe, 1994), 135–45, and the CCP's 1987 campaign against "bourgeois
liberalization" in Merle Goldman, *Sowing the Seeds of Democracy in China* (Cambridge: Harvard University Press, 1994).

was, moreover, linked to the country's greatest external threat, the United States.[10] This view was only held by a portion of the political elite, however, and liberals were a powerful force from the beginning of Mexico's independent political history. Indeed, by the middle of the nineteenth century liberalism had become the dominant political doctrine in Mexico. Despite this, it never escaped the taint of utopianism and remained divorced from actual political practices.

Thus democracy has been a stronger force in Mexico than in China. Resistance to democracy in Mexico during the latter half of the twentieth century was not primarily legitimized by ideology, but was almost entirely grounded in pragmatic arguments. Indeed, the Mexican government never denied the moral virtue of democracy while justifying the authoritarian arrangements of the Mexican political system as necessary responses to Mexico's "idiosyncrasies" and history. Chinese regimes either defended "people's dictatorship" on Leninist grounds or redefined democracy so far from the Western meaning as to make *minzhu* (literally, "people's rule," the Chinese translation for democracy) closer to political participation under Nationalist Socialism of the European Fascist regimes than to anything recognizable as liberal democracy.

Moreover, unlike China, Mexico possesses many of the factors typically cited as facilitators for democracy. Mexico has an autonomous bourgeoisie, possesses a so-called instrumental culture, and is subjected to powerful external influences favoring democratization, including the spread of democracy throughout the rest of Latin America and proximity to the United States.[11] In part, as a consequence, Mexico has moved toward ever more democratic elections, especially since 1994. China, on the other hand, is an almost paradigmatic example of an environment that is hostile to democracy. It still does not possess an autonomous bourgeoisie, has a consummatory culture, and has been much more insulated from external forces promoting democratization. China's size, power, and internal focus, joined to its greater

---

10. The most articulate and powerful exponent of these views was Lucas Alaman. The most important of his writings is his monumental *Historia de Mexico*.

11. For the role of these factors see Huntington, "Will More Countries Become Democratic?" 198–209. An instrumental culture/religion separates intermediate and ultimate ends while a so-called consummatory religion does not. By seeking to explain and guide all social spheres, a consummatory religion encourages monism and is less tolerant of pluralism. For these reasons, instrumental culture tends to be more tolerant of diversity and hospitable to democracy. See David E. Apter, *The Politics of Modernization* (Chicago: University of Chicago Press, 1965), 85.

distance from the democratic powers, make it less susceptible to such pressures than Mexico.

The comparison of two cases with notable similarities and significant differences offers the opportunity to undertake a comparative contextual analysis and to understand why certain elective affinities, in the true Weberian sense, can arise in otherwise widely divergent polities. In the present case these elective affinities are precisely the shared historical resistance to a *Rechtstadt* (substantive rule of law) and the *habitus* of liberal participatory politics. Understanding the genesis, persistence, and current evolution of these elements provides, in turn, insights into how different social and cultural contexts create a predilection or resistance to certain political forms—in short, why market liberalization sometimes leads to democratization and sometimes not.

The Mexican Political System

Democracy has flowered only infrequently in Mexico's history. Throughout much of the nineteenth century, political turbulence and strife, joined to the lack of effective government, nurtured a powerful desire for strong, central authority.[12] The advocates of centralized, unitary government, who also believed in the preservation of church privileges and glorified the colonial period and Mexico's Hispanic traditions, were joined together into a Conservative party. Opposing them, the Liberal party advocated free market economics, the curtailment of church privileges, the separation between church and state, and democracy. This larger ideological schism overlaid additional conflict produced by regionalism and personal ambition, promoting repeated sultanistic coups. Although the Liberals finally won their struggle with the Conservatives on the battlefield during a long struggle marking much of the 1850s and 1860s, Mexico's social, political, and economic reality continued to effectively preclude democracy. Regionalism, militarism, banditry, and the persistence of personal political fiefdoms and armies prevented economic development and made governability a much more pressing issue than liberty. The triumph of liberalism conjoined to the overwhelming need for a Leviathan created a highly paradoxical political situation in which liberal forms including federalism, separated government, and constitutionalism became

---

12. Several excellent studies examine the Liberal/Conservative conflict in Mexico, including Charles Hale's two excellent books, *Mexican Liberalism in the Age of Mora, 1821–1853* (New Haven: Yale University Press, 1968) and *The Transformation of Liberalism in Nineteenth Century Mexico* (Princeton: Princeton University Press, 1989).

a veneer, overlaying a deeper drive to concentrate and centralize power. This disjunction, which has run through Mexican political life over most of the last one hundred years, was perhaps inevitable given the impossibility of reconciling Hobbes and Locke.

The dictatorship of Porfirio Díaz, which governed Mexico from 1877 to 1910, when the Mexican Revolution erupted, dramatically epitomized this disjunction, producing order by concentrating and centralizing power while also trying to preserve a liberal facade marked by a formally federal structure, rigged elections, and constitutionalism. In the economic realm, the regime pursued liberal policies, opening up the country to foreign investors and promoting trade. Economic liberalism during the Porfiriato emphatically did not encourage democracy but supported an authoritarian dictatorship.

The same disjunction between formally liberal forms and a unitary, authoritarian substance characterized the regime created after the Mexican Revolution. The tension between the triumph of Locke and the persistence of Hobbesian fears and convictions led both the Porfiriato and the postrevolutionary regime to affirm their commitment to liberalism and democracy, while also arguing that Mexico's socioeconomic and political reality precluded their institutionalization. Positivism, explicitly during the Porfiriato, justified this apparent disjunction, for it permitted the affirmation and postponement of democracy until Mexico had evolved into a country capable of sustaining a democratic political system. Until then, democracy would be an exercise in utopianism because the country's reality required a set of aggregating, albeit authoritarian, institutions and ruling practices.

These philosophical and pragmatic arguments against democracy were sustained not only by historically grounded concerns about anarchy and disorder but by Mexico's few experiences with truly democratic government, including the liberal governments from 1867 to 1877 and the Madero administration (1911–13). In both cases, factionalism, regionalism, and political violence flourished, seemingly confirming the need for strong, central government. The turbulence confronting the Madero administration, in particular, after the long, peaceful, although extraordinarily inegalitarian interregnum created by the Díaz dictatorship, furthered the belief that order and stability could only be maintained through strong central authority, with power overwhelmingly concentrated in the executive. Persisting factionalism and violence after the revolution, pitting different revolutionary leaders and groups against each other, acted as the final confirmation of these arguments.

This situation, joined to the desire to consolidate power, led Plutarco Elías Calles to create the ruling party in 1929. This party, initially called the PNR (National Revolutionary Party), controlled political strife by aggregating different groups into a single structure. In the 1930s, the ruling party, currently called the PRI (Party of the Institutionalized Revolution) was redesigned along corporatist lines to incorporate different political groups and interests and to absorb a significant portion of the organized working population. The three sectors of the party—workers, peasants, and middle-class groups—permitted the regime to segmentally incorporate several critical social forces playing a key role in the construction and preservation of political stability.[13]

However, the creation of intermediary organizations from above by the regime also had an enervating effect on political participation and on the development of autonomous organizations and interests. The early development of these organizations preempted and effectively replaced the formation of autonomous groups from below. Moreover, because the ruling party's sectors were primarily designed to maximize political control and manage interest articulation, they had a strongly demobilizational effect on mass-based organizations, including those of workers and peasants. Ironically, this demobilization, although it initially strengthened the regime, later became an increasingly serious problem. The inevitable, accompanying rise in political apathy meant that the government had to rely on support that was more passive than active. This lack of engagement undermined the nexus between regime and society, raising nagging questions about legitimacy.

Nonetheless, the discipline promoted by this structure encouraged conciliation and compromise, civilizing the struggle for power. In effect, negotiation and power-sharing replaced the naked use of force. A set of tacit, but long-established, rules governed behavior among the concatenation of groups and interests who were part of the so-called "Revolutionary family" included in the ruling party and the bureaucracy.[14] Party discipline was further cemented by the widespread distribution of benefits and elite circulation.[15] Real perquisites and opportunities for upward mobility created by elite circulation also promoted acquiescence and cooperation.

---

13. The size of the PRI is another factor: between 15 and 20 million party members in a general population of about 95 million. The CCP's membership is some 57 million but in a population of 1,250 million (i.e., 1.25 billion).

14. The term "Revolutionary family" was coined by Frank Brandenburg in *The Making of Modern Mexico* (Englewood Cliffs, N.J.: Prentice-Hall, 1964), to describe the concatenation of groups composing the ruling party and the political elite.

15. The best study of elite circulation in Mexico is Peter Smith, *Labyrinth of Power* (Princeton: Princeton University Press, 1979).

Harmony within the constellation of interests composing the Revolutionary family was also partially preserved through the avoidance of ideological conflict. Political recruitment de-emphasized ideological credentials, making loyalty and political ability the most important determinants of success within the regime. In addition, an ideologically amorphous political and economic program prevented the intensification and expression of ideological differences by placating distinct groups.[16] Small and occasionally larger policy shifts across different presidential administrations also helped to reward and address the demands of divergent constituencies.[17]

While this structure created and preserved political stability, it also effectively eliminated real contestation. The size, organizational capacity, and power of the ruling party, combined with the huge resources at its disposal, gave it an enormous electoral advantage. All of these factors also debilitated the already small and poorly organized opposition, helping to turn elections into largely pro forma, ritualistic affairs, the outcome of which was assured from the outset. As a consequence, they became part of the democratic veneer rather than the authoritarian substance of the political system. It was only in the mid-1980s when the corrosive effects of a profound economic crisis conjoined to other factors finally turned elections, especially in the northern part of the country, into real contests. Greater competitiveness was also initially accompanied by increases in both real and putative electoral fraud. These charges of fraud deepened cynicism and skepticism, tainted all electoral results, and ensured that elections at that time continued to lack legitimacy despite their greater competitiveness.

The aggregating, centralizing urge underlying this system directly contradicted the liberal elements included in the Constitution of 1917. As a consequence, federalism, the separation of powers, and other elements formally established by the constitution became largely empty shells, existing in theory but ignored in practice. Real power in Mexico was entirely concentrated in the executive branch of the central government. The president dominated the federal bureaucracy, and largely

---

16. In this sense the PRI could be the CCP's future much more than a Chinese Yeltsin being Deng's successor. The PRI shows how a "formally" revolutionary regime can carry on without a living ideology.

17. For a long time scholars argued that these shifts were indicative of an ideological pendulum. This "pendulum theory" has been largely rejected since "rightist" interludes and groups have lasted longer and been stronger than "leftist" elements. Nonetheless, the regime pursued a "rolling agenda" of sorts across different administrations designed to address distinct groups and issues. For details, see Daniel Levy and Gabriel Szekely, *Mexico: Paradoxes of Stability and Change* (Boulder, Colo.: Westview, 1987), 116–18.

controlled the ruling party, the legislature, and the judiciary. It was only in 1997, when the opposition finally gained control of the legislature, that this power began to weaken.

State governments, lacking independent sources of revenue and largely dependent on federal largesse, were also subordinated to the president's will. Indeed, states were virtual dependencies of the central government. Moreover, the president, through the medium of the ruling party, also effectively appointed governors. The only exceptions to this rule have come in recent years when the opposition has won governorships and begun to gain control of some state legislatures.

Despite the constitutional provisions, the federal legislature was stripped of many of its most important functions, especially the initiation of law. The executive branch assumed these functions, while the legislature, because of the ruling party's dominance, became a rubber stamp body, invariably ratifying presidential initiatives. This situation changed after 1997, when the opposition gained a majority for the first time in the Chamber of Deputies. The judiciary also lacked institutional independence, effectively acting as an extension of the executive branch. For example, the Supreme Court not only was appointed by the executive but never ruled against a presidential initiative.

Other features of the political system reinforced overwhelming executive power. Each president, whose term is limited to six years with no reelection, personally selected his successor.[18] In sum, power was largely concentrated in the executive branch. The president enjoyed a measure of control over the political system unimaginable in a liberal democratic polity. Policy initiatives flowed from the top down, confining most groups and interests to a reactive role.[19] In addition, the president made all high-level appointments, controlled the ruling party, and set policy direction.

The president's huge power, however, did encounter some checks. While institutional restraints on the president were virtually non-existent, bureaucratic inertia and long-established practices affected his ability to implement policy. The president's power was also restrained by the need to respect vested interests, both within and outside the regime. This last, prudential factor provided the most important limit to his policy latitude.

This system has faced increasing stresses over the last twenty years. Deepening economic problems, marked by growing inflation, indebtedness, and stagnation steadily eroded the regime's legitimacy. Con-

---

18. This process is known as the *dedazo*, or finger-pointing.
19. See Susan Kaufman, *The Mexican Profit-Sharing Decision* (Berkeley: University of California Press, 1976).

comitantly, these economic problems reduced policy space, forcing the regime to adopt measures that engendered and exacerbated cleavages within the government. Straitened economic circumstances, moreover, necessitated the implementation of a set of policies, including privatization and other market reforms, that gave the regime an ever more rightist identity, alienating more leftist groups in the party. Additionally, growing pressures for reform spawned cleavages within the elite over the desirability of change. The regime's response to persistent economic crises produced real and putative winners and losers, creating and inflaming conflict.

In addition, these difficulties exposed and highlighted the regime's central, long-term, structural problems. Decades of economic growth, running from the 1940s through the mid-1970s, had modernized and diversified Mexican society. The regime's structure and ruling style, however, remained largely unaltered, inevitably widening the gap between government and society. The ruling party faced the difficulties produced by this disjunction especially strongly, in part because the simple, functional scheme informing its corporatist sectors no longer reflected Mexico's social reality. As a consequence, the party's efficacy as an instrument of aggregation and political control steadily declined.

The party's difficulties were clearly evident by the late 1980s. These problems first, and most dramatically, evidenced themselves during 1986 and 1987, when much of the leftist branch of the party split away to contest the 1988 presidential elections against the official candidate. Though this schism was extremely serious, its impact on the regime during subsequent years was initially attenuated by several factors. Most importantly, the rightward drift of the population at first made the loss of the center-left much less politically consequential. At the same time, the efficacy of the left was notably reduced by its additional, internal problems. Historically, ideological conflicts, organizational problems, and tactical and strategic mistakes limited its appeal. These problems, which had long plagued Mexico's left, disappeared briefly before the 1988 elections when these leftist parties and groups united with the dissident former members of the PRI to create an electoral front, called the FDN (National Democratic Front). These problems reappeared, however, after the election with the FDN's transformation into a political party—the PRD (Party of the Democratic Revolution). It was only in 1997 that the PRD once again emerged as an especially significant political force. Although the FDN garnered more than 30 percent of the vote in 1988, the PRD only received 16 percent of the vote in the 1994 presidential elections. The overall showing of the left in the 1994 elections was somewhat stronger than this figure, since it included the vote totals of two other parties—the PPS

(Popular Socialist Party) and the PARM (Authentic Party of the Mexican Revolution.) Their votes, joined to the PRD's, raised total support for the left to more than a quarter of the electorate. Although significant, this is still somewhat less than the left's showing in 1988. In 1997, however, they won the first elections for mayor of Mexico City and garnered the second largest share of seats, after the PRI, in the Chamber of Deputies.

On top of losing the left, additional internal struggles have arisen within the ruling party. These conflicts, although colored by ideology, primarily reflect deeply contending interests. Shifts in political recruitment toward an ever more technocratic elite marginalized older cadres whose position is further threatened by political reform and change.[20] The threat to their positions, careers, and perquisites deepened the passion fueling their opposition to change. Their control of the ruling party's membership base has made their resistance especially difficult to overcome. The resultant conflict between these so-called dinosaurs and reformers within the government has intensified over the years. A peasant uprising in the state of Chiapas, the assassination of key political figures (notably the party's candidate for president and the secretary general of the party in 1994), national disgust with corruption, the rapaciousness of the country's judicial system, and scandals touching some of the most important families in Mexico—all have deepened the regime's troubles.

The regime's difficulties have contributed to the steady growth of opposition strength on the center-right as well as the left. The PAN (National Action Party) has been the most important beneficiary of revulsion against the government on the center-right. Over the last several years, it has gained important electoral victories around the country, acquiring control of several important statehouses and an ever-larger presence in the legislature.

However, despite these stresses the PRI still enjoys residual support and strength. This support stems from several sources, including fear of change, the appeal of the familiar, deep-seated concerns about political disorder, and the paucity of available alternatives at the national level. Disorder and violence, except for strife within the regime, strengthen support for the ruling party and the extant political system, which are still seen by a substantial portion of the population as the only forces capable of preventing wider instability.

Nonetheless, democratizing pressures have steadily grown. These

20. On this shift in political recruitment and its implications, see, for example, Juan Lindau, *La elite gobernante mexicana* (México, D.F.: Joaquin Mortiz, 1993).

pressures forced the regime to reform electoral procedures before the 1994 and 1997 elections and pursue negotiations with the opposition. The reforms produced by these negotiations ruptured the financial relationship between the ruling party and the government, gave different parties equal access to the media, and ended the government's control of elections, among other things. However, the broader impact of electoral reform still remains somewhat unclear. Alterations in the executive and in the judiciary promised by these reforms, if they are enacted, do offer hope of truly substantive change. However, the government's ability and willingness to implement these reforms remain suspect.

The Chinese Political System

Liberal democracy as a political system has never worked in China. As an idea it has had a checkered and unhappy career. Imperial dynasties ruled China from the third century B.C.E. to the early twentieth century. The ideas of political democracy and limited government were introduced into China during a cataclysmic century of foreign intrusion and domestic anomie. From the end of the first Opium War in 1842 when the Qing Dynasty conceded treaty port rights (including the right to trade opium) to the British in the Treaty of Nanking to the reunification of China under the CCP and the People's Republic in 1949, China faced a broad-ranged cultural crisis that compressed the four centuries of Mexican history from Spanish contact with the Aztecs to the 1911 Mexican Revolution into a single century. In that period, China's traditional Confucian Emperor system and self-perception as center of the physical and moral universe collapsed, and the survivors had to cope with a new, strange economic, diplomatic, and cultural system: the treaties of Christian European nation-states.[21]

Market and political changes in China over the past century cannot be understood out of the context of this violent clash of cultures and the revolutionary compression of time—the transition from the ancien régime that took four or five centuries in Europe or the Americas was radically quickened in Asia. The driving force for China's economic and political reformers since the late nineteenth century has been the search for "wealth and power" (*fuguo qiangbing*) in order to resist the encroachment of European (and later Japanese) interests. In fact, the history of market reform (of China's centuries-old and extensive com-

---

21. The best general overview of this history is Spence's *In Search of Modern China*.

mercial system to a capitalist and industrial system)[22] and political change since the late nineteenth century is one in which market liberalization emphatically did *not* coincide with or promote democratization. Late Qing reforms sought to revive the failing dynasty through market liberalization and state support of industrialization efforts. After the fall of the empire and the founding of the Republic in 1911, Sun Yat-sen, the ideological leader of the Republic, emphasized "political tutelage" (continued by his successor, Chiang Kai-shek, into the 1960s). Under that system, the ideal of liberal democracy was acknowledged but, as in the Mexican case, deferred in the name of practicality: China's peasant majority was too uneducated and China's feudal culture too antiquated for the rigors of electoral democracy.

The traumatic Taiping Rebellion (1850–64) against the Qing and the disastrous Boxer Rebellion of 1900 against foreign interests buttressed philosophical arguments and cultural predilections toward the efficiency and coherence of authoritarian regimes.[23] The first parliament of the Republic collapsed by 1913 and saw the rise of the first of the warlords, Yuan Shikai. For the next twenty-five years, over half of China was controlled by a variety of militarists, despite the formation of a reasonably stable Republican government in Nanjing under Chiang Kai-shek in 1927. Added to the regional disunity and the depredations of local militarists, the contenders for national leadership engaged in bloody competition for the two decades following 1927. The government party (the single ruling party) was the Nationalists. They engaged in near-constant warfare with the small CCP. Even though two periods of "United Front" were accepted by the two parties in the early 1920s and the late 1930s, the two remained mortal enemies. Domestic order did not return until one, the CCP, had expelled the other, the Nationalists, from the China mainland.

The 1911–49 period is generally considered the Republican period for China (though the Republic of China continues to administer Taiwan). The legacy of those years was deeply mixed. Despite Communist claims, the Nationalist government was not pro-business.[24] It was na-

---

22. Most scholars agree that China's economy has been highly commercialized since the eleventh century (Song Dynasty). See, for example, Dwight Perkins, ed., *China's Modern Economy in Historical Perspective* (Stanford: Stanford University Press, 1975).

23. And all this built upon authoritarian political thought of early nineteenth century Chinese reformers, such as Wei Yuan. See Philip Kuhn, "Ideas Behind China's Modern State," *Harvard Journal of Asiatic Studies* 55, no. 2 (1995): 295–337.

24. See Parks Coble, *The Shanghai Capitalists and the Nationalist Government, 1927–1937* (Cambridge: Harvard Council on East Asian Studies, 1980).

tionalist first and anything else as circumstances dictated (for example, Chiang Kai-shek became a public church-going Methodist, much to the delight and good publicity of Henry Luce of *Time* magazine). The Republican government's attitude toward both capitalism and democracy was instrumental—if either or both contributed to Chinese independence and national "wealth and power," then well and good. If not, they were dispensable.

In any event, the Nationalist government failed. It neither protected China from the Japanese invasion of 1937 (arguably no Chinese government of the time could have) nor produced wealth. Rampant inflation and renewed civil war with the Communists marked the allied victory of World War II for China. Within a few years the new Communist government had taken control of the mainland. The Nationalists, who had been supported by the United States, fled to Taiwan. Democracy and free markets went, in disgrace, with them.

The Communists came to power with great popular support. Compared to the corruption and incompetence of the Nationalist administration of the 1940s, these rugged revolutionaries from the countryside seemed to be China's best hope. The Nationalist party was, in fact, a Leninist party, but it had stressed its liberal democratic trappings in order to curry favor with the United States. The Communists brought ideological zeal to the Bolshevik organization and thus tapped its full mobilizational potential. The transformative ideology that propelled the CCP to national power was hammered out in the dusty hills of northwest China during the war years. This synthesis of the German-Russian ideology and Chinese political experience is generally called the "Yan'an Way" after the CCP's wartime capital. The ideology is called "Mao Zedong Thought" after the party's charismatic leader.

The keys to Maoism were its utopian goals and practical organizational practices. It promised not only wealth and power for China but equality for China's citizens, land to the tiller, industrial modernization, and growing respect for China in the world. It did so on clearly Marxist-Leninist lines, being anti-imperialist, anti-market, and anti–"bourgeois democracy."[25] Using Marxist class analysis the Chinese communists declared the free market to be a tool of oppression by which capitalists extracted the surplus labor of China's workers and peasants, and they decried liberal democracy as a sham to convince the same exploited laborers to accept their oppression as fair. The CCP proposed in their stead the virtues of a "scientific" Stalinist command

---

25. For a sense of the inspirational power of Yan'an communism, see David Apter and Tony Saich, *Revolutionary Discourse in Mao's Republic* (Cambridge: Harvard University Press, 1994).

economy in which the means of production were nationalized and production determined by a state plan *and* the morality of "democratic
dictatorship" in which the working classes would practice democracy
amongst themselves but exercise dictatorship over enemy classes.[26]
These Marxist conceptions of revolution were implemented in their
Leninist-Stalinist form. That is, the party leadership as the "vanguard
of the proletariat" exercised the democracy as well as the dictatorship.
In short, "democracy" meant doing what the party told you to do.
However, as in the Mexican case, the implications of the ideal—now
the attributes of a future communist society—remained as ultimate
goals to be tapped by other leaders in changed circumstances.

The demise of the great charismatic authority of the CCP and state
socialism came from the twin blows of the Great Leap Forward (1958–
60) and the Cultural Revolution (1966–69). These two mass campaigns
were initiated by the CCP and resulted in disaster for China. In the
first, the ill-conceived and overly ambitious plans to convert China's
abundant labor supply into capital through mass irrigation and construction campaigns produced three years of man-made famine that,
by conservative estimates, killed thirty million Chinese. After creating
the world's worst famine the CCP careened into a fratricidal cultural
and political fight that made a mockery of the hallowed ideals of Maoism and decimated the party organization. A key result of this factional
warfare was the creation of teenage gangs called the Red Guards.[27]
Supposedly Chairman Mao's vanguard in continuing the revolution,
they became in fact pawns for the power struggle and tormentors of
nearly every neighborhood. Hardly a family in China today lacks a
victim of the Cultural Revolution.

Mao died in 1976, bringing an end to the direct repercussions of the
Cultural Revolution (indeed, most date it 1966–76 even though Mao
declared it victorious at the 9th Party Congress in 1969). The key drives
of the CCP leadership in the post-Mao period have been precisely economic reform and political control. Deng Xiaoping, the paramount
leader from 1979 to 1996, sought to correct the errors of radical Maoism. He put an end to the communes and returned land to the tiller,
thus reaping a windfall jump in production. He ended political slogan-
mongering, stressed the rules and regulations of party discipline, and
made promising noises about "the rule of law." He opened China to

---

26. See Mao Zedong, "On the People's Democratic Dictatorship" (June
1949), in *Selected Works of Mao Zedong* (Peking: Foreign Languages Press, 1969),
vol. 4, 411–24.

27. See Michael Schoenhals, *Not a Dinner Party: A Documentary History of the
Chinese Cultural Revolution* (Armonk, N.Y.: M. E. Sharpe, 1996).

foreign trade and cultural intercourse. Finally, he produced political stability by ending the extreme factional infighting within the CCP and by withdrawing excessive ideological monitoring by party cadres from businesses and enterprises. All of this, however, was based on a reaffirmation of party dictatorship, what Deng identified in 1980 as the Four Cardinal Principles (keeping the socialist road, upholding the dictatorship of the proletariat, party leadership, and Marxism-Leninism–Mao Zedong Thought).[28]

This history has left China's political system with enduring tensions. The charismatic legitimacy, the "salvationary mission," of the CCP is gone, yet there are no practical competitors to run the government. While the comparison of the CCP—a real Bolshevik party—and Mexico's PRI may strike many as forced, it is precisely, as James Williams points out, the non-charismatic and wounded party of the post–Cultural Revolution period in China that so resembles Mexico's *Institutional* Revolutionary Party.[29] This is because what most powerfully remain of China's revolutionary party are the institutions of the party-state.

The central government is inseparable from the CCP even though there is formal separation between party and state organs. What the politburo of the CCP says, the government does.[30] Yet the pressing necessity for such political monotheism (the Chinese call it *yiyuanhua*) and prestige of the CCP to carry it out well are both gone. In addition, the elaborate (frankly, paranoid) Stalinist security systems of the PRC provide a headless monster of secret police and public regulations fit to tie down any giant. The centralized bureaucracy of the Leninist party-state has been eroded over the past fifteen years, but it is a long way from evaporation. More to the point, China has no viable alternative administrative or legal system to replace the Maoist-Stalinist structure. The much vaunted rural reforms in which the communes were disbanded and land returned to the tiller have run up against the hard fact of unwieldy state factories and distribution "companies" and a

---

28. Carol Lee Hamrin, *China and the Challenge of the Future: Changing Political Patterns* (Boulder, Colo.: Westview Press, 1990), and Joseph Fewsmith, *Dilemmas of Reform in China: Political Conflict and Economic Debate* (Armonk, N.Y.: M. E. Sharpe, 1994).

29. Thanks are due to James Williams for raising and pressing this comparison between the CCP and the PRI. See his essay "Mexico and NAFTA" (unpublished essay) and discussion of his work in Cheek's chapter.

30. The best introductions to China's political system are James Townsend and Brantly Womack, *Politics in China* (Reading: Addison-Wesley, 1986) and Kenneth Lieberthal, *Governing China: From Revolution Through Reform* (New York: W. W. Norton, 1995).

personalized legal administration system that requires the good will of local party secretaries for financial success.

The system is corrupt. Deeply corrupt. But too many people are making too much money out of it to expect quick change. This is not only a matter of high officials seeking rents in exchange for licenses or police protection. A new class of entrepreneurial "fixers" has arisen to bridge the gap between the command economy structures of Maoist China and the market aspirations of Dengist China. Tony Saich calls this "Nomenklatura capitalism." Others see in this state corporatism with Chinese characteristics. The chapters in this volume examine just these issues through case studies. But what is clear is that the political heritage of China's recent history does not contribute to the easy equation of market reform and political democratization.

Neither does the political culture of daily life in China. Confucian culture never set much store by formal laws, relying instead on a mix of moral ideals and thick interpersonal obligations glued together by family ties. Buffeted by Maoist excesses and market attractions, many in China today lack a sense of what is appropriate behavior in a market economy. Values and practices that have served Chinese communities (and businesses) very well in more stable times are now threatening the wealth and power goals of the government. *Guanxi* (personal relations/obligations) was part of the Confucian cement, but now serves as collusion against the legal regimes of markets—corruption, smuggling, tax evasion, engrossment.[31] Lack of legal protection of property discourages capital investment and promotes a "slash and burn" style of quick profit-taking. Most large investments, in fact, are godfathered by major bureaucratic interests. This is why we read of major international hotels in Beijing or Guangzhou being "owned" by the Ministry of Public Security or the People's Liberation Army.

For all its troubles, however, the CCP regime enjoys widespread support, if not great respect. The reason is simple: The only alternative seems to be the anarchy that is taking over the former Soviet Union. In this sense, Gorbachev was Deng Xiaoping's best ally. The prospect of a weak center seems to most Chinese a recipe for a Russian disaster rather than western European delights. The CCP can still deliver the minimum necessities: reasonable stability and a possible path toward further modernization, increased wealth, and political reform. Therefore, the greatest worry today is what will become of the CCP and

---

31. Mayfair Mei-hui Yang, *Gifts, Favors, and Banquets: The Art of Social Relationships in China* (Ithaca: Cornell University Press, 1994). Readers should know that Professor Yang sees *quanxixue* as more of a factor promoting democracy than we do.

China with the recent death of Deng Xiaoping. While guessing about future leadership is beyond the scope of this volume, it is our hope that comparative contextual analysis will provide a clear sense of the likely range of developments in China and Mexico.

Areas of Focus

In both countries a mixture of self-interest and conviction has driven advocacy and resistance to change. Supporters of democratization have been motivated by resentments against the existing political system, the desire for power, and the belief that democracy is a more humanitarian system that promotes the rule of law, preventing the impunity and unrestrained use of power inherent in authoritarianism. In Mexico, although reformers typically portray advocates of the status quo as narrow, self-interested dinosaurs who are unwilling to surrender power, supporters of the postrevolutionary political system have also been motivated by concerns about instability and disorder and the conviction that the regime is still the most efficacious response to Mexico's particular political situation. In contrast, supporters of democratization, always tarred by the taint of utopianism, have effectively argued since the late 1980s that democracy offers the only hope for long-term stability. This argument represents a truly new development in Mexican political discourse. Advocates of centralization and authoritarianism had always owned pragmatism, given the widespread conviction that the compression and aggregation produced by these measures offered the only remedy for centrifugal tendencies. For the first time since the end of the Porfirian dictatorship, however, supporters of the political system were challenged on these views, especially after the 1988 elections. With increasing effectiveness, advocates of democratization asserted that political change was the only way to avert instability because it offered an outlet and voice to divergent political interests. By extension, they argued that the frustration accompanying the prolongation of authoritarianism would increasingly promote extra-systemic and violent political behavior. This partial inversion of traditional positions has offered one of the most important sustenances for democratization. In China, too, "democracy" has been captured by advocates of political reform in recent years. Both maverick senior party theorists like Su Shaozhi and Yan Jiaqi and political outsiders among China's intelligentsia have articulated versions of democracy that strip the term of both its "liberal" shame and Leninist sham. The student demonstrations and popular protests of 1989 centered in Beijing's Tiananmen Square crystallized this development. The state repression of those protests and discussions of democracy have muted but not halted the new discourse on democracy in China.[32]

The studies in this book seek to make sense of this well-known political history of democratic struggle. It is easy to misconstrue the intent of advocates and opponents and the likely results of their efforts without a strong grounding in the history of political thought on the relationship between markets and democracy, the international and regional systems with which each polity must deal, and a clear sense of the institutional, social, and cultural realities in each polity based on its history. The major sections of this book address these three areas of analytical focus.

In a recent work, Haggard and Kaufman adopt a similar approach and explicitly consider "the impact of the [economic] adjustment process on political economy" in their chapter in *The Politics of Economic Adjustment*.[33] Drawing on detailed country studies in an earlier project,[34] they examine the relationship between economic reform and political change in three steps: the impact of international shocks of the 1980s, the effects of economic adjustment policies on the pattern of political conflict, and the possibilities for alternative political systems to reconcile democratic politics with market-oriented economics. They identify three empirical patterns: economic reform first, political reform first, and simultaneous economic and political reform.

Their analysis is extremely helpful to the project of this book because they introduce a more complex and empirically based three-way refinement of the Δ democracy = Δ market equation. Furthermore, they identify two key variables that modify—even reverse—the impact of the market on democratization. Haggard and Kaufman conclude their assessment by noting that "the principal danger to democratic consolidation in the 1990s is less likely to be a reversion to military rule than a decay of state institutions and in the capacity of groups within civil society to engage in sustained and constructive collective action."[35] We too have found that state institutions, especially an independent judiciary capable of enforcing a rule of law, are one key to answering the

---

32. See Bill Brugger and David Kelly, *Marxism in Post-Mao China* (Stanford: Stanford University Press, 1990); Goldman, *Sowing the Seeds of Democracy*; and Barret L. McCormick and David Kelly, "The Limits of Anti-Liberalism," *Journal of Asian Studies* 53:3 (August 1994): 804–31.

33. Haggard and Kaufman, "Economic Adjustment and the Prospects for Democracy," 319–50.

34. Published in Joan Nelson, ed., *Economic Crisis and Policy Choice: The Politics of Adjustment in the Third World* (Princeton: Princeton University Press, 1990).

35. Nelson, *Economic Crisis*, 349.

question of the prospects for democracy in Mexico, China, and other nations undertaking market reforms. This variable is necessary for the consolidation of the other essential condition for democracy, a civil society that allows the expression of diverse social interests. Haggard and Kaufman did not set out to and do not offer substantial descriptions of these two key variables. It is our hope that the present collection does.

The first area of focus, consisting of this introduction and the following chapter by Jorge Domínguez, provides the historical context for each country and a theoretical examination of the relationship between market reform and democratization. Jorge Domínguez's chapter, in particular, explores the historical discussion about the impact of economic liberalization on political change since Thomas Hobbes.

The second area of focus analyzes China's and Mexico's regional contexts and both common and idiosyncratic factors in each country's recent social experience. The first chapter, by Robert Packenham, helps to locate Mexico's experience with economic liberalization through an extended discussion of the countries of the Southern Cone. Packenham constructs a continuum running from socialism to "raw, savage capitalism" and then locates countries along it. This approach is especially useful because it allows a much more nuanced examination of economic liberalization. It also debunks the myth that Latin American liberalizers, in their rush to abandon statist policies, have embraced an undiluted, neoclassical form of capitalism. Instead, all of these countries have retained, albeit to different degrees, significant elements of the welfare state. The second chapter in this section, by Gaye Christoffersen, provides an East Asian referent for China's experience with market reform. She compares the experience of privatization without reform in Russia to developments in China and the "East Asian model" of development in South Korea and Taiwan. While both China and Mexico share elements with other polities in their region, they also have certain distinct traits highlighted by comparison with their neighbors. It turns out that some of these particular traits are common to Mexico and China.

The third area of focus pursues the elective affinities shared by Mexico and China that we see as the two most fundamental impediments to institutionalizing democracy. Both societies possess to a degree much greater than their neighbors a weak tradition of a rule of law and a vacant public sphere. The key variables for democratization in this analysis emerge as the judicial system, which serves as the "rudder of democracy," and political participation with a "civil society," which permits the twin goals of limited government and the development of individual social responsibility, which is, of course, intimately linked to the rule of law. The first two chapters in this section examine the rule of law and the judiciary in Mexico and China. The first, by Lorenzo Meyer, discusses the evolution of the Mexican judiciary and the difficulty of constructing a *Rechtstadt* in Mexico. Meyer argues that the creation of an overwhelming executive and the concomitant lack of a separation of powers made the rule of law impossible. The second chapter in this section, by Pitman Potter, discusses legal culture in China and the relationship between law and entrepreneurship. By addressing the concept of "legal culture," Potter is able to show how a relatively alienated group, the *getihu* entrepreneurs of Shanghai, takes up the formal claims of legal procedure superficially offered by the government and pushes to have it serve as substantive law. However, as in Mexico, Potter's Shanghai is still not governed by the rule of law.

Political culture, the focus of the next two chapters in this area of focus, is a fundamental mediating variable in the formation of the legal system and civil society. The first, by Juan Lindau, examines the presumed development of civil society in Mexico. He argues that the reach and scope of civil society continue to be exaggerated and concludes that its relatively slow growth is a product of certain features of Mexican society and political culture. The second chapter, by Timothy Cheek, analyzes civil society in China, rejecting the traditional normative approach to civil society of Habermas and arguing in favor of a functional Gramscian approach. Cheek suggests that this approach shows that non-democratic corporatism may produce more humane results in China than the "vulgar liberalism" of local entrepreneurs.

Finally, in the concluding section of the book, two chapters extend the application and findings of our analysis. David Hendrickson considers what these views on China and Mexico and the relationship between market and democracy mean for U.S. foreign policy. After discussing the evolution of U.S. policy during the nineteenth and twentieth centuries, he explores the current use of economic vehicles—from NAFTA to MFN to sanctions—to promote democratization. He is not sanguine about the effectiveness of economic sanctions. David Finley extends our approach to the example of post-Soviet Russia. He concludes that our two central themes of the judiciary and civil society indeed do explain many of Russia's difficulties in effecting a transition to democracy.

Conclusions

In terms of theory, we suggest that a conscientious balance of contextual detail and appreciation for the particularity of each case study, combined with the effort to articulate generalizations susceptible to testing, provides the best approach to understanding the dynamics of market and democracy in the late twentieth century and the recent history of our two case studies. We have articulated those generalizations as specific questions that other approaches to the question of democracy and civil society have neglected: a weak tradition of the rule of law and an empty (vacant or directed) public sphere. Our two central questions from this analysis are: How does the market promote the rule of law and civil society along with the political *habitus* to support them? And how does the market help create an independent judiciary? At best the market does this by highly indirect means. Our analysis directs critical attention to just those previously glossed over steps between market forces and political actions, including the pressures of regional context. We do not deny the power of markets, as Huntington and others have long since pointed out, but we hope to have laid to rest the easy equation of market liberalization and political democratization. In its stead, we offer these questions and an example of the inductive but generalizing method to encourage their application and refinement in other case studies.[36]

In terms of our case studies, our most striking conclusion is that Mexico's PRI could be China's CCP's future much more than a Chinese Yeltsin might be Deng Xiaoping's successor. The PRI shows how a "formally" revolutionary regime can carry on without a living ideology—for decades and decades. The PRI translated market forces in Mexico into a sort of corporatist patronage system which Clark Reynolds called an "alliance for profits."[37] An ideologically amorphous political and economic program prevented the intensification and expression of ideological differences by placating distinct groups that have each gotten a cut of the economic pie. The PRI also "civilized" the struggle for power through this form of state corporatism. The structural results for the Mexican polity have been twofold. First, a sustainable institutional corruption in which the distribution of wealth followed the de facto line of power among the PRI's leaders and their constituencies rather than the formal de jure liberal social forms. Yet, this distribution was done in a way that sustained admirable macroeconomic development for several decades. It was more sustainable

---

36. It is clear, furthermore, that there is an interesting line of questions to be pursued in comparing successful transitions to market and more liberal democratic institutions from Franco's Spain in the 1980s to Japan in the post–World War II period. In both cases the moment of authority—the monarchy—bridged the disruptive changes.

37. Clark Reynolds, *The Mexican Economy: Twentieth Century Structure and Growth* (New Haven: Yale University Press, 1970).

and thus to be distinguished from warlord ravishing of resources in 1920s China or drug lord rapaciousness of the 1990s. Second, the Mexican polity has had a weak public sphere—that crucial social space in which the positive forces of market liberalization are supposed to do their democratizing work. This deficiency pushed out independent actors from the public arena who are necessary for the Δ market $= \Delta$ polity equation. In Mexico the PRI's state corporatism combined with the political culture to produce a vacant public sphere, a gap made more ominous by a security apparatus unchecked by effective electoral or judicial constraints.

What about Mexico's future and the PRI itself? Drug money has increasingly brought the Jamaicanization of politics in Mexico with the unsustainable corruption of the gang. Forty years of "institutional revolution," as well, has brought social changes and forces to bear on Mexican society that do not yet appear in China. There are a substantive number of non-governmental organizations (NGOs), and other citizen's groups in Mexico, aligned around a plethora of issues. The rise of these groups in however nascent a form and the simultaneous dismemberment of a once-invincible political apparatus have launched Mexico into a profound political transition, the outcome of which is still difficult to discern. Most recently we have seen the opposition parties gain a majority in the lower house of the legislature. However, taming the country's security apparatus and constructing a *Rechstadt* remain the most intractable problems complicating a transition to a full democracy.

China in the 1990s shares these twin characteristics of the market-liberalized, non-democratic polity. The CCP is moving toward the same sort of sustainable institutional corruption that has long marked the PRI. The post-Mao and certainly the post-Deng CCP has come to offer a similarly ideologically amorphous political and economic program that prevents the intensification and expression of ideological differences by placating distinct groups who have each gotten a cut of the economic pie. Rather than demonstrating an unsustainable corruption (as many China commentators suggest), the comparison with the PRI gives us the example of decades' worth of energy in this state corporatist model. Second, China too has a weak public sphere. While in the Mexican case there was a vacant public sphere into which the state stepped, China has had a directed public sphere running along harsh Leninist-Stalinist lines which has forcibly pushed out independent actors from the public arena. The weakening and gradual dismemberment of the institutional sinews of China's propaganda state, combined with Chinese culture's own inward-looking familism (a fault long bemoaned by Sun Yat-sen as "the shifting sheet of sand" problem, for instance), are more likely to produce a vacant public sphere than a robust civil society. Thus we may reasonably anticipate the development of China's political economy in the next twenty years to look more like the Mexican of the past twenty years.[38] Differences in size, military power, and geopolitical strength (such as China's seat on the UN Security Council) should not blind us to this fundamental similarity between Mexico and China in certain key aspects of political culture and organization.

---

38. The longer term may, indeed, lead toward democratic forces in China as seems to be the case in Mexico today—as long as economic disaster or ethnic rivalries do not draw these polities in less happy directions. Still, we find even a nuanced consideration of the forces at play in China as that by Tony Saich erring on the hopeful side that discounts the variable our analysis has raised. See Saich, "The Search for Civil Society and Democracy in China," *Current History* (September 1994): 260–64.

2

Market Economics and Political Change: A Historical and Theoretical Examination

Jorge I. Domínguez

What is the relationship between free politics and free markets? In what ways does the achievement of market freedoms increase the likelihood of the achievement of political freedoms? To what extent may the accomplishment of political freedom and democracy improve the prospects for a market economy? Does democracy increase or decrease the likelihood that markets will operate effectively and that economic growth will be sustained? The hoped-for connection between free politics and free markets is a key issue underlying the momentous changes in eastern Europe and the former Soviet Union in the late 1980s and early 1990s. Many citizens of those countries thought that the transition toward democracy would lead them also to a transition to market-based economic prosperity.

In this chapter, I lay out themes from various traditions of thought to set a baseline for subsequent chapters which focus on these issues in China and Mexico. I trace the history of the ideas about these connections as well as the stylized experiences of various countries over time. I concentrate on asking whether markets increased the likelihood of democracy—the question that the Mexican and Chinese cases, some might argue, seem to answer in the negative—but near the chapter's end I also consider whether democratic politics may help improve market efficiency in the long term. (These fundamental questions are raised as well in this book by Timothy Cheek and Juan Lindau in chapter 1.)

Mine is a common conception of democracy, namely, a political system in which the decision about who shall rule is determined through active contestation in a political arena, itself characterized by extensive participation (at a minimum, universal suffrage), and in which the government and its policies are responsible to the people's elected representatives in the legislature. There is a connection among those who rule, how they are chosen to rule, and the policies that they pursue.[1]

Thinking About the Effects of Capitalism Before Its Triumph

The consequences of market freedoms have been debated for centuries. Attention has centered on private property as a key institution to define the relationship between the citizen and the state, to set the requirements for and the foundations of public order, and to unleash the dynamics of economic growth. This debate began as a conversation held in English in the seventeenth century, when the connection was first drawn between limited constitutional government and free markets. At issue was the nature of the state and the extent of its powers.

The opening salvo of this debate was fired by Thomas Hobbes. Hobbes argued that the sovereign must be very strong; he described what today we would call an authoritarian regime in a strong state. The sovereign had to be all-powerful to prevent war, to create the conditions for peace, and thus to ensure the foundations for a public order that would permit the consolidation of private property. The sovereign's powers would guarantee persons in their property and would make market activity possible: "in all kinds of actions by the laws permitted, men have the liberty, of doing what their own reasons shall suggest, for the most profitable to themselves."[2]

The notion that an authoritarian political regime and a strong state are a solution to the problems posed by a permanent state of war surfaced in Mexico in the closing years of its revolution earlier in the twentieth century, as Lorenzo Meyer makes clear in chapter 5 of this book. In 1929, Mexico's military and political elites made a deal to end the state of war and founded the political regime and the political party that (after various metamorphoses and name changes) still governs Mexico.[3] That Mexican "leviathan" was mild compared to the much

---

1. For the classic contemporary statement, see Robert A. Dahl, *Polyarchy: Participation and Opposition* (New Haven: Yale University Press, 1971).

2. Thomas Hobbes, *Leviathan*, ed. Michael Oakeshott (New York: Collier, 1962), 161. It was first published in 1651. See also chapter 22.

3. See Lorenzo Meyer's "Historical Roots of the Authoritarian State in Mexico," in *Authoritarianism in Mexico*, eds. J. L. Reyna and R. S. Weinert (Philadelphia: Institute for the Study of Human Issues, 1977).

stronger and more severe Chinese "leviathan" founded in 1949 at the end of the long, bloody, and destructive national and international wars that ravaged China during the second quarter of the twentieth century.[4]

In these two countries, an important intellectual tradition has long made a version of this argument: Authoritarian order is essential for their governance. Only a strong sovereign makes economic growth possible. This argument remained compelling for many during much of the second half of the twentieth century. As the century ends, fewer and fewer Mexicans (as Meyer reminds us in chapter 5) believe the leviathan's claims to ensure prosperity through authoritarian rule, but the argument is still invoked by the rulers of both countries. And, as Timothy Cheek shows in chapter 8, even in the closing years of the twentieth century China's political and economic elites work in concert to maintain order and generate prosperity. In contemporary Mexico, moreover, those citizens who tell pollsters that they support the ruling party because it best ensures "social peace"[5] articulate Thomas Hobbes's centuries-old proposition in the language of our times; they also support Juan Lindau's insights in chapter 7 that Mexican civil society remains weak.

John Locke differed in his answer to the same question. Locke agreed that public order and the absence of war were necessary for markets: "The great and chief end, therefore, of men's uniting into commonwealths, and putting themselves under government, is the preservation of their property." Government, in Locke's view, provides "the standard of right and wrong," a "known and indifferent judge, with authority to determine all differences according to the established law," as well as "power to back and support" judicial decisions.[6] Locke suggested, however, that limiting the power of the state by adopting constitutional government would further the likelihood that markets would function more dynamically and efficiently. Locke's reasons on behalf of constitutional government emerged from his political theories, but he also believed that the prospects for operating market systems would be enhanced by governments that did not claim or make

4. Benjamin I. Schwartz, *Chinese Communism and the Rise of Mao* (Cambridge: Harvard University Press, 1951).

5. See Jorge I. Domínguez and James McCann, *Democratizing Mexico: Public Opinion and Electoral Choices* (Baltimore: The Johns Hopkins University Press, 1996).

6. John Locke, "An Essay Concerning the True Original, Extent and End of Civil Government," in *Treatise of Civil Government and A Letter Concerning Toleration*, ed. Charles L. Sherman (New York: Appleton-Century-Crofts, 1937), 82–83. It was first published in 1690.

every decision of significance to human beings. Locke's principal arguments on behalf of limited government, and against arbitrary government, concerned the rights of property holders to make use of their property as they deemed best.[7] Thus Locke laid the foundations of the case that freer politics would lead to freer and more effective markets—the case that the citizens of formerly communist central and eastern Europe so desperately wish to be true.

A stronger economic case for limiting government intervention in the economy was made famous by a third author, Adam Smith. Not only should government be limited in its capacity to dictate to the rest of the society, the economy, and the polity but, in addition, for the most part the government was an obstacle to the proper functioning of markets. Free markets demanded limited government. Capitalism was the midwife of democracy.[8]

The strongest political case on behalf of the virtues of the market was made by Montesquieu, as the debate engaged thinkers in continental Europe.[9] As compared to other human endeavors, markets are boring. Market activity is less heroic than making war, less saintly than martyrdom, less righteous than actions on behalf of God. The pursuit of economic interest in a market environment is also, however, less threatening to civility and public order than the pursuit of struggles based on religious passion and resolved by recourse to warfare: "Commerce is a cure for the most destructive prejudices." In Europe, the scourge of such extreme passions had devastated nations and impeded prosperity. Montesquieu argued that people should pursue the peaceful and boring endeavors of getting rich instead of those that engage their passionate beliefs. The pursuit of interest would restrain the passions that might lead to war. The market, according to Montesquieu, was good for political stability: "Peace is the natural effect of trade. Two nations who traffic with each other become reciprocally dependent. . . . their union is founded on their mutual necessities."[10]

Montesquieu developed the notion of limited government as a means to restrain the passions within the state as well as within the larger society. He argued forcefully for the separation of executive, legislative, and judicial powers as a means to restrain state power.[11] He

<hr>

7. Locke, "An Essay Concerning the True Original, Extent and End of Civil Government," 89–93.

8. Albert Hirschman, *The Passions and the Interests: Political Argument for Capitalism Before Its Triumph* (Princeton: Princeton University Press, 1977).

9. I owe this reading of Montesquieu to Hirschman's *The Passions and the Interests*.

10. Baron de Montesquieu, *The Spirit of the Laws*, tr. Thomas Nugent (New York: Hafner, 1966), 316. It was first published in 1748.

11. Montesquieu, *The Spirit of the Laws*, Book XI, 149–82.

made the double connection forcefully: Peace is essential for markets, while markets are the most likely to lead to peace. Limited government may foster markets; markets may foster limited government.

By the end of the eighteenth century, therefore, one school of thought in Britain and France argued on behalf of narrowing the claims concerning the utility of the state for markets. All agreed that the state had to provide public order but, beyond that, several authors argued that the state should attempt to interfere no further in the economy. The more the state would attempt to meddle in the economy, the worse the outcome would be.

In some of these texts, there is also the birth of an intellectual suspicion about the propensities of democratic government, namely, that democratic government might be too intrusive. Governments based on the consent of the governed could enjoy such wide and massive support that they would endeavor to intervene more in the economy to redress apparent wrongs.

Thinking About the Effects of Capitalism as It Was Triumphing

A century later, leading European intellectuals turned that suspicion into their predominant concern; they agreed that capitalism and democracy were incompatible.[12] As a vibrant capitalism spread through western Europe, views on the relationship between free politics and free markets converged: Markets and democracy did not go together.

For Alexis de Tocqueville, the issues were quite practical. The sweep of democratic force through France in 1848 affected him as a scholar and as a government official. In de Tocqueville's own preface to the twelfth edition (published in 1848) of *Democracy in America,* he revealed his motivation in writing the original work: to understand "the advent of democracy as governing power in the world's affairs, universal and irresistible." Then he recalled his introduction to the original work, wherein he had expressed one chief concern: "Can it be believed that the democracy which has overthrown the feudal system and vanquished kings will retreat before tradesmen and capitalists? Will it stop now that it is grown so strong and its adversaries so weak?"[13]

For de Tocqueville, the rise of democracy in Europe threatened both

---

12. I owe this insight to Claus Offe's essay, "Competitive Party Democracies and the Keynesian Welfare State," in *Contradictions of the Welfare State,* ed. Claus Offe (Cambridge: MIT Press, 1984).

13. Alexis de Tocqueville, *Democracy in America* (New York: Vintage Books, 1945), vol. I, ix, 6. It was first published in 1835.

order and liberty. Part of de Tocqueville's interest in the United States derived from his thinking about how it could ever function; he set for himself the task of understanding this exotic "exception" where democracy, liberty, and markets seemed to coexist, albeit not always easily. In the United States, de Tocqueville found enough order, enough liberty, and enough prosperity: "Almost all Europe was convulsed by revolutions; America has not had even a revolt. The republic there has not been the assailant, but the guardian, of all vested rights; the property of individuals has had better guarantees there than in any other country of the world; anarchy has there been as unknown as despotism."[14] But he remained skeptical that markets and democracy could coincide and strengthen each other, especially in Europe. For him, the values and structures of markets contended with the values and structures of democracy.

In Karl Marx's writings, free competition through markets even more clearly concentrated economic and political power in the hands of the few (the bourgeoisie), thus temporarily impeding the achievement of democracy, understood as government of the majority (the proletariat).[15] The state's guaranteed public order ensured that public and private power remained in the hands of the few. As Marx wrote with regard to the 1848 revolutions in France, the government of the bourgeoisie was a "state whose admitted object is to perpetuate the rule of capital, the slavery of labor."[16] Only the overthrow of such order could bring about democracy—a political regime that responded to the wishes of the vast, immiserated majority. In a democracy, Marx believed, the largest number of citizens should shape the circumstances of their lives and determine their private and public conduct. The relatively few owners of property stood in the way of such exercise of majoritarian democracy. The freer the market, the stronger the property principle, the less likely that the majority of citizens could exercise popular power. Free markets stood in the way of majoritarian democracy.

Equally convinced of the importance of this analytical relationship (though for different reasons) was John Stuart Mill. As democracy spread in Britain, in continental Europe, and in the United States, the liberty for which he cared deeply seemed threatened everywhere. Democracy threatened personal as well as economic liberty, that is, the

---

14. de Tocqueville, *Democracy in America*, x.

15. Karl Marx and Friedrich Engels, "Manifesto of the Communist Party," in *Marx and Engels*, ed. Lewis S. Feuer (New York: Anchor, 1959). It was first published in 1848.

16. Karl Marx, *Class Struggles in France, 1848–1850* (New York: International Publishers, 1964), 58. It was first published in 1850.

capacity of individuals to operate on their own. "Democratic feeling," Mill feared, would increase the spread of "the notion that the public has a right to a veto on the manner to which individuals shall spend their incomes." On the contrary, he argued, governments should not "fix prices and regulate the processes of manufacture" because "the cheapness and the good quality of commodities are most effectually provided by leaving the producers and sellers perfectly free, under the sole check of equal freedom to the buyers for supplying themselves elsewhere." The principle of free trade, he averred, "rests on grounds different from, though equally solid with, the principle of individual liberty."[17]

Mill's concerns about the threat that democracy posed for liberty led him to ponder the design of representative government.[18] Representative government had various purposes and features, in Mill's view, one of which was to stop the broad and unfettered exercise of mass democratic power from impeding the consolidation of constitutional liberty and to destroy the free operation of markets. Majoritarian democracy stood in the way of free markets.

The values and structures of democracy contend with the values and structures of the market. The stronger the democratic impulse and power, the greater the threat of liberties and markets, feared de Tocqueville and Mill. The stronger the impulse and power of markets, the greater the impediment for the achievement of majority rule, averred Marx. Though their reasons differed, these intellectuals, and many others, believed that markets and democracy were incompatible.

The High Point of Optimism: The Hopes for Markets and Democracy

The immediate aftermath of World War I was the empirically based high point of optimism about the proposition that markets increase the likelihood of democracy. At varying speeds, freer markets had been spreading throughout Europe during the preceding two centuries, but especially since the French Revolution. The detailed government regulation of the economy that had characterized mercantilist Europe began to give way, as governments intruded less in specific market transactions in the United States and British North America, the United

---

17. John Stuart Mill, *On Liberty*, ed. Currin Shields (New York: The Liberal Arts Press, 1956), 107, 115. It was first published in 1859.

18. John Stuart Mill, *Consideration on Representative Government* (London: Longman, Green, and Co., 1872).

Kingdom, southernmost South America, and, less rapidly, parts of continental western Europe. Even where governments still played a significant role in the direction of the economy—central Europe, especially Germany, the Tsarist empire, and Japan—market forces had gained great strength.

In the same regions of the world where market forces spread the most, so too did constitutional, limited government. There is constitutional government when a stable political order has lasted for decades, where the power of the chief executive is limited, and where chief executives are chosen following procedures that are agreed upon by the contestants for power. Constitutional governments had gained strength not just among the English-speaking nations of the North Atlantic but also in the closing years of imperial Germany, Tsarist Russia, and Meiji Japan. After World War I, the trend toward constitutional government was interrupted in Russia, but it deepened in Germany with the establishment of the Weimar Republic, as it did in Japan. Universal male suffrage spread as well in the late nineteenth century and in the early twentieth century, from Sweden to Argentina and many countries in between. Soon thereafter, women obtained the right to vote in western Europe and North America (women's suffrage would spread through Latin America mainly after World War II). Opposition political parties could and did win elections, and took power, in western and central Europe, North America, and southernmost South America—the strongest test of democracy. Even where the extension of the suffrage stopped short of democracy's standards (Brazil, Chile, or Colombia), in the first three decades of the twentieth century, there were constitutional governments nonetheless.

In the politics of those days, markets and democracy were seen to evolve together because the rise of one seemed to foster the emergence of the other. Their mutual consolidation rested on the vitality of each of the components of this marriage made through historical practice. Liberal[19] (market-conforming) economic policies called for a reduction of the role of the state in the economy, and especially deregulation. Those policies had generated good economic growth rates, creating a business class and a larger middle class. These new social actors, in turn, pressured government to limit its intervention in the economy, thereby strengthening the political foundations of limited government. This business class sought to deconcentrate government power and to disperse it among private agents. Deconcentrating political power shifted decisionmaking from the bureaucracy toward individuals and firms.

---

19. I am using this word as it is employed everywhere except in the United States.

To accommodate the extension of the suffrage while also reassuring economic and political elites, representative government was invented. At the outset, the electoral laws on which representative government was founded in western Europe and the United States in the nineteenth and early twentieth centuries sought to constrain the spread of mass political power that could overwhelm the state. That was why the Senate of the United States was elected indirectly for over a century; why the United Kingdom retained the House of Lords; and why proportional representation election rules sought to guarantee to the long-governing, now-declining elite parties some substantial parliamentary representation as they faced the onslaught of large socialist parties. In the early days of the consolidation of democracy in Europe, the history of electoral laws demonstrates that their purpose was to contain the power of the masses from winning political power while protecting declining, older political forces.[20]

Representative institutions were first designed by elites, therefore, to ward off the dangers feared by de Tocqueville and Mill—the rule of the mob, which might destroy order and make prosperity impossible. Later on, the same representative institutions protected the elites from their utter replacement by new political forces.

In the long term, the fears of Mill and de Tocqueville, and the hopes of Marx, turned out to be unfounded. The strong participation and political engagement of organized workers did not prove lethal to constitutional order or to markets. Throughout much of Europe and North America, the working class turned out not to be revolutionary. Workers supported reformist parties to set the conditions that would enable them to participate in prosperity.

An implicit bargain was struck between economic and political power. Social Democrats gained political power through elections in many western European countries; they used it not to abolish capitalism but to found the welfare state with the profits of capitalists. The welfare state could only be financed if capitalists were to prosper. Social Democrats became reformers as well as protectors of capitalism. Capitalists, in turn, could not rule alone nor impose their power if they wanted a stable order, and only through democratic institutions and mass suffrage could such order be guaranteed. Markets and democracy had discovered each other in the real world. The one could not

---

20. See Seymour Martin Lipset and Stein Rokkan, "Cleavage Structures, Party Systems, and Voter Alignments," in *Party Systems and Voter Alignments*, ed. S. M. Lipset and Stein Rokkan (New York: The Free Press, 1967); and Douglas Rae, *The Political Consequences of Electoral Laws* (New Haven: Yale University Press, 1971).

survive without the other, or so many believed at this euphoric high point.[21]

One key test was World War I. The Socialist International asked its members, and all workers, to refuse to participate in that capitalist war. The call went unheeded; the Socialist International came to an end. The workers became the soldiers whose blood was the casualty of war. The workers were loyal to the homeland, not to the revolution. The socialist parties of Europe, too, decided that they were the parties of the French, the German, and the British people and that they would support their nation more than internationalist socialist solidarity. These parties remained more interested in reform than in revolution, with the single exception of the faction that seized power in Moscow in 1917 and brought the Tsarist empire to its end. The war indicated that the workers were nationalists, that the socialists were reformists, and that neither was revolutionary.

This was, then, the empirical high point of optimism—the belief that markets would increase the likelihood of democracy and that democracy did not stand in the way of the market economy. This optimism did not last long.

The Birth and Growth of Pessimism

On empirical grounds, soon many became pessimists, believing that democracy and prosperity could not coexist for long. During the 1920s and 1930s, many came to think that democratic institutions were a recipe for social chaos, prevented the development of markets, and impeded the resumption of economic growth. In the strife and torment of the interwar world, democratic governments were seen as unreliable guides to the future. In the 1920s in Italy, in Portugal, and in Spain, mild forms of fascism rejected democratic institutions for the sake of a tougher order and a greater likelihood of prosperity and even grandeur. Military and business elites abandoned their flirtation with freer politics.

Soon the authoritarian trend spread harshly to Germany, where the Nazis overturned the Weimar Republic, and to Austria and elsewhere in eastern and western Europe, and it became harsher in the pioneer "soft authoritarians" of southern Europe. In Latin America, constitutional governments tumbled nearly everywhere in the 1920s and 1930s.

---

21. See Adam Przeworksi, *Capitalism and Social Democracy* (Cambridge: Cambridge University Press, 1985); and Offe, "Competitive Party Democracies and the Keynesian Welfare State."

In Japan, a military dictatorship displaced the practice of limited government.[22] (In Mexico, the revolution engulfed the second decade of the twentieth century. In the decades that followed, Mexican government institutions became more stable, war subsided, and the economy recovered, but there was no liberal democracy at any point.)

Social Science Scholarship: Toward Pessimism

In the aftermath of World War II, the torch of optimism about the positive relationship between markets and democracy again flickered briefly. Some social scientists and historians argued that the prospects for growth under a market economy improved the chances for democracy. This proposition was put forth most forcefully by Seymour Martin Lipset in two related ways, each based on a straightforward statistical correlation.[23]

One of Lipset's arguments was robust, namely, that democracies are most likely to be found in countries that have a high level of economic development.[24] Less persuasively, he argued, unstable democracies are likely to be less unstable in countries that have higher levels of economic development. Lipset's other arguments triggered an intellectual thunderstorm, however. He proposed that the existence of markets helped to "cause" democracy for reasons that are now familiar (and persuasive): Market economies are more likely to generate prosperity, thus more likely to diversify the social structure, thus more likely to create a business and a middle class that would foster limited government, thus more likely to deconcentrate political power, thus more likely to set the foundations for liberal democracy. A market economy also created a large working class, but these workers were prosperous and contented, too. They were not interested in revolution; they wanted secure access to food, shelter, clothing, and schools for their children. Markets led to democracy through the embourgeoisement of the population; those who were not bourgeois aspired to become so.

Other scholars countered that there was impressive empirical evidence that authoritarian governments could coexist and prosper along with market economies. Indeed, some authoritarian governments in central Europe, Germany above all, had grown powerful thanks to the

---

22. Juan J. Linz, "Totalitarian and Authoritarian Regimes," in *Handbook of Political Science*, eds. F. I. Greenstein and N. W. Polsby (Reading, Mass.: Addison-Wesley, 1975), vol. 3.

23. Seymour Martin Lipset, *Political Man* (New York: Doubleday, 1960).

24. See also Samuel Huntington, *The Third Wave: Democratization in the Late Twentieth Century* (Norman: University of Oklahoma Press, 1991), chapter 2.

workings of the market economy. One example of the symbiotic relationship between markets and authoritarian politics in the years when
Lipset published was, of course, Mexico.

The most intellectually influential response came from Barrington
Moore, who explored the social origins of dictatorship and democracy.[25] Moore argued that capitalism could lead either to democracy or
fascism. Markets are indeterminate with regard to the form of the political regime. Moore sought to specify the causal paths that led certain
countries to install the kind of market economy that would evolve
toward democracy or the sort that would lead to authoritarianism. The
key "track switch" was the form of the shift toward markets. Where
labor was repressed, as in Prussia, the groundwork was laid for authoritarian rule through the alliance among the landlord, the urban
bourgeoisie, and the aristocratic and militaristic state; where peasants
disappeared as a class, as in England through the enclosures, a different pattern of class coalitions would form. For Moore, it was not
markets in general but the specific form of the turn toward the market—and the kinds of coalitions that such a shift made possible—that
set the foundations for the evolution of the political regime toward
authoritarian or democratic rule.

In Latin America, the most influential response to Lipset's argument
was Guillermo O'Donnell's exploration of the foundations of bureaucratic-authoritarianism.[26] O'Donnell challenged what he called the optimistic equation, namely, that (market-based) economic development
would lead to democracy. O'Donnell argued that there was an "elective affinity" between a form of political regime that he dubbed bureaucratic-authoritarianism, on the one hand, and capitalist economic
growth, on the other. Democracies could exist in some countries at
fairly low levels of economic development, which lacked dynamic
markets. As rates of economic growth rose and the level of development increased, the economic task required the deepening of the
industrial economy. Governments sought to foster economic development beyond light industry to nurture capital goods-producing industries. Only the latter, he believed, would fully develop a country's
economy. O'Donnell argued that Latin American states relied upon
bureaucratic-authoritarian methods to deepen their economies. Therefore, at higher levels of economic development, there would be not

25. Barrington Moore, Jr., *The Social Origins of Dictatorship and Democracy*
(Boston: Beacon Press, 1966).

26. Guillermo O'Donnell, *Modernization and Bureaucratic-Authoritarianism*
(Berkeley: Institute of International Studies, University of California, 1973), 53–
114.

Lipset-like democratic nirvana but the harsh rule of bureaucrats and soldiers. These new authoritarian regimes did not rely on the classic "man on horseback"; rather, they were installed by a military coup launched by the armed forces as an institution. Their style of operation was bureaucratic, micromanaging various economic activities in conjunction with business, while repressing labor, in order to speed up economic growth.

This intellectual debate can be summarized as follows: Without markets, democracy is impossible. The scholarly and political debate of the 1970s had fully overcome the alleged intrinsic contradiction between markets and democracy common in the political thought of the middle of the nineteenth century. Scholars and politicians from many different perspectives came to the same conclusion. This consensus shaped much of the thinking associated with the democratization of southern and central Europe, Latin America, and the democratizing steps in eastern Europe that would unfold from the mid-1970s to the 1990s.

The debate remained vibrant, however, on a second point: If there are markets, there was no consensus on the most likely shape for the political regime. For some who thought as Barrington Moore, the issue remained the pattern of coalitions at the time of the original shift toward a market economy, which defined the path that would carry the nation's politics for generations. Those who agreed with O'Donnell rejected the argument about the salience of founding coalitions and, instead, focused on the political effects of the changes in the level of development as countries passed through different stages in the organization of production. For yet others, if there are markets, the likelihood of democracy remained indeterminate and impossible to specify.

The High Point of Pessimism: Free Politics versus Free Markets

The apogee of the antidemocratic moment occurred between the mid-1960s and the end of the 1970s. In Argentina, Brazil, Chile, and other Latin American countries, entrenched dictatorships held power (see also Robert Packenham's discussion in chapter 3). In Turkey, democratic regimes were replaced by military regimes. In east Asia, some authoritarian regimes, such as those in South Korea, Singapore, and Taiwan, had become stunningly successful in accelerating the rate of economic growth, as Gaye Christoffersen points out in chapter 4 of this book.

Several Latin American countries as well as South Korea and Turkey had experienced populist democratic politics. Democratic populists had won national elections and, as the elite nineteenth-century intellectuals feared, used their democratic legitimacy to intervene in the economy thoroughly and intrusively.[27] As Mill and de Tocqueville would have expected, these economic policies were disastrous for both the economy and for democracy. Democratic regimes tumbled thereafter, as the belief spread especially in business and military circles that democracy and markets were incompatible in Africa, Asia, and Latin America.

A related but different argument was Hobbes's intellectual heir: Only a leviathan can guarantee prosperity. Only when the government is all-powerful and credibly committed to protect private property and the functioning of markets can sustained prosperity be ensured, even if at the sacrifice of political liberty. This view spread in Singapore, South Korea, Taiwan, Hong Kong (in what came to be known as the Brazilian economic "miracle"), General Augusto Pinochet's Chile, and even in Mexico in the 1960s. Democracy was seen with disdain, at best. For those who wanted economic growth, Hobbes's ideas had resurrected.

A third antidemocratic argument was invoked through the word "Eurosclerosis," in vogue during the 1970s. Western Europe's economies and politics were not faring well, suggesting serious trouble in the relationship between democracies and markets even in the one region of the world where they had embraced each other. A wider term was "stagflation," applied to western Europe, the United States, and Canada. Fairly high rates of inflation coincided with relatively low rates of economic growth. The democratic governments in these countries did not do a good job of generating economic growth.[28] Why should those interested in market-based growth emulate democratic governments that produced stagnant, sclerotic economies?

To maintain social peace under those conditions and to permit the smoother functioning of the economy, some scholars and politicians suggested that benign "corporatism" was the solution, that is, the state's detailed licensing and management of the forms of societal representation and its supervision of the pattern of relations between labor and management. Though most scholars eschewed recommending the tough "state corporatism" evident in Brazil, the wide social compacts and inter-class formal agreements evident in Austria, Sweden, and Switzerland came in for analysis and praise. The remedy for stagfla-

27. For a sharp critique, see Rudiger Dornbusch and Sebastian Edwards, "Macroeconomic Populism," *Journal of Development Economics* 32 (1990): 247–275.
28. Douglas A. Hibbs, Jr., *The Political Economy of Industrial Democracies* (Cambridge: Harvard University Press, 1987).

tion, some argued, was government economic micromanagement with a soft touch; they demanded statist activism in the hope of generating order and growth.[29]

In the 1970s, moreover, communist Europe still seemed successful. Eastern Europe had recovered economically from the ravages of World War II. Its rates of economic growth were fairly high in the 1950s and 1960s, more so in some countries than in others. Communist central planning seemed one plausible and rational way to organize backward economies for a great leap forward.[30]

The last claim of the antidemocrats made recourse to political culture arguments. Democracy might work in the United Kingdom or in the United States, but "not with my people." The politician who has sustained this view the longest and most successfully has been Singapore's Lee Kwan Yew.

In short, the antidemocrats were apparently triumphing because democratic governments in Europe and North America had a poor record of economic management, while democratic governments in what was called "the Third World" had an even worse record. In contrast, cultural authoritarians in East Asia and communist authoritarians everywhere held up their models of order and progress—the words emblazoned on the Brazilian flag since the nineteenth century—while European scholars and politicians endorsed or at least tolerated forms of corporatism that, in fact, constrained both free politics and free markets as means to rescue enough of each. For many, the leviathan

---

29. Suzanne Berger, ed., *Organizing Interests in Western Europe* (Cambridge: Cambridge University Press, 1981); Philippe Schmitter and Gerhard Lehmbruch, eds., *Trends toward Corporatist Intermediation* (Beverly Hills: Sage Publications, 1979); Ruth Berins Collier and David Collier, "Inducements versus Constraints: Disaggregating Corporatism," *American Political Science Review* 73 (December 1979): 967–86; Mancur Olson, *The Rise and Decline of Nations* (New Haven: Yale University Press, 1982), chs. 2 and 3; Claus Offe and Helmut Wiesenthal, "Two Logics of Collective Action: Theoretical Notes on Social Class and Organizational Form," in *Contradictions of the Welfare State* ed. Offe; Peter Lange and Geoffrey Garrett, "The Politics of Growth: Strategic Interaction and Economic Performance in Advanced Industrial Democracies, 1974–1980," *Journal of Politics* 47 (1985): 792–827; Peter Swenson, "Bringing Capital Back In, or Social Democracy Reconsidered: Employer Power, Cross-Class Alliances, and Centralization of Industrial Relations in Denmark and Sweden," *World Politics* 43, no. 4 (July 1991): 513–44; and David Held, "Pluralism, Corporate Capitalism and the State," in *Models of Democracy* ed. Held (Stanford: Stanford University Press, 1987), 186–220.

30. On the effect of communist economics on workers, see Charles F. Sabel and David Stark, "Planning, Politics, and Shop-Floor Power: Hidden Forms of Bargaining in Soviet-Imposed State-Socialist Societies," *Politics and Society* 11, no. 4 (1982): 439–75.

seemed the only sure path to prosperity. Consequently, as Cheek makes evident in chapter 8, learning from the successful leviathans of the day, in the late 1970s Chinese leaders adopted new policies: communist politics persisted but now with East Asian, strong-state, market-oriented policies.

The Tarnished Promise of Authoritarian Rule

In the 1980s, three sets of empirical events terminated the antidemocratic movement. The slowdown in the growth rates of the economies of communist Europe led to a scholarly and political reassessment of their histories since World War II. The spurt of growth in eastern Europe in the 1950s and 1960s came to be seen as the economic recovery from World War II, not as a genuine process of growth. The growth rates lasted into the 1960s not because such economies were dynamic but, on the contrary, because they took much longer to recover from a much lower base than the economies of western Europe. The gross inefficiencies of central planning in communist Europe came to be better understood. These states did not allocate resources efficiently; they stood in the way of innovations in society, economics, and politics, retarding the technological revolution already evident elsewhere in Europe, North America, and East Asia.

The second major set of events occurred in Latin America. Authoritarian governments failed spectacularly in their macroeconomic management. The failure was truly catastrophic in Argentina, Bolivia, and Peru, and bad enough in Brazil. Even Pinochet's Chile—which looks good in the folklore of some of the international business press—faced a very severe economic downturn. Chile's economy crashed in 1982–83; the rate of decline of its gross domestic product was worse than elsewhere in South America at the birth of the international debt crisis. The Chilean government responded by seizing many of the banks and other financial institutions.[31] The Mexican government, too, grossly mismanaged its economy, which crashed in 1982; it took the remainder of the decade barely to recover. Many came to believe, therefore, that authoritarian regimes were much less effective in practice than they had seemed on the eve of their installation.

The third major shift was the recovery of the economies of the industrial democracies in the North Atlantic region and Japan. The hope

---

31. V. Corbo, J. de Melo, and J. Tybout, "What Went Wrong with the Recent Reforms in the Southern Cone," *Economic Development and Cultural Change* 34, no. 3 (April 1986): 607–37.

was reborn that democracies and economic growth could coexist and reinforce each other.

In short, there was a marked change in political and scholarly perceptions about the relative efficacy of democratic governments, of communist governments, and of non-communist authoritarian governments. This most recent change set the intellectual and policy environment that prevailed in the 1990s: free politics and free markets go together. Democracy and prosperity reinforce each other and best sustain the peace within and among countries.

Explanatory Puzzles

At the analytical level, nevertheless, skepticism has persisted, and with good reason. Scholars must attempt to explain the nature of the relationship between democracy and markets, not just note their coincidence in some cases, while remaining alert to cases that do not fit the "happy" relationship. The difficulties can be illustrated through four analytical puzzles.

Does the spread of markets explain the emergence of democratic political systems? If the political system of Country X has democratized, is that because of the prior spread of a market economy? In the early 1990s, the evidence poured in: the answer is no. Democratization spread through most of eastern Europe, not just to those countries (such as Poland or Hungary) where markets had played a stronger role. All eastern European communist regimes collapsed in 1989. The change in these political systems cannot be explained in terms of the prior injection of some market forces as compared to their complete absence: Communism was toppled in Albania and Romania even in the absence of prior market reforms.

Democracy can result from reasons other than the spread of market forces. In chapter 9 of this book, David Hendrickson assesses the role of various international factors in advancing or retarding democratic politics. Democratic politics may result from defeat at war, as was the case in Germany, Japan, and Italy at the end of World War II, in Greece after its defeat by Turkey in 1974, in Argentina after its defeat by the United Kingdom in 1982, or in Grenada in 1983 and Panama in 1989, respectively, after the defeat of their governments by the United States. An international political explanation (the change in Soviet policy toward its neighbors) explains the collapse of European communist regimes between 1989 and 1991. The prior existence of the market was neither necessary nor sufficient to explain change in eastern Europe.

Communist regimes fell independently of the content of their prior economic policies.

Can the spread of a market economy facilitate the emergence of democratic politics? The answer to this much weaker formulation of the previous question is yes. The spread of market forces probably facilitated political openings in South Korea and Taiwan in the 1980s and 1990s (as Christoffersen notes in chapter 4) as it did in Spain during the 1960s and 1970s, among other countries. It took a couple of decades for this process to unfold, however. It may also be premature to assert that all of these countries have been inoculated forever against the authoritarian temptation; markets once fostered political openings in Germany, Italy, and Japan, only to be reversed during the 1930s.

Does the fact that authoritarian regimes have lingered for a very long time invalidate the possible link between markets and democracy? The answer is no. Consider Mexico and China. Important democratizing forces in both countries have followed, and were to some extent caused by, "market-enough" experiences. In each case, ruling elites had to prevent the transition toward greater democracy. This was most evident in China at Tiananmen Square in 1989 after the stunning growth of the market economy during the preceding decade, but it happened as well in Mexico with the repression of urban protest in 1968 after impressive growth of the market economy since the 1940s. As Meyer notes in chapter 5, elite action in Mexico delayed the full installation of democratic practices through electoral fraud, selective and limited repression, and the generalized practice of cooptation to disarticulate the opposition.[32] In both countries, markets facilitated the coming of democracy, but elites did not, and the latter prevailed through the 1990s.

Why can markets coexist for so long with authoritarian politics? They have in Bismarckian Germany and among the so-called "Asian Tigers" (Singapore, South Korea, Hong Kong, and Taiwan) as well as in Mexico and China. Let us distinguish, however, between the concept of markets as economists use it and markets as political scientists, sociologists, and historians may observe them; the latter I will call business markets. Business markets are often characterized by private monopolies and private oligopolies. In small countries with small economies, business markets—contrary to the idealized markets in the writings of some economists—do not deconcentrate economic or political power. Business markets often depend on the informal, occasionally corrupt,

---

32. A growing number of ordinary Mexicans supported democratic values and practices in the 1990s. See Domínguez and McCann, *Democratizing Mexico*, chapter 2.

but normally lawful representation and advancement of business interests to lock in relations between business and the state that reduce the likelihood of democratic outcomes. Where economic and political power remain concentrated and where informal means of interest representation prevail, there is no "responsible" government: Governments are not chosen democratically, but, even if they are, they enact policies that respond to the interests of the influential few. In the long run, nonetheless, markets do increase the probability of democratic politics, for the general reasons already stated.

The Evolving Intellectual Consensus

What has increased the likelihood of an elective affinity between democracy and markets? (By "elective affinity" I mean not a hard or deterministic relationship but a correspondence of choices—Max Weber's original formulation.) What has improved the odds that democrats would choose markets and that economic actors would choose democracy as their preferred form of economic and political organization, respectively? For this section, I will focus exclusively on Latin American countries in the 1990s (see also Packenham's comments in chapter 3).

In Latin American countries, many who had not believed in the appropriateness and efficacy of markets have changed their views. This shift required only modest intellectual adjustments in the case of Alejandro Foxley, former finance minister of Chile, whose views in the late 1960s and early 1970s suggested a stronger government intervention in the economy to achieve socially valued objectives. A larger change occurred in the thinking of Brazil's President Fernando Henrique Cardoso, whose belief in markets in the 1960s and 1970s was, at best, weak; in the 1990s, he has energetically reoriented Brazil's economic policy to make greater use of markets.

Some who had not believed enough in the utility of democracy changed their views as well. Argentina's former economy minister, Domingo Cavallo, exemplifies this shift. In the early 1980s, Cavallo served as central bank president during an inept military government. The failure of authoritarian regimes in the formulation of effective economic policies made it easier for those who had believed in efficient markets, but not necessarily in democracy, to change their minds, too.[33]

---

33. Javier Corrales, "Why Argentines Follow Cavallo: A Technopol Between Democracy and Economic Reform," João Resende-Santos, "Fernando Henrique Cardoso: Social and Institutional Rebuilding in Brazil," and Jeanne Kinney Giraldo, "Development and Democracy in Chile: Finance Minister Alejandro Foxley and the Concertación's Project for the 90s," in *Technopols: Freeing Politics and Markets in Latin America in the 1990s*, ed. Jorge I. Domínguez (University Park, Pa.: Pennsylvania State University Press, 1997).

In the 1990s, democrats who chose markets and economic decision-makers who chose democracy, though neither had done so before, converged as well on the belief that freer markets contribute to a less arbitrary state. Markets dispersed power more than state firms and agencies did, thus helping to curtail the inept and arbitrary state, a legacy from the 1970s and early 1980s. For both democracy and markets, this change was long overdue.

The logic of democracy strengthened the new consensus. This logic sets rational expectations for market actors more effectively than its alternatives. Compared to authoritarian regimes, in the 1990s democratic political systems could set rules and fashion institutions that were more likely to endure even after there are personnel and partisan changes. Non-monarchical, non-communist authoritarian regimes, though often market-friendly, have never managed political succession well. The principal way military governments replace presidents is by military coup (Brazil between 1964 and 1985 was an exception). Non-monarchical, non-communist, market-friendly authoritarian governments do not, therefore, give reliable long-term guarantees. Democracies do so more credibly, and thus investors can have rational expectations about the future behavior of governments.

Chinese leaders, too, are aware that they must provide stable long-term conditions so that rational economic actors would foster China's economic development. As Pitman Potter shows in chapter 6, Chinese leaders have sought to link legal to market reforms as China's answer to this problem of rational expectations. Not surprisingly, a key difficulty in relying on law as the source for stable rule is the potential for arbitrariness that persists under the Communist Party and the uncertainties still evident in the process of political succession.

Many non-communist authoritarian regimes also tend to be politically less stable in the contemporary world because there is often an organized opposition, labor unions, and other means of citizen resistance. Democracies are more likely to handle the opposition more effectively, thus lowering the market transaction costs that otherwise stem from political instability and repression.

In the long term, democracy is more likely to permit the consolidation of market-friendly rules. The long-term guarantor of market rules and institutions is, above all, the political opposition. If the opposition endorses the rules and institutions of the market along with the parties in government, then economic actors can infer rationally that they can expect such a market framework to continue even if the opposition were to win the next elections. Government and opposition dispute power not over these fundamental issues but over policy choices within the framework of a market economy. Only a democratic political system can embody the compromises and commitments that bind the government and the opposition freely to a market economy. In Latin America in the 1990s, only through the consent of the governed could governments signal credibly to economic actors that the market economy would persist. Democracy, as Montesquieu would remind us, restrains the passionate extremism of government officials: only democracy permits credible and enduring commitments bound by constitutional norms and limited powers.

Reinventing the Keynesian Bargain

In the years following World War II, scholars of European countries analyzed the relationship between democracy and markets as what was called the Keynesian bargain. This bargain, so it was argued, helped to link democratic politics to a market economy, making them mutually reinforcing. The Keynesian bargain had three fundamental features. First, workers recognized the right of capitalists to profit. Second, capitalists save, invest, generate economic growth, create jobs, and raise wages in response to improve productivity. Third, the state provides order, enforces the bargain between workers and capitalists, and smooths out the economic cycles while collecting taxes from profits in order to create the welfare state for the workers.[34]

The Anglo–American "faith" differed somewhat. From Adam Smith and Thomas Jefferson to Margaret Thatcher and Ronald Reagan, it was better summarized in the slogan that the government that governs least governs best. In contrast to both the Keynesian bargain and the Anglo–American faith, Latin American governments had long ago constructed the capacious but hollow state whose tasks were as ambitious as its capacities were limited. In the early 1990s, Latin American politics shifted from the feeding of the fat state to muscle-toning the fit state. The fat state had sought to do everything, to control and to regulate many activities, but to do so badly. The fit state seeks to do fewer things but to do them more effectively.

The new Latin American state, with a democratic political regime and a market-oriented economy, differs from the Reagan–Thatcher formulation. In the U.S. presidential campaign in 1988, Republican candidate George Bush pledged, "Read my lips, no new taxes." In contrast, Economy Minister Cavallo in Argentina and Finance Ministers Foxley and Cardoso in Chile and Brazil, respectively, represented an alterna-

---

34. Offe, "Competitive Party Democracies and the Keynesian Welfare State."

tive slogan: "Read my lips, pay your taxes." One stunning change in Latin America in the 1990s was increased tax revenues. This was accomplished mainly by improved tax collections (though taxes were raised slightly in Chile). These states are not withering away. They seek to remain capable and strong, different from the Anglo–American leaders to whom they are sometimes compared. The new Latin American state has fashioned a novel Keynesian bargain between democracy and the market: the investment in "human capital," that is, spending more on public schools and public clinics. Only healthy and better-educated labor forces make the economy efficient and competitive.

Conclusion

The existence, growth, and consolidation of a market economy increase the likelihood that democratic politics can similarly emerge, grow, and become consolidated, but there is no guarantee that democracy and markets have an easy or readily predictable relationship.

Most democratic regimes in the 1990s serve markets better than most authoritarian regimes because only democratic regimes can credibly set rational expectations for the long-term future. Not all kinds of democratic regimes do that; the Latin American experience from World War II to the 1980s reminds us that democratic governments can and often have malperformed in their economic policies. But democracy in its logic is useful for markets because only democracy can bind the nation's future to the market by means of the nation's consent.

Democracy does not automatically create prosperity; it has not in most of eastern Europe and the former Soviet Union. But democracy can be strategically useful for markets, as Argentina's Economy Minister Cavallo demonstrated: He chose a democratic procedure—an act of Congress—to bind his hands on the exchange rate policies that he would or would not pursue. He wanted to signal that Argentina would have a stable and invariant exchange rate and a steady monetary policy. He realized that his own word would not be credible beyond a few weeks; he could not guarantee stability by decree. Instead, he sought and obtained an act of Congress (the so-called convertibility law of 1991) which mandated that the exchange rate could not be changed by the central bank, the economy minister, or the president except through another act of Congress. That decision demonstrates how democratic institutions can be employed to send credible, long-term market signals.

Markets are strategically useful for democracy as well because they can deconcentrate power. The challenge is how to create "real" economists' markets, not just to endure business markets with monopolies and oligopolies.

Difficult questions remain. How can one foster the voluntary choices required for a democratic opening and help those decisions to succeed? This has yet to occur sufficiently in either China or Mexico. Meyer in chapter 5 and Lindau in chapter 7 call our attention to important cultural traditions and to the weaknesses in Mexican civil society that have retarded a democratic transition. Cheek in chapter 8 notes severe problems in the articulation of civil society in China. How can one avoid behaviors that became common throughout much of South America in the late 1980s and early 1990s, namely, that candidates campaigned for president (in Argentina, Brazil, Peru, and Venezuela, among others) on a given set of promises, won the election, and proceeded to implement policies that were the exact opposite of those promises? What are the incentives to reward truth tellers?

In 1852, Karl Marx wrote that "men make their own history but they do not make it just as they please."[35] The construction of democracy and markets occurs only within historically constrained possibilities. It results from a combination of structure and choice. The structure of markets makes it possible for individuals to choose democracy. The choice of democracy makes it possible to consolidate the workings of the market economy. In the long term, democracy and markets increase their respective likelihood of joint occurrence, and this, too, may well be the torch that lights the path to the future in Mexico and in China.

---

35. Karl Marx, *The Eighteenth Brumaire of Louis Bonaparte* (New York: International Publishers, 1963), 15.

Part II
REGIONAL CONTEXT

3

Market-Oriented Reforms and National Development in Latin America

Robert A. Packenham

E conomic liberalism has been rejected in Latin America during most of the region's history. Colonial mercantilism lasted three centuries and left an illiberal legacy. There was a "liberal pause" from, say, 1850 to 1930,[1] but, even during that period, significant spaces for the state in development were maintained.[2] After 1930 economic liberalism was again discarded in favor of import substituting industrialization and other non-liberal economic strategies and philosophies. The traditional Latin American distaste for economic liberalism was certainly not reversed by its association with the military regime in Chile after 1973. In most other countries various forms of state capitalism stayed in place throughout the 1970s and most of the 1980s despite partial (e.g., Colombia) or failed (e.g., Martinez de Hoz in Argentina) attempts to change them.[3]

---

1. Claudio Veliz, *The Centralist Tradition of Latin America* (Princeton: Princeton University Press, 1980).

2. Peter H. Smith, "The State and Development in Historical Perspective," in *Americas: New Interpretive Essays*, ed. Alfred Stepan (New York: Oxford University Press, 1992), 30–56.

3. For overviews, see Enrique Krauze, "Old Paradigms and New Openings in Latin America," *Journal of Democracy* 3, no. 1 (January 1992): 15–24, and Sebastian Edwards, *Crisis and Reform in Latin America: From Despair to Hope* (New York: Oxford University Press, 1995), 43–48. For a summary of the Colombian case, see Miguel Urrutia, "Colombia," in *The Political Economy of Policy Reform*, ed. John Williamson (Washington, D.C.: Institute for International Economics, January 1994), 285–315. On the failed efforts of Martinez de Hoz in

At the end of the 1980s and in the 1990s, however, the policies of Latin American governments suddenly and dramatically changed. Everywhere the stated policy models of state-market relations moved in a liberalizing direction.[4] It did not matter what the political trajectory, ideology, generation, political party, or (in some cases) campaign promises of the leader and his new government had been before; once in power, almost all of them—de la Madrid and especially Salinas and Zedillo in Mexico; Collor, Franco, and especially Cardoso in Brazil; Menem in Argentina; Fujimori in Peru; Andrés Pérez in Venezuela; Aylwin and Frei in Chile; even Castro in Cuba—moved, at least at the level of policy rhetoric and often in reality as well, in the direction of freer trade and investment policies, privatization of state enterprises, reductions in governmental deficits and state subsidies for private enterprises, deregulation, and other "neoliberal" development strategies.[5]

To be sure, the amount of rhetorical change was much, much less in quantity—and much less enthusiastic and far-reaching in quality—in Cuba than in, say, most other Latin American countries. To be sure, the degree of implementation of the rhetoric also has varied enormously: The most notable contrast is between Brazil, where implementation has been slow, and Chile, Argentina, and Mexico, where it has gone much faster and farther. The causes, consequences, and permanence of the changes may also vary greatly from country to country; on the latter point, time will tell the full story.

Nevertheless, a revolution has occurred in Latin America—not the kind most frequently dreamed about and predicted, but a revolution all the same—that was unforeseen and even unimagined by most analysts only a few years ago. This chapter surveys and analyzes this unexpected revolution for both its intrinsic interest and its implications for the broader field of development theory and specific cases such as

---

Argentina, a summary with citations is Jeffry A. Frieden, *Debt, Development, and Democracy: Modern Political Economy and Latin America, 1965–1985* (Princeton: Princeton University Press, 1991), 206–215. There were other partial exceptions and failed efforts in smaller countries such as Bolivia, Ecuador, and Peru before 1990; see, for example, Catherine M. Conaghan and James M. Malloy, *Unsettling Statecraft: Democracy and Neoliberalism in the Central Andes* (Pittsburgh: University of Pittsburgh Press, 1994).

4. There were a very few exceptions: e.g., Honduras, Uruguay after its referendum of late 1992, the administration of Rafael Caldera in Venezuela from 1994 to about 1996. But the overwhelming trend is the one indicated.

5. By far the most thorough survey at the economic level of these changes is Edwards, *Crisis and Reform*.

Mexico (and perhaps also China, though that is a larger leap). The aim is to clarify issues and concepts as well as to offer analytic perspectives.

More specifically, there are eight questions to take up in this chapter. It is worthwhile to state them at the outset not only to give a preview of what is coming but also because formulating good questions is no less important than giving good answers. These questions are designed to separate issues that need to be separated, not conflated and blurred together in ways that obscure analysis. The questions are: 1) How should we conceptualize and define development? 2) How should we conceptualize and define state-market relations and economic liberalization (so that we can later assess their relationship to development)? 3) What was the baseline, that is, what models of state-market relations were used in Latin America before the surge of market-oriented reforms? 4) What has happened to state-market relations since the late 1980s? 5) What have been the observable effects of economic liberalization on national development? 6) Have the reforms been good or bad for development and how should one think about such matters? 7) What are the implications of the foregoing for existing theories about development? 8) What are the implications of the foregoing for the case of Mexico? We shall devote most of our attention to questions 5, 6, and 8, but it is also important to address the others at least briefly.

Dimensions of Development

Scholars and policymakers put a variety of "things" or "items" or "dimensions" under the umbrella of the word "development." Often they refer, as I do in this chapter, explicitly or implicitly to three or four main dimensions: economic, social, political, and (sometimes) international. The economic dimension has mainly to do with aggregate economic productivity as measured by levels of GNP, GNP per capita, industrialization, and like indicators. It is about the size of the economic pie. The social dimension has mainly to do with social and economic equality and the status of the poor. It is about how the economic pie is divided up and how those at the lower ends of socioeconomic stratification systems are doing. The political dimension is multifaceted. It is about regimes that are, among other things, either democratic or authoritarian (or totalitarian), stable or unstable, civilian or military. The international dimension has mainly to do with issues of national autonomy and dependence. It involves a variety of economic and non-economic ingredients related to the size and character of external influences on national development and the capacities of national governments to steer their own course in their domestic and foreign policies.[6]

When we think about development, it is necessary to consider any single dimension or aspect not only by itself but also in relation to other dimensions. Failure to address the interrelatedness of dimensions can produce theoretical and analytic fallacies and policy disasters. For instance, it is often said that what really matters is basic human needs such as food, shelter, and health care and that, wherever these needs are met, the essentials of development are being realized. Such a perspective has often been used to justify the Castro regime in Cuba; it has also been used (less often and usually not by the same people) to justify the apartheid regime in South Africa. But note that food, shelter, and health care are provided in any well-run prison. A prison is not a good model for national development, and neither is Castro's Cuba or South Africa under apartheid. It is necessary to think about several dimensions of national development, not just one.

Once development is defined the next question is: What brings development about? A big part of the answer to that question has to do with the relationship between the state and the market.

A Continuum and Four Models of State-Market Relations

Imagine a continuum along the dimension "degree of state control of the private sector of the economy." At one end of the continuum is total state control; at the other end is no state control at all. This single continuum is in fact made up of a number of elements or sub-dimensions, such as the degree of state control over productive enterprises, open or closed trade and investment regimes, regulation or deregulation of ongoing private-sector enterprises, increases or decreases in state subsidies, size of budget deficits/surpluses and state bureaucracies, and moves toward bureaucratic centralization or decentralization. The degree of control by the state over the market and the private sector is an aggregate concept that can include any or all of these or other

---

6. These are not, of course, the only dimensions that might be considered under the heading of development. Environmental, ethnic, gender, cultural, religious, kinship, security, and/or military dimensions, and doubtless others, could also be used. It is legitimate to argue that one or more of them or others should for some purposes displace one or more of the dimensions used here. However, as a practical matter, the number that can be employed at one time is limited. The dimensions used here are clearly very central and widely employed by other development scholars and by policymakers. Moreover, as will be seen, they provide plenty of complexity, both empirical and moral.

similar dimensions. Economic liberalization can occur on some of these dimensions without necessarily occurring in others. It can go up on one dimension and down on another. But the elements can also be aggregated into one single continuum conceptually and empirically.

Thus the economist Robert M. Solow, a Nobel laureate writing in a nonscholarly journal, observed in 1986 that "we can imagine a line segment with pure capitalism at its right end point and pure socialism at its left end point; and we can think of arraying existing and possible social-economic arrangements along that line, depending on how closely they resemble one ideal type or the other. There might be dispute about the relative placement of certain hard cases. (I think this is . . . [because] we are reducing a two-or-more-dimensional classification to a one-dimensional array.) In practice, however, we will be able to talk comfortably in these terms most of the time."[7] And so we do— both ordinary citizens and, increasingly, professional economists and other social scientists.

For example, a number of studies have appeared recently that have used increasingly sophisticated, systematic, and complex concepts and data to measure the degree of control of the market by the state (in other words, the degree of economic freedom or liberalization). The first of these used ten measures for a single point in time. They were vivid snapshots that yielded aggregated index numbers incorporating all ten measures for as many as one hundred countries.[8] In 1996 the first edition of *Economic Freedom of the World* appeared.[9] It had seventeen measures aggregated into four clusters and also into one aggregated summary indicator of economic freedom for each of 100 countries. Even more significantly, it had such information for not just one year but five points in time: 1975, 1980, 1985, 1990, and 1995. For the first time, analysts of the subject have a series of snapshots, a very crude moving picture, of the degree of state control or economic freedom for one hundred national cases based systematically on seventeen different indicators which are also aggregated into one overall number.

Now that we have a conceptual continuum of state control/economic freedom for which data exist to locate countries over time in a

---

7. Robert M. Solow, "Dollars and Democracy," *The New Republic*, 15 & 22 September 1986, 50–52, quotation at 51.
8. See Williamson, *The Political Economy of Policy Reform*; Bryan T. Johnson and Thomas P. Sheehy, *The Index of Economic Freedom* (Washington, D.C.: The Heritage Foundation, 1995); and Harry Rowen, "World Wealth Expanding," in *The Mosaic of Economic Growth*, eds. Ralph Landau, Gavin Wright, and Timothy Taylor (Stanford: Stanford University Press, 1996), 92–125.
9. James Gwartney, Robert Lawson, and Walter Block, *Economic Freedom of the World: 1975–1995* (Vancouver: Fraser Institute, 1996).

fairly precise and replicable fashion, we can move on to the next step, which is to identify some types along the spectrum. To that end, let us divide the continuum into four spaces, sections, or types: from left to right, very high state control, high state control, low state control, very low state control. We can attach conceptual or theoretical names or labels to each of these four spaces or types; let us call them, in order, socialism, state capitalism, social capitalism, and pure market capitalism. (Of course, different labels could be used.) So far the exercise is still abstract; no cases have been identified yet. But now let us use the four types a) to locate Latin American cases in the past and b) as a way to characterize the massive changes in development models in the last few years.

From the 1930s to the Late 1980s:
State-Capitalist and Socialist Models of Development

From the 1930s to the late 1980s, most Latin American countries, while capitalist, had high levels of economic control by the state. In other words, during that period most of them were in the state-capitalist category. This certainly was the case for Mexico after the presidency of Lázaro Cárdenas (1934–40), Brazil after the first presidencies of Getúlio Vargas (1930–45), and Argentina after the first presidencies of Juan Domingo Perón (1946–55).[10] Most other Latin American countries also fell into the state-capitalist category during this period. There were some exceptions: Cuba after 1960 fell into the socialist category, while Chile (1970–73) and Nicaragua (1979–90) also moved strongly in the socialist direction. An exception of the opposite sort was Chile after 1975, which moved vigorously in the direction of economic liberalization. There are other possible exceptions; for example, one might argue that Costa Rica or Colombia had moved into the social capitalism category. But there were not many exceptions, and even the Colombian and Costa Rican cases are debatable.

During the half century from the 1930s to the 1980s, there were many policy and academic debates in Latin America (and among foreign Latin Americanists) about what kind of state capitalism to have and whether to move from state capitalism to socialism, but many fewer policy and academic debates about moving to social capitalism. The

10. In Argentina the Yacimientos Petroliferos Fiscales (YPF), the first state-owned oil monopoly in Latin America, was founded in 1922. But many aspects of a liberal economic regime remained in place until the Perón governments after 1945.

thinking of the vast majority of decisionmakers and intellectuals within most Latin American countries was so firmly embedded in the range of state capitalist models and socialist alternatives to them that they seldom considered moving to social capitalism—never mind pure market capitalism. Relatively small minorities of policymakers and thinkers within most countries did call for greater liberalism, but they were never successful in moving their countries' policies out of state capitalism into social capitalism. They were usually designated "monetarists," later "Chicago Boys," or simply "liberals," which in Latin America tended strongly to connote elitism, authoritarianism, and reaction; with a few notable exceptions they were usually marginal players in both the political arena and the academy during the period from the 1930s to the 1980s.

If Latin American development models during those fifty years or so did not move into the social liberalism category, then they were even less likely, obviously, to move into the category of pure market capitalism. The latter model, with very low state involvement, did sometimes operate in reality in certain sectors of the economies of many countries—particularly in the poorest and most socially retrograde countries and areas—but nowhere was it a model of national development endorsed or favored by influential political leaders or intellectuals. (Anyone who thinks that Chile after 1973 is a case of pure market capitalism needs to think again. The copper industry remained in state hands throughout the Pinochet period and remains so at this writing. While most of the state enterprises that existed in 1973 were privatized by the 1980s, some of the largest ones remained in state hands. The state took over a number of private banks in the economic crisis of 1982–84, and state regulation of the economy increased overall after 1985.)

As a model of national economic and social development, pure market capitalism has been and remains not a widely desired, practiced, or realistic political option but rather a negative symbol for proponents of state capitalism and socialism to beat upon. Pure-market capitalism simply does not exist in Latin America, or anywhere else, in the former sense. By contrast, in the latter sense—that is, as a negative symbol—it is very much alive in both the political and the scholarly world.

In sum, during the fifty years or so before the middle and late 1980s, policy and intellectual debates in Latin America were, broadly speaking, about two main questions: First, what kind of state capitalism should be used? And second (especially after 1959), should state capitalism be retained or should there be a move in a leftward direction to socialism? Defenders of more market-oriented models of economic development certainly existed, but during those years they were in a distinct and rather small minority in policy debates and even more so in academic discussions. In the relatively few instances when their policies were adopted, as in Argentina in the late 1970s, they usually did not last long because they were politically unsustainable or for other reasons. The major exception to this, of course, was Chile after 1975, but even there the trend never went as far as pure market capitalism; and after the economic crisis of 1982–84 the model was modified in a statist direction for both economic and political reasons. There were virtually no defenders or national exemplars of pure market capitalism, and even exponents of social capitalism were on the defensive vis-à-vis the two options on the left-hand side of the spectrum.[11]

Since the Late 1980s: The Trend Toward Economic Liberalization

In the last few years those patterns, in place for fifty years, have changed dramatically. The socialist model has largely disappeared as a widely desired option in policy and theoretical debate, at least for the moment. The state-capitalist model, so long dominant, is now on the defensive. The model of social capitalism is now admissible to the debate. In fact, wherever countries were located on the spectrum before, by the early 1990s most of them were moving at varying speeds toward a smaller state role and a larger private sector role than they had previously. Whether this means movement only as far as the right end of the state capitalism category or actually into the social liberalism category, the direction of the change is clear. In short, a process of economic liberalization has been going on that is unprecedented since the 1930s. It constitutes a revolution in ideas and policies regarding state/private-sector relations.

The first country to move in the liberalizing direction was, of course, Chile under the military regime that came to power in a coup in 1973.

11. Full documentation would require citations to studies of individual countries. For overviews see Joseph Love, "Economic Ideas and Ideologies in Latin America Since 1930," in *Cambridge History of Latin America*, vol. 6, ed. Leslie Bethell (Cambridge: Cambridge University Press, 1994), 393–460; and Albert Fishlow, "The State of Latin American Economics," in *Changing Perspectives in Latin American Studies*, ed. Christopher Mitchell (Stanford: Stanford University Press, 1988), 87–121. Among Fishlow's five approaches the most procapitalist one is export-led growth; it is notable that in it he gives no Latin Americans as exemplars but only North Americans (Bela Balassa, Jagdish Bhagwati, William Cline, Anne Krueger, Jeffrey Sachs). The other approaches he offers, which are more statist or socialist, all include Latin Americans prominently as exemplars.

It broke with not only the historical trajectory of Chilean political economy but also the Latin American pattern in which military governments followed statist policies as much as civilian governments did.[12] But the Chilean case alone could not make a Latin American revolution. For one thing, a widespread view outside Chile through the middle and even the late 1980s was that the neoliberal experiment in Chile was a failure.[13] In addition, Chile's pariah political system made it virtually impossible for policymakers and thinkers in most Latin American countries explicitly and publicly to use the Chilean economic innovations as a model for their countries.[14]

With hindsight we can see that a strong hint of what was coming occurred in Mexico in 1985 when the de la Madrid government moved dramatically to liberalize trade and investment. Although this effort was stalled by earthquakes both geological and political between 1985 and 1988, it was extended, deepened, and consolidated by the administration of President Carlos Salinas de Gortari after he took office in December 1988. Then as now the Mexican political system, though opening up, was still on balance authoritarian.

Even clearer and more decisive indicators of the revolution in national economic policies in the region came all in a rush in 1989 and 1990 in more democratic contexts. In a period of a year or so the following events took place:

- Carlos Saúl Menem took office in Argentina and shortly thereafter embarked upon an astonishing reversal of virtually the entire economic program his Perónist Party had represented for nearly a half-century.
- In Brazil's first popular election for president in twenty-nine years, a center-right candidate (Fernando Collor de Mello) promising economic "modernization" (his term for state reform and eco-

---

12. Thus the military governments in Brazil from 1964 to 1985, far from weakening state influence in the economy, in fact maintained and increased it. So did those in Argentina, even though a few of them tried unsuccessfully to liberalize.

13. "Chile has often been hailed as an experiment—a successful one by its proponents until 1982 and a failed one by both detractors and others thereafter." Pan A. Yotopoulos, "The (Rip) Tide of Privatization: Lessons from Chile," *World Development* 17, no. 5 (1989): 698. The negative Latin American evaluation is discussed in Edwards, *Crisis and Reform*, 53–54.

14. However, according to Enrique Iglesias, Latin American political leaders privately paid more attention to the Chilean case as a model in the 1980s than they were willing to state publicly. See his interesting comments in "Economic Reform: A View From Latin America," in Williamson, *The Political Economy of Policy Reform*, 493.

nomic liberalization) defeated a leftist (Luis Inacio da Silva or "Lula") committed to maintaining and expanding the state's role in the economy.

- The newly elected government of César Gaviria instituted the most "coherent and radical"[15] set of liberalizing economic reforms in Colombia's history.

- Venezuela's President Carlos Andrés Pérez, elected in December 1988 to his second term after an earlier one in the 1970s when his policies were vigorously in the mainstream of state capitalism, by 1990 had reversed that earlier course and put in place the most radical policies of trade liberalization, deregulation, and privatization, accompanied by state action to achieve fiscal balance, macroeconomic stabilization, and direct social assistance, in modern Venezuelan history.

- The social-democratic president-elect of Chile, Patricio Aylwin, committed his administration to maintaining and elaborating the basic features of the neoliberal development model put in place by the military government.

- In the election of February 1990, Nicaraguans surprised the world by throwing out the Sandinistas and voting in a president committed to the kind of economic reforms that were sweeping the rest of the continent.

- In the Peruvian election of 1990 the standard-bearer of economic liberalism, novelist Mario Vargas Llosa, was defeated; the victor, Alberto Fujimori, once in office launched a radical restructuring of the Peruvian economy along the lines of neoliberalism.

In short, between mid-1989 and the end of 1990 the seven largest Latin American countries (Brazil, Mexico, Colombia, Argentina, Peru, Venezuela, Chile), plus one smaller country of enormous symbolic political significance (Nicaragua), plus assorted other cases not covered here, all moved suddenly and dramatically away from state capitalism and socialism in the direction of more liberal economic policies and structures. This was a revolution.[16]

No one predicted this revolution in 1975 or 1980 or even 1985 or 1988; anyone who did would have been regarded as hopelessly unin-

---

15. Urrutia, "Colombia," 285.

16. The way these events cluster in time makes irresistible the hypothesis that the dramatic events in central and eastern Europe and the Soviet Union starting in spring 1989 were very significant in bringing them about. This linkage has not been studied (or even noted) very much but it should be. The whole issue of the causes of the revolution in state-market relations in Latin America is very important but too complex to be addressed in this chapter.

formed or ideological, if not a denizen of the lunatic fringe. Yet it happened.

One of the striking features of the revolution is that no matter what the party, ideology, generation, previous history, personality, etc., of the leadership of the various national governments, the broad trend toward liberalization is the same. Not only the right but most of the center and the left have spoken of liberalizing the economy. Pinochet and Aylwin and Frei, Alfonsin and Menem, Belaunde Terry and Vargas Llosa and Fujimori, Carlos Andrés Pérez, the Collor and Franco and Cardoso governments with a weak party base, or the Salinas and Zedillo governments with a stronger party base—no matter what these or other differences, the overall direction of the change has in very recent years been nearly everywhere the same, that is, to move toward more reliance on the market and less on the state.

Consider one of the clearest and most dramatic examples, the administration of President Fernando Henrique Cardoso that took office in January 1995 in Brazil. As a prestigious academic sociologist from the 1950s and into the 1980s, Cardoso insisted on socialism and nationalism as the only desirable or acceptable solutions to Latin American ills. In the late 1970s, for example, Cardoso believed, "It is not realistic to imagine that capitalist development will solve basic problems for the majority of the population. . . . The important question . . . is how to construct paths toward socialism."[17] Reflecting in 1991 on why he held such views, Cardoso stated, "I was trained . . . to conceive relationships among nations and among classes within nations that were based on the idea of exploitation. The principal theories of political organization and domination are based on the idea of exploitation. The same is true regarding internal social structures within each country."[18]

However, as a practical man of affairs in Brazil after 1982—a federal senator from São Paulo, candidate for mayor of São Paulo in 1985, minister of foreign affairs and of economics in 1993 and 1994, presidential candidate in 1994, and president from 1995 to the present—Cardoso has taken a very different course. As senator he favored privatization

---

17. Fernando Henrique Cardoso and Enzo Faletto, *Dependency and Development in Latin America* (Berkeley: University of California Press, 1979), xxiv. See also Robert A. Packenham, *The Dependency Movement: Scholarship and Politics in Development Studies* (Cambridge: Harvard University Press, 1992), chapters 1–5.

18. Fernando Henrique Cardoso, "Surprises and Challenges for Democracy in Latin America," Panel on Prospects for the Hemisphere in Symposium on Global Peace and Development: Prospects for the Future (Notre Dame, Ind.: Kellogg Institute, September 13, 1991), 1.

of state enterprises and introduced legislation to that effect in the early 1990s. As economics minister he formulated the economic stabilization plan that tamed Brazil's galloping inflation in July 1994. As president he is seeking to lead Brazil into a new economic era in which low inflation, privatization, fiscal reform, administrative reform, tax reform, social security reform, lower tariffs, and a more open foreign investment regime are high priorities. Regarding Brazil's Landless Rural Worker's Movement (MST), President Cardoso deplored the fact that "they are not fighting only for agrarian reform but against the capitalist system."[19] It is a remarkable turnaround: he has championed policies he condemned when he was an academic sociologist and has condemned policies he intensely supported in those earlier days.[20] At the same time, consistent with the theme that overall economic liberalization is compatible with maintaining or increasing state action in some areas, he has also pledged a program of direct social action, Comunidade Solidaria, broadly similar to the Solidaridad program (PRONASOL) in Mexico and directed by his wife, the anthropologist Ruth Correa Leite Cardoso.

We have seen how widespread the market-oriented reforms in Latin America have been. The next question is, what have been the consequences of the reforms for economic, social, and political development in these countries?

The Effects of Economic Liberalization

Identifying Effects: Some Cautions

Even at this early stage it is possible to learn important lessons from the record about the consequences economic liberalization has had and may have in the future on economic, political, and social development. Doing this, however, is not easy or simple. The effects of economic liberalization are even more difficult to identify than is its extent. The time frame that is selected for measuring effects is particularly important. Since in most countries it has occurred very recently, until more time passes it may be risky to draw firm conclusions about effects. Even if short-term effects are discernible, which may not always be the

19. Cardoso as quoted in Jack Epstein, "Land Grabbers Under Fire in Brazil," *San Francisco Chronicle*, 28 June 1997, 10 (A), 12 (A).

20. For a brief catalogue of such contrasts, see Ken Brown, "Having Left Campus for the Arena, Winner in Brazil Shifts to the Right," *New York Times*, 11 November 1994. For fuller treatments see Susan Kaufman Purcell and Riordan Roett, eds., *Brazil Under Cardoso* (Boulder, Colo.: Lynne Rienner, 1997); and Packenham, *The Dependency Movement*, esp. 95–96, 216–219.

case, middle and longer term effects may not be. Additionally, other causal mechanisms besides the ones we want to study may be operating, and some of those other variables may affect outcomes in ways we cannot estimate or measure.

Consider the case of Mexico. Events there since January 1, 1994, put to rest the idea, if anyone held it, that economic liberalization can have only positive features and effects. No one doubts that the list of crises and setbacks since then is long and significant: from the rebellion in Chiapas, to the devaluation of the peso on December 20, 1994, to the intense struggles within the ruling Institutional Revolutionary Party, as well as between it and other parties and entities, for the very soul of Mexico's polity and economy. Clearly market reforms can be associated with instability and economic difficulties. Some analysts seem prepared to infer generalizable effects from the Mexican experience. Indeed it seems doubtful that features like the following are limited in their applicability only to the case of Mexico:

> As the economic and financial situation became more serious . . . the public began rapidly to lose confidence in the government policies. The sustainability of the exchange rate was questioned, and in spite of several official statements, a strong speculation against the peso developed. Economic agents readjusted their portfolios toward a higher proportion of assets denominated in foreign exchange. . . . the government finally decided . . . to pursue a more active policy. The peso was devalued. . . . However, this was too little and too late. At this point the loss of credibility in the government policies was almost complete, and the devaluation accelerated the speculation against the peso, with a resulting large loss of international reserves in the following weeks. The international financial community reacted negatively to these measures, and the flow of foreign funds . . . was further reduced.

Can one be confident that, in the wake of economic liberalization, scenarios such as this one and the devastating economic, political, and social consequences that flow from them can and will reveal themselves only in Mexico? Clearly not. Therefore opposition to economic liberalization has intensified, and calls for a return to statist policies are heard in the land.

The Mexican experience surely reminds one not to reach conclusions about those effects sweepingly or prematurely. But this cautionary note has more than one facet or implication in substantive terms. Whether or not the post-1994 Mexican crisis signals the failure of economic liberalization and the need for a return to statism depends on (among other factors) the time frame one uses to assess costs and benefits. In Mexico economic liberalization began rather slowly in 1985 and picked up speed rapidly after 1988. Are the seven to ten years from 1985 or 1988 to 1995 enough time to make such an assessment? It is instructive at this juncture to point out that the scenario quoted in the previous paragraph was written to describe not Mexico in 1994 but Chile in 1981–82![21] The lines of the scenario fit Mexico almost word for word, but they are not about Mexico. And why is that very significant? Because the Chilean crisis of 1981–82 led not only to economic decline and suffering in 1982–84 but also to the best performance of economy, society, and polity of any country in Latin America after 1984. In other words, the Chilean developmental profile since then is the envy of every other country in the region and many outside it. Far from being a harbinger of failure, the Chilean crisis of 1981–84 was followed by unparalleled success.

Chile's liberalizing economic reforms began in earnest in 1975. The big economic crisis occurred in 1981–84.[22] On the evidence six to nine years after the reforms began, that is, as of 1981–1984, it is understandable that some scholars concluded that the Chilean reforms were a major failure.[23] But the government made adjustments—still following the liberalization project but in less extreme ways—and Chile recovered from the crash. From 1985 to the present Chile has had steady, strong economic growth and has achieved by nearly universal agreement the most successful overall profile of economic, political, and social development in Latin America. The economic model was so effective that two democratically elected center-left governments accepted its basic premises and main lines of policy (with some adjustments, of course) no less firmly than the military governments that

21. Sebastian Edwards, "Stabilization with Liberalization: An Evaluation of Ten Years of Chile's Experiment with Free-Market Policies, 1973–1983," *Economic Development and Cultural Change* 33 (1985): 223–254, quotation at 247–248.

22. For useful descriptive and analytic accounts from varying perspectives, see Frieden, *Debt, Development, and Democracy*, 169–77; Eduardo Silva, "Capitalist Coalitions, the State, and Neoliberal Economic Restructuring: Chile, 1973–1988," *World Politics* 45, no. 4 (1993): 548–55; Arturo Fontaine Aldunate, *Los economistas y el presidente Pinochet* (Santiago: Zig-Zag, 1988), 141–79; David Gallagher, "Chile: la revolucion pendiente," in *El Desafío Neoliberal: El fin del tercermundismo en America Latina*, ed. Barry B. Levine (Bogotá: Grupo Editorial Norma, 1992), 141–78; and Barry P. Bosworth, Rudiger Dornbusch, and Raul Laban, eds., *The Chilean Economy: Policy Lessons and Challenges* (Washington, D.C.: Brookings Institution, 1994), passim.

23. Alejandro Foxley, *Latin American Experiments in Neo-Conservative Economics* (Berkeley: University of California Press, 1983); Joseph Ramos, *Neoconservative Economics in the Southern Cone of Latin America, 1973–1983* (Baltimore: Johns Hopkins University Press, 1986); and Yotopoulos, "The (Rip) Tide of Privatization," 683–702.

preceded them (which also continuously made adjustments, some of them in a strongly statist direction). In short, it makes all the difference whether one views the effects of economic liberalization in Chile after ten years[24] or after twenty years.[25]

This does not mean, of course, that Mexico will duplicate Chile's experience. The two countries had very different histories before they made market-oriented reforms, and for that reason and others their post-reform histories will also be significantly different. Nevertheless, the preceding discussion should make analysts cautious in drawing overly negative conclusions about Mexico and other countries. Will the consequences of Mexico's economic reforms not appear to be more positive (should one say "even more positive"?) in 2005 than they did in 1995? Will the time frame not make all the difference in Mexico as it did in Chile? It is still true that one should avoid exaggerating the positive effects of market reforms or reaching premature conclusions about those effects. But equally one should avoid exaggerating the negative effects and recall that the caution about judging too quickly cuts both ways: not only against but also in favor of the reforms.

Despite such difficulties and notwithstanding the need for caution, it is still necessary and worthwhile to learn what we can from the experience so far. So let us proceed following the advice of (among others) John Locke, John Stuart Mill, John Dewey, and Mao Zedong: seek truth from facts.

Identifying Effects: A Few Facts

We begin by looking at the region as a whole. The baseline is the 1980s when, in most Latin American countries, state-capitalist models were still in place and economies were either declining or stagnant. Economic liberalization took off at the very end of the 1980s and in the early 1990s partly as a way to exit the economic crisis that occurred under state capitalism. Market-oriented reform was not the cause of the economic crisis of the 1980s, as some commentators have claimed; it was an effort to escape the crisis. Given the liberalizing reforms, what has been achieved?

On the economic front, here is what a review of economic performance through 1994 published by the Economic Commission for Latin America and the Caribbean (ECLAC) has to say:

In 1994, Latin America is completing the fourth year of what appears to be a new pattern of economic performance. The pattern has three main

---

24. For example, Foxley, *Latin American Experiments*.
25. For example, Alejandro Foxley, *Economia politica de la transicion: El camino del dialogo* (Santiago: Dolmen, 1993).

elements: 1) modest economic growth rates of around 3% in aggregate
terms and slightly over 1% on a per capita basis; 2) increased control over
inflation, which (excluding Brazil) should fall to around 16% in 1994; and
3) a large and growing current-account deficit, financed by capital inflows
that are likely to reach some US$ 55 billion this year.[26]

The previous year's ECLAC annual report had begun in a similar fashion except that its third point emphasized not the current-account
deficit but rather "the support of a plentiful supply of foreign capital"
as a positive factor.[27]

In Latin America as a whole (twenty countries), in the *ten* years between 1981 and 1990, GDP increased by a *total* of 12.5 percent and per
capita GDP *decreased* by a total of 9.0 percent; in the *four* years between
1991 and 1994, GDP increased by a total of 14.3 percent and per capita
GDP *increased* by a total of 5.7 percent![28] The same upward trend is
apparent even if one extends the analysis into the next year, 1995, after
the Mexican crisis of December 1994 and its so-called Tequila Effects.
In the five years between 1991 and 1995, GDP increased by a total of
17.2 percent and per capita GDP increased by a total of 6.9 percent.[29]
Comparing the periods 1981–90 and 1991–95, in terms of average annual rates of change in GDP and GDP per capita in nineteen Latin
American countries, one sees that GDP changes go from an annual
average of 0.9 percent in the first period to 3.0 percent in the second
period, and that GDP per capita goes from an annual average of −1.1
percent in the first period to 1.1 percent in the second period.[30]

It seems clear that, in the first years of economic liberalization, overall economic performance in the region in aggregate terms was positive
by any standard and extremely positive in comparison to the results
associated with state capitalist policies and structures. Although these
facts by themselves cannot establish a positive causal relationship from

26. Economic Commission for Latin America and the Caribbean (ECLAC),
Economic Panorama of Latin America 1994, U.N. Doc. LC/G. 1369/1994 (Santiago: ECLAC, September 1994), 5.

27. ECLAC, *Balance preliminar de la economia de America Latina y el Caribe
1993*, Documento informativo (Santiago: ECLAC, 17 de Diciembre 1993), 1. The
full statement is, "In 1993, for the third consecutive year, we have moderate
economic growth in most Latin American and Caribbean countries. In most
countries one finds relative price stability, that is, relatively low levels of inflation, and a plentiful supply of foreign capital."

28. ECLAC, *Economic Panorama of Latin America 1994*, 11, Table 1.

29. CEPAL, *Panorama Economico de America Latina 1995* (Santiago de Chile:
United Nations, September 1995), Table 1, 13.

30. CEPAL, *Panorama Economico de America Latina 1996* (Santiago de Chile:
United Nations, September 1996), Table 1, 14.

liberalization to performance, they are consistent with one. It is important to note that they are flatly inconsistent with the widely held hypothesis that liberalization causes economic hardship.[31] They seem to support what Tommasi and Velasco call a more "optimistic" view, namely, that "the recessionary consequences of stabilization have been much milder than anybody anticipated. . . . If anything, reforms are proving to be both more popular and more lasting *ex post* than many analysts predicted *ex ante*."[32] As Tommasi and Velasco recognize, this issue will continue to bear watching, but they are surely right that the conventional wisdom that market-oriented reforms necessarily brought about economic austerity that made them politically hard to sustain is less clear than it once seemed.[33]

Politically, the trend toward democracy since the late 1970s and the 1980s continued in the great majority of countries. The main exception was Cuba. The democratic regimes were, to be sure, imperfect—in some cases very imperfect. There were some partial reversals, as in Peru's so-called presidential coup in 1992, and others may occur in the future. But none of the major democracies has collapsed so far. Peru had another democratic election in 1995. There were attempted military coups, as in Venezuela (twice in 1992), but no successful military coups occurred in any major country. The overall record showed a remarkable maintenance of democracy in the face of many serious challenges in both the bust years of the 1980s and the growth years of the 1990s. Contrary to some predictions, economic liberalization did not end political liberalization. To the contrary, cases such as Argentina after 1990 (and perhaps Brazil after 1990 and especially after 1995) showed dramatically that the two faces of liberalism were compatible, that authoritarianism was not necessary to achieve higher levels of economic freedom (or economic development).

What about social development? Until very recently the prevailing view has been that capitalism has extremely high costs in terms of its effects on increasing inequality and absolute poverty. Since the 1930s, large state sectors were justified in part as means to reduce socioeco-

---

31. See, for example, the statements cited critically by Mariano Tommasi and Andres Velasco in their excellent article "Where Are We in the Political Economy of Reform?" *Policy Reform* 1 (1996): 187–238, esp. 213.

32. Tommasi and Velasco, "Where Are We?" 211–12.

33. For additional evidence and analysis on these matters see Carlos H. Gervasoni, "El Impacto Electoral de las Politicas de Estabilizacion y Reforma Estructural en America Latina," *Journal of Latin American Affairs* 3, no. 1 (1995): 46–51; and idem, "Economic Policy and Electoral Performance in Latin America, 1982–1995," M.A. Thesis, Center for Latin American Studies, Stanford University (September 1995).

nomic injustice and poverty. Much of the intellectual and political critique of the recent trends toward economic liberalization has continued to make those kinds of arguments. Many facts, however, do not support them.

The first set of facts that does not support such arguments is the development record associated with the state-capitalist and socialist models and policies in place from the 1930s to the 1980s. In the half century they were in place, the state-capitalist models and policies did little to reduce the massive socioeconomic inequalities of the region, which remains one of the most unequal in the world. The evidence from the 1930s to the 1980s is overwhelming that, as a strategy to reduce inequality in Latin America, state capitalism was a failure. So was (and is) socialism, a lingering mythology to the contrary notwithstanding. In Latin America as elsewhere, socialism's "egalitarianism' has turned out to be the short-term redistribution of the wealth that capitalism created combined with the destruction of the ability to continue to create such wealth. Socialism is also inextricably associated, in Latin America as everywhere it has been tried, with a "new class" of party and bureaucratic elites whose inegalitarianism is different in form but similar in degree to that which occurs in capitalism.

There were reductions of absolute poverty in Latin American cases at various times from the 1930s through the 1970s, but they may have been due more to the capitalism than to the statism of the state-capitalist model. As for socialism, for decades its proponents argued that it would reduce poverty better than capitalism; it is now clear, given a seventy-year record in the USSR and almost forty years' experience in Cuba, that socialism creates poverty for almost everyone except the party and military-bureaucratic elites who have political power.

The second set of facts that has assaulted the preference for statist models as ways to address issues of inequality and poverty is the record in more recent years—both the so-called lost decade of the 1980s under state capitalism and the 1990s when economic liberalization began to take hold. These new facts are even more surprising than those from the earlier period. They show that the main cause of poverty resolution is not government policies of redistribution but whatever gets the overall economy moving. Thus Morley, in a systematic review of the evidence since the 1980s about poverty and distribution, states the "lessons that can be learned" as follows:

> The first and foremost lesson is that changes in the level of per capita income are the key determinant of changes in the level of poverty. Anything that slows down the growth rate or causes a recession will hurt the poor. Indeed, since inequality typically rose during recession, Latin

America's recessions hurt the poor more than they hurt other groups in society.

Second, no social emergency program or special antipoverty social policy can completely offset the effect on the poor of a macroeconomic downturn. . . . Such policies are palliative and should never be thought of as a substitute for a solid recovery. The only truly effective policy is to get the economy growing again—and in a sustainable way.

Third, it is misleading and unfair to blame all the increase in poverty during the 1980s on the adjustment process. It would be as reasonable to blame it on the unwise policies and excessive borrowing that made that adjustment necessary.[34]

Similar conclusions are found in a recent ECLAC study on Latin American social development. It reported that between 1990 and 1992 six Latin American countries achieved significant reductions in poverty: Argentina, Bolivia, Chile, Mexico, Uruguay, and Venezuela. These reductions occurred in both urban and rural areas. Key factors associated with the reduction in poverty were "a slowdown in inflation . . . [which] contributed to a recovery in the real incomes of the working population, especially wage-earners. . . . All these improvements were achieved in a context of growth in per capita GNP."[35] Like Morley's survey, the ECLAC study said that it was overall economic growth much more than redistribution programs by the state that explained poverty reduction:

The progress achieved in combating poverty during the 1990s is largely due to the growth in household income. Changes in income distribution made little or no contribution to that progress, as the highly unequal patterns which have characterized the region remained unchanged in most of the countries.[36]

Other surprising conclusions in the area of social development are revealed by recent studies of the effects of market-oriented reforms. Tommasi and Velasco find that "the often-predicted social 'explosion' that would presumably follow the application of drastic reforms has, with some notable exceptions, never materialized." The exceptions in

---

34. Samuel A. Morley, *Poverty and Inequality in Latin America: Past Evidence, Future Prospects*, Policy Essay No. 3 (Washington, D.C.: Overseas Development Council, 1994), 69–70.

35. ECLAC, *Social Panorama of Latin America: 1994 Edition*, LC/G. 1844 (Santiago: ECLAC, Statistics and Economic Projects Division and Social Development Division, November 1994), 2, 5.

36. Ibid., 13. The only exception is Uruguay, where state-led redistribution of income led to decreases in poverty.

Latin America they cite are the Chiapas uprising in 1994, the Venezuelan riots of 1989, and "the much less serious upheaval in northern Argentina (Santiago del Estero province) in 1993." It is "sadly revealing about the state of politics," they say, "that the two most successful attempts at targeting the poor through safety nets in Latin America were made by Pinochet in Chile and by the (far less harsh but still authoritarian) government of Mexico under Carlos Salinas."[37] Tommasi and Velasco's conclusions about Chilean poverty programs are broadly consistent with those of Graham and Foxley. Graham writes:

> Poverty indeed exists in Chile. In absolute terms, however, it is much less severe than in most countries on the continent. Despite the severity of the economic crises of the late 1970s and early 1980s, progress was made in lowering the incidence of extreme poverty. . . . By making inroads on extreme poverty as well as implementing a far-reaching program of economic reform, the military government left its democratic successors a firm base on which to implement diverse and innovative antipoverty efforts like FOSIS [Fund for Solidarity and Social Investment, set up by the Aylwin administration in 1990]. Indeed, without sustained economic reform and renewed growth, programs like FOSIS would have a marginal, if any, impact.[38]

Chilean economist Alejandro Foxley, who was minister of finance in the Aylwin government, notes that the percentage of the Chilean population living in poverty fell from 44.6 in 1987 to 40.1 in 1990 to 32.7 in 1992.[39]

Another way to gauge effects is to ask which countries liberalized the most and which the least, and then see what their development records have been. At the end of 1993 the countries that had done the most to liberalize their economies were, in alphabetical order, Argentina, Chile, Colombia, Mexico, and Venezuela; those that had done the least were Brazil, Cuba, and Peru.[40] The rates of growth in per capita internal gross product of the first group of countries in the period 1991–93 inclusive were 21 (Argentina), 17.9 (Chile), 4.8 (Colombia), 0.7 (Mexico), and 9.3 (Venezuela) percent, respectively; the rates in the same period for the second set of countries were −0.5% (Brazil), −0.5 percent (Peru), and Cuba.[41] Although ECLAC does not provide data on the Cuban case, we know from many sources that the Cuban economy

37. Tommasi and Velasco, "Where Are We?" 220.
38. Carol Graham, *Safety Nets, Politics, and the Poor: Transitions to Market Economies* (Washington, D.C.: Brookings Institution, 1994), 53.
39. Foxley, *Economia politica de la transicion*, 223.
40. Johnson and Sheehy, *Index of Economic Freedom*, 249–51.
41. ECLAC, *Balance preliminar 1993*, Table 3, 33.

was collapsing during these years largely because of the end of Soviet subsidies but also because of the nondynamic character of its socialist economic institutions. In short, it is clear that there is a strong positive correlation between economic liberalization and economic performance.[42]

In what Latin American country has economic liberalization been most extensive and profound over the longest period of time? The answer, clearly, is Chile. What Latin American country today has the best overall development profile in economic, political, and social terms? Again, clearly, the answer is Chile. Economic performance has been steady and strong each year in the period since 1985. During these years a military regime gave way to a democratic regime in which two scrupulously fair, free, and participant elections produced two highly legitimate governments. Chilean democracy is as strong and stable as any in the region. Absolute poverty is declining. Income distribution data are more ambiguous.[43] Even if the record on the latter score is not as impressive, and it probably is not, still the overall profile is the envy of every other country in the region.

By contrast, in Cuba and Brazil, the countries that had done the least in the liberalizing direction through December 1993, development did not go well. Cuba was by that time an economic catastrophe. Its much-vaunted social services also were in shambles. Only a few sectors—such as party and bureaucratic elites, black marketers, tourism—avoided the general stagnation and deepening immiseration. The political system remained totalitarian or nearly so. Overall the Cuban way of socialist development no longer had appeal among developing countries as a desirable model. In the early 1990s Brazil was much, much better off than Cuba in economic and political terms, but still its slowness to implement the rhetoric of economic liberalization was associated with galloping inflation, huge fiscal deficits, and sluggish rates of economic growth, to say nothing of continuing socioeconomic elitism and other problems. It was only in the last half of 1994 that Brazil conquered (at least temporarily) its galloping inflation, which

---

42. This relationship is equally strong if not stronger in subsequent years in Latin America; see CEPAL, *Balance Preliminar de la Economia de America Latina y el Caribe 1996* (Santiago de Chile: United Nations, December 1996), Table A.1, 39, and Table 2, 6. In a worldwide sample of 100 countries, the relationship is stronger still; see the stunning correlations in Gwartney et al., *Economic Freedom of the World 1975–1995* (1996), Exhibit S-2, xxii.

43. The best summary and analysis I have seen appears in Mario Marcel and Andres Solimano, "The Distribution of Income and Economic Adjustment," in *The Chilean Economy*, 217–55, which includes valuable commentary by Eliana Cardoso and Carol Graham at 241–52.

fell from 45 percent a month to 1 percent a month between July 1 and
December 31. Finally it seemed as if Brazil might have a good chance to
achieve significant economic expansion, social reform, and democratic
consolidation—*if* it could keep going on fiscal, administrative, and judicial reform, privatization, educational and social infrastructure, and
electoral and political party reform.[44]

What in summary can be said about the effects of economic liberalization in Latin America—remembering that it is still fairly early to
judge and the data are, as always, incomplete? In general it seems to
have enhanced economic efficiency and productivity, reduced absolute
poverty, and strengthened democracy without having consequences
for social equality much worse than those that accompanied the state-
capitalist models of development that came before. Most policymakers
in the region now take this view; as a result, their support for economic
liberalization is overwhelming. Academic scholars are more divided.
Some, especially economists, tend to agree with the policymakers (and
vice versa). Others perceive a less positive set of effects and continue
to emphasize statist models and strategies and attack market-oriented
reforms and strategies.

This brings us to our next topic: The issues involved in assessing
economic liberalization are not only empirical but also normative or
prescriptive.

Normative Issues

So far in this treatment of the recent trends toward economic liberalization in Latin America, we have been addressing empirical questions,
that is, questions in the sphere of positive theory: What has happened,
and with what effects? Now we turn to questions in the sphere of normative theory, that is, questions about what ought to happen: Is economic liberalization good or bad, and how should we think about such
matters?

States and Markets: Either/Or or Both/And?

In discussions of market-oriented reforms, it is frequently assumed
that if one stresses the virtues of markets, or has anything good to say
about them, that means one is unwilling to say anything good about

44. See Peter Flynn, "Brazil: The Politics of the 'Plano Real,' " *Third World Quarterly* 17, no. 3 (September 1996): 401–27, and Kaufman and Roett, *Brazil Under Cardoso*, passim.

the state. But the latter part of the statement does not logically follow and such thinking is not fruitful. As we explained earlier, state-market relations can usefully be conceived as a continuum that is the aggregate of several dimensions on which changes need not and probably will not all go in the same direction. Either/or normative models, whether they are of the all-state variety or the all-market variety, are not very useful in this conceptualization (or many others). Development requires activities by both state and market and cannot proceed without something from both.

The real questions are how to combine states and markets and how to think about combining them. From this perspective it is certainly possible to move in a liberalizing direction on some dimensions, in order to get away from the kinds of state capitalism (or socialism) that were in place for half a century but have exhausted themselves, while at the same time maintaining or increasing the activities and influences of the state in other selected areas. There is nothing inconsistent, and should be nothing surprising, about such a combination. Liberalizing state-market relations on some, many, or most dimensions surely need not mean liberalizing them on every dimension. What would be surprising would be to insist that at any moment of significant historical change every phenomenon has to move in the same direction. Those who stress the virtues of the state are indignant, understandably, if readers assume that they necessarily deny any positive features of and effects from the market. *Yet those same analysts often deny to defenders of the market the same opportunity for systematic, comprehensive, differentiated thinking they claim for themselves.* In a serious discussion it has to be possible to refer to market-oriented reforms without being thought to imply that the state never has any role on any dimension.

A few examples may help to clarify the point. Not long ago I was having lunch with a friend, a political theorist, in a restaurant overlooking a *praça* (public square) in Rio de Janeiro. My friend, who in general is supportive of the state as an instrument of development, said to me, "Look, it's ridiculous that in this *praça* if the local authorities want to change some trees or a statue, or make some other routine adjustment, they must go not only to the local level and the state level of government but all the way to the national level in Brasília to make the change. For a small alteration in a local *praça*! It's absurd." Though in general he was critical of the trend toward economic liberalization, in this instance he thought the level of state involvement was ridiculous, as indeed it appears it was.

On the other hand, abiding by the same principle that both increased and decreased state controls in different areas are possible and consistent with the overall trend to liberalization, there are other areas where greater regulation seems clearly to be in order. For example, horrible accidents have occurred in recent years in and around refineries and gas lines in Santos, Brazil, and in the Federal District and Guadalajara in Mexico. In these instances, improved government regulation might have saved hundreds of lives. (After the latest white-knuckle ride in a Rio de Janeiro taxi, one is tempted to say something similar about the subject of driving rules and customs and their effects.) In Brazil and Mexico one can buy over the counter in *farmacias* and supermarkets types and varieties of pharmaceutical drugs and "medicines" that boggle the mind of the foreign visitor. What you can easily purchase might cure you, might harm you, or might do nothing except lull you into a false sense of security, but often it is hard to know because there is relatively little regulation of retail drug sales. Those who know stock markets around the world say that while those in Latin America are less imperfect than they once were they still need greater above-board state monitoring and regulation (as well as changes in cultural norms and self-policing). Privatization of state-owned enterprises may require new regulatory activities to ensure transparency and avoid corruption as well as antitrust legislation and enforcement to prevent private monopolies.

In short, those who in general favor economic liberalization including deregulation can also argue, quite consistently, that there should be more state activity and/or regulation in some areas. Indeed, a number of policymakers and social scientists who have championed economic liberalization have recently urged a "second stage" of reforms to improve social conditions (especially health and education for the poor), courts, police, bureaucratic capability and transparency, tax collection, infrastructure (roads, power generation, water supply, telecommunications systems), local and state government capacities, financial institutions, electoral laws, and the like.[45] In making these recommendations, they do not reject the earlier market-oriented strategies (to the contrary), and they think that many of the second-stage reforms should be done in the private sector; but they readily acknowledge that the state may be needed to implement some of them.[46] Granting

---

45. See, for example, Moises Naim, "Latin America: The Second Stage of Reform," *Journal of Democracy* 5, no. 4 (1994): 32–48; Tommasi and Velasco, "Where Are We?" 226–29; Sebastian Edwards, "Latin America's Underperformance," *Foreign Affairs* 76, no. 2 (March/April 1997): 93–103; Maria Dakolias, *The Judicial Sector in Latin America and the Caribbean: Elements of Reform,* Technical Paper No. 319 (Washington, D.C.: World Bank, June 1996).

46. The challenge, of course, is to do these things without lapsing into the same inefficiency, particularism, and corruption that made market-oriented

all this, my argument is still very different from the one that has been dominant in development theory and continues in many quarters, namely, the idea that development by definition always and everywhere requires primary reliance on the state.[47]

State-Market Mixes: Optimal Equilibria or Satisficing Oscillations?

Many analysts implicitly and sometimes explicitly look for the right mix of state and market. Their effort is to find "the" optimal equilibrium point. Debates in this mode are over whether the putative optimal point should be here, or there, or somewhere else. I am inclined to think that such searches are fruitless, not only overall but in any particular sector. The amounts of information, analytic capacity, and theoretical understanding needed to be able to identify such "optimal" points are beyond most of us, maybe any of us.[48] Moreover, such points of optimal equilibria, even if they could be identified, would be inherently unstable because they would create vested interests and other features that would immediately render them suboptimal.[49] Still further, even if all the foregoing problems could be solved, there are still important differences in culture, developmental circumstances, etc., in different cases that affect the feasibility of generalized prescriptions in different places and times; not everything that works in Japan or Korea or Taiwan will work equally well in Argentina or Brazil or Mexico.[50]

---

reforms necessary in the first place. That is usually difficult and may be impossible in many instances. All this creates serious dilemmas. For a brief discussion of these issues see Naim, "Latin America: The Second Stage," 43–45.

47. For an intellectual history and continuing endorsement of the latter view, see Colin Leys, *The Rise and Fall of Development Theory* (Bloomington: Indiana University Press, 1996), esp. chapter 1.

48. A neglected source on this subject is Robert A. Dahl and Charles E. Lindblom, *Politics, Economics, and Welfare* (New York: Harper and Row, 1953). See also the works of Herbert Simon and of Albert O. Hirschman.

49. See especially Hirschman, *Exit, Voice, and Loyalty: Responses to Decline in Firms, Organizations, and States* (Cambridge: Harvard University Press, 1970).

50. See especially Douglass North, *Institutions, Institutional Change, and Development* (Cambridge: Cambridge University Press, 1990); see also Francis Fukuyama, "Virtue and Prosperity," *The National Interest*, no. 40 (Summer 1995): 21–27; Sun-ki Chai, *A Cognitive Approach to Rational Action* (Ann Arbor: University of Michigan Press, forthcoming). I definitely do *not* agree with Chalmers Johnson and E. B. Keehn, "A Disaster in the Making: Rational Choice and Asian Studies," *The National Interest*, no. 36 (Summer 1994): 14–22, who take the extreme view that the principles of capitalist economics "do not work" (p. 20) in Japan and elsewhere in Asia. I agree with those like North, *Institutions*, 7, who accept "the standard constraints of economic theory" and supplement them with institutional and cultural analysis.

On the other hand, the question of what direction to move in mixing state-market and state–private sector activities is often much less difficult to answer. This is especially the case at historical moments like the present one. After fifty years or more of state capitalism and socialism, it is time for the pendulum to swing in the other direction. This is a prescription one can make with a relatively high degree of confidence; it is the answer to a relatively easy question (as these matters go in the social sciences). The question of how far to go to reach optimal equilibrium—of when and where to stop the reverse swing of the pendulum—is much more difficult. The need to address the easy question of what direction to move rather than the hard question of exactly where to stop and rest in equilibrium is greatest in the early stages of a new swing of the pendulum; after the pendulum has gone in the same direction for a certain period of time, then it may become more desirable and feasible to ask the tougher questions about optimality again. (To be precise and systematic it is necessary to add that it is legitimate to address the optimality question at any time because the satisficing strategy can also fail. Indeed it is probably a good idea that at least a few analysts always ask optimality questions. The point remains that one should not use *only* the optimality strategy.) In general, one should address the easier questions (there is plenty to do about them) rather than the harder ones, and avoid making the unattainable perfect the enemy of the achievable good.

Although as discussed earlier the image of a single swinging pendulum is an oversimplification that represents the aggregate of a number of different elements or dimensions, this fact does not obviate the relevance and utility of the principle of satisficing oscillations being advocated here. Indeed, this principle applies to the different dimensions as well as to the overall aggregate tendency or tendencies. After a half century or more of state capitalism in Latin America, it was time in the 1980s and 1990s to cut fiscal deficits, privatize state enterprises, lower tariffs, and reduce barriers to foreign investment. But in areas where the state for decades had been negligent, such as safety conditions for industrial workers and residents, or consumer protection, to say nothing of health care and elementary education for small children from low-income families, it was time for the state to be more active—provided that the institutional foundations and personnel base for a technically competent, honest cadre of regulatory officials are achievable.

The Order of Economic and Political Liberalization

The third issue in the sphere of normative discourse is what ought to be the order of economic and political liberalization. Which should come first, political liberalization or economic liberalization? Or should they come together? Again, how would one know?

These are complex issues. There are also prior questions of the internal order of economic liberalization[51] and of the internal order of political liberalization,[52] which are vast topics in themselves, before one even gets into the matter of how they ought to relate to each other. Other prior questions are a) the relationship between economic performance and economic liberalization, and b) the relationship between economic performance, on the one hand, and democracy or authoritarianism, on the other. One can argue, therefore, that the question of the order of economic and political liberalization ought to be addressed only after one has made considerable progress on these prior questions and others noted earlier. On the other hand, in many countries today the order of the two kinds of liberalization is also a pressing policy concern that cannot in practical terms await the results of other analyses. Therefore, it is fitting to give some attention to this question.

To begin to come to grips with this topic, I want to postulate that for most countries the trend toward economic liberalization tends to be good for economic performance. Most economists would agree with that proposition; some economists and many more political scientists would not. It is possible to point to cases where economic liberalization has been associated for some time period with low or negative economic productivity (e.g., Chile 1982–85) and where state capitalism (e.g., Brazil 1968–74) or even socialism (e.g., the USSR from the 1920s to the 1950s) has produced rapid growth. But the overall empirical association between economic liberalization and economic performance is strong. Barro puts it well: "With respect to the determination of growth, the cross-country analysis brings out favorable effects from maintenance of the rule of law, free markets, small government consumption, and high human capital."[53] Therefore for discussion purposes and to simplify matters I am prepared to make this assumption. This enables us to turn to the question of the relationship between

51. For differing views on economic liberalization, see Ronald McKinnon, *The Order of Economic Liberalization* (Baltimore: Johns Hopkins University Press, 1992); and Anders Aslund, "The Case for Radical Reform," *Journal of Democracy* 5, no. 4 (October 1994): 63–74.

52. There is a vast literature in political science on political liberalization. At one extreme is the view that mass participation through revolution should precede political liberalization; at the other extreme is the view that successful transitions are more likely if they are top-down, gradual, and nonviolent. In the last twenty-five years the latter view has been dominant among scholars.

53. Robert J. Barro, *Democracy and Growth*, Working Paper Number 4909 (Cambridge, Mass.: National Bureau of Economic Research, October 1994), 25. See also "Identifying Effects: A Few Facts," above.

economic performance and political democracy or authoritarianism, which in turn is central to the issue of the order of economic and political liberalization.

Imagine a two-by-two, four-cell table where one variable is economic performance (strong, weak) and the other is political regime (authoritarian, democratic). I hypothesize that if one were to locate empirical cases in such a table one would find the following patterns and relationships. (All the hypotheses about relationships postulate ceteris paribus conditions.) First, there are some cases in all four cells. In other words, authoritarian regimes can be associated with either strong or weak economic performance; so can democratic regimes. Second, historically there have probably been more cases of strong economic performance with authoritarian regimes than with democratic regimes—in other words, more cases in cell 1 than in cell 3. Third, what unites the cases in cells 1 and 3, aside from their economic policies, is probably the kinds of features that explain successful implementation of economic liberalization programs, that is, features such as the perception of crisis, a legitimate government, organizational capacity of parties or other political institutions, skillful political leadership, and public opinion and interest group preference structures with at least the possibility of agreement with the policy innovations.[54]

Fourth, democratic regimes characterized by features such as those identified in point three are about as likely to be associated with strong economic performance as with authoritarian regimes. Fifth, although historically authoritarian regimes may have been more likely to have had the kinds of features conducive to strong economic performance than democratic regimes, increasingly in the contemporary world this difference between authoritarian and democratic regimes has declined.[55] Thus today democratic regimes, especially newly democratic ones, may be only slightly less likely than authoritarian regimes to be associated with strong economic performance. Barro concludes from his rigorous study of a panel of one hundred countries from 1960 to 1990 that once other variables are held constant, "the overall effect of democracy on growth is weakly negative." He adds, however, that "there is some indication of a nonlinear relation in which more democracy enhances growth at low levels of political freedom but depresses

---

54. List based on author's unpublished research. See also Packenham, "The Politics of Economic Liberalization: Argentina and Brazil in Comparative Perspective," Working Paper No. 206 (Kellogg Institute for International Studies, University of Notre Dame, April 1994).

55. For this view see chapter 5 by Lorenzo Meyer.

growth when a moderate level of political freedom has already been attained."[56]

The final conclusions about the order of economic and political liberalization also come from Barro:

> More democracy is not the key to economic growth, although it may have a weak positive effect for countries that start with few political rights. . . . The more general conclusion is that the advanced countries would contribute more to the welfare of poor nations by exporting their economic systems, notably property rights and free markets, rather than their political systems, which typically developed after reasonable standards of living had been attained. If economic freedom can be established in a poor country, then growth would be encouraged and the country would tend eventually to become more democratic on its own. Thus, in the long run, the propagation of western-style economic systems would also be the effective way to expand democracy in the world.[57]

Implications for Development Theory

What can be said in general terms about the implications of the foregoing for development theory? The trends reported and analyses offered support some theoretical perspectives more than others. These trends and analyses are inconsistent with the claims of dependency authors such as Cardoso, Evans, dos Santos, and Frank, world-system theorists such as Wallerstein, and "Bringing the State Back In" writers like Evans, Krasner, and Skocpol. (In saying this, I refer to such claims in a form in which they could in principle be falsified; in their nonfalsifiable form, of course, which is the way some of them are written, such claims are consistent with any facts.) In short, they do *not* support the ideas and practices that were hegemonic among U.S. academic Latin Americanists from the late 1960s through the 1980s and that remain influential today, although now often without the labels and terminology used earlier.

The trends and analyses reported in the previous sections *do* support the claims of such theorists as Douglass North on institutions; Peter Berger on the effects of capitalism compared to socialism; Samuel Huntington, Albert Hirschman, and Robert Jackman on the importance of

---

56. Barro, *Democracy and Growth*, 25. An influential theoretical explanation for the second part of this phenomenon is Mancur Olson, *The Rise and Decline of Nations* (New Haven: Yale University Press, 1982).

57. Barro, *Democracy and Growth*, 26.

political will, skill, capacity, and institutions; and Robert Dahl, Huntington, and Scott Mainwaring and Timothy Scully on democratization. They also vindicate the claims of so-called "modernization theorists" (Lerner, Lipset, Inkeles) who argued in the 1950s and 1960s that economic development would tend to lead to political democratization and other good things. The modernization theorists were intensely criticized in the late 1960s and the 1970s. But today we can see that many of the relationships they identified using the more limited data available in the 1950s stand up over time. Although those relationships weakened in the middle and late 1960s and early 1970s, a trend that gave rise to the critiques, they were not destroyed and were strengthened again in the 1980s and 1990s. The modernization approach remains anathema to many scholars, but overall it is still one of the most empirically and historically well-grounded theories in the scholarly literature.[58]

Implications for the Case of Mexico[59]

Are the empirical trends and theoretical and normative analyses of this chapter consistent with the case of Mexico? Or does Mexico show that market-oriented reform may not be necessary or desirable or likely to encourage the emergence of democracy, and that it is wrong and possibly dangerous to think that it is? Many observers believe that the second view or something like it may be more nearly correct.[60] Their concerns are legitimate, especially given events in Mexico after December 1994. Nevertheless, I will argue that these analyses are relevant for Mexico as well—not mechanically or rigidly but still meaningfully. Or, to put the point a different way, the foregoing trends and analysis have

58. An important restatement of modernization theory based on systematic evidence from surveys in countries representing 70 percent of the world's population is Ronald Inglehart, *Modernization and Postmodernization: Cultural, Economic, and Political Change in 43 Societies* (Princeton: Princeton University Press, 1997). He agrees with earlier modernization theorists "on their most central point," namely, "that economic development, cultural change, and political change are linked in coherent and even, to some extent, predictable patterns." But he differs with them on what he says are its assumptions of linearity and determinism and equation of modernization with Westernization (10–11).

59. This section on Mexico was written before the important elections of July 6, 1997, in which opposition candidates won for mayor of the Federal District and for governor in the states of Nuevo León and Querétaro, and for the first time the PRI did not get a majority in the lower house of the federal Congress.

60. For example, see chapter 5 by Lorenzo Meyer and, to a lesser extent, chapter 1 by Juan Lindau and Timothy Cheek in this volume.

relevance and meaning for Mexico, and perhaps (more distantly) even China—though not necessarily all at once. Market-oriented reforms do not guarantee development, but they are more likely to lead to it than state capitalism and socialism are.

Let us review some of the reservations analysts have expressed about Mexico's current course and then take up the responses that can be made to each of them.

The first big set of reasons to doubt Mexico's current course is obvious, namely, the series of dramatic events and crises Mexico experienced beginning about January 1994: the Zapatista rebellion in Chiapas, the assassination of PRI presidential candidate Luis Donaldo Colosio, the kidnappings of businessmen Alfredo Harp Helu and Angel Losada Moreno, the assassination of PRI president Jose Francisco Ruiz Massieu, the peso devaluation and ensuing financial crisis, the government austerity plan and recession, the accusations against President Carlos Salinas's brother Raul Salinas for Jose Francisco Ruiz Massieu's murder, the charge that former deputy attorney general Mario Ruiz Massieu tried to thwart a government investigation into his brother's death, former president Carlos Salinas's break with President Ernesto Zedillo and eventual foreign exile, growing concerns about drug traffic and its potential influence on the Mexican government, etc.

Although this list of considerable length and severity could easily be longer, it hardly means that market-oriented reforms are at fault and ought to be abandoned. At this point no one can rightly make firm judgments on empirical grounds about the consequences of the new economic policies for Mexico's development. In temporal terms Mexico is no further along in its process of reform than Chile was in the early 1980s when its crisis hit. That crisis hurt Chile at least as badly as this one is likely to damage Mexico, which is to say very seriously indeed.[61] Yet Chile not only survived the crisis but emerged a far stronger economy and in time a less authoritarian polity than it had been before. The same may be said ten years from now about Mexico, or not, but it is too early to know either way now.

What do we know now? For one thing, we know that most of Mexi-

---

61. In fact in the first two years at least the damage was quite a bit greater in Chile than in Mexico. In Mexico, GNP declined by almost 7 percent in 1995 but was already back to a positive rate of more than 4 percent in 1996. In Chile, by contrast, the decline in GNP the first year of the crisis, 1982, was 14 percent; and the next year, 1983, it was still negative (minus 0.7 percent). For the Mexican data see CEPAL, *Balance Preliminar de la Economia de America Latina y el Caribe 1996* (Santiago: Naciones Unidas, Diciembre de 1996), Cuadra A.1, 39. For the Chilean data see Bosworth, Dornbusch, and Laban, *The Chilean Economy*, Table 1.1, 32–33.

co's developmental ills, including the recent afflictions just listed, are caused not by Mexico's policies of economic liberalization but by other factors. Mexico's authoritarianism, socioeconomic inequality, widespread poverty, and overall economic dependence on the United States hardly can be said to be due to the very recent trend toward economic liberalization. These features have been in place for many decades, even centuries, during which Mexico has never had a truly liberal economic order—not even during the so-called liberal period in the late nineteenth and early twentieth centuries. So the negative aspects of Mexican development have to be understood as having illiberal roots much more than liberal ones.

To other arguments against economic liberalization in Mexico, some responses can and should be made. One set of these is about its allegedly negative political effects. For example, it is said that Mexico disproves the idea that there is an association between economic liberalization and democracy, or more broadly between level of economic development and the incidence of democracy. It is true that Mexico, despite notable political changes and reforms, still has not crossed the threshold from an essentially authoritarian political system to an essentially democratic one. It is closer than it has ever been but not there yet, and it's still a question whether or when it will cross that threshold.[62]

It is wrong to deny, however, that economic liberalization and increasing economic development have put pressures on the political system in a democratizing direction. The evidence that they have done so is strong. By the mid-1990s, after the liberalizing economic policies of the de la Madrid and Salinas administrations, the political system of Mexico—while on balance still properly classifiable as authoritarian—had more democratic features than at any other time in its history. Political competition was keener and more authentic. Elections were more honest. Political discussion was freer. Political communication, though still highly asymmetrical between the PRI and the opposition parties, was more open and pluralistic.

As a result the votes for opposition parties dramatically increased in the 1988 and 1994 presidential and congressional elections compared to their pre-1988 counterparts. Opposition candidates for governor won elections *and* took office afterwards in four states in 1994–1995. President Zedillo made dramatic and unprecedented moves to challenge the practice of legal impunity for the highest PRI officials, including the brother of former President Carlos Salinas de Gortari. He

---

62. The elections of July 6, 1997, seem initially to have strengthened the case that democratization is occurring.

pledged to continue Mexico's transition to democratic politics, create a more independent judicial branch, and move generally toward the rule of law. We still cannot know how much he will be able to implement these pledges. Opposition will be fierce and perhaps prevail in the short term and perhaps even longer. We can say, however, that in a number of ways the market reforms have increased the pressures for democratization and the rule of law and on balance will probably continue to do so.

Another argument against economic liberalization is the allegation that it is unpopular and would not be politically sustainable if popular support were necessary. However, it is essential not to ignore strong evidence that popular support for and acquiescence in Mexico's economic liberalization have often been high in recent years. In the 1994 presidential election, for example, 77 percent of the popular vote went for the two candidates—Zedillo and Diego Fernandez, the candidate of the PAN—who most strongly supported the market-oriented reforms; indeed, by 1994 (as contrasted with 1988) even Cuauhtémoc Cárdenas, who finished third in the 1994 presidential election, supported parts of the liberalization agenda. These facts are an astonishing change from earlier years. Judging by the 1994 election it is not social-liberal strategies but state-capitalist and socialist strategies that more clearly fail to meet the test of popular support. The Mexican case supports those who have challenged the conventional wisdom about the supposed unpopularity and political costs of market-oriented reforms.

Criticisms of economic liberalization are also based on its alleged negative consequences for social aspects of development. The argument is that the new liberal policies have inegalitarian results and are especially damaging to the poor. The revolt in Chiapas that began January 1, 1994, is often cited as a case in point, as are popular demonstrations in Venezuela and Argentina. This argument has elements of truth but is partial and misleading. It is true that the leaders of the EZLN (Zapatista National Liberation Army) have had objectives such as "the construction of housing in all of Mexico's rural communities with electricity, roads, potable water, and the like." But they also want "the advantages of the city like television, stoves, refrigerators, washing machines, etc."[63] In other words, as elsewhere the poor in Chiapas want the consumer goods that are produced most effectively and efficiently by a market economy.[64] Moreover, the Chiapas rebellion had at least

---

63. Point 11 of agreement between EZLN and Mexican government signed March 2, 1994, as reported in *New York Times*, 3 March 1994, A4.

64. On the general phenomenon, see Inglehart, *Modernization and Postmodernization*; and for Latin America, see Claudio Veliz, *The New World of the Gothic Fox: Culture and Economy in English and Spanish America* (Berkeley: University of California Press, 1994), esp. chapter 9.

three other major causes and objectives besides those attributed to it by critics of economic liberalization. First, the rebellion in Chiapas was a protest against political authoritarianism and corruption on local, re-gional, and national levels. Second, it was a protest against prejudice and discrimination by mestizos and whites against Indians. Neither of these two goals of the protest was in any sense against economic liberalization; indeed, each is perfectly compatible with economic lib-eralization. Third, the Chiapas rebellion was not just a regional phe-nomenon with social causes and goals but also part of a national political strategy against the ruling PRI system. The leader of the EZLN, Subcommandante Marcos, is not from Chiapas and has little in common regionally, ethnically, and culturally with those he claims to represent. Rather he was born and raised in the Gulf Coast city of Tam-pico, Veracruz, the son of a prosperous furniture store owner. His real name is not Marcos but Rafael Sebastian Guillen Vicente. A university graduate (the National Autonomous University, 1980) in philosophy and sociology said to have been "infatuated with the works of Marxist French philosopher Louis Althusser," and a former instructor at the Metropolitan Autonomous University, Xochimilco campus, Marcos has lived and traveled abroad and speaks some English and French and perhaps Italian as well as Spanish. He fits a classic pattern of a political activist socialized and trained outside the revolting state who moves into a position of influence for wider strategic political reasons as well as for reasons of social justice related to Chiapas.[65]

Another argument against economic liberalization on social grounds is that efforts by the Mexican government to supplement marketization with direct social programs to reduce poverty and inequality were in-adequate or dishonest and hypocritical. The main focus of such criti-cism was the so-called Solidarity program or PRONASOL (Programa Nacional de Solidaridad) whose activities were allegedly cosmetic, tac-tical, manipulative, and inconsequential in terms of outcomes.[66] What can be said about such criticism?

It is important first to identify the phenomenon being criticized. The National Solidarity Program was "an umbrella organization in charge of coordinating health, education, infrastructure, and productive proj-

---

65. See newspaper reports and Andres Oppenheimer, *Bordering on Chaos: Guerrillas, Stockbrokers, Politicians, and Mexico's Road to Prosperity* (New York: Little, Brown, 1996), 236–37, 249–53. The passage in quotation marks is on 250.

66. Denise Dresser, "Bringing the Poor Back In: National Solidarity as a Strategy of Regime Legitimation," in *Transforming State-Society Relations in Mexico: The National Solidarity Strategy,* ed. Wayne C. Cornelius, Ann L. Craig, and Jonathan Fox (San Diego: Center for U.S.-Mexican Studies, 1994), 143–65.

ects designed to improve living conditions of the poor."[67] It was a "demand-driven" (as contrasted with "top down") program[68] based on the principles of community initiative and participation, shared responsibility between beneficiaries and state authorities, and transparency in administration; its "overarching goal" was that of "promoting justice, pluralism, and democracy in everyday life."[69] But it was also well described as "a targeted, compensatory relief program whose capacity for reducing extreme poverty and social inequality is limited."[70] Thus no one thought that Solidarity by itself could alleviate poverty, let alone create democracy in Mexico. Not even the whole of federal expenditures in the social sphere, which from 1989 through 1992 were between eight and thirteen times larger than those devoted to Solidarity,[71] could do that. A successful assault on Mexican poverty must depend heavily, indeed mainly, on macroeconomic and other factors rather than government programs of direct action like Solidarity.[72]

Nevertheless, as Cornelius, Craig, and Fox rightly pointed out, "in specific communities and among selected segments of the population, Solidarity can alleviate some of the worst symptoms of the country's uneven development."[73] By this standard, Solidarity's activities can be seen fairly positively. As many as 90 percent of Mexican communities are said to have been reached by at least one Solidarity program and about 200,000 projects are said to have been completed as of early 1995. President Salinas de Gortari's interest in the concept went back to his Ph.D. dissertation completed at Harvard in 1978. As president (1988–94) he spent massive amounts of time and prestige supporting Solidarity programs; according to one analyst he visited Solidarity sites an average of about three days per week during his presidential term.[74] The percentage of the Mexican population suffering from extreme poverty declined from 14 percent to 11 percent between 1988 and 1992.[75]

67. Nora Lustig, "Solidarity as a Strategy of Poverty Alleviation," in *Transforming State-Society Relations*, 79–96, quotation at 83.

68. Lustig, "Solidarity," 79.

69. Wayne Cornelius, Ann Craig, and Jonathan Fox, "Mexico's National Solidarity Program: An Overview," in *Transforming State-Society Relations*, 3–26, at 6–7.

70. Cornelius, Craig, and Fox, "Mexico's National Solidarity Program," 22.

71. Lustig, "Solidarity," 88–89.

72. See notes 34–35 and the text accompanying.

73. Cornelius, Craig, and Fox, "Mexico's National Solidarity Program," 22.

74. Gregory Greenway, "Democratization, Economic Liberalization, and Social Policy: The Case of Mexico's National Solidarity Program," Seminar Presentation, Stanford University, 22 February 1995.

75. Jose Cordoba, "Mexico," in Williamson, *The Political Economy of Reform*, 268–72; and Greenway, "Democratization, Economic Liberalization, and Social Policy."

Thus, while the argument that Mexican social programs in general and Solidarity in particular have failed cannot be firmly rejected, neither can it be firmly sustained. Research to date on Solidarity's effects indicates mixed, uncertain results and the plausibility of contrasting, mutually incompatible interpretations.[76] Those supporting the "Solidarity failed" argument may find some empirical support but they also must confront many inconvenient facts. It is scarcely credible to say that Solidarity failed simply because it could not correct in a few years the results of social ills in place for centuries.

In short, the evidence again compels the conclusion that it is too early to declare market reform in Mexico to be a failure. There is no reasonable warrant for attributing the post-1994 bad news entirely to market-oriented reforms. The assassinations and kidnappings surely had other major causes. So did Chiapas. As for the devaluation crisis, was it triggered by too much economic liberalization or by too little? After all, the peso was overvalued because it was fixed within a narrow band rather than floating freely and thus correcting incrementally as it should have done in a free market. As for the political turmoil in the dominant PRI and the political system more broadly, they were indeed partly (though by no means entirely) caused by economic liberalization. But was that all bad? Government corruption and illegality did not begin with market-oriented reforms. By the mid-1990s, Mexico was closer to being a democratic political system than it had ever been in its entire history. And the record does not support the allegation that nothing was done to address social questions.

---

76. Cornelius, Craig, and Fox, *Transforming State-Society Relations*, passim, esp. chapter 1.

4

Socialist Marketization and East Asian Industrial Structure: Locating Civil Society in China

Gaye Christoffersen

D oes market liberalization in East Asian economies promote democratization in these societies, where the social base for political reform, an autonomous middle class, is weak? Can we account for the shifting public-private space in post-communist societies in transition without referring to an autonomous middle class? What kind of Northeast Asian international political economy is China becoming increasingly embedded in?

The current intellectual trend is to focus on the "strong state" in East Asia to explain economic and political change. The "new institutionalism" explains East Asian economic reform and socialist economic reform without reference to societal forces, emphasizing the role of political institutions in fostering economic growth through state interventions, restructuring the economy toward marketization. It is an explanatory framework that excludes the necessity for a strong base of social forces, the middle class, to support economic change and is a framework especially suited for East Asia, where industrialization tends to coopt the newly emerging middle class, undermining its autonomy, while the state remains "strong" in relation to this relatively weak society.

China, as prelude to further economic liberalization before joining the World Trade Organization (WTO), is in the process of considering means to protect its economy from being swamped with foreign imports, especially autos and electronics, after liberalizing it in conformity with WTO rules. Chinese planners admire and plan to emulate the

Japanese and South Korean governments' structuring of industry and commerce in a way that protected their economies from foreign economic penetration through non-tariff barriers while simultaneously claiming to be liberalizing.

The transformation of China's industrial structure in a fusion of socialist marketization and the East Asian model of industrialization could not be expected to sustain the conditions for an autonomous economic or political life. How this might impact on the prospects for a Chinese civil society and where that civil society might be located, if it can be located, are the focus of this chapter.

This argument can be situated in an extensive literature that yields four approaches:

1. structural explanations that view the democratic transition as shaped by economic and social structures;
2. explanations focused on human agency; strategic, process-oriented explanations of governmental and oppositional elites' actions and choices promoting democratization;
3. the explanation of state theory, a third approach which finds forces within the state negotiating a restructuring of the state and which views democratization as the result of the state reforming itself rather than the outcome of a struggle between state and society; and
4. a fourth explanation which emphasizes the influence of the international system on economic and political change, presented as the consequences of a globalizing civil society or as the result of incorporation into an international political economy.

Recent scholarship leans toward the second approach, in which democratization follows an autonomous trajectory rather than being the result of socioeconomic forces, called the "Third Wave" of democratization.[1] The study of Latin American democratic transitions from authoritarian rule has adopted this approach, which focuses on political elites and their strategic interactions and choices. Scholarship on East Asian democratic transitions emphasizes the role of the state, de-emphasizing the role of oppositional elites even though successful East Asian transitions to democracy have been led by oppositional elites in South Korea, Taiwan, and the Philippines, all of whom had a broad social base.

---

1. For a review of the literature, see Doh Chull Shin, "On the Third Wave of Democratization: A Synthesis and Evaluation of Recent Theory and Research," *World Politics* 47, no. 1 (October 1994): 135–70.

Current scholarship has shifted from the first approach because it is closely associated with "modernization theory," an explanatory framework of the 1950s and 1960s that had real world consequences in the policies of the U.S. Agency for International Development. Modernization theory assumes: (1) a linear path extends from tradition to modernity, forming a continuum on which all countries could be situated at some point; (2) modernization is the result of domestic processes, and the units of comparison, nation-states, are responsible for their own development or underdevelopment; and (3) economic modernization and democratic politics depend on the rise of an urban, educated, middle class.

Resistance to modernization theory was led by proponents of dependency theory and world-systems theory, both theoretical frameworks that emphasized the world economy's influence and responsibility for the underdeveloped state of the Third World. Modernization theory was rejected for the ideological and Western biases embedded in it, considered inappropriate for non-Western countries. A further resistance to modernization theory, and a reaction to world-systems theory, was led by scholars who discovered the autonomous role of political institutions in modernization—earlier called "state theory," most recently referred to as the "new institutionalism," concerned with "Bringing the State Back In."[2]

The analytical focus of this chapter is on the interaction of state, society, and the international system. This approach differs somewhat from Robert Packenham's chapter in this volume, which makes a strong argument for "Bringing Modernization Theory Back In." His focus is on the domestic processes of Latin American countries' shift to economic liberalization since the late 1980s, giving less emphasis to external influences such as the World Bank or the diffusion of economic and political models through a process of global learning.

This chapter concurs that societal factors contribute to marketization and political change, but resists the wholesale adoption of modernization theory. In more precise terms, the actual shift to economic liberalization in Latin America was from import-substitution to export-led growth policies. This shift was the result of global learning from the East Asian model of development, a model based on export-led growth and extensive state intervention in an economy that is market-driven. Learning suggests foreign ideas are transcending national boundaries.

If learning from the East Asian model is taking place in the international system, countries, as the units of analysis, cannot be placed on

2. Peter B. Evans, Dietrich Rueschemeyer, and Theda Skocpol, eds., *Bringing the State Back In* (Cambridge: Cambridge University Press, 1985), 193–94.

the linear path of modernization theory, moving from tradition to modernity, insulated from global processes. Modernization theory is confronted with Galton's dilemma: Increasing global interdependence erodes the autonomy of the nation-state, reducing its utility as the unit of analysis. The nation-state exists in a time-dependent, dynamic relationship with other nation-states. Change in whatever variable is to be explained, such as the shift to economic liberalization, is not really independent but rather the result of an underlying process of global diffusion, such as international learning.

The East Asian model of economic development and democratization poses problems for both structural and strategic explanations of democratization because very few resources exist outside the state's control. The East Asian model of development blurred the boundary between state, market, and civil society, creating a corporatist and clientelist relationship between political and economic elites that permitted little autonomy for capital. Societal factors in the "new institutionalism" approach drop out of the analysis, yielding only a partial account of political and economic change that cannot explain the significance of that defining moment when the middle class in South Korea or Taiwan joined street demonstrations, decisively moving their countries toward wider political participation.

The East Asian model of economic development poses less of a challenge to world-systems theory, representing an Asian variant of world-systems theory when the argument is made that this model has its origins in the Japanese colonial empire that spanned East Asia. The incorporation of the region into Japan's political economy has been sustained since then by the "flying geese pattern" in which the industrial product cycle passed from Japan to South Korea and Taiwan, and later to China and Southeast Asia. More recently, Japanese foreign investment in the newly industrializing countries (NICs) of China and Southeast Asia has encouraged the regionalization of the East Asian economy.

This approach contrasts with the chapter in this volume by David Hendrickson, which finds the international wave of democratization not a result of a globalizing civil society or the result of incorporation into a regional political economy, but rather a democratist project of the U.S. government. He considers this imposition of an alien concept from afar with coercive means, e.g., economic sanctions, to be counterproductive. His implied preference is for the first explanatory approach emphasizing economic structures: If democratization emerges in countries such as China, it will occur because liberalizing economic structures promote reduced state control and a growing middle class. He does not consider viable the second approach of strategic choices promoting democracy, producing an effective transnational alliance between the international system and domestic oppositional elites.

In the East Asian case, the role of the United States has been definitive in nudging smaller client states South Korea and Taiwan toward more democratic processes and in establishing political institutions in Japan after Word War II, when it was a vanquished power. The influence of U.S. political culture on China, however, took root only in the urban intelligentsia, leaving peasants indifferent and conservative party cadres alarmed.

This Chinese intelligentsia could be the nucleus of an oppositional elite, but China poses problems for the strategic, process-oriented approach to Chinese democratization, as governmental political elites are intolerant of ideas that promote "peaceful evolution" away from Chinese Communist Party (CCP) domination. Oppositional political elites, the urban intelligentsia, continue to have a very narrow and weak social base, making them vulnerable to authoritarian measures. They magnify this weakness when they seek to affect the democratic transition within the state rather than through an oppositional civil society (see Cheek's dour assessment of the role of such intellectuals in chapter 8).

China poses difficulties for an argument based on such domestic social and economic structures because the Chinese middle class is small and not autonomous. Thus the new institutionalism approach might appear to have explanatory value for understanding Chinese political and economic change. World-systems theory, framed in its Asian variant as the flying geese pattern, also makes a compelling argument. But both approaches offer only partial explanations.

This chapter's thesis is that despite the strength of the East Asian state, the state-centered approach cannot construct an adequate explanation of political change in East Asia without reference to the influence of state-society relations and the impact of the international system. It is this focus on state, society, and the international system that provides the most adequate account of markets and politics in China.

Comparison with the Russian Case

A comparison with the situation in the Russian Far East as a point of reference offers some insight into the process of the post-communist transition to a market economy when the East Asian model is grafted onto the Leninist state. Unlike in China, privatization in Russia has outpaced the creation of institutions supportive of marketization, and political reform preceded economic reform. It is quite common for managers of state enterprises to appropriate property rights in their enterprises at their own initiative, referred to as "spontaneous privatization." By 1993, two-thirds of Russian privatized state enterprises had been acquired by insiders. Because significant public assets end up in the private hands of the old communist nomenklatura, it is called "nomenklatura capitalism." Although these enterprises are privatized, they are not subjected to hard budget constraints, still receiving state subsidies that accounted for 22 percent of Russia's GNP in 1993. State theory explains this condition of privatization without marketization as the result of a weak Russian state, a state unable to act autonomously from dominant societal interests, unable to define and implement policy in the national interest.[3]

Privatization in socialist economies can reinforce the power and privileges of the old system's elite rather than create a new entrepreneurial class as orthodox economics would suppose. In Primorye territory in the Russian Far East, the nomenklatura capitalists, managers of the military-industrial complex aligned with the security forces and sometimes the Mafia, have formed themselves into a business association, *PAKT*, that intends to model itself on Japanese *keiretsu* industrial organization. The political consequences of this alignment of economic, criminal, and paramilitary elites are their ability to control the public sphere in Primorye and its capital, Vladivostok, and the ability to put their candidate, Governor Nazdratenko, into office. Ordinary citizens live in terror, appearing outwardly quiescent as a survival strategy. Under such conditions, civil society would appear to be an idea whose time has not yet come. This nomenklatura has supported the communists and the extreme nationalists and would support a red-brown coalition.

Intellectuals in Moscow have debated the advantages of the Japan model versus the Western model, arguing that Russia's dual identity of being Asian and Western justifies considering both. It is the old nomenklatura, however, that is drawn to state-guided capitalism, as it provides the formula by which they can hold on to political and economic power during the post-communist transition.

It was surprising, therefore, when Primorye's silent majority in June 1993 brought into office their first democratically elected mayor in Vladivostok, a retired naval officer and honest individual opposed to *PAKT* and the Mafia. In less than a year, under instructions from the governor, this mayor was dragged out of office after a siege of city hall and a floor-to-floor search of the building by OMON (Interior Ministry

---

3. Michael McFaul, "State Power, Institutional Change and the Politics of Privatization in Russia," *World Politics* 47, no. 2 (January 1995): 210–43.

troops). The deputy mayor was literally thrown out feet first. Some of Vladivostok's citizens stood vigil outside city hall in support of the mayor, but most citizens were home watching a Mexican soap opera, *Prosta Maria* (Simply Maria), a TV series meant to encourage romantic fantasy and apolitical quiescence. The democratic leaders, oppositional elites to the governor and *PAKT*, appeared to lack a viable social base.

In the 1996 Russian presidential elections, Primorye's government vocally supported the communist and nationalist candidates. The relatively democratic candidate, Yeltsin, seemingly had minimal support. Yet, the quiescent citizenry once again surprised everyone, including Yeltsin, by giving him a plurality in the territory's vote. Yeltsin may eventually purge Primorye's territorial administration after his political base is secure, thus justifying his support in the territory. In the Russian case, political institutions in the form of fair elections empower the ordinarily quiescent citizen, while economic structures on the Japan model disadvantage the powerless.

It is this shift from Leninist command economy to an industrial structure modeled on the *keiretsu* and *jaebol* that leaves no public sphere for an autonomous economic and political life that could sustain oppositional elites. This autonomy is necessary for civil society to emerge and democratization to take place in China.[4]

U.S.-Japan Differences over State Intervention

The United States promoted privatization and reduced state intervention in the economy of Third World countries during the 1980s as a solution to their debt crisis, and continues to promote privatization. Under U.S. influence, the World Bank requires a study on the feasibility of privatization before it releases funds to a recipient country. The underlying rationale of the United States and the World Bank is that the private sector allocates goods and services more efficiently than the public sector and that it is less corrupt and less inclined toward rent-seeking behavior. World Bank policy always had advised against state intervention in the economy.

During this same period, the 1980s, the world's fastest growing economies in East Asia practiced extensive state intervention in their economies. Japanese industrialization had depended on state interven-

---

4. Gu Xin, "A Civil Society and Public Sphere in Post-Mao China? An Overview of Western Publications," *China Information* 8, no. 3 (Winter 1993–1994): 38–51.

tion, or state guidance, to create rapid economic growth. The major characteristic of Japanese industrial organization is the business group (*kigyo keiretsu*), a group of companies formed on the foundation of the old *zaibatsu*, with cross-shareholding and vertical integration, and centered around a bank. Within this grouping, large enterprises subcontract out work to their smaller subsidiaries. Long-term agreements between industries to do business at fixed prices create cartels, illegal but widely practiced, buffering domestic industries from international competition. The *keiretsu* networks give the Japanese state numerous access points to the private sector.[5]

The ability of the Japanese *keiretsu* to protect Japanese domestic markets has been a source of tension in U.S.–Japan relations. American exporters feel these inter-industry buyer-seller cartels block American access to the Japanese domestic market, creating non-tariff barriers. The U.S. strategy of *gaiatsu* (external pressure) on Japan to liberalize and open its domestic economy requires a transnational alliance with the Japanese middle class (as consumers) aligned against the *keiretsu*.

The extent to which economic success in Japan or South Korea is the result of state interventions or marketization remains contested terrain. In the debate over the role of state intervention and market forces, many Asian researchers credit a strong state and state intervention for East Asian successes. Many Western researchers argue that it was market forces that produced these "East Asian Miracles," that is, that these countries' industrial policies were market promoting. When state intervention does not promote marketization, it often leads to clientelist patronage networks and crony capitalism, to privatization without market liberalization, which can transfer and concentrate public assets in private hands, creating monopolies.

This U.S.–Japanese difference found a forum within the World Bank, centering on the question of the appropriate economic model for developing countries: the U.S.-supported model of market liberalization and privatization or the Japan-supported model of some degree of state intervention. This opposition occurred at the time that Japan had enlarged its position as a donor nation, challenging the United States' dominant position within the World Bank. Both drew on the success of the East Asian development experience, but put different emphasis on whether it was market forces or state intervention that accounted for East Asian success. This disagreement produced a volume, *The East Asian Miracle: Economic Growth and Public Policy*, that was intended to resolve the issue by acknowledging the successes of the Japan model

---

5. Daniel I. Okimoto, *Between MITI and the Market: Japanese Industrial Policy for High Technology* (Stanford: Stanford University Press, 1989), 132–52.

and the role of state intervention in industrialization.[6] Instead, the volume produced a compromise, stating that the East Asian economies were successful because of the creation of strong state institutions that promoted growth, intervening selectively in the market with public policies that promoted market liberalization. Recent work by World Bank researchers suggests that China, with state intervention that is shifting from "market supplanting" to "market fostering," is following a pattern similar to the East Asian NICs.[7]

The U.S.–Japan difference over state-economy relations found another arena in China, differing over how liberal or authoritarian the Chinese state should be. This split has also led to conflicting advice on the degree to which the Chinese state should intervene in the economy. Following the 1989 massacre at Tiananmen Square, the U.S.–Japan difference centered on the need for political and economic liberalization in China, with human rights a much more volatile issue than economic development strategies. Several projects attempted to coordinate U.S.–Japan policies toward China to prevent policy differences from escalating, a situation that China would have exploited.[8]

Japanese question whether marketization in China is beneficial for Japan if, for example, marketization undermines authoritarian stability in China or if its failure leads to mass emigration throughout East Asia. To maintain stability, Japanese prefer the "developmental-authoritarian" state in China, maintaining parts of the planned economy through macroeconomic controls and resorting to authoritarian interventions when necessary. According to a Japanese analyst, the Chinese Communist Party must retain its dictatorial power for the state to have the capacity for authoritarian interventions. Consequently, he felt Japan's response to China's marketization should be to increase Sino–Japanese economic interdependence, further enmeshing China into the international system. China's recent emulation of Japan and South Korea as reference models for development he considered positive, hoping that "if China adopts an economic system that resembles that of Japan, then Japan may well be able to exercise greater influence on China."[9]

6. World Bank, *The East Asian Miracle: Economic Growth and Public Policy* (New York: Oxford University Press, 1993).

7. Yan Wang and Vinod Thomas, "Market Supplanting Versus Market Fostering Interventions: China, East Asia and Other Developing Countries," *China Economic Review* 4, no. 2 (1993): 243–58.

8. See, for example, the Asia Society, *U.S.-Japan Policy Dialogue on China: Economic Issues*. Report on the first meeting of the U.S.-Japan Consultative Group on Policies Toward the People's Republic of China, New York, 18–19 December 1991.

9. Hisahiro Kanayama, *The Marketization of China and Japan's Response: Prospects for the Future* (Tokyo: Institute for International Policy Studies, November 1993), 26.

In contrast to official U.S. advocacy of reduced state intervention in China, Japanese economists studying China advocate a slow, cautious movement to removing state controls and liberalization, advising that the Chinese state build and control China's market economy for a long time rather than wait for its spontaneous emergence. Japanese economists find similarities in the state intervention of Japan's regulated capitalism with the state intervention of China's guided socialism, holding up Japan's experience as relevant for China.[10]

Reflecting the World Bank's policy preferences, a study by the IMF on China's market liberalization argued that the role and functions of the Chinese government should be changed. The government should withdraw from its tight control over enterprises and focus on macro-economic management of the economy. The IMF was hopeful that the streamlining and restructuring of the government bureaucracy since 1992 indicated a more limited role for government with less intervention. On the formation of enterprise groups, the study assessed them as a rationalization of the industrial structure that took advantage of economies of scale by creating large conglomerates that could efficiently compete internationally. There was no indication of an awareness that enterprise groups facilitated state interventions.[11]

Explaining the South Korean Model

What is the East Asian model of industrialization and what is its appeal to China? South Korea more than any other East Asian NIC closely resembles Japanese *keiretsu* arrangements in the formation of Korean *jaebol* (*chaebol*) as a legacy of the Japanese colonial period. China, in turn, is at present actively engaged in transforming itself from a planned economy with state enterprises to having an industrial structure resembling other East Asian economies. Chinese analysts compare Chinese industry to the *jaebol* of South Korea and the *keiretsu* of Japan.[12]

The South Korean state represents one of the strongest developmental states with coercive and allocative authority that penetrated far

10. Kyoichi Ishihara, *China's Conversion to a Market Economy* (Tokyo: Institute of Developing Economies, 1993).

11. Michael W. Bell, Hoe Ee Khor, and Kalpana Kochhar, *China at the Threshold of a Market Economy* (Washington, D.C.: International Monetary Fund, September 1993), 29.

12. Zeyuan Liu, "Zhong han ri jingji fazhan bijiao yanjiu" (Comparative Research on the Economic Development of China, Korea, and Japan), *Dongbei ya* no. 4 (1993): 10–15.

into Korean society, suppressed labor, and maintained strict regulatory discipline over Korean industry, the *jaebol*, until the 1980s. Analyses that make a strong statist or institutionalist argument claim that the shift to export-led economic growth in the 1960s and economic liberalization in the 1980s was not the result of social coalitions but rather the result of economic, legal, and institutional reforms initiated by the state.[13] Thus the emergence of a strong bourgeoisie was not a prerequisite to democratization and economic growth.

It was initially Chinese democrats in the late 1980s who hoped China would follow the path of the East Asian developmental states: economic liberalization under the guidance of a strong authoritarian government that would eventually lead to political reform, the "new authoritarianism." In the 1990s, following the Tiananmen experience, it is younger technocrats who want China to follow the East Asian development path, although there is a lowered expectation that a strong authoritarian state would give way to democratization in China.[14]

The emulation of South Korea is the result of China learning during the 1980s as it watched South Korea's export-led growth produce a prosperous economy. The World Bank also recommended that China follow the Korean model of marketization. Chinese economists began serious study of the South Korean model in the mid-1980s, producing many volumes that acknowledged the achievements of this developing country's export-led growth. All of the East Asian NICs' economic success had a major impact on Chinese decisions to pursue economic liberalization, but South Korea had the largest impact.[15] It was at this time that discussions began regarding Northeast Asian regional economic cooperation and industrial coordination that required industrial reorganization to facilitate cooperation.

Chinese have also studied the Japanese economy, perceiving the Japan model of state-guided industrialization and large enterprise groups a means to preserve China's state-owned enterprises even while forcing them to face market competition and thereby disciplining them to be more efficient and profitable.[16] Formation of enterprise

---

13. Stephen Haggard, *Pathways from the Periphery: The Politics of Growth in the Newly Industrializing Countries* (Ithaca: Cornell University Press, 1990).

14. Tony Saich, "The Search for Civil Society and Democracy in China," *Current History* (September 1994): 260–64.

15. Fu Dedi, ed., *Nan chaoxian jingji de jueqi* (The South Korean Economy's Rise) (Beijing: Zhongguo guoji rencai kaifa yanjiusuo yanjiu fazhanbu, June 1990).

16. Niu Jiangtao and Cai Xingyang, "Riben guanting zhudao xia de shichang jingji yunzuo ji qi qishi" (Operation of a Market-oriented Economy under the Guidance of the Japanese Government and Its Inspiration), *Dongbeiya luntan*, no. 2 (1993): 30.

groups would preserve the economies of scale and other advantages of state-owned enterprises.

A major factor in Korea's liberalization during the 1980s was the U.S. government's pressure on Korea, especially in 1985–87, to import more from the United States. The institutionalist approach to Korea makes the argument that the international system during the 1980s imposed economic liberalization on an unwilling Korea even though it was inappropriate for Korea and loosened the state's control of the *jaebol*. State-led capitalism under Park Chung Hee had produced rapid industrialization and economic growth through the creation of a powerful bureaucratic organization and business groups, the *jaebol*, that cooperated with the state's industrialization strategy. By the 1980s, the state sector accounted for 40 percent of total investment. After Park's death, the Fifth and Sixth Republics "mistakenly" (in the view of the current regime) abandoned this strategy and tried to replace it with the American model of economic liberalism during the 1980s under the Chun Doo Hwan and Roh Tae Woo administrations. The share of the state sector was brought down to 16 percent of total investment. Analysts using this approach argue that the American model was institutionally inappropriate for Korean conditions, leading to friction, contradictions, and a loss of state control over the big business groups, the *jaebol*. These authors advocate that Korea return to the Japanese model of industrialization and reassert state control over the business groups. The economic liberalism of the Fifth and Sixth Republics saw many state corporatist institutions survive the 1987 political democratization, continuing to dominate the Korean economy. This led to contradictions between a foreign-imposed liberalism and state corporatism, resulting in a loss of Korean international competitiveness that produced a trade deficit.[17]

One account of the 1980s liberalization phase takes this argument further, stating that the Korean Development Institute dominated national economic policy, that it was staffed by thirty-five economists with Ph.D.s from U.S. universities, and that thus this was the access point for an alien influence.[18] Another author remains critical of this Korean drift toward liberalization and stresses the need to reassert state control over the *jaebol* to make industry more accountable to the Korean people.[19] The 1980s liberalization, therefore, is viewed as inimical to democratic control of the economy.

17. Lee-Jay Cho and Yoon Hyung Kim, eds., *Korea's Political Economy: An Institutional Perspective* (Boulder, Colo.: Westview Press, 1994).

18. Jung-en Woo, *Race to the Swift: State and Finance in Korean Industrialization* (New York: Columbia University Press, 1991).

19. Alice H. Amsden, "The Specter of Anglo-Saxonization Is Haunting South Korea," in *Korea's Political Economy*, 87–125.

In resistance to the state-centered approach, a minority of analysts argue that it is the complex, dialectical interaction between state and society that produced these specific outcomes rather than the state as the primary factor. The critique of the state-centered approach is that it is too narrowly economistic in its focus on state-market relations, tending toward a reification of the East Asian developmental state and ignoring the broader social transformations and other elements of Korea's civil society within which its political economy is embedded.[20] Korean society has not been quiescent, having a history of peasant rebellions, student demonstrations, and labor protests. It was when the South Korean middle class joined massive street demonstrations by students and labor in 1987 that strongman Chun Doo Hwan was forced to transfer power through direct presidential elections, thus bringing about a democratization initiated by an active civil society.

Controversy remains over whether to emphasize the state alone or state-societal interaction in an explanatory framework of South Korean economic liberalization and democratization, but it is clear that an autonomous middle class was able to emerge despite the corporatist alliance dominating society—a state corporatism that enmeshed emerging social forces in clientelist patronage networks. This autonomous middle class had assistance from the international system in the form of U.S. pressure in the 1980s. This transnational alliance of domestic and international forces drove the democratic transition in South Korea.

If China should follow the path of other East Asian economies, relying on a strong state to promote market liberalization, we can predict that this kind of industrial structure will make democratization difficult but not impossible, and that it will impede but not preclude the emergence of an independent middle class as a force for democracy.

State and Society in Taiwan

Taiwan represents a somewhat different model of Northeast Asian industrialization. Despite the fact that Taiwan (Republic of China) is in the Northeast Asian regional political economy and has been part of the region's product-cycle industrialization pattern,[21] Taiwan's indus-

---

20. Hagen Koo, "Introduction: Beyond State-Market Relations," in *State and Society in Contemporary Korea*, ed. Hagen Koo (Ithaca: Cornell University Press, 1993), 7.

21. Bruce Cumings, "The Origins and Development of the Northeast Asian Political Economy: Industrial Sectors, Product Cycles, and Political Consequences," in *The Political Economy of the New Asian Industrialism*, ed. Frederic C. Deyo (Ithaca: Cornell University Press, 1987), 44–83.

trial structure is different. In Taiwan, government-business relations and state-society relations followed a trajectory different from Korea's. All these factors contributed to a different process of political liberalization.

The manner in which the Kuomintang (KMT) took power in Taiwan, with the "2–28 incident" in 1947, which liquidated ten to twenty thousand Taiwanese political, economic, and intellectual elites, produced a weak, quiescent, leaderless Taiwanese society under a strong KMT party-state. This party-state was backed by a large military and internal security apparatus that penetrated this weak society. The civilian and military administrative structures were staffed by mainlanders who had no property interests in Taiwan and no connections with a landlord class, many of whom had been removed with the 1947 liquidation. This left the KMT party-state more autonomous from societal influence than governments were in other East Asian economies. With few local Taiwanese capitalists and a state sector created out of former Japanese enterprises, Taiwan could have been expected to form a government-business relationship similar to that in South Korea. However, investment capital that shifted from the mainland to Taiwan after the KMT defeat in the civil war went into private enterprises, creating the basis for an autonomous middle class.

The economic bureaucracy that guided Taiwan's economic development was staffed by technocrats intent on reform. The KMT land reform produced an agricultural sector with rising living standards. The conservative wing of the party-state was interventionist ideologically because of concern that economic development would produce a strong, autonomous ethnic Taiwanese middle class. Therefore, KMT conservatives promoted a large state-run sector and the state enterprises supported import-substitution policies. The United States, however, promoted the private sector. KMT technocrats, in alliance with the U.S. AID mission, pushed for a shift to export-led growth, the sale of state enterprises, trade liberalization, and exchange rate reform. The United States had sufficient leverage to pressure Taiwan to liberalize its economy, promote economic development, and recruit more Taiwanese. Taiwan began to take some liberalization measures in 1958 and by the mid-1960s had shifted to export-led growth.

Japanese colonial rule had developed heavy industry in Korea to a greater extent than in Taiwan. In the early years of colonial rule, Taiwanese could not form enterprises without Japanese participation. Later on, Taiwanese were permitted to form only small-scale enterprises not in heavy industry. Businesses in Taiwan tend to be family-run, small, self-financed, or financed through a *hui* (a group of people who pool their money) independent from the state. Therefore, the financial and monetary policy instruments that the Japanese and South Korean states have used for administrative guidance of industry were less available to the Taiwan government. The KMT party-state in the late 1970s and early 1980s attempted to merge the many small and middle-size enterprises into a few giant corporations in the auto and steel industries to emulate Korean industrial structure. Taiwanese businessmen resisted being incorporated into a Taiwanese *jaebol* and had the financial autonomy to resist.[22] Taiwanese government–private sector relations have been more distant than such relations are in Japan or South Korea.

Production from these small and medium-size enterprises accounts for 60 percent of total exports. These Taiwanese firms are more responsive to world market conditions than are Korean *jaebol* and are part of the reason Taiwan has had trade surpluses while South Korea has continually had trade deficits except for the late 1980s.

The KMT party-state kept Taiwanese society weak by creating many associations to incorporate social groups into the state. Under the threat of an invasion from the mainland, martial law forbade the formation of independent parties. Labor was suppressed and dissidents were pulverized. The KMT party-state made no pretense to being a democracy during this time and resisted pressure to democratize.

During the 1970s, conservatives and reformers in the KMT promoted conflicting policies regarding democratization and Taiwanization (the incorporation of ethnic Taiwanese into the state and KMT). This elite conflict created an opening. The turning point in which societal forces emerged and confronted this state has been situated at the 1977 Chung-li incident, in which ten thousand people rioted in response to KMT rigging of a local county election. During the thirty years that had passed since the 2–28 incident, Taiwanese society had renewed itself. During the decade from the 1977 Chung-li incident until 1987, when opposition parties were legalized and martial law was lifted, the *dangwai* (opposition parties) organized, demonstrated, and represented the ethnic Taiwanese sector of the middle class.[23] This activism outside the domain of the state, and in defiance of the state, produced a stronger society.

In the late 1980s, Taiwan underwent political liberalization, characterized by expanded political participation, the rise of a Taiwan independence party, the Taiwanization of the state bureaucracy, and

---

22. Chien-kuo Pang, *The State and Economic Transformation: The Taiwan Case* (New York: Garland Publishing, Inc., 1992), 251.
23. Thomas B. Gold, *State and Society in the Taiwan Miracle* (Armonk, N.Y.: M. E. Sharpe, Inc., 1986).

expanded freedoms of speech and association giving voice to opposition parties. The official KMT explanation of this transformation is that former president Chiang Ching-guo decreed political liberalization in 1988, thus claiming that the KMT party-state had reformed itself. Taiwan is held up as an example of the new authoritarianism, which guides a country from authoritarianism to democracy by transformations within the state.

Did the Taiwanese state reform itself, or should the state's interaction with societal forces be credited with this transformation? And within the general framework of state-society interaction, should we emphasize the importance of economic and social structures, or does a focus on the strategic choices of oppositional elites and their interactions with governmental elites better explain Taiwan's liberalization?

Research that conforms to the KMT's self-understanding regarding Taiwan's democratization adopts the statist approach, focusing on the transformation of formal political institutions and electoral politics rather than socioeconomic forces as the impetus to democratization. The legitimizing of oppositional parties and the rising role of the Legislative Yuan and its transformation purport to demonstrate that Taiwan has become more democratic. It is argued the KMT party-state created an environment that permitted electoral politics to take place, completing Taiwan's democratization by the December 1992 elections.[24]

The literature on Taiwan's democratization is characterized by extensive study of the minute details of the constitutional issues involved while avoiding harder questions about the relevance of electoral politics to the exercise of power in Taiwan. Irregularities in the electoral process point to state assistance to the KMT by the security apparatus and enormous private and public funding far exceeding the financial support of the Democratic Progressive Party (DPP). Elected officials still do not have control over government policy, suggesting that the state administrative apparatus remains autonomous from the electoral process.

Progress toward democratization in Taiwan has been incremental but steady. The December 1991 elections to choose a National Assembly created a legislature that was accountable to the people of Taiwan rather than maintaining the fiction of representing all the provinces on the Chinese mainland, as had been the case before the elections. This previous legislature was dominated by KMT delegates who were very elderly, having been elected to their positions in 1947. The author remembers Taiwan TV in 1978 inadvertently catching some of the elderly

---

24. Jurgen Domes, "Taiwan in 1992: On the Verge of Democracy," *Asian Survey* 33, no. 1 (January 1993): 54–60.

delegates in their eighties asleep during a legislative session, with some appearing to be embalmed in their chairs. The 1991 elections were the first where KMT dominance was not rigged and the Democratic Progressive Party's campaign platform could speak of Taiwan as an independent republic, previously an act of sedition.

Nevertheless, the KMT obtained a landslide in the 1991 election.[25] The DPP was routed because it is only a loose coalition of oppositional elites, and its party platform has been gradually co-opted by the KMT, except for the issue of independence from the mainland. More important, the KMT represented stability to the middle class. Because the DPP's program generally stresses the pro-independence and ethnic Taiwanese issues, it is not seen by the middle class as a force for stability.

Responding to this middle-class distrust, the DPP in the December 1994 elections targeted its party platform to discredit the KMT on what are considered middle-class issues of corruption and environmental pollution. While the KMT will try to win back this important sector of the electorate through promises to eliminate the corruption, the DPP will attempt to widen its base of support through programs appealing to the middle class. The first direct elections for Taipei mayor, held in December 1994, voted a DPP candidate into office, indicating the strategy's success.

The DPP characterizes Taiwan's democratization as a joint project of governmental and oppositional elites, thus placing Taiwan's transformation in the Third Wave of democratization, providing a strategic, process-oriented explanation.[26] Some studies identify four groups of political elites led respectively by Chiang Ching-kuo, Lee Teng-hui, the KMT, and the DPP, and argue it was the interaction of these groups that produced constitutional reforms, placing the exercise of political power under the rule of law.[27]

Both the DPP's and KMT's explanations of Taiwan democratization are self-serving and suspect. The evidence leans toward state-societal interaction to account for Taiwan's political outcomes. There is ample evidence to argue that autonomous social movements emerging in the 1970s and 1980s—including the student movement, labor, the consumer movement, the rural farmers' movement, and the environ-

25. Simon Long, "Taiwan's National Assembly Elections," *China Quarterly* no. 129 (March 1992): 216–28.

26. Shao-chuan Leng and Cheng-yi Lin, "Political Change on Taiwan: Transition to Democracy?" *China Quarterly* no. 136 (December 1993): 805–39.

27. Linda Chao and Ramon H. Myers, "The First Chinese Democracy: Political Development of the Republic of China on Taiwan, 1986–1994," *Asian Survey* 34, no. 3 (March 1994): 213–30.

mental movement—produced a civil society in Taiwan.[28] A question remains regarding how autonomous these associations are from the KMT or the DPP. Evidence such as the official *Taiwan Statistical Data Book*, listing civic organizations as numbering 2,500 in 1952 and 11,000 in 1987, is not always credible.

The statist approach applied to Taiwan is a hard argument to make.[29] The KMT had a repressive state, at least until the late 1980s, but not so dominating that it could account for Taiwan's economic development and political reform without reference to the influence of society. The state has not dominated private industry to the same extent it historically did in Korea or Japan.

With regard to the international system, world opinion and U.S. influence on Taiwan to democratize have always been strong dating back to the 1940s. In the 1980s the U.S. Congress held hearings on the KMT's martial law and abuses of human rights. Exposure of abuses has a singular significance because Taipei is continually in a propaganda war with Beijing to demonstrate its moral superiority. The struggle for world opinion is part of the ongoing civil war. If U.S. pressure alone could have changed the KMT, that would have happened in the 1940s. Many scholars argue that international pressure combined with domestic change pushed Taiwan toward democratization.[30]

Taiwanese democracy received further influence from the international system in spring 1996, during Taiwan's first presidential elections. Beijing's threatening stance toward Taiwan's implicit shift toward independence undermined support for both the pro-Beijing party and the DPP's independence agenda. The U.S. policy toward China and Taiwan of "calculated ambiguity" undermined the DPP. The KMT candidate, Lee Teng-hui, having never openly suggested independence for Taiwan, represented stability and won by a landslide.

Taiwan may contribute a political rather than an industrial lesson to China's incorporation into the Northeast Asian political economy. In the summer of 1995, Beijing organized a conference on the transition to democracy, inviting foreign participants from several countries to explain their own experience with democratization. The Taiwanese participants discussed Taiwan's experience with democratization, the

---

28. Kuo-wei Lee, "The Road to Democracy: Taiwan Experience," *Asian Profile* 19, no. 6 (December 1991): 489–504.

29. Joel Aberbach, David Dollar, and Kenneth Sokoloff, eds., *The Role of the State in Taiwan's Development* (Armonk, N.Y.: M. E. Sharpe, 1994).

30. Andrew J. Nathan and Helena V. S. Ho, "Chiang Ching-kuo's Decision for Political Reform," in *Chiang Ching-kuo's Leadership in the Development of the Republic of China on Taiwan* (Lanham, Md.: University Press of America, 1993), 31–62.

institutionalization of electoral politics, including the use of unortho-dox means for managing electoral outcomes. The Chinese Communist Party planned to implement lessons learned from Taiwan in the village electoral system being constructed by the party-state.[31]

The Political Economy of Chinese Civil Society

Can the institutional approach favored in the study of Japan, South Korea, and Taiwan be adapted to the study of China? The institutional approach to Chinese economic reform has only been explicitly used by one study, which argues that state intervention managed by the Chi-nese Communist Party, rather than societal forces, produced the eco-nomic reforms of the 1980s. This study examines the continuity and resilience of communist bureaucratic authoritarian institutions that supported a planned economy prior to 1978 and economic reform after 1978. This approach argues that economic reform policies were shaped by their institutional setting following a political logic rather than an economic logic.[32] The institutional approach shifts emphasis from soci-etal coalitions as the force for economic reform, arguing it was the party-state rather than a middle class that led marketization.

Within U.S. scholarship on China, however, the dominant intellec-tual trend reflects a belief that political change is the result of state-society interactions, and thus societal factors must have explanatory value. Research explains the absence or emergence of a civil society by focusing on societal forces and their relationship to the state. This approach encounters conceptual difficulties because the boundary be-tween state and society in China is blurred by extensive party-state control of economic life.

Because the Chinese cadre/businessman is neither solely a bureau-crat nor a merchant, one study refers to cadres and businessmen as "mutually interpenetrated semiclasses" which manage rural and urban enterprises. The economic reforms have generated institutions such as enterprise groups which advantage bureaucrats in the use of state assets to create economic power. These kinds of institutions pro-long or "freeze" the transition to marketization.[33]

---

31. As related by Anne F. Thurston, author of (in collaboration with Li Zhi-sui) *The Private Life of Chairman Mao: The Memoirs of Mao's Personal Physician* (New York: Random House, 1994).

32. Susan L. Shirk, *The Political Logic of Economic Reform in China* (Berkeley: University of California Press, 1993).

33. Dorothy J. Solinger, "Urban Entrepreneurs and the State: The Merger of State and Society," in *State and Society in China: The Consequences of Reform*, ed. Arthur Lewis Rosenbaum (Boulder: Westview Press, 1992): 121–41.

Chinese Enterprise Groups

Western analysts, unlike Japanese researchers, have not seriously studied the formation of Chinese industrial groupings (*qiye jituan*) during the 1980s and 1990s based on the Korean *jaebol* and the Japanese *keiretsu*. An enterprise group is a merger of small and large state-owned enterprises backed by a financial institution, forming a union based on cross-shareholding by corporate bodies. Enterprise groups can also emerge out of the subcontracting arrangements state-owned enterprises have had with township and village enterprises.

When these enterprises are grouped around a trading company, they are the basis for a transnational corporation. The goal of this type of enterprise group is to better integrate trade with industry. They are formed in response to the increasing liberalization of the Chinese domestic market. It is hoped that these groups can operate as *keiretsu* do and "protect" China's economy from foreign (Japanese and U.S.) economic penetration after Beijing joins the WTO regime, just as the Chinese have witnessed Japanese *keiretsu* arrangements protect the Japanese economy from U.S. trade and investment.

According to Li Lanqing, head of the Ministry of Foreign Economic Trade and Cooperation, international market competition creates pressures on Chinese enterprises to reorganize themselves defensively, to become more competitive in the world market.[34]

The Chinese government has been forming socialist transnational corporations through industrial restructuring and enterprise groups since the 1980s.[35] Chinese transnational corporations create a worldwide marketing network, contributing to export competitiveness.[36] In Shanghai, 480 overseas enterprises reorganized themselves into five large transnational groups. By 1992, in China as a whole, there were thirty-five groups formally established and twenty groups in the process of being formed at the state level. Some reports note 1,600 enterprise groups at varying levels throughout China but find only 430 could be considered enterprise groups that intermingle their assets. The rest were business associations. The State Council's Economic and Trade Office, the State Planning Commission, and the State Commission for Restructuring the Economy jointly supported these experi-

---

34. Li Lanqing, "Foreign Trade Enterprises Should Rapidly Change Their Operational Mechanisms," *Guoji shangbao* (3 December 1992): 1–2, in Foreign Broadcast Information Service-CHI-93–004 (7 January 1993), 38.

35. Lu Jiarui, "Lun shehui zhuyi kuaguo gongsi" (On the Socialist Transnational Corporation), *Xuexi yu tansu* no. 4 (1990): 84.

36. Lu Shengliang, "Shilun waimao jingying jituanhua" (On the Grouping of Foreign Trade Enterprises), *Guoji maoyi wenti* no. 5 (1991): 19.

mental enterprise groups, creating a domestic and foreign legal regime that permitted them to operate with more autonomy and granting them preferential policies with independence from central ministries and local governments.

Japanese economists have advised Chinese industry to reorganize the industrial structure into industrial and trade groups.[37] In contrast, advice by World Bank researchers is that the Chinese government should limit its strong state intervention in the formation of these enterprise groups and let them form voluntarily. In any case, Western research has focused on the creation of shareholding companies rather than enterprise groups, although the latter control vastly larger assets than the former.[38]

The formation of Chinese enterprise groups portends a trend toward East Asian state corporatism rather than economic liberalization. An examination of the township and village enterprises and the state-owned enterprises that make up the enterprise groups should help us better understand to what extent there is space for autonomous economic life.

China's Township and Village Enterprises

The most important fact of the Chinese economic reforms is the devolution of economic decision making power from the center down to the locality, the province, county, and village. This devolution led to expanding economic activity outside the planned economy as each level of government created enterprises to meet its local needs of consumption and employment. China's township and village enterprises (TVEs) have been the most dynamic sector of the Chinese economy, now producing 60 percent of China's GNP, and represent the most successful area of economic liberalization and marketization. It is in this economy outside the plan that autonomous social forces would be expected to be found in the form of rich peasants and private entrepreneurs.

Close examination of China's TVEs, however, reveals them to be controlled by local government, a relationship referred to as "local state corporatism."[39] Local governments tend to provide the initial cap-

---

37. Ryoshi Minami, *The Economic Development of China: A Comparison with the Japanese Experience* (New York: St. Martin's Press, 1994), 37–38.

38. Peter Harrold and Rajiv Lall, *China: Reform and Development in 1992–93.* World Bank Discussion Paper no. 215 (Washington, D.C.: World Bank, 1993), 45.

39. Jean C. Oi, "Fiscal Reform and the Economic Foundations of Local State Corporatism in China," *World Politics* 45 (October 1992): 99–126.

ital, help build the physical plant, and are essential for finding needed production inputs such as raw materials or energy when the market is in short supply. One study examined the extent to which TVEs responded to market signals and were market-oriented enterprises. It found that local governments set up TVEs to achieve communal objectives and thus limited their ability to be profit maximizers responding to market signals.[40]

Chinese marketization should be seen as reassignment of property rights between state agencies, a devolution of property rights over assets from the central to the lower levels of government administration.[41] This downward reassignment led to the emergence of township and village enterprises (TVEs). The local party-state retains tight control over the TVEs, as communist cadres manage their local enterprises.

Private entrepreneurs (*getihu*) represent a potential, emerging, autonomous middle class. After Tiananmen, the central government closed down many private enterprises between 1989 and 1991. Since then, there has been a growing recognition of the contributions *getihu* make to China's economy and revenue collection. A *getihu* is allowed to employ up to seven people. Enterprises with eight or more employees are *siying qiye* (private enterprises). Owners of either type of enterprise were initially required to be from certain categories: a displaced farmer, a retiree, or an unemployed worker.

The relationship between private entrepreneurs and the local party-state is blurred. Localities have broadened the definition of those eligible to form *getihu* to include employees of state-owned enterprises. Because registration is difficult, private entrepreneurs often register with a TVE and pay the TVE a fee to use its name, called *gua kao* (hang-on enterprise). Private entrepreneurs also establish a collective as a facade, *dai hong maozi* (wearing the red hat) with the assistance of the local government.[42] Local governments subcontract the use rights of public assets to private individual entrepreneurs, receiving in return a share of the profits.

Because entrepreneurs are so dependent on local government, they

---

40. Zhang Gang, "Government Intervention vs Marketization in China's Rural Industries: The Role of Local Governments," *China Information* 8, no. $^1/_2$ (1993): 45–73.

41. Andrew G. Walder, "Corporate Organization and Local Government Property Rights in China," in *Changing Political Economies: Privatization in Post-communist and Reforming Communist States*, ed. Vedat Milor (Boulder, Colo.: Lynne Rienner Publishers, 1994), 53–66.

42. Susan McEwen, "New Kids on the Block," *The China Business Review* 21, no. 3 (May–June 1994): 35–39.

are susceptible to being squeezed through excessive taxation and demands for bribes. Their dependence on the local party-state undermines our ability to refer to them as autonomous. TVEs themselves are examples of marketization without privatization, thus preventing the emergence of an autonomous middle class in rural areas.

China's State-Owned Enterprises

In China, economic liberalization (meaning reduced state intervention in the economy) has several components: separating the state from state-owned enterprises; privatization of these enterprises by selling shares in them; reducing and eliminating their state subsidies, thus reducing the heavy burden on the central state's budget, which has led to a fiscal crisis of the state; and the state's role shifting from micromanaging these enterprises to macroeconomic management of the economy.

American studies of Chinese economic reform probe for signs of marketization unencumbered by state interventions. One study argues that contrary to the general view of the Chinese state-owned enterprise (SOE) as subsidized, loss-making enterprises with soft-budget constraints, Chinese enterprises are becoming increasingly responsive to market forces even without being privatized. This pattern allows China to gradually move out of the planned economy through marketization without privatization, an aberrant but still viable path to economic liberalization.[43] Marketization without privatization, however, will not provide the economic base for an autonomous middle class.

Two schools of thought have emerged on the future of China's SOEs: One school expects them to disappear gradually, displaced by the TVEs, arguing that nothing needs to be done because the SOEs will evolve in response to their external environment; another school expects the party-state to continually obstruct reform of them and argues that nothing can be done to circumvent bureaucratic vested interests in the SOEs. Both schools have been proven correct in that the external environment is changing toward marketization and the party-state is unwilling to relinquish its control of SOEs. China's situation resembles Japan's and South Korea's from the 1950s to the 1970s, with the difference that China does not have the strong and efficient state that these other East Asian countries had that could remain autonomous from special interests.[44]

---

43. Thomas G. Rawski, "Progress Without Privatization: The Reform of China's State Industries," in *Changing Political Economies*, 27–52.
44. Dwight H. Perkins, "Summary: Why Is Reforming State Owned Enterprises So Difficult?" *China Economic Review* 4, no. 2 (1993): 149–151.

The approach of Beijing to reforming SOEs has been protracted and limited since the introduction of the economic reforms in 1979. The reform began as technical reform to renovate facilities and introduce improved technology into existing enterprises. Beijing requested Japanese assistance in factory modernization in 1980 from MITI during the first Japan–China Ministerial Conference in Beijing. Japanese assistance had two channels: governmental through the Japan International Cooperation Agency (JICA) and private through the Japan–China Association on Economy and Trade. Of the 3,000 enterprises renovated in 1982, ninety were renovated with machinery and technology from Japan as model factories to serve as examples for other enterprises. JICA and other agencies began accepting hundreds of Chinese trainees in enterprise management. This effort by the Chinese was to improve technical efficiency as the means to improving SOE performance, putting aside the question of economic efficiency, although the Japanese did point out its necessity.[45]

The introduction of the urban industrial reform, announced in October 1984, gave enterprises the right of self-management and replaced the old system of enterprises turning over all profits with a new tax payment system. Government agencies would contract with enterprise managers, giving them autonomy to manage the enterprise and the right to retain a percentage of the surplus production to invest or distribute as bonuses. It was meant to boost productivity and introduce a profit incentive with the expectation that market mechanisms would emerge as a result and SOEs would respond to them.

In 1985, the proportion of industrial output governed by mandatory planning (direct government control) decreased to 20 percent of total production. The rest was under guidance planning (indirect government control). In practice, most state-owned enterprises produced simultaneously for the mandatory plan, the guidance plan, and the market, giving them opportunities to obtain inputs at subsidized prices from the planned economy and sell their outputs on the higher-priced market. This produced high profits, but SOEs still depended on government subsidies. In December 1986, an enterprise bankruptcy law was introduced to liquidate the worst enterprises and reduce the burden on the state budget, but it was never really implemented.

Until 1987 China officially had a mixed economy in which the market was subordinated to the planned economy. In that year Zhao Ziyang announced that the market was no longer subordinated but rather interacted with the state, "state guidance of the market and mar-

---

45. Sueo Kojima, "Japan-China Economic Interchange and Enterprise Reform," *China Newsletter* no. 40 (September–October 1982): 18–23.

ket guidance of enterprises."[46] The system of management by contract was introduced into all SOEs that year with the intent to replace direct control by government officials.

Nevertheless, despite a decade of reform efforts, government agencies continued to intervene in enterprise management, enterprises continued to receive subsidies in the soft budget constraint, and the number of SOEs in deficit rose with very few bankruptcies. The retrenchment policy of September 1988 strengthened the central government's control over economic liberalization and marketization, signaling a disillusionment with the ability of marketization alone to reform SOEs. The March 1989 industrial policy further legitimized government intervention to manage imbalances created by liberalization. The June 1989 Tiananmen Square massacre resulted in reformers such as Zhao Ziyang being put out of office and the momentum of reform slowed.

Deng Xiaoping's tour of South China in January 1992 appeared to reemphasize economic reform, but that did not include reduced state control. In October 1992 at the 14th Party Congress, the term "socialist market economy" was introduced. Although there is uncertainty as to its meaning, it appears to support stronger government intervention and reflects recognition that strong central government macroeconomic control is necessary to form a market economy and to promote adjustment of the industrial structure. The use of an industrial policy to guide marketization was modeled on Japan's MITI and its industrial policy. It was argued that strong government intervention was needed to push state-owned enterprises into the market. An influential Chinese economist, Lin Zili, developed theoretically the concept of socialist market economy. Lin advocated marketization but not privatization, arguing that the socialization of property rights in the stockholding system (*gufenzhi*) should be the goal only after marketization.[47]

Although the "Regulations on Overhauling the Operational Mechanism of State-owned Industrial Enterprises" was adopted in 1991, it took until 1994 to complete supplementary documents to the regulations. By that year, state-owned enterprises were responsible for one trillion yuan of bad debt with 60 percent of them operating at a loss. The problem of triangular debt, in which intercorporate nonpayment of debt has a chain effect on an expanding number of enterprises, has become critical in China.

---

46. Morio Matsumoto, "China's Industrial Policy and Participation in the GATT," *China Newsletter* no. 112 (September–October 1994): 2–5.

47. Lin Zili, *China: Going Toward the Market*. Translated in Joseph Fewsmith, ed., *Chinese Economic Studies* 27, no. 1–2 (January–February/March–April 1994): 17–19.

China's vice premier, Zhu Rongji, recently stated that foreign analysis focuses on the SOEs' defects and ignores their strengths. His claim that the SOEs' real problem is bad management, not state ownership, indicates a continued reluctance to privatize and to reduce the party-state's control of them. Officials claimed the government's top priority in 1995 was to introduce a "modern management system" into these enterprises, once again promising to give managers more autonomy, but in fact not really breaking up the nexus of managers, cadres from the party-state, and local bankers willing to continue bank loans. Other means of saving the SOEs continue to be selling shares, obtaining foreign investment, and merging them into enterprise groups. Although state subsidies for the SOEs account for 60 percent of China's budget deficit and fuel a high inflation rate, bankruptcies and shutdowns are threatened but not expected.[48] Beijing's current emphasis on reforming the management system as a solution to failing SOEs is not that different from strategies pursued in 1980.

The World Bank had recommended that Beijing transform the SOEs into joint stock companies to privatize. From 1984 to 1989, thousands of enterprises introduced the joint stock system and issued nearly four billion yuan of shares, much of this generated by conversion of existing state-owned assets rather than the raising of new capital. Most of the stock was issued in non-public offerings to employees or related companies. The intent was to create new revenue sources to alleviate the large burden of state subsidies to the SOEs. The Shanghai and Shenzhen stock exchanges were opened in 1991 to issue shares to the general public. It is possible to conceive of an autonomous middle class emerging out of corporate shareholders, but to date the party-state remains the largest shareholder in the SOEs.

World Bank reports advocate reform of the SOEs as a major priority for East Asian economies, both socialist economies in transition and capitalist economies with large public sectors, in order for them to sustain their rapid economic development. The World Bank definition of enterprise reform entails privatization, market competition, and corporate financing on the basis of commercial criteria rather than government subsidies. For these World Bank analysts, Chinese enterprise groups that merged state enterprises with a financial enterprise met the criteria of reform on two counts, marketization and commercialization of credit, even though they omitted privatization.[49]

---

48. "Asia's Ailing State Enterprises: China," *Far Eastern Economic Review*, 23 February 1995, 48–54.

49. *Sustaining Rapid Development in East Asia and the Pacific* (Washington, D.C.: The World Bank, 1993), 32.

Locating China's Civil Society

The political economy of China's industrial structure does not give much hope for the emergence of a civil society and an autonomous middle class. Nevertheless, there is much that goes on in China that is outside the control of the state, unrelated to China's urban and rural industry, and it is that activity that attracts research intent on uncovering civil society. The core of that activity is the enormous number of non-governmental organizations (*minjian*) forming outside the central state's control. Most analyses that locate a civil society do so in the more than 1,000 national associations and 100,000 local associations in China. These NGOs (to the extent they actually are NGOs and not GONGOs, government-organized non-governmental organizations) may represent the basis for an emergent civil society in the future but at present give China the characteristic of being a "sheet of loose sand" rather than a strong society autonomous from the state. Margaret Pearson addresses the nature of NGOs by examining Chinese business associations and asking to what extent did they represent societal forces and to what extent have they been incorporated into the party-state through clientelist patronage networks. The study finds that the business associations are Janus-faced in the position they retain between state and society, a pattern Pearson calls "socialist corporatism." The state continued to control and penetrate these associations, but they retained autonomy within the narrow realm of their expertise.[50]

Because the CCP is controlling the establishment of village elections, skeptics would expect them to be a mechanism for socialist corporatism rather than the means for an autonomous political and economic life. Nevertheless, the village elections might provide sufficient public space to allow civil society to emerge at the local level sometime in the future despite the pervasive presence of the CCP.

Conclusion

China's marketization without privatization is not an aberration in the transition to a market economy, but rather the result of the party-state's policies to retain state control over the economy combined with the activities of the lower-level cadre-merchants over whom it may have little control. For the Chinese leadership, the Russian case of a

---

50. Margaret M. Pearson, "The Janus Face of Business Associations in China: Socialist Corporatism in Foreign Enterprises," *The Australian Journal of Chinese Affairs* no. 31 (January 1994): 25–46.

weak state losing control over privatization remains the negative example of the socialist transition to a market economy, while the East Asian
model justifies the retention of strong state intervention in the economy. China's marketization has not produced a nomenklatura capitalism as in the Russian case because the state-owned enterprises have
not privatized as rapidly as in Russia. The state is still the largest shareholder even in those enterprises that have issued shares. Although
many cadres have appropriated use rights of public property, they
have not appropriated state-owned property itself to the same extent
as in Russia.

The "new institutionalism" provides theoretical justification for
state control, omitting the need for societal forces, an autonomous middle class, or a civil society to drive economic development. This approach treats the middle class that has emerged in Asian industrialized
and industrializing countries as the result of, rather than the driving
force behind, industrialization. It does not adequately explain the processes by which this autonomous class formed, emerged, and ultimately became the deciding factor in the democratization of several
East Asian countries.

Comparing Chinese, South Korean, and Taiwanese political change,
two differences are most relevant:

1. Both South Korea and Taiwan have a middle class that ultimately
    sustained the transition to democracy, in alliance with student
    dissidents and striking workers. China has produced student dis-
    sidents and striking workers, but has an economic and industrial
    structure that impedes the formation of an autonomous middle
    class.
2. When South Korea experienced tremendous pressure from the
    United States to liberalize its economy and democratize its polity
    during the 1980s, it responded because of its continuing need as
    a client state for the U.S. security alliance. U.S. pressure on Taiwan
    has a history of more than half a century. U.S. pressure on Japan,
    gaiatsu, has produced mixed results in Japan's economic liberal-
    ization. U.S. pressure on China has produced some results in
    moving toward greater economic liberalization because of Chi-
    na's need for American markets and plans to join the WTO. Exter-
    nal pressure by the United States for increased democratization
    in China, however, has not produced results to the same extent
    because there is no domestic societal base to support the external
    pressure and no autonomous middle class within which external
    pressure would resonate other than a narrow strata of urban
    intellectuals.

I would argue that civil society requires both a domestic societal base and an international environment that pressures the authoritarian developmental state to conform to international standards. The strong state arguments that attempt to account for economic development and liberalization with a focus entirely within the state inflate the capacity of the state and miss the contributions of society and the international system to political and economic outcomes. Explanations of democratization need to look more closely at the interactions of state, society, and international system.

Despite its inadequacies, the strong state argument will probably remain attractive in East Asia because it represents an indigenous alternative to the Western model and is more representative of Asian values. Chinese prefer to identify with the East Asian model rather than the Western model, and autonomous social forces are not easily identified or located.

Although East Asian industrial structure would appear to be a form of market liberalization, *keiretsu* and *jaebol* industrial structures inhibit rather than promote the emergence of a civil society. On the contrary, they promote close ties between political and economic elites in industry and government, a corporatism that dominates ordinary citizens and suppresses civil society. Nevertheless, in Taiwan, South Korea, and Japan, a middle class did eventually emerge to support democratization despite the *keiretsu* and *jaebol*. In a similar pattern, the Chinese shift from a Leninist party-state to a strong East Asian state would delay but not prevent political reform.

Part III

JUDICIAL SYSTEM, CIVIL SOCIETY, AND POLITICAL CULTURE

5

Mexico: Economic Liberalism in an Authoritarian Polity

Lorenzo Meyer

[Democracy] is a great word, whose history, I suppose, remains unwritten, because that history has yet to be enacted.

—Walt Whitman

This chapter inquires into the nature of the relationship among economics, politics, and law in Mexico. More specifically, it focuses on the impact of the substantial and rapid transformation of an economic system on the legal and power structures of an authoritarian regime that tried to resist and delay change without resorting to open and systematic violence.

Mexico's traumatic experience from 1982 to 1997 included repeated economic crises, rapid privatization and internationalization of the economy, a deterioration of the living standards of the working and middle classes, an erosion of the legitimacy of the political system, a free trade agreement with the United States and Canada, a protracted political transition, signs of ungovernability, violent internal struggle among the state party elite, a small but persistent guerrilla movement, a new economic crisis (1994–96), and a modest recuperation. These experiences permit the investigation of the impact of rapid economic liberalization on the political and legal institutions and practices of an old authoritarian political system. More precisely, how and to what extent is a state party system that embraces market economics subjected to pressures to open up its political life and reshape its legal framework?

The impulse to change rapidly in one arena, the economy, and to move very slowly in others, the polity and legal practices, has had consequences not anticipated by the authoritarian Mexican elite that was forced to start a process of economic transformation in 1985. By that time, Mexico's economic model based on a protected, but weak, internal market was in a profound structural crisis. The Mexican experience was a kind of *perestroika* without *glasnost* aimed at avoiding the fate of the former Soviet Union: the evaporation of power from the hands of the *nomenklatura* and the simultaneous breakdown of the regime and the state.[1] "Democracy, but within reason" appeared to be the motto of a technocratic elite interested in introducing market economics as a way of renovating its legitimacy and avoiding the danger of losing power by adopting an open and competitive political system.[2] However, by the second half of the 1990s this process of relying on economic manipulation to postpone regime transformation began to unravel. When the economic reforms did not deliver expected results for the many, signs of ungovernability increased. Pressures also mounted to accelerate the transition from authoritarianism to some kind of democracy. The worsening of the contradiction between change and resistance became the essence of Mexican politics immediately after Ernesto Zedillo's inauguration in December 1994 as the thirteenth consecutive president belonging to the same political party.

Mexico and Its Dilemmas

Mexican authoritarianism is the immediate product of a violent political and social revolution at the beginning of the century (1910–20). In a couple of decades this system became centered on a very strong executive power presiding over a corporatist state party that governed for sixty-eight years. This party, created in March 1929 as the Partido Nacional Revolucionario (National Revolutionary Party), was reorganized in 1938 as the corporatist Partido de la Revolución Mexicana (Party of the Mexican Revolution) and reformed again in 1946 when it became more conservative and was renamed the Partido Revolucionario Institucional (Institutional Revolutionary Party), or PRI.

---

1. Lorenzo Meyer, "Aquí, Perestroika sin Glasnost," *Excelsior*, 13 December 1989.

2. A good study of the original idea to use technocratic Mexican elite's authoritarianism to implement an economic revolution and to subsequently begin a slower and controlled political liberalization is in Miguel Angel Centeno, *Democracy within Reason: Technocratic Revolution in Mexico* (University Park: Pennsylvania State University Press, 1994).

The Mexican state party came into being long after the revolution that started in 1910 had defeated the forces of the *ancien regime*. At the time there was no real alternative to the revolution, opposition from right and left was extremely weak, and the only real political struggle took place within the ruling revolutionary group. From time to time this internal struggle of the elite ended in a split with an insurgent faction claiming to be the real bearer of revolutionary ideals. Until very recently, all the revolts within the "revolutionary family" ended in failure, but the last one, started in 1987, crystallized in a new center-left opposition party (PRD) that together with the old center-right PAN are now central to the process of political transition.

The state party's original objective was not to be just another political actor competing within a democratic framework. A victory won on the battlefield was not going to be exposed to the uncertainties of the ballot box. Therefore, the new governing party was not an electoral organization but something very different: a bureaucratic machine designed to help the revolutionary elite reintroduce centralization and discipline among the ranks in order to avoid divisions and violence in the internal struggle for power.[3]

However, during the last quarter of a century, the legitimacy of Mexico's authoritarian political arrangements based on a very strong presidency, a state party, and non-competitive elections increasingly came under attack from within and outside Mexico. This assault became especially pronounced after the arrival of the "third wave of democracy" to Latin American shores and the subsequent fall of almost all the authoritarian regimes in the region.[4]

The Achilles Heel

From the very beginning, the new regime had to live with a dangerous, intrinsic contradiction: the real rules of the political game were systematically contradicted by its formal, legal rules. The revolutionary constitution of 1917, still in force despite roughly 400 amendments, was a mixture of liberal and collectivist principles, but enshrined basic liberal, democratic political principles. The new Mexico envisioned by the constitution makers would have a strong presidency able to implement

---

3. The best study of the origins of the state party is Luis Javier Garrido, *El partido de la revolución institucionalizada: medio siglo de poder en México. La formación del nuevo estado, (1928–1945)* (México: Siglo XXI, 1982).

4. The nature of worldwide trends toward democratization is best developed in Samuel P. Huntington, *The Third Wave: Democratization in the Late Twentieth Century* (Norman: University of Oklahoma Press, 1991).

revolutionary reforms, but free and competitive elections would be the source of its political legitimacy. The new constitution also retained the classical liberal idea of the division of power among the executive, legislative, and judicial branches and among federal, state, and local governments. Individual freedom of association, a free press, and due process of law were also enshrined. It was only in religious matters, as a consequence of the conflict between the Catholic church and the revolutionary regime, that the constitution departed from democratic liberalism and denied any political rights to churches and clergymen.

An *Estado de Derecho*, or a state of law, postulates that nobody should be above the law. Modern political life requires a constitution and a real separation of powers to prevent disequilibria and permit the creation of an independent judiciary.[5] In postrevolutionary Mexico, the presidency overwhelmed the legislative and judicial branches of government. It also overpowered local and state government. In these conditions a real state of law was, and still is, impossible, because the presidency made frequent use of metaconstitutional and even anticonstitutional powers.[6] Only the construction of a real separation of powers can create the rule of law, the most formidable obstacle still confronting the democratization of the country.

Historically, Mexico's legal regime has been problematic. Spanish legal institutions never fit well in an Indian, non-Western society. If legality had serious difficulties during colonial times, the problem increased after independence in 1821. A radical liberal elite imposed its theoretical conceptions on a corporatist society with few elements to transform former subjects of the king of Spain into citizens.[7] The gap between those two worlds increased because the nature of Mexican society (corporatism and wide cleavages between social classes) was antagonistic to liberal and democratic institutions. After the enactment of the new regime's constitution in 1917, the contradiction between the legal framework and the real rules of the political and judicial game increased and became a key characteristic of Mexico's civic life in the twentieth century.

A real state of law became impossible after the consolidation of a

---

5. Guillermo Cabanellas, *Diccionario enciclopédico de derecho usual* (Buenos Aires: Editorial Helestia, 1986).

6. In regard to supra- and anticonstitutional powers of the Mexican presidency, see Jorge Carpizo, *El presidencialismo mexicano* (México: Siglo Veintiuno, 1978).

7. The lack and impossibility of a widespread sense of citizenship in nineteenth-century Mexico has been explored by Francis-Xavier Guerra in *Mexico: del antiguo régimen a la revolución* T.I. (México: Fondo de Cultura Económica, 1988), 182ff.

strong presidency at the end of the nineteenth century. The Mexican Revolution did not alter this situation; instead it helped to concentrate power in the hands of the executive. After 1935, the president became the undisputed leader of the state party, and it was through that party that he controlled Congress, state governors, and municipal governments. Without an independent Congress, the judicial branch of the government became helpless and finally marginal.

A subservient legislature and judiciary produced an unaccountable presidency. Unaccountability has, as a necessary outcome, endemic corruption of high and low public officials and of public life in general. If, in spite of this, the new regime was regarded as legitimate by key political actors, this was due not to its democratic and law-abiding nature but to its social reforms and its creation of economic development from the 1940s to the beginning of the 1980s. This economic development improved the material conditions of important sectors of Mexican society.

New Medicine for Old Symptoms

Since the end of the 1960s, changes in the social, demographic, economic, and cultural arenas have eroded the regime's political legitimacy. In the last twenty years, Mexico has also experienced a chain of economic crises. As a reaction to them and since the mid-1980s, the powerful presidency forced the country to change from a non-competitive, protected, nationalistic, and state-directed economy to a relatively open market economy where privatization of state enterprises has been systematic and foreign investment enjoys equal legal footing with national private capital. Moreover, on the first day of 1994 Mexico became the third member of the North American Free Trade Agreement (NAFTA) along with the United States and Canada. At about the same time it was accepted into the Organization of Economic Cooperation and Development (OECD). Unfortunately, all these changes, with their high social toll, have not restored Mexico's economic health. On the contrary, the addiction of Mexico's open economy of the 1990s to foreign speculative capital brought another spectacular economic crisis.[8]

For about half a century, the essence of Mexican economic strategy was centered around economic nationalism and a protected internal

8. Alternative views of contemporary Mexico's economy are presented by Macario Schettino, *Para reconstruir México* (México: Océano, 1996), and Nora Lustig, *Mexico: The Remaking of an Economy* (Washington, D.C.: Brookings Institution, 1992).

market. The strategy after World War II was to use the local market as the platform to create a strong native industrial class and to build an industrial complex able to survive U.S. dominance and competition. Such industrialization required, among other things, high tariff barriers and an active and interventionist state that could provide not only infrastructure but direct support to producers.[9]

Industrialization through government support was a relative success in terms of growth, producing average increases in GNP of 6 percent per year from 1940 to 1970, but it could not achieve international competitiveness. Trade deficits became unsustainable, and by the second half of the 1970s economic development based on a relatively small internal market was no longer viable. After an intense debate and struggle within the corridors of power, a young group of market-oriented economists lead by Carlos Salinas, a member of Mexico's power elite and a Harvard-trained social scientist, captured the all-powerful and authoritarian presidency and began a rapid implementation of a new economic policy.[10]

Under the impact of market economics, the old dogma of Mexican revolutionary nationalism evaporated. What happened, then, to the political regime? Did it also transform itself and go from limited pluralism to liberal democracy and a state of law, or did the key political variables remain more or less impervious to macroeconomic changes? The answer is neither. The technocratic elite tried to use the old authoritarian tools at their disposal to overcome obstacles to economic liberalization. At first they succeeded beyond anyone's expectations, but by 1994, the situation began to unravel and demands mounted to re-examine the economic formula and speed up political reform. By the midterm elections in 1997 the main issue on Mexico's agenda was regime transformation. The struggle between the old state party and the opposition was especially bitter because for the first time in more than eighty years the presidency had lost Congress.

The Strong Historical Roots of Mexican Authoritarianism

The authoritarian nature of Mexico's political system and civic culture are deeply rooted in its history, specifically in three centuries of colo-

---

9. A general picture of Mexico's economic strategies and achievements in the period of economic protectionism is presented by Clark W. Reynolds, *The Mexican Economy: Twentieth-Century Structure and Growth* (New Haven: Yale University Press, 1970).

10. For an analysis of the structural nature of the economic crisis of the 1980s, see the collection of essays in Carlos Bazdresch et al., *México: Auge, crisis y ajuste*, 2 vols. (México: Fondo de Cultura Económica, 1992).

nial domination and the failure of political liberalism in the nineteenth century. In the sixteenth century, the newly created Spanish national state found in present-day Mexico one of the largest and most sophisticated demographic concentrations in the Americas, between ten and twenty-five million strong, with urban concentrations larger than those of Europe.[11]

Mesoamerican civilization based on the cultivation of corn was entirely original; all its achievements and weakness were the product of internal developments without any external influences. The very idea of an external world was completely alien. The unexpected and violent presence of Europeans in the sixteenth century was a cosmic catastrophe from which Indian civilization was unable to recover.[12] Spanish conquest signified the sudden destruction of a whole worldview, a total military, political, cultural, and religious defeat from which native Mexicans never fully recovered.[13]

By the end of the sixteenth century the domination of what is today central Mexico was over. The effective occupation of the land by Spaniards and the subordination of the natives was an irreversible fact. For three hundred years of colonial domination, the Europeans, never more than a few hundred thousand strong, totally and completely dominated the native societies of central and southern Mexico, which were divided in small communities with different languages and traditions, and implanted in them a Christianity that, together with the Spanish language and legal framework, became the foundations of a future sense of nationhood. Religion, language, and law were not the only elements brought by the European minority to native Mexicans; they also carried a sense of the natural intellectual and moral superiority of Spaniards and creoles.

Racial discrimination was an integral part of the colonial system. After a bitter legal and theological fight in Madrid, the thesis of the humanity of the Indians was accepted but at a price: the new subjects of the king received nonage status in perpetual need of protection and supervision by royal authorities and the church.[14] The Kingdom of New Spain was divided by the Spanish crown into two republics occupying the same space: the Republic of the Indians and the Republic of

11. Sherburne F. Cook, and Woodrow Borah, *Essays in Population Study*, 2 vols. (Berkeley: University of California Press, 1973).

12. Enrique Florescano, *Memoria mexicana*, 2nd ed. (México: Fondo de Cultura Económica, 1994), 321–90.

13. Guillermo Bonfil, *México profundo: Una civilización negada* (México: Secretaría de Educación Pública, 1987).

14. David Brading, *Orbe indiano: De la monarquía católica a la república criolla* (México: Fondo de Cultura Económica, 1991), 90–108.

the Europeans. Their inhabitants lived in the same territory and both communities were subjects of the king, but each was governed by a different set of laws.[15] For three centuries, complete domination of the natives by a very small minority of Europeans or European descendants was the core of the political and legal development of Mexico. Colonial domination formally came to an end in 1821, but some elements of the original social cleavage are still alive.

A Legality More Formal Than Real

In the original nation-states of Europe and in the United States, the legal frameworks that evolved into constitutions were the result of a long evolution from the times of Roman domination to the end of Middle Ages in which rules were the crystallization of centuries-old practices. Mexico's situation was totally different.

Legal institutions in New Spain were not the result of internal evolution but an external imposition. Spanish legal ideas and practices confronted a completely alien social environment. The Council of the Indies in Spain had to draft laws for a reality thousands of miles away that had very little in common with the Roman legal tradition prevailing in the Iberian Peninsula. The result was a complex set of legal rules that tried to accommodate local reality with the principles and interests of the Spanish crown, but never fully succeeded. This gap between legality and reality became permanent.

Part of New Spain's legal and political reality is captured by the dictum of local authorities trying to be obedient officials while working with laws enacted far away in the metropolis: *"se obedece, pero no se cumple"* ("the order is accepted but not implemented"). The inconsistency between legality and reality became systematic not only because of a deep contradiction between the traditions and interests of conqueror and conquered, but also because of conflicts of interest between the crown and church and the few but powerful private individuals, the *conquistadores* and their descendants. The king and the church were interested in the preservation of Indian communities, but private individuals objected to obstacles preventing the rapid exploitation of nature and natives.[16]

---

15. José Miranda, *Las ideas y las instituciones políticas mexicanas* (México: National University of Mexico, 1978).

16. A classic study of Spanish institutions in the New Spain is José Miranda's *Las ideas y las instituciones políticas mexicanas* (México: Universidad Nacional Autónoma de México, 1978). See also Mark A. Burkholder and D. S. Chandler, *From Impotence to Authority: The Spanish Crown and the American Audiencias, 1687–1808* (New York: Columbia University Press, 1977).

The violent imposition of the interests of one civilization upon the other produced a profound incompatibility between the legal and moral frameworks and the actual behavior of Indian communities, authorities, and the colonial power elite. The gap separating what is from what ought to be continued after Mexico became independent in 1821. Liberal constitutionalism never became real, for a society of corporations and Indian communities was unfit for individualism, and this chapter of Mexican history became just another example of a disencounter between principles and practice.

Nationhood in an Unintegrated Society

By the eighteenth century the contradictions between creoles (native-born whites) and peninsular Spaniards were evident—peninsulars got the best offices in government and church and controlled trade—but these differences did not evolve into open confrontation. It was the invasion of Spain by Napoleon, the imprisonment of the king, and the discussion of sovereignty in the Spanish empire in America that precipitated a rupture at the top of the power structure. In 1808 a preemptive coup in Mexico City led by a wealthy peninsular Spaniard, Gabriel Yermo, against possible creole domination of local government, accelerated the power struggle between Spaniards and locals. In 1810, a handful of creoles, a priest, and military officers plotted against the Spaniards in central Mexico, and their actions led to something unexpected: a race war, a general and bloody revolt of the lower classes, Indians, and mestizos against Spanish domination.[17] However, by 1815, Spaniards and native loyalists had managed to reimpose, through blood and fire, the authority of the crown. If independence finally took place in 1821, it was not as a result of an insurgent victory but of a conservative reaction by the upper classes against a liberal government in Spain.

External events, the French Revolution and the Napoleonic wars in Europe, created a power vacuum in the Spanish colonial empire, triggering a chain of events that concluded in the independence of Mexico and Latin America in the 1820s. Unfortunately, the economic, social, and cultural cleavages among creoles, Indians, and mestizos made nation-building in nineteenth-century Mexico long and painful. Given

---

17. Hugh M. Hamill, *The Hidalgo Revolt: Prelude to Mexican Independence* (Gainesville: University of Florida Press, 1966), 117–216; John Tutino, *De la insurrección a la rebelión: Las bases sociales de la violencia agraria, 1750–1940* (México: Ediciones Era, 1990), 45–184.

these cleavages, and the country's institutional fragility, a state of law continued not to exist.

An Improbable Nation

For the first fifty years after independence, the main political conflict in the new nation was between a liberal and republican elite and the conservative and monarchical elements of the upper classes and the church. The Indian and mestizo majority were more objects than subjects of this chaotic and bloody process that negatively affected almost all regions and social groups.

One of the few political changes accepted or at least tolerated by all sides as a result of independence was an end to the legal distinctions between Indian and non-Indians: to finish the colonial political and judicial distinction between the "Republic of the Indians" and the "Republic of the Europeans." It was the necessary first step to create a sense of nationhood and a single political entity. However, cultural, social, economic, and political discrimination and abuse against the Indians not only persisted but deepened.

The lack of social and political cohesiveness transformed the new Mexican nation into a mosaic of unlinked local societies. Centrifugal forces were dominant. As demonstrated by the war against the United States in 1847, only a minimum of political solidarity and sense of national interest existed among classes, parties, and regions to confront a foreign enemy.[18]

The political dream of the Mexican liberal elite was to shape out of colonial Mexico a new nation of individuals, of free citizens and successful capitalists just like the United States. That is why they enthusiastically adopted a revolutionary political framework: a democratic, presidential, and federal political system systematized in the 1857 constitution. However, the project was a virtual sociological impossibility in a nation of corporations, church, army, craftsman guilds, trade monopolies, universities, and Indian communities looking for survival in a market economy and without an individualistic tradition. Moreover, legal traditions and practices did not support individual rights, further preventing the realization of the liberals' dream.

In the 1860s, a bloody civil war between liberals and conservatives produced a brief empire headed by Maximilian of Austria and sup-

---

18. Ramón Eduardo Ruiz, "La guerra de 1847 y el fracaso de los criollos," in *De la rebelión de Texas a la guerra del 47*, ed. Josefina Zoraida Vázquez (México: Nueva Imagen, 1994), 79–103.

ported by a French expeditionary force. However, local resistance by liberals under the leadership of Benito Juárez, along with U.S. government pressure, put a dramatic end to the conservative project. After a while, the liberal hegemony produced much needed order and social discipline but not a modern democratic polity.[19]

The original liberal dream soon became a nightmare for the Indians when their communal lands and communal savings, the material bases of their very way of life and civilization, were forcefully placed on the market along with church property. By the end of the century, what was supposed to be a community of individual entrepreneurs and free citizens had become a landholding oligarchic society embarked on a modernization process resisted or resented by a large segment of the population.[20] For a very large portion of the country's inhabitants, law, used to defend and extend private property, was not a source of protection but an instrument of oppression. This inevitably promoted views of law that further complicated the creation of a state of law.

The Way to the Stability: A Liberal Dictatorship

The liberal utopia inscribed in the 1857 constitution and the liberal resistance to the imperial interlude of Maximilian, the French, and the conservatives concluded in a personal dictatorship. For more than three decades (1877–1911), General Porfirio Díaz shaped the collective life of Mexicans. Díaz's government was economically liberal and successful, but was not politically liberal or democratic.

The economic system presided over by Díaz was centered around a massive influx of American, British, and French capital and technology, while the political system revolved around an all-powerful president. Díaz, a hero in the war against the conservatives and the French, co-opted his former enemies, diminished the political influence of the army, overcame the resistance of local political bosses, reduced Congress to silence, and kept the press under tight control. It was the personal nature of power in Díaz's Mexico that explains the very poor political institutionalization characterizing the period. Díaz always ob-

---

19. Alfred Jackson Hanna and Kathryn Abbey Hanna, *Napoleon III and Mexico* (Chapel Hill: University of North Carolina Press, 1971); and Ralph Roeder, *Juárez and His Mexico*, 2 vols. (New York: Viking Press, 1947).

20. The utopia and reality of Mexican liberals in the nineteenth century are analyzed with great depth by Charles Hale in two books: *Mexican Liberalism in the Age of Mora, 1821–1853* (New Haven: Yale University Press, 1968), and *The Transformation of Liberalism in Nineteenth-Century Mexico* (Princeton, N.J.: Princeton University Press, 1989).

served the democratic forms of the liberal constitution but never its substance. He held non-competitive elections. After 1888, with the help of a relatively small army and police and of a subservient landed oligarchy, he destroyed the beginning of a constitutional division of powers, ended any possibility of state and local autonomy, and effectively inhibited the formation of an opposition party.

While Díaz controlled daily political developments, the system functioned well for foreign investors and the landed Mexican gentry, but when old age created a succession problem and the elite could not work out an effective internal agreement, dissidents mobilized popular opposition and the whole system collapsed by the beginning of 1911. It was the beginning of the Mexican Revolution.[21]

Porfirian modernization and liberalism negatively affected the communal land systems of Indian communities and concentrated land and wealth as never before. The legal system was heavily loaded in favor of the landed classes and foreign investors. This only deepened suspicions about the legal and judicial apparatus, creating additional barriers to a state of law. After three decades, the oligarchic agreement created by Díaz created two uprisings: one, in the north, demanding political change and the opening up of the system; another, in the south, demanding the return of communal lands. After a while both developments melted into one and Díaz was forced into exile. Political change through violence developed after a couple of years into a real revolution.

Economic Modernization without Political Change and Revolution

The terrible civil war that devastated Mexico between 1910 and 1920, the Mexican Revolution, was more an antioligarchic movement and a reaction to the negative effects of economic liberalism in an agrarian society than a cry for something unknown: political democracy. Nevertheless the original banner of the revolution was centered on political democracy: *"sufragio efectivo y no reelección"* ("effective suffrage and no reelection"). In any case, peasant communities, labor unions, the emerging middle class, a set of popular armies, the church, and local political bosses were some of the main actors in the revolutionary drama. In the 1920s and 1930s, representatives of organized peasants,

---

21. James D. Cockcroft, *Intellectual Precursors of the Mexican Revolution, 1900–1913* (Austin: University of Texas Press, 1968); and Alan Knight, *The Mexican Revolution,* vol. I, (Cambridge: Cambridge University Press, 1986), 1–170.

workers, and middle classes were incorporated into the new regime, an uncommon situation in Latin America.

In contrast with the Russian Revolution, the Mexican Revolution had no clear-cut ideology. However, the Constitution of 1917 can be taken as the best summary of the Mexican revolutionary utopia. The new constitution preserved some of the liberal elements of the old one, but it also had a very strong nationalistic and anti-liberal component. Private property was subordinated to the interest of the collectivity, foreigners could not have agrarian property, rural communal lands had precedence over individual landholdings, labor rights were as important as or even more important than those of capitalists, state intervention in the economy was presented as indispensable to secure the common good and the national interest, oil deposits belonged to the nation, and church participation in the school system and in the political arena was restricted.[22]

The revolution tried again to end the historical division between Indians and non-Indians. Agrarian reform and a cultural revolution through public education injected an element of social justice and pride into the Mexican masses. Populism and nationalism in the 1930s elevated the Indians, the workers, and the poor into depositories of the essence of nationhood.[23]

The New Regime

After the military and political victory in 1916 of the *Carrancistas*, the least radical revolutionary faction, Mexico became a classic case of limited pluralism or authoritarianism as defined by Juan Linz.[24]

The Constitution of 1917 provided for a strong presidency but within a democratic framework: division of powers, federalism, and a strong municipal government. However, the fact that the revolutionary armies had obliterated the old political order and that one revolutionary faction, the Carrancistas, had militarily defeated all others, made

22. Hanz Werner Tobler, *La revolución mexicana. Transformación social y cambio político 1876–1940* (México: Alianza Editorial, 1994), 347–71.

23. A general interpretation of the Mexican Revolution is provided by Héctor Aguilar Camín and Lorenzo Meyer, *In the Shadow of the Mexican Revolution: Contemporary Mexican History, 1910–1989* (Austin: University of Texas Press, 1993).

24. The concept of an authoritarian political system was developed by Juan Linz in his seminal work, "An Authoritarian Regime: Spain," in *Cleavages, Ideologies and Party Systems: Contributions to Comparative Political Sociology,* ed. Erik Allardt and Yrje Littunen (Transactions of the Westermarck Society, X 1964), 291–342.

competitive elections—the necessary base for a modern democratic political system—a formal exercise without real content. Victorious revolutionaries had no effective opposition at the ballot box or anywhere else and very little use for a competitive party system. In those conditions, division of power was not based on Montesquieu but only existed between regional political bosses and the president and central government. The rule of law had little chance of surviving when confronted by revolutionary generals, strong labor unions, or any person or group able to get the support of the new leadership.

Beginning in 1916, elections were more formal than real. National and local elections were an opportunity for revolutionary leaders and forces to dispute power while excluding all outsiders. Victory belonged not to those who got more votes but to those with more effective internal support from the army or mass organizations. Disagreements about results were not settled through legal institutions but through pressure or even violence. The regime's basic source of legitimacy was not party competition (before 1929 there were several hundred parties) and the ballot box but the capacity of the leadership to respond to the demands of key constituencies: the army, organized peasants and workers, and certain segments of the middle class.

Effective power in the new regime was first kept within the small circle of the revolutionary generals and the leaders of mass organizations. After 1946, dominance passed to civilians.[25] From 1920 to the present, presidential power has been transferred to a member of the cabinet of the outgoing president, by force at the beginning and more or less peacefully since the 1930s. The principle of no reelection for the presidency and governorships has been faithfully observed since 1928 and has been a very effective instrument for the periodic internal renovation of the elite, a source of stability in a system that prefers co-optation to repression.

While Mexico's constitutional framework makes it a federal republic, this legal regime does not operate because of the existence of a *de facto* state party system. As a consequence, Mexico is a centralist, authoritarian polity where the only limits to presidential powers are time, the six-year period with no reelection, and external factors: U.S. power and international economic forces.

Since the party's creation almost seventy years ago, the Mexican presidency has remained in the hands of its members, and until 1989 all state governments and almost all municipal governments were also under its control. After 1989, the president and his party were forced by opposition mobilizations to accept a handful of governorships con-

---

25. Camín and Meyer, *In the Shadow of the Mexican Revolution.*

trolled by the old center-right Acción Nacional Party (PAN), an unexpected partner in the transformation of the economic system along market lines and away from state control. For the same reasons, for more than half a century local and federal legislatures were overwhelmingly dominated by the president through his party, but in recent years the presence of sizable opposition minorities has introduced an element of change in federal and some state congresses.

A strong presidency, a system of non-competitive elections, a powerless Congress, and a federation that is, in fact, a highly centralized system have, as a natural outcome, a judiciary that has no independence vis-à-vis the presidency and state governors. For the same reasons, police, judges, and tribunals are very independent from society. In fact, public officials are accountable only to the holders of executive power and the president enjoys complete immunity. This situation of unaccountability is the root of endemic public corruption.[26]

The patrimonial tradition of government established in colonial times remains alive in present-day Mexico. A bureaucracy that is not supervised by Congress, a judiciary that is totally subservient to the presidency, and a police force that is badly paid and trained and preys on society, especially the poor and the powerless, have produced the opposite of a state of law.[27]

Political and bureaucratic corruption in Mexico is both the origin and result of entrenched authoritarianism. Pervasive corruption is a significant problem in Mexico's public life because it has a very negative effect on governmental performance and legitimacy. But this problem becomes even more serious and difficult to control when a powerful external agent intervenes, such as drug trafficking. By the mid-1990s there was strong evidence that drug money had reached the highest levels of Mexico's security apparatus, including the army, and some signs of ungovernability began to appear.[28]

From 1917 to the present, the transfer of power at the highest level in Mexico has taken place within the small circle of the president and his cabinet. In the few cases of competitive presidential elections (1929, 1940, 1946, 1952, and 1988), fraud impeded credibility. In 1994 open fraud was not detected, but the result was far from democratic because the campaign remained extremely unfair to the opposition. Therefore,

---

26. Héctor Fix Fierro, ed., *A la puerta de la ley: El Estado de derecho en México* (México: Cal y Arena, 1994).

27. Stephen D. Morris, *Corruption and Politics in Contemporary Mexico* (México: Cal y Arena, 1994).

28. Eduardo Valle, *El segundo disparo: La narcodemocracia mexicana* (México: Editorial Océano, 1995).

the Mexican political system remains the oldest authoritarian regime in the world.

Liberal economic policies began to be introduced in Mexico after 1985. This change produced great tensions and contradictions in the social system and were immediately experienced by the old authoritarian political structure based on traditional populist policies. In 1988 and 1994, official results of presidential elections gave the state party its lowest results ever: around 50 percent of the vote. In the second half of the 1990s, anti-authoritarian pressures mounted along with the sense of an approaching end of regime. Nevertheless, the old state party used all means to cling to the privileges of power.

Market Economics within an Authoritarian Framework

After World War II, Mexico, in common with the rest of Latin America, started a rapid process of industrialization based on import substitution. This economic system was relatively successful until the mid-1970s, when the weakness of the internal market and the structural inefficiencies of the manufacturing sector produced large external deficits that led to devaluation and inflation. For a while, oil exports seemed to be the answer, but sudden negative changes in the world price of oil precipitated a final collapse in 1982.[29] In the 1980s, an increasing foreign trade deficit and a mounting foreign debt (it reached the $100 billion mark) ended what for forty years had been a successful process of economic growth, if not development.

Without the material resources to answer the demands of its different and contradictory constituencies—industrialists and workers, middle class and squatters, peasants and agribusiness, students and pensioners—the Mexican government began to lose its legitimacy. Local elections in the northern state of Chihuahua produced an unexpected victory of the center-right opposition, and in 1986, the government had to resort to open fraud in that region to sustain the dominance of the state party.[30]

Around 1985, the structural economic crisis permitted a small group of young technocrats under the leadership of Carlos Salinas, then secretary of budget and planning and later president from 1988 to 1994, to displace traditional politicians from key decisionmaking positions.

---

29. For an analysis of the crisis of the old economic model see Jaime Ros, "La crisis económica: un análisis general," in *México ante la crisis*, comp. Pablo González Casanova and Héctor Aguilar Camín (México: Siglo XXI, 1985).

30. Alberto Aziz Nassif, "Chihuahua: historia de una alternativa," (México: *La Jornada-CIESAS* 1994).

They also began reforms designed to change the old economic model to a market-oriented economy.

The technocratic group lost no time in introducing drastic economic transformations. Initially, they opened up the economy to foreign trade and investment, especially from the United States. Before this economic revolution, the Mexican market was one of the most protected in the world: import licenses were required for almost every product, and import tariffs on certain goods were 100 percent. Ten years later, licenses had virtually disappeared and the average import tariff was only 9.5 percent.[31]

Shortly thereafter, the nationalistic Foreign Investment Law of 1973 was quietly dismantled, and foreign capital was welcomed in almost every sector of the economy. As a consequence, foreign direct and portfolio investment in Mexico surpassed the 90 billion dollar mark during the 1989–94 period.[32] An open market and the demise of economic nationalism were institutionalized in a grand manner with the ratification in 1993 of the North American Free Trade Agreement (NAFTA) by the United States, Canada, and Mexico.

Since the emergence of the active Mexican state at the end of the 1930s, direct government involvement in the economy provided the main impulse for growth. But, after 1985, governmental expenditure diminished, and a broad range of public enterprises, including banks, highways, a telephone company, and airlines, were privatized. In 1982 there were 1,155 state-owned enterprises, but ten years later there were only 223.[33] By the end of Salinas's presidential term in 1994, there were only three important economic activities under state control: Mexican Oil (Pemex), the Power Commission (CFE), and Mexican Railways (FF.NN.). However, railways were about to go, generation of electric power was no longer a state monopoly, and Pemex began to accept private capital, foreign and Mexican, in exploration and drilling and in its petrochemical production.

Rapid Change at a High Social Price

The dismantling of an economic system that had lasted from World War II to the mid-1980s had to overcome the resistance of very powerful vested interests that were, at the same time, the social bases of the

---

31. Robert A. Pastor, *Integration with Mexico: Options for U.S. Policy* (New York: The Twentieth Century Fund Press, 1993), 17–20.

32. *La Jornada*, 4 July 1994.

33. Organization for Economic Cooperation and Development, *OECD Economic Surveys, Mexico* (Paris: OECD, 1992), 89.

state party system, including labor unions, agrarian organizations, middle-class professional organizations, commercial and industrial organizations, and the bureaucracy entrenched in the public sector.

For roughly fifty years, the private Mexican industrial establishment had subsisted with strong governmental guidance, protection, and subsidies. In order to break down the resistance of key industrialists to change, the government permitted and supported the creation of monopolies in certain sectors, including television, telephones, banking, cement, and glass. The rationale for this policy was that only Mexican giants could withstand foreign competition or get a share of foreign markets. However, this policy also destroyed thousands of medium, small, and micro industries, the basic source of employment, that were unable to compete with imported products.

Labor unions, the very core of the state party corporative structure, were forced to accept a new and precarious situation: declining real wages and reduced job security. President Salinas had no problem using the army in early 1989 to arrest and jail the leadership of the powerful, and corrupt, oil union. This action warned all other labor bosses not to oppose a policy that allowed prices to fluctuate freely but set a ceiling on salary increases through a formal pact among government, entrepreneurs, and labor unions.

At the end of 1994, job creation was nil, but Mexicans entering the labor market for the first time numbered around 1.2 million. Even those who did not lose their jobs had reasons to complain: Real wages in the manufacturing sector were close to 1975 levels. In addition, the minimum wage had lost roughly 50 percent of its value during the same nineteen-year period. Of the 35 million in Mexico's labor force, 2.3 million were unemployed, and at least another 7 or 8 million were part of the underground economy; the numbers in both categories are growing.[34]

In spite of the hardship for the average worker, there were few strikes or movements advocating labor independence from government. With unemployment or underemployment on the rise and very few jobs available, union workers were very vulnerable. Employers emphasized productivity increases and not job creation. Unemployment and decreases in real salaries were two of the high prices Mexican society has paid for market economics. By the mid-1990s, the formal sector of the economy was not able to absorb more than one-third of the new workers entering the labor force every year.[35]

Poverty remains a central characteristic of Mexican society and is

34. *La Jornada*, 18 July 1995; *El Financiero*, 21 May 1995.
35. José Luis Calva, *El Financiero*, 18 November 1994.

increasing. According to official figures, 13.6 million Mexicans (about 12 percent) live in what is called "absolute poverty," and 40 percent of the total population is classified as poor.[36] The market economy and politics are working against a large sector of less fortunate Mexicans. In 1992, the poorest 40 percent got less than 13 percent of the total income available to Mexican families, while the top 20 percent got 56 percent.[37] For the poor, economic modernization and globalization have been an unmitigated disaster. Mexican demography demands 1.1 million new jobs a year, but net job creation in the formal sector in the 1990s has been less than half that number. In the 1990s the formal sector of the economy has only accommodated 50 percent of new entrants into the labor force. In a very real sense, if today's economic tendencies prevail, a sizable number of Mexico's poor, the unskilled and uneducated, will be permanently marginalized. The dual society, characteristic of modernization in underdeveloped countries, is now even more evident. This deepening chasm makes the construction of legal equality, a necessary condition for the state of law, even more difficult.

Support and Resistance

The frustrations of small industrialists and merchants unable to compete in the new global market economy of Mexico, of union workers whose real salaries had gone down, of peasants losing government subsidies and protection, of unemployed and underemployed professionals and of unskilled workers created a political environment where opposition began to gain ground and develop in new ways and places. At the beginning of the 1980s, the center-right Partido Acción Nacional, or PAN, began to mount a regional, but real, challenge to the authoritarian system, especially in the more developed north, where the middle class is stronger.[38]

Opposition also developed within the political elite. In 1987, a handful of PRI members who identified with nationalism and the left and felt marginalized by the young technocrats in charge of the central government openly demanded the beginning of a real internal democracy and a genuine debate about market economic policies and the selection of the next presidential candidate. President De la Madrid (1982–88) rejected and dismissed what he rightly saw as a challenge

36. *El Financiero,* 25 October 1994.
37. *El Financiero,* 24 May 1994.
38. Juan Molinar, *El tiempo de la legitimidad: Elecciones, autoritarismo y democracia en México* (México: Cal y Arena, 1991), 53–214.

not only to the traditional authority of the presidency but to the very essence of Mexican authoritarianism. After all, since 1935 the state party had been an organization that was unconditionally subservient to the president's will, regardless of his personal political orientation and ideology. In such circumstances, Cuauhtémoc Cárdenas, the son of a popular former president and himself a former governor of the state of Michoacán, along with Porfirio Muñoz Ledo, a former cabinet member and ex-president of the PRI, and a handful of other dissidents, left the PRI and began the difficult and painful process of shaping a center-left coalition to support Cárdenas as an opposition candidate in the 1988 presidential election. Small existing leftist organizations from the former Communist Party to the Mexican Workers Party also joined Cárdenas.[39]

The 1988 election shook the political system as no other schism in the state party. In contrast to earlier formal and bureaucratic elections, this time the election became a real contest among the government's candidate, Carlos Salinas; the PAN's candidate, Manuel Clouthier, a northern businessman and former member of the PRI; and the center-left coalition, Frente Democrático Nacional (National Democratic Front, or FDN), led by Cuauhtémoc Cárdenas. This political struggle pitted the all-powerful PRI machine, illegally but effectively supported with government resources, against two poorly equipped opposition forces headed by former priistas.

During the afternoon of election day on July 6, 1988, a somber secretary of the interior announced that unspecified "weather conditions" prevented the ultramodern computerized voting information center in Mexico City from providing preliminary results. After a tense waiting period of several days, the government finally declared Salinas the winner with 50.74 percent of the vote. Cárdenas was credited with 31.06 percent, the highest official figure ever for an opposition presidential candidate in the twentieth century, and Clouthier received 16.81 percent. It was the eleventh consecutive presidential victory of the PRI, but it was a victory without any credibility. Examples of fraud abounded and Cárdenas refused to accept defeat.[40] The PAN, however, after some vacillation, reached an informal but effective *modus vivendi* with Salinas based on common interests: the struggle against the leftist coalition, the introduction of market economics, and the privatization of state enterprises and *ejido* (communal) lands. After a tempestuous

---

39. Luis Javier Garrido, *La ruptura: La corriente democrática del PRI* (México: Grijalbo, 1993).

40. José Barberán et al., *Radiografía del fraude: Análisis de los datos oficiales del 6 de julio* (México: Nuestro Tiempo, 1988).

debate, Congress declared Salinas president and Cárdenas began the difficult process of trying to transform his political coalition into a mass-based opposition party.[41]

With the PAN as the loyal and cooperative opposition, Salinas, the PRI, and the whole state apparatus used legal and illegal means to try to reduce Cárdenas and his newly created *Partido de la Revolución Democrática*, Party of the Democratic Revolution (PRD), to a meaningless force. From the point of view of the government and its allies (the majority of the press and the TV monopoly), Cárdenas was the representative of a populist past, unwilling and unable to face the challenges of the future. During the six Salinas years, 290 members of the PRD were assassinated and many more were arrested.[42] In those years, the PRD was denied victories in several state and municipal elections, while the PAN was allowed, for the first time in its history, to win state governorships. The PRD managed to survive a frontal and brutal attack by the powerful Mexican presidency, but in the 1991 mid-term elections it lost three-quarters of its supporters and dropped to the third political force in Mexico, well behind the PRI and the PAN. In the 1994 presidential election, Cárdenas ran again but only received half of his total in 1988: 16 percent.[43]

Immediately after his inauguration, Carlos Salinas began to use all the force available to an all-powerful authoritarian presidency to create a new and strong coalition around himself. The natural allies of *salinismo* outside Mexico were the United States and other foreign governments, international financial institutions, and multinational corporations with interests in Mexico. Within Mexico, the banking and financial community, the powerful service monopolies, and the big exporting and importing interests strongly supported the young technocratic politicians. The press was occasionally critical but not the electronic media, the source of political information for 90 percent of the adult population. The conservative Catholic church, expelled from the political arena in the mid-nineteenth century, but attracted by favorable changes in the constitution and the establishment of formal relations with the Vatican, also supported Salinas. The PAN was by nature anti-

---

41. Pablo González Casanova, coordinator, *Segundo informe sobre la democracia: México el 6 de julio de 1988* (México: Siglo XXI-UNAM, 1990).

42. Isabel Molina, *Un sexenio de violencia política* (México: Congreso de la Unión, Grupo Parlamentario del PRD, 1993).

43. A critical but well-informed analysis of the PRD 1994 political campaign that shows the extreme internal and external difficulties of a party that confronts the hostility of Mexican authoritarianism is Adolfo Aguilar Zínser, *Vamos a ganar: La pugna de Cuauhtémoc Cárdenas por el poder* (México: Editorial Océano, 1995).

cardenista, as it had been born in 1939 out of a confrontation between the middle classes and the populist forces led by Lázaro Cárdenas, the father of Cuauhtémoc.

The informal alliance between Salinas and the PAN led the president to force the PRI to accept its first defeat at the state level in the twentieth century. In 1989, the central government accepted the PAN's victory in Baja California. In the next few years, the government also permitted the PAN to win the governorships of Guanajuato and Chihuahua. In exchange for regional power, the PAN not only supported Salinas's economic revolution but was also instrumental in isolating the PRD. The systematic and effective co-optation of the center-right opposition by the authoritarian presidency prevented a repetition in Mexico of the Spanish or Chilean path to democracy: a temporary common front of the opposition parties to bring about the end of the authoritarian regime.

To balance its conservative coalition and keep the traditional support of the poorer classes, Salinas created and personally supervised a National Program of Solidarity (PRONASOL). With an annual budget of two to three billion dollars, part of it the product of the privatization of state enterprises, PRONASOL supported thousands of local committees engaged in small projects. It introduced electricity, potable water, sewage systems, paved roads, small enterprises, schools, school lunches, and scholarships to poor rural communities and urban neighborhoods. Everything was done in the name of the president and with a logo very similar to the PRI's.[44] PRONASOL was an effective way to regain the old type of populist legitimacy by manipulating the needs of the rural and urban poor without interfering with the essential agenda of market economics.

Mid-term legislative elections in 1991 were a great success for Salinas and his policy of *perestroika* without *glasnost*. The PRI, bolstered by PRONASOL and the traditional support of government money and manpower, needed less fraud than in 1988 to garner 61.48 percent of the vote. In these elections the PAN received 17.73 percent and the PRD only 8.25 percent of the vote. The state party as well as the de facto center-right coalition headed by Salinas, PRI-PAN, were again in full command of the situation, or so it seemed at the time.[45]

After the electoral recuperation of the PRI, preparations for the 1994

44. Denise Dresser, *Neopopulist Solutions to Market Problems: Mexico's National Solidarity Program* (La Jolla, Calif.: Current Issue Brief Series, no. 3, Center for U.S.-Mexican Studies Center, University of California, 1991).

45. Alberto Aziz and Jacqueline Peschard, coordinators, *Las elecciones federales de 1991* (México: National University of Mexico and Porrúa, 1992).

presidential election began in an atmosphere of government and business confidence. In November 1993, President Salinas selected as his successor Luis Donaldo Colosio, an economist, secretary of social development (SEDESOL), former president of the PRI, and protégé of the president. Following tradition, the PRI's leadership immediately and without question accepted the president's decision. Through Colosio, Salinas sought to ensure the continuity of market policies and preserve the technocrats' control of the presidency and the whole authoritarian system. By then, many suspected that Salinas and his group wanted to control the presidency well beyond the year 2000.[46] This was a violation of a golden unwritten rule that allowed those members of the ruling party left on the margins for a presidential term to have a real chance to trade places with those who had enjoyed power for six years.

Economic Policies and Regime Crisis.

At the very moment when the complex process of power transference had begun, an unexpected resistance to Salinas and to authoritarian politics appeared. In the early hours of January 1, 1994, a group of perhaps two or three thousand Indians in Chiapas, supported by their communities and organized into the Zapatista Army of National Liberation (EZLN), captured several towns in the southern part of the state. Chiapas is located in one of the poorest regions of the country, where market economics, in particular the beginning of the privatization of communal lands, has had a very negative impact.[47] The insurgents objected to the regime's authoritarianism, racial discrimination, and systematic violation of the letter and the spirit of the law. They accused Salinas of electoral fraud and corruption and of pursuing economic and social policies that had extremely negative impacts on most Mexicans' standard of living, especially indigenous people. Almost from the beginning, the rebels stated that their goal was not to assume power but to help galvanize society into ending the state party system, create the rule of law, and open up Mexico to political democracy, authentic social justice, and moral development.[48]

---

46. Alejandro Ramos, coordinator, *Sucesión pactada: La ingeniería política del salinismo* (México: Plaza y Valdés, 1993).

47. To understand the roots of the Chiapas rebellion, it can be very useful to consult Thomas Benjamin, *A Rich Land, a Poor People: Politics and Society in Modern Chiapas* (Albuquerque: University of New Mexico Press, 1989). A well-documented book on the *zapatista* rebellion is Carlos Tello Díaz, *La rebelión de las cañadas* (México: Cal y Arena, 1995).

48. The insurgents in Chiapas have published a great many documents explaining their position and objectives the best collection is *La palabra de los arrmados de verdad y fuego*, 2 vols. (México: Editorial Fuenteovejuna, 1994–95).

After ten days of fighting between the army and the EZLN, accompanied by a growing public clamor for a truce, the government declared a cease-fire, and direct negotiations with the *zapatistas* started. In the post-communist world a military campaign against the poorest of the poor, the Indians of southern Chiapas, had no legitimacy. The first round of negotiations between the government and the rebels ended in failure, but after the 1994 presidential elections, with a new administration in power, the talks resumed in early 1995.

When the new round of negotiations started, using prominent civilians and legislators as mediators, the government enjoyed uncontested military superiority because sudden military movements at the beginning of the year had drastically reduced the *zapatistas'* territory. Nevertheless, the central issue was not military but political; the legitimacy of the rebels' demands could only be politically neutralized. EZLN representatives insisted on discussing national issues of political significance, especially demanding a change of regime and local autonomy, while the government wanted to talk about concrete local issues and grievances. Both sides were buying time: the rebels waiting for the regime crisis to deepen after the 1997 elections and the government waiting for the *zapatistas* to become irrelevant after a new economic recuperation. But by 1996, the *zapatistas* were joined by a new rebel group, a more classical guerrilla movement, the EPR, or Popular Revolutionary Army, that began operations in Guerrero, another state in the poor south.

The Chiapas social and political explosion was a complete surprise for many inside and outside of the government. The astute insurgent leadership, part Indian and part white, was able to transform a small and poorly armed military force into a national political entity by exploiting the regime's weaknesses: its lack of democratic legitimacy, its insensitivity to extreme poverty, its permanent marginalization of Indian communities through market economic policies, and its creation of a corrupt judicial system systematically loaded against Indians and the poor.

A few months after the eruption of the Chiapas rebellion, Luis Donaldo Colosio, the PRI's presidential candidate, was assassinated in Tijuana. The same fate awaited the secretary general of the PRI, Francisco Ruiz Massieu, a few months later. Not since the murder of president-elect Alvaro Obregón in 1928 had the Mexican political elite experienced political assassinations of such magnitude. The reasons behind these two political killings remain a mystery. In any event, the killing of Salinas's successor was a direct challenge to the old rules governing the internal struggles of the elite and an indicator of the decay of the regime's vitality.

It was obvious to all impartial observers that the 1994 election, won by the PRI's candidate, Ernesto Zedillo, another economist from the inner circle of market technocrats, was not fair. The state party used all its traditional legal and illegal advantages to the fullest. However, widespread and open fraud did not play the central role it had six years before. In the end, half of the voters supported the PRI's candidate and his slogans "for the well-being of your family" and "I vote for peace." The image of prosperity at the moment of elections was possible thanks to an overvalued peso, a concomitant consumer boom, and a very low rate of inflation. When, in December 1994, the weakness of such a situation ended up in a new economic crisis (a 7 percent drop in the GNP), the elections were a thing of the past. Finally, Solidarity program expenditures in key political regions plus the government's control of television helped to convince half of Mexican voters to continue their support of the state party system and reject the call for political democracy and social justice promoted by the center-left or those for political and moral transformation from the center-right.

With the PRI commanding the support of half of the electorate, and with the opposition unable to join forces to mount the final assault on the weakened but still impressive fortress of Mexican authoritarianism, a transition to democracy still seemed a distant possibility at the end of Salinas's presidential term in December 1994.

A Protracted Transition

Why did half of the Mexican voters, although well aware of the anti-democratic nature of the regime and the absence of a state of law, prefer the status quo to the promises of change? Part of the answer lies in the manipulation of the fear produced by the *zapatista* rebellion and Colosio's assassination and in the overwhelming superiority of the state party's resources.[49] However, another part of the explanation lies in history.

The main achievements of the Mexican Revolution were the redistribution of wealth through agrarian reform and unionism, the creation of a strong sense of popular nationalism, the expansion of public education, and the incorporation of popular masses into the new regime through agrarian reform and labor policies. These political, economic,

---

49. An unknown source gave the files of the 1994 electoral campaign expenditures of the PRI to the leadership of the PRD in the state of Tabasco. They amounted to sixty times the legal limit and more than four hundred times the expenditures of the PRD, the most important opposition party in that state. *La Jornada*, 15 to 19 June 1995.

social, and cultural transformations were a significant, historical break with Mexico's recent and distant past. On the other hand, the revolution did not represent a real break with the authoritarian use of power. As a matter of fact, the new elite perfected authoritarian traditions and gave them new life.

Unlike the Porfirian dictatorship, power in post-revolutionary Mexico was not centered on the person, the president, but on the institution, the presidency. The principle of no reelection was introduced to ensure the permanent, impersonal character of the new power structure and to allow for a systematic, nonviolent renovation of political personnel. This principle was the golden rule of the authoritarian *modus operandi* of the political elite. An all-powerful and centralist presidency that renovates itself at a precise time is not subject to biological decay, as was the case with the caudillistic presidents of the nineteenth century or the first stages of post-revolutionary Mexico.

Institutionalization of authoritarianism in the presidency and the incorporation of the rural and urban masses to the regime through a state party gave the postrevolutionary Mexican system a strength that was absent from personal and excluding authoritarianisms such as Franco's Spain or Salazar's Portugal. A comparison between the excluding and bureaucratic military authoritarianisms dominant in Latin America during the 1970s and the Mexican system, where repression plays a secondary role to co-optation, helps explain the resiliency of Mexico's non-democratic form of government.

The revolutionary transformation of Mexico ended in 1940, but the essence of the political system created by the revolution has persisted to the present, although it is losing ground to the internal and external forces of democracy. Until very recently the executive had an absolute predominance and control over the legislative and judicial branches, as well as over state and local governments. Through a very active and direct state role in the economy, the presidency played the central role in economic development and growth, subordinating the private sector as much to presidential power as labor unions or peasant organizations.[50]

If the state of law was systematically violated by the absence of an effective division of power, and elections and political democracy were only a facade, what provided the effective legitimacy that the system needed to survive for sixty-six years? For a long time, authoritarian

50. A good analysis of Mexican post-revolutionary authoritarianism can be found in Roger D. Hansen, *The Politics of Mexican Development* (Baltimore, Md.: The Johns Hopkins University Press, 1971).

legitimacy in Mexico was based on pragmatism, on the economic out-comes of the system: economic growth and distributive populist poli-cies. It was populism that permitted every collective and organized social actor—whether workers, peasants, the middle class, entrepre-neurs, or squatters—to receive a relatively satisfactory answer from the government to some of their demands. The government, namely the presidency, became the great dispenser, the great arbiter of social con-flict, and the essence of the Mexican political system.

The Crisis of Mexican Authoritarianism

In the summer of 1968, a student movement developed in Mexico City as a protest against police brutality. In two months, it had evolved into a middle-class, peaceful movement for political democracy, not unlike the Chinese student movement of 1989. Under the circumstances, the desire for an open and plural political system was, in fact, a demand for a change of regime. The reaction of the government in general and the presidency in particular was to portray the protesters as tools of a foreign conspiracy. In the name of legality and national security, the president ordered police and the army to end the challenge. On the evening of October 2, the army opened fire on a peaceful students' meeting in Tlatelolco Square. In political and human terms, this was a tragedy very similar to the June 3 Tiananmen Square massacre in Beijing, twenty years later.[51]

In the short run, presidential power was reasserted and Gustavo Díaz Ordaz (1964–70) was able to end his administration in full com-mand of the political structure. However, today it is clear that the re-pression of peaceful and legitimate demands for democracy signaled the beginning of the structural crisis of Mexican authoritarianism. After 1968, armed opposition to the regime appeared, including urban and rural guerrillas in the 1970s and the Indian uprising in Chiapas in 1994. In addition, peaceful opposition grew in the 1980s, and in the midterm elections of 1997, for the first time since the Mexican Revolu-tion, the president lost control of the Chamber of Representatives and opposition took charge of local government in six states and Mexico City.

Beginning in 1976 all presidential administrations have ended in cri-sis. These crises—in 1976, 1982, 1987–88 and 1994–95—have been the

---

51. A description and analysis of Mexican presidentialism is in Jorge Car-pizo, *El presidencialismo mexicano* (México: Siglo Veintiuno, 1978).

product of a complex mixture of economic and political failures and contradictions.[52] However, the recurrence of failure at the end of every administration in the last quarter of a century is an indication not only of unexpected circumstances or personal limitations of the leadership but of an institutional, systemic malfunctioning.

The Mexican political system confronts a vastly different country than the one that existed when it was constructed. Half a century ago, Mexico had about 18 million people, illiteracy affected almost half of the population fifteen years of age or older, 60 percent of Mexicans lived in rural areas, per capita income was 180 U.S. dollars, and agriculture represented about 23 percent of GNP. By 1993 Mexico had quadrupled its population (to 91 million), 71 percent of Mexicans lived in urban areas, 85.9 percent of the population age fifteen or over was literate, and per capita income was 3,750 U.S. dollars, while agriculture represented only 7 percent of GNP.

An urbanized, literate Mexico, connected to internal and international communications networks, still lives in a political suit made for a very different country. The pressures coming from civil society to force the transition to a real pluralistic and democratic system and create a genuine state of law are increasing. However, vested interests of the old political guard are fighting a rear guard struggle and producing a very messy and protracted transition.

In the mid-1980s, Carlos Salinas and his technocratic group were confident that renewed economic growth, produced by the introduction of a market economy, would postpone the necessity for a regime change until the next century. In order to influence electoral results in 1994 in favor of yet another PRI victory, Salinas's government overvalued the peso and began to run a systematic and increasing trade deficit that reached 25 billion U.S. dollars in 1994. Speculative foreign investors attracted by high interest rates on Mexican government paper sensed the weakness of the situation and began to leave the country, forcing a dramatic devaluation of the peso on December 20, three weeks after Ernesto Zedillo's inauguration.

The ensuing recession in 1995 produced general frustration and strongly negative reactions against the government and the regime from all groups. Market economics had been unable to create a solid

---

52. Evelyn P. Stevens, *Protest and Response in Mexico* (Cambridge: The MIT Press, 1974). The chain of political and economic crisis from 1968 to 1988 is presented and analyzed in Camín and Meyer, *In the Shadow of the Mexican Revolution*, 186–187 and 199–267, and Luis Medina Peña, *Hacia el nuevo estado: México, 1920–1993* (México: Fondo de Cultura Económica, 1994), 168–295.

foundation for future economic development and to propel Mexico into the First World as Salinas promised. Recession, inflation, unemployment, uncertainty, worsening income distribution, corruption, and a dramatic rise in urban and rural violence eliminated the government's ability to use economic outputs as the main source of legitimacy and as an alternative to a democratic transition. Pressures for change were increasing.

At the beginning of 1997, in the midst of a fragile economic recovery, a truly historical change in Mexico's political development appeared possible. While the result of some local gubernatorial elections in Yucatán and Tabasco were still clouded by fraud, elections in 1995–96 in Jalisco, Guanajuato, and Baja California were won by the center-right opposition, while some municipal and local legislative elections were won by the center-left. All of this is a very strong indication that the old state party dominance in Mexico is close to an end.

The mid-term elections of 1997 produced a somehow unexpected resurgence of Cuauhtémoc Cárdenas, this time as the first elected mayor of Mexico City. The PRD also became the second largest party in the Chamber of Representatives. Congress became the arena of a real and bitter struggle between the forces of the old system and the emerging opposition of right and left. The backlash against Salinas's corruption and the negative effects of market economics were stronger than expected by the government as well as the opposition.

Democratization is not always the result of pressures exerted by the beneficiaries of market economics. The electoral insurgency of July 1997 shows that anti-authoritarian politics can also be the product of a reaction. Many of those who supported the PRD were negatively affected by the market revolution imposed from above. Regardless, Mexico's democratic transition and the weakening of a formerly all-powerful presidency presents many dangers. If the transition is not well managed through a truly national agreement among the main political actors, local resistance of traditional interests to modernization and accountability may increase the symptoms of ungovernability and can trigger an authoritarian reaction of a different kind, one based more on repression than co-optation.

Among the main obstacles Mexican political leaders have to overcome in the immediate future are the resistance of vested interests; the effects of economic depression on all social classes; the weakness of political parties and social organizations; the widening of the gap between rich and poor;[53] the EZLN and EPR guerrilla activity and the

---

53. Julieta Campos, *¿Qué hacemos con los pobres? La reiterada querella por la nación* (México: Aguilar, 1995), 437.

militarization of some regions; the breakdown of governability as a result of common criminal violence and the penetration of the state security and judicial apparatus by drug organizations; the lack of a democratic tradition; and finally, the difficulty of creating an effective legal system out of an extremely corrupt and incompetent police and judiciary.

Ten years ago the young technocratic elite of Mexico thought they were smarter than their Soviet counterparts, that they could do better than Gorbachev. Their strategy was quite simple: Because there was no ideological commitment in Mexico's regime, it was possible to use the old authoritarian tools to speed up economic modernization. Economic success was its own justification. In the initial stage Mexican technocrats succeeded, much to the envy of many leaders in the underdeveloped world. However, the economic transformation of Mexico, centered around the free trade agreement with the United States, did not perform as promised.

Mexico's political transition at the end of the twentieth century is going to be costlier than it could have been ten or twenty years earlier, at a time when the authoritarian model first began to show clear signs of fatigue. Today the problems have increased, and Mexico confronts three formidable tasks: to build modern democratic political institutions out of a non-democratic tradition; to reshape market economic policies to generate employment and avoid the widening of the gap between the extremely rich and the extremely poor; and to rebuild all its judicial and legal institutions and create a genuine state of law.

Elsewhere in this book, Pitman B. Potter states that the notion of rule of law in China has been very instrumentalist. The situation has not been very different in Mexico. The current constitution has been continually amended. Until now, every president has forced upon a powerless Congress the amendments he needs to remove political obstacles. Under these circumstances, law is not more than what the ruling elite requires to justify and legitimize its policies. The legacy of this instrumental use of law is widespread cynicism about the law and a deepening of the gap between the formal and the real. All of this has been worsened by the extraordinarily arbitrary, partial, and corrupt practices of a judiciary subordinated to the presidency. To transform this pragmatic notion of law into something different, to implant in society the notion that law is something that relates to its dignity and well-being, is going to require a great effort on the part of democratic forces and an authentic revolution in Mexican civic culture.

With the new political environment produced by the 1997 elections, the first free, competitive, and almost fair elections in twentieth-century Mexico, the authoritarian presidency can be dismantled, an authentic division of power can emerge, and the beginning of a state of law becomes a possibility. Mexican civil society has had to overcome its traditional weakness to defeat the strong "imperial presidency" in the words of Enrique Krauze.[54] This process took almost thirty years, but victory at the ballot box in 1997 created the possibility of a virtuous circle in favor of civil society in the next century.

The Mexican agenda for the twenty-first century is formidable: to implant democracy and a state of law. Without either of these two elements, viable economic development and a civilized way of life are impossible.

54. Enrique Krauze *La presidencia imperial: Ascenso y caída del sistema político mexicano, 1940–1996* (México: Tusquest, 1997).

6

Economic and Legal Reform in China: Whither Civil Society and Democratization?

Pitman B. Potter

T he theme of this volume concerns the relationship between market reforms in the developing economies of China and Mexico and the possible emergence of democratization. As Cheek and Lindau suggest in chapter 1, the issue of whether market liberalization promotes democracy has been much debated. In the case of China, assumptions about the linkage between market economic policies and the inevitability of democratic reforms have underpinned foreign aid projects managed by the Western industrial democracies.[1] And, not surprisingly, private interests have been only too keen to suggest that they be free to pursue their commercial interests in China unfettered by concerns over the less savory features of Beijing's authoritarianism, on the grounds that market-oriented reforms will one day beget political liberalization.[2]

On the other hand, an emerging coterie of scholars has challenged assumptions about markets and democracy in China. Drawing on the discourse of "new institutionalism," Gaye Christoffersen suggests, for example, in chapter 4 of this volume that marketization in China has not resulted in a significant diminution of the state's leading role and,

---

1. See, e.g., Canadian International Development Agency, *China: Country Development Policy Framework* (1994); Asia Pacific Foundation of Canada, *Canada Asia Review* (1997), 72–77; and Asian Development Bank, *Law and Development at the Asian Development Bank* (1997).
2. Human Rights Watch, "Commerce Kills China Criticism Says Human Rights Watch," 3 April 1997.

therefore, should not be expected to engender civil society and democratization in the short term, although political reform may be possible
in the long run. The lesson of Taiwan suggests that the will of the state
is critical in permitting a transition to democratic reforms, even in the
context of market-oriented economic policies and the social pressures
for political liberalization that they raise.[3] For just as market reforms
require the state to disengage from its hegemony over the economy, so
too does democratization require the state to disengage from political
hegemony and cede significant authority to the popular will.[4]

Thus, any analysis of the potential emergence of civil society and
democratization in China would seem to require an evaluation of the
state's commitment to withdraw from its hegemonic position in social,
economic, and ultimately political terms. Of particular interest are the
institutions established to support the economic reforms, as well as the
attitudes of those who interact with these institutions. The legal reforms adopted in China have served explicitly as a complement to the
market-oriented economic reform effort and thus have particular significance for assessing the extent to which the reforms support a withdrawal by the state from socioeconomic and political hegemony. This
chapter focuses on norms and institutions of Chinese legal reform and
on the attitudes that make up Chinese legal culture,[5] in an effort to
reach preliminary conclusions as to the possibility of the state retreating from hegemony. This, it would seem, is an essential first step to

---

3. The comparison to Taiwan is often made in this regard, but it is instructive to remember that the democratization effort there occurred largely as a
result of the government's quest for international legitimacy in its relations
with the mainland—and was generally opposed by the dominant Taiwanese
economic actors. For discussion of the origins of Taiwan democracy, see Wang
Hao, "The Ruling Party and the Transition to Democracy: The Case of the
Chinese Nationalist Party (KMT) on Taiwan," (Ph.D. diss., University of British
Columbia, 1996).

4. By "hegemony," I mean domination not merely of the institutions of rule
but also of the norms and ideology that construct and inform popular interactions with such institutions. Obviously, this approach owes much to the legacy
of Antonio Gramsci. See Gramsci, *Selections from the Prison Notebooks*, ed. and
tr. Hoare and Smith (New York: International Publishers, 1971); and "Edward
Greer, Antonio Gramsci and 'Legal Hegemony,' " in *The Politics of Law*, ed.
David Kairys (New York: Pantheon, 1982). Also see Alan Hunt, *Explorations
in Law and Society: Toward a Constitutive Theory of Law* (New York: Routledge,
1993).

5. For discussion of legal culture as embodying attitudes and behavior about
law, see Lawrence M. Friedman, *The Legal System: A Social Science Perspective*
(Englewood Cliffs, N.J.: Prentice-Hall, 1975), 15. For discussion of the utility of
this approach as applied to China, see Stanley Lubman, "Studying Contemporary Chinese Law: Limits, Possibilities and Strategy," *American Journal of Comparative Law* 36 (1991): 293, at 333.

assessing potential linkages between market liberalization and the emergence of civil society (and possibly even democracy).

Norms and Institutions of the Chinese Socialist Legal System

The explicit orientation of the Chinese legal reforms has been to support the policies of economic reform. This perspective reflects the instrumentalist norms that inform the Chinese socialist legal system, which are supported by norms of formalism. These norms in turn dominate the structure and operation of the major institutions of the socialist legal system. The following review of norms and institutions in the legal system of the People's Republic of China (PRC) suggests that rather than retreating from hegemony, the state continues to play a dominant role.

Underlying Operative Norms

The operative norms that underpin the Chinese legal reform effort reflect basic norms of instrumentalism and formalism. Law is conceived of as an instrument of rule, while the effectiveness of this instrument is subject to formalistic assessments that emphasize content over performance.

Instrumentalism in the Role of Law

The Chinese government's approach to law is fundamentally instrumentalist,[6] meaning that laws and regulations are intended to be instruments of policy enforcement. Legislative and regulatory enactments are not designed as expressions of immutable general norms that apply consistently in a variety of human endeavors; neither are they constrained by such norms. Rather, laws and regulations are enacted explicitly to achieve immediate policy objectives of the regime. Law is not a limit on state power; rather it is a mechanism by which state power is exercised.

This approach to the role of law derives from a long tradition in Chinese history in which law has been aimed primarily to achieve so-

---

6. See, e.g., Lubman, "Studying Contemporary Chinese Law," and Yu Xing-zhong, "Legal Pragmatism in the People's Republic of China," *Journal of Chinese Law* 3 (1989): 29. Also see, generally, Ronald C. Keith, *China's Struggle for the Rule of Law* (New York: St. Martin's Press, 1994), 218–221.

cial control but also in pursuit of economic goals.[7] Ideologies of rule through recent Chinese history, whether derived from the Confucianism of imperial China, the republicanism of China under the Kuomintang, or the Marxism-Leninism of China after 1949, have emphasized law as an instrument of control. Throughout the 1950s in the PRC, law and regulation were used to transform the economy and society to achieve the revolutionary goals of the Maoist regime.[8] The instrumentalism of that regime was amply illustrated when, just at the time law began to be taken seriously not simply as an instrument of rule but as a source of norms and principles of general applicability that might give rise to rights and protections for the populace, it was subjected to criticism for obstructing the policy goals of the party and state.[9]

In the post-Mao era, efforts at legal reform have been couched mainly in the language of instrumentalism—in part so as to enlist the support of conservative members of the regime who question the benefits of a legal system that intrudes on the party's monopoly on power.[10] The resilience of the instrumentalist notion of rule by law, as opposed to a universalist approach to the rule of law, is widely acknowledged today by the legal communities in China as a matter severely in need of reform.[11]

One consequence of legal instrumentalism as practiced in China is that laws and regulations are intentionally ambiguous so as to provide policymakers and implementing officials alike significant flexibility in interpretation and implementation.[12] Many Chinese laws and regula-

---

7. See Derk Bodde and Clarence Morris, *Law in Imperial China* (Philadelphia: University of Pennsylvania Press, 1967); and Michael Dutton, *Policing and Punishment in China: From Patriarchy to "The People"* (Hong Kong: Oxford University Press, 1992).

8. See, generally, Stanley B. Lubman, "Methodological Problems in Studying Chinese Communist 'Civil' Law," in *Contemporary Chinese Law: Research Problems and Perspectives*, ed. Jerome A. Cohen (Cambridge: Harvard University Press, 1970).

9. See, e.g., Victor H. Li, "The Evolution and Development of the Chinese Legal System," in *CHINA: Management of a Revolutionary Society*, ed. John Lindbeck (Seattle: University of Washington Press, 1970), esp. 240–41.

10. For example, see Peng Zhen, "Guanyu qi ge falu caioan de shuoming" (Explanation of seven draft laws), in Peng Zhen, *Lun xin shiqi de shehuizhuyi minzhu yu fazhi jianshe* (On the establishment of socialist democracy and legal system in the new period) (Beijing: Central Digest Publishers, 1989), 1.

11. For example, in October 1991, the Law Institute of the Chinese Academy of Social Sciences hosted an International Symposium on the Rule of Law in Social and Economic Development, which addressed this issue specifically.

12. In theory, the flexibility and discretion conferred on Chinese decisionmakers are controlled through ideological training in much the same way that the discretion of imperial Chinese officials was controlled through Confucian

tions are replete with vague passages that do not lend predictability or transparency to the regulatory process. While this ambiguity does free the hands of central policymakers to modify the policy foundations for these measures and permits local implementing officials to use broad discretion in ensuring that regulatory enforcement satisfies policy objectives, it also makes uniform interpretation and enforcement difficult if not impossible to obtain.

The Role of Formalism

The instrumentalist bent of current policies of legal reform is complemented by the role of formalism in the assessment of the effects of law. Formalism in this sense means that the content of law is assumed to represent reality, with little if any inquiry permitted into gaps between the content and operation of law.[13] Law is not only seen as a tool by which desired social, economic, and political goals can be attained but also presumed to be an *effective* tool. When a policy is agreed upon and then expressed through law or regulation, the law or regulation serves as a conclusive indicator that the policy is being enforced.

To a large extent this formalism is a predictable consequence of the instrumentalism that drives the enactment of law and regulation. While consensus is difficult enough to achieve concerning the legislative and regulatory enactments that are expressions of policy ideals, it is nearly impossible to achieve in the area of implementational details due to the numerous political trade-offs that accompany policy enforcement.[14] As a result, policies and the laws and regulations that ex-

---

training. See, generally, Joseph Levenson, *Confucian China and Its Modern Fate* (Berkeley: University of California Press, 1958).

13. See James Feinerman, "Economic and Legal Reform in China, 1978–91," *Problems of Communism* (September-October, 1991), 62–75; and Stanley B. Lubman, "Emerging Functions of Formal Legal Institutions in China's Modernization," in *China Under the Four Modernizations*, ed. Joint Economic Committee of U.S. Congress (Washington, D.C.: U.S. Government Printing Office), 235. Elsewhere, I have suggested an alternative approach to legal formalism as one that interprets justice as compliance with formal rules regardless of substantive consequences. See Pitman B. Potter, "Riding the Tiger: Legitimacy and Legal Reform in Post-Mao China," *The China Quarterly* 138 (June 1994): 325. Also see Thomas C. Grey, "Langdell's Orthodoxy," *University of Pittsburgh Law Review* 45 (1983): 1.

14. For a discussion of the problem of policymaking and trade-offs, see Susan Shirk, *The Political Logic of Economic Reform in China* (Berkeley: University of California Press, 1993), in which the author uses the term "particularistic contracting" to describe a policy process by which consensus is reached through a series of agreements ("particularistic contracts") that confer on contending elite groups benefits sufficient to induce their support for the policy

press them are replete with thinly veiled compromises that represent programmatic ideals rather than implementational details. Where elaborate inquiry into implementation is likely to raise issues that may threaten the political consensus or even the policy ideals, such inquiry is not pursued. Rather, the content of law is seen as coterminous with its operational effects. In China's contentious policy environment, the ideal and its implementation become one.

Institutions

The formal institutions of legal reform in China represent the organizational face of socialist legalism. The new attention given to legislative, judicial, and administrative institutions suggests a commitment to subjecting the state's governance authority to a modicum of legal restraint. Upon closer examination, however, it appears that the state's hegemony over legislative, judicial, and administrative power remains intact.

Legislation and Rule-making

Legislative institutions are important as a source of formal rules (laws and regulations) which, if taken as a source of private rights, can support greater social autonomy and potentially the emergence of civil society and democratic reforms. A key requirement, however, is the procedural rigor and ultimately the legitimacy of the legislative process. Particularly in the context of potential links between markets and democracy, formal legitimacy for the processes for enacting market-governing rules may strengthen the prestige of the legislature generally and may elevate public expectations for the role of law. This can serve as a basis for popular calls for government accountability and greater empowerment of popular will.

During the reform era under Deng Xiaoping, the National People's Congress (NPC) has been transformed from a "rubber stamp" parliament into a vibrant institutional component of political authority.[15]

of the day. Also see Murray Scot Tanner, "Organizations and Politics in China's Post-Mao Law-Making System," in *Domestic Law Reforms in Post-Mao China*, ed. Pitman B. Potter, (Armonk, N.Y.: M. E. Sharpe, 1994), 56.

15. See Kevin O'Brien, "China's National People's Congress: Reform and Its Limits," *Legislative Studies Quarterly* 13, no. 3 (1988): 343–74, and *Reform Without Liberalization: The National People's Congress and the Politics of Institutional Change* (New York: Cambridge University Press, 1990); Tanner, "Organizations and Politics in China's Post-Mao Law-Making System"; and Murray Scot Tanner, "How a Bill Becomes Law in China: Stages and Processes in Lawmaking," *The China Quarterly*, no. 141 (1995): 39–64.

Due to the influence of norms of instrumentalism and formalism, however, the NPC has been the site of much bureaucratic wrangling over legislation intended to effectuate the economic reform policies. Examples of the Bankruptcy Law and the State Enterprise Management Law are particularly noteworthy, although not unique.[16] The Bankruptcy Law was formally enacted by the 18th Session of the NPC-SC in December 1986. The law raised particularly sensitive issues about the fate of inefficient state enterprises and particularly the disposition of their assets and employees. Because it had the potential to operate at the interstices of the planned and market economies, the law gave rise to a number of policy and ideological conflicts. These came to the fore during the course of bureaucratic infighting over the legislation, which in turn ultimately delayed its enactment and undermined its implementation.

Although the Deng Xiaoping–led reformist coalition saw enterprise reforms and bankruptcy legislation as essential to their broader economic reform goals, significant apprehension and resistance emerged from CPC traditionalists and from the line ministries responsible for state enterprises and their assets and employees. These institutions had largely been bypassed by the reformist coalition whose supporters proposed the Bankruptcy Law. However, they found receptive voices among the leadership of the NPC and its Standing Committee, which played a significant role in delaying enactment and ultimately implementation of the proposed legislation. The delays in enacting the Bankruptcy Law and the State Enterprise Law reflected the extent to which bureaucratic politics affected the legislative process.

The bureaucratic politics that dominates NPC legislation is also in evidence in the processes of administrative rule-making that follows— even to the extent of nullifying or diluting the thrust of NPC enactments. The story of the enactment of rules on protection of computer software pursuant to the PRC Copyright Law is illustrative.[17] The Ministry of Electronics Industry (MEI), which had coordinated the drafting of the rules, was not given implementational authority and, as a result, was less than an enthusiastic supporter of implementation. The State Copyright Administration was ultimately appointed as implementing

---

16. See, generally, Da-kuang Chang, "The Making of the Chinese Bankruptcy Law: A Study in the Chinese Legislative Process," *Harvard International Law Journal* 28 (1987): 333. Also see Tanner, "How a Bill Becomes Law in China."

17. This discussion is drawn in part from Michel Oksenberg, Pitman B. Potter, and William B. Abnett, "Advancing Intellectual Property Rights: Information Technologies and the Course of Economic Development in China" (Seattle: National Bureau of Asian Research, 1996).

agency, but this office is not housed in a strong and supportive bureaucracy, but rather is within the Press and Publication Administration, which in turn is part of the Propaganda system of the CPC. These factors together with the personal relations among the officials who competed and ultimately won or lost the bureaucratic struggle for control over computer software protection have had a marked effect on enforcement of the administrative rules themselves. Thus, factors affecting the implementation of legislation extend well beyond the confines of the NPC and are intimately connected with the bureaucratic politics attendant to administrative rule-making.

The tendency for the NPC to be used as a resource in elite politics may work to elevate the stature of China's legislative apparatus over the long run. However, as the legislative process remains the product of bureaucratic politics, formal process norms remain subordinate to substantive policy prerogatives. Moreover, legislation remains subject to CPC control and intervention. Under such conditions, policy-driven statutes quickly become marginalized as the policy imperatives that gave them birth are discarded and/or paralyzed in the course of bureaucratic and political conflict. The result is a legislature characterized by politicized enactment of laws with limited effect. This seems unlikely to elicit significant popular legitimacy or expectations that formal law can be a meaningful source of norms for regulating social, economic, and political relationships.

Dispute Resolution

Dispute resolution is essential to the potential linkage between market policies and democratization, where the key issues involve rights and rights enforcement. Just as the legislative process is key to popular expectations as to the meaning and effect of law, so too does enforcement dictate popular expectations about the significance of the private rights that are central to market-oriented economic policies. To the extent that legislation aimed at effecting market reforms has recognized the importance of private rights, enforcement through dispute resolution organs is critical. The Chinese economic reforms have contributed to increased levels of commercial disputes, as the bureaucratic compromises that had worked effectively under the state planning system in preventing and resolving these conflicts have become less acceptable to economic actors increasingly concerned with profit and loss. As a result, increased attention has been paid to building institutions for dispute resolution, particularly the courts and the arbitral institutions.

Unfortunately, the Chinese court system remains relatively ineffective. The generally low level of political status and authority of formal legal institutions derived from traditional Chinese attitudes as well as from Maoist ideology impedes the capacity of courts to compel production of evidence and enforce awards.[18] The often parochial view taken by courts toward enforcement of judicial awards from outside the immediate area of jurisdiction reflects ingrained traditions of localism and the centrality of personal relations as the basis for behavior. Judicial processes of internal and informal fact-finding and decision-making mean that disputants are seldom protected against abuses of power and political connections by their adversaries. As well, the Communist Party continues to play a dominant role through the "adjudication committees" that are attached to each court and that in effect review and approve judicial decisions notwithstanding official directives ordering that the intervention of adjudication committees be curtailed.[19] Thus, the politicization, low level of professionalism, and local protectionism of the Chinese courts have largely made them inadequate to handle the increased level of commercial disputes that have accompanied economic reform.

Arbitration of disputes has emerged as a workable compromise between the overly lax procedures of informal mediation and the problematic formalism of the judicial system.[20] Arbitration of disputes involving Chinese domestic enterprises is handled by various administrative departments with jurisdiction over the subject matter: For example, labor disputes are handled by the local Labor Administration, while contract disputes are under the authority of the State Administration for Industry and Commerce. Under the Arbitration Law of the PRC (1994), arbitration committees are being established under the local people's governments to handle a wide array of economic disputes. Maritime disputes are subject to the China Maritime Arbitration Commission. Arbitration and conciliation of disputes involving foreigners are most often handled by the China International Economic and Trade Arbitration Commission (CIETAC), although the provincial government arbitration bodies also have jurisdiction to handle these types of cases.

While arbitration proceedings are often perceived as reasonably fair

---

18. See, generally, Donald C. Clarke, "Dispute Resolution in China," *Journal of Chinese Law* 5 (1991): 245; Lubman, "Studying Contemporary Chinese Law," and Potter, "Riding the Tiger."

19. See Stanley B. Lubman, "Introduction," in *Domestic Law Reform in Post-Mao China.*

20. See, generally, Albert H. Y. Chen, *An Introduction to the Legal System of the PRC* (Hong Kong: Butterworth's, 1993), 175ff.; and Guiguo Wang, *Business Law of China: Cases, Texts and Commentary* (Hong Kong: Butterworth's, 1993), 538–44.

and effective, problems remain. Requests for cooperation by other administrative units in the collection of evidence, seizure of assets, production of witnesses, and other matters often go unheeded. As well, arbitrators are known to engage in what are essentially *ex parte* contacts with the disputants, either during the course of the mediation process that previously was intertwined with arbitration or during the course of preparing the matter for hearing.[21] While rules have been enacted requiring fairness and impartiality by arbitrators,[22] such activities continue—supported by traditional Chinese norms regarding the judge/arbitrator, who is expected to meet regularly with disputants and personally investigate facts.[23] Bureaucratic politics have also played a role, as Chinese courts continue to insist on subjecting arbitral decisions to extensive review prior to enforcement.

The increased numbers of commercial disputes brought on by the market reforms has created a certain degree of institutional competition for a share of the dispute resolution "market." This competition may bode well for the emergence of independent and effective dispute resolution processes both in the courts and in arbitration. However, so far there is little to indicate that the competition for dispute resolution cases has motivated courts or arbitral organs to increase their autonomy and/or procedural rigor. Instead, institutional competition seems to be taking the form mainly of increased efforts to strengthen ties with government departments.[24] Thus, the institutions of dispute resolution seem not to herald a withdrawal of the state but instead suggest its continued dominance.

Administrative Reform

An important element contributing to the potential for market policies to give rise to democracy is the notion of accountability in the market regulatory system. The enactment of the Administrative Litigation Law (ALL) signaled an effort to make administrative agencies

21. For examples, see Huang Yanming, "The Stylization and Regularization of the Management and Operation of the Chinese Arbitration Institute," *Journal of International Arbitration* 11, no. 2 (1994): 77; and Huang's "Mediation in the Settlement of Business Disputes," *Journal of International Arbitration* 8, no. 4 (1991): 23.

22. See Huang Yanming, "The Ethics of Arbitrators in CIETAC Arbitration," *Journal of International Arbitration* 12, no. 2 (1995): 5.

23. See generally, Bodde and Morris, *Law in Imperial China*, 5–6; Austin Coates, *Myself a Mandarin* (London: Frederick Muller, 1968); and Robert Van Gulik, *Celebrated Cases of Judge Dee* (New York: Dover Publications, 1976).

24. For a preliminary discussion, see Stanley B. Lubman, "Setback for the China-Wide Rule of Law," *Far Eastern Economic Review* 17 November 1996, 38.

more accountable through provisions for limited judicial review.[25] Under the ALL, individuals and enterprises may challenge in court the legality of decisions by Chinese administrative organs. While only the administrative organizations themselves may be defendants under the ALL, a cause of action may arise as a result of an individual official's act. The ALL permits judicial review of a variety of regulatory decisions, including the imposition of fines, restrictions on property rights, interference in business operations, and denial of business licenses. In addition, the ALL permits challenges against administrative agencies to be filed as a result of individual officials abusing their official powers to elicit graft from business enterprises.

However, the ALL remains a weak basis for private challenges against government behavior. The law does not extend to review of decisions by Chinese Communist Party departments and officials. Nor does it permit review of discretionary decisions by administrative agencies. In light of the textual ambiguities of Chinese laws and regulations, discretionary decisions are widespread and abuses of discretion are common. Nonetheless, these are outside the scope of ALL review. In addition, ALL review does not extend to the lawfulness of administrative regulations themselves, and as a result administrative agencies can in effect legislate their own immunities from ALL review. Finally, applicants seeking judicial review must first exhaust administrative remedies within the department being challenged, and under the Regulations of the PRC on Administrative Reconsideration, administrative agencies have virtually unlimited power to dictate the governing procedures and to limit the availability of appeal to the courts. Thus, in the area of administrative law, the state remains largely insulated from judicial review.

Summary

The Chinese legal reforms carried out since late 1978 have operated in conjunction with reforms in the economic system aimed at introducing market-oriented policies. The legislative record has been impressive in terms of scope and breadth. And to a significant extent, the enactment of formal laws and legal institutions permits the standards for economic behavior to become part of the public discourse. These standards are then more open to popular scrutiny than were the secretive policy pronouncements of the Maoist regime, which were

---

25. See Pitman B. Potter, "Judicial Review and Bureaucratic Reform: The Administrative Litigation Law of the PRC," in *Domestic Law Reforms in Post-Mao China*, 270.

grounded in ideological presumptions that were always monopolized by the regime. An increasingly public discourse over the rules governing economic life might possibly form the groundwork for popular demands for greater autonomy in other spheres, for greater government accountability, and for other attributes of civil society and democratic reform.

However, underlying norms of instrumentalism and formalism tend to reinforce the state's hegemony in interpretation and application of law and thus undermine the potential for law to serve as an autonomous body of objective norms governing socioeconomic and political behavior. And rather than suggesting a withdrawal of the state, the institutions of the legal system reveal and in many instances support the state's determination to retain control. In neither the institutions nor the norms of the socialist legal system do we find a meaningful commitment by the state to withdraw from its hegemonic position.

Popular Attitudes About Socialist Law

I have suggested elsewhere that popular support for legal reform in China has proceeded from an essential distrust of the state and, rather than serving as a basis for legitimacy of the regime, may in fact imply a degree of alienation from official norms on the structure and consequences of legal relationships.[26] Popular attitudes serve as important indicators of the extent to which various social groups respond to marketization in ways that conform to or depart from the formal ideology of the state.[27] While the retention of state control through the institutions of the socialist legal system remains a key obstacle to the emergence of civil society in China, popular attitudes that challenge the normative hegemony purporting to legitimate such control have particular significance for assessments about the potential for political change.

The Getihu: Indicia of Receptivity to Legal Reform[28]

Of particular interest are the attitudes of small-scale independent business operators (*getihu*) who have emerged in response to the mar-

---

26. See Potter, "Riding the Tiger."
27. See, e.g., James and Ann Tyson, *Chinese Awakenings: Life Stories from Unofficial China* (Boulder, Colo.: Westview, 1995).
28. This section draws upon the author's "Socialist Legality and Legal Culture in Shanghai: A Survey of the *Getihu*," *Canadian Journal of Law and Society* 9, no. 2 (1994): 41.

ket reform policies. The *getihu* are independent business operators engaged mainly in small retail and service activities, ranging from selling vegetables and dry goods to providing machinery and vehicle repairs.[29] Gaye Christoffersen, in chapter 4, notes the potential role of the *getihu* to emerge as an autonomous middle class, but suggests that this potential is limited due to continued reliance on the local party-state. Yet the *getihu* are perhaps the most autonomous of China's emerging "private sector," as their activities involve the formation and enforcement of private commercial relationships that contrast with the state-centered public relationships that characterize the state enterprise sector.[30] In this regard it is helpful to remember that the autonomy of business interests is seldom absolute, as corporate actors even in the "civil societies" of the West remain heavily dependent on state support through favorable tax regimes, shared ideologies on such matters as private property and contract autonomy, and the frequent sharing of specialized knowledge through direct participation in the regulatory process and the intertwined career patterns of government and corporate officials.[31] Thus, while the *getihu* are creations of the regime's economic reform policies and remain heavily dependent on the regime's continued commitment to the development of independent markets, they are also outsiders[32] whose attitudes about the norms and operation of the socialist legal system can be expected to reflect a significant degree of independence.

This section examines attitudes about legal regulation of commercial

29. For general discussion of the *getihu*, see Thomas B. Gold, "Guerrilla Interviewing Among the *Getihu*," in *Unofficial China: Popular Culture and Thought in the People's Republic*, ed. Perry Link, Richard Madsen, and Paul G. Pickowicz, (Boulder, Westview, 1989), 175; and "The Golden Ghetto of Individual Businesses," *China News Analysis*, no. 1476 (1 January 1993): 1–9.

30. As Professor Christoffersen notes, by reference to the work of Jean Oi ("Fiscal Reform and the Economic Foundation of Local State Corporatism in China," *World Politics* 45 [October 1992]: 99–126), much of the so-called private sector in China is actually controlled if not owned outright by party and state interests. Also see Kristen Parris, "Local Initiative and National Reform: The Wenzhou Model of Development," *The China Quarterly* 34 (June 1993): 242–63.

31. See, e.g., George Cooper, "The Avoidance Dynamic: A Tale of Tax Planning, Tax Ethics, and Tax Reform," *Columbia Law Review* 80 (1980): 1553; Duncan Kennedy and Frank Michelman, "Are Property and Contract Efficient?" *Hofstra Law Review* 8 (1980): 711; and R. Mahon, "Regulatory Agencies: Captive Agents or Hegemonic Apparatuses?" in *Class, State Ideology and Change: Marxist Perspectives on Canada*, ed. P. Grayson (Toronto: Holt, Rinehart and Winston, 1980).

32. See, generally, Alison W. Conner, "To Get Rich Is Precarious: Regulation of Private Enterprise in the People's Republic of China," *Journal of Chinese Law* 5 (1991): 1; and Edward J. Epstein and Ye Lin, "Individual Enterprise in Contemporary Urban China: A Legal Analysis of Status and Regulation," *The Inter-*

relationships among small-scale *getihu* in Shanghai's Jingan District.[33] Attitudinal data for this study were obtained through use of a survey questionnaire distributed to fifty registered *getihu* through the assistance of the Law Institute of the Shanghai Academy of Social Sciences (SASS). Of the fifty participants, nineteen were female and thirty-one male. The average age was thirty-eight for female respondents (ranging from age twenty to age sixty-seven) and thirty-nine for male respondents (ranging from age twenty to age sixty-two). Income levels ranged from a low among both male and female respondents of less than 3,000 yuan per year to a high of more than 10,000 yuan per year.[34] The average income for male respondents was higher than 5,000 yuan per year, while the average income for female respondents was less than 5,000 yuan per year. The education levels of the respondents centered mainly on high-school or equivalent technical school; only one respondent (male) indicated college training. The personal information obtained from the respondents, while not necessarily representative of China as a whole, still provides useful context for the survey results. Additional context comes from comparing the responses of the *getihu* surveyed with those from the general population of Jingan, of which 154 individual residents received and answered the questionnaire, again through the assistance of the SASS Law Institute and the cooperation of the Huashan street committee.

Responses of the *Getihu* on Norms of Equality, Justice, and Private Obligations

The responses to the survey among *getihu* in Shanghai's Jingan District suggest limits to assimilation of official Chinese doctrines of legal reform. These may be identified by specific reference to questions addressing matters of equality, justice, and private law relations, norms that are central features of the Chinese socialist legal system.[35] This section compares official doctrines on these norms with the responses obtained from the *getihu* survey.

---

national Lawyer 21 (1987): 396, esp. 412 et seq. Also see "The Golden Ghetto of Individual Businesses."

33. Field research for this chapter was carried out during my residency at the Shanghai Academy of Social Sciences (SASS) Law Institute during June–August 1993, as well as during numerous visits in 1990–92.

34. While the official exchange rate during the summer of 1993 when the survey was taken was 5.67 yuan: US$1.00, the semi-official Shanghai swap center rate hovered around 8 yuan: US$1.00.

35. See Potter, "Riding the Tiger."

Equality

Official Norms. With the onset of legal reform after 1978, official doctrine emphasized legal equality to a degree not seen at least since the 1950s. The doctrine of legal equality was expressed in the context of economic relations in the 1981 Economic Contract Law (ECL), which provided that contracting parties enjoyed equal rights.[36] Judicial decisions applying the Economic Contract Law have stressed the equality of contracting parties operating at hierarchically unequal organizational positions.[37] The doctrine of legal equality was formally entrenched in the 1982 Constitution of the PRC, which granted all citizens equality before the law.[38] Notions of legal equality have been extended to a broad array of civil relations under the 1986 General Principles of Civil Law (GPCL), which granted rights to all natural persons without regard to organizational, family, or class status.[39] The GPCL also recognized economic actors as legal persons with equal rights regardless of ownership, structure, or form of operations.[40] Judicial decisions applying the GPCL to contract and inheritance cases enforced the notion of legal equality between the parties.[41]

---

36. See Economic Contract Law, Article 5. This principle was reiterated in the revisions to the Economic Contract Law that were issued in September 1993. See Economic Contract Law 1993, *China Law and Practice* (December 1993). Also see Pitman B. Potter, "Note," *China Law and Practice* (December 1993), 46–8.

37. For discussion of agricultural contracts, see "Gongya xian fayuan caijue yi qi hetong jiufen" (The Gongya County Court Arbitrates a Contract Dispute), *Sichuan Ribao* (Sichuan Daily), 10 April 1984, 3; "Fayuan caijue peichang sunshi" (The Court Decides That Losses Should Be Compensated), *Sichuan Ribao* (Sichuan Daily), 18 April 1984, 3. For discussion of commercial contracts, see "Nanjing zhong ji fayuan renzhen zuo hao jingji shenpan gongzuo" (The Nanjing Middle Level Court Conscientiously Does a Good Job in Economic Adjudication Work), *Renmin ribao* (People's Daily), 24 June 1984, 4.

38. Constitution of the People's Republic of China, Articles 33–34. This provision had its origins in the 1954 constitution. See Constitution of the People's Republic of China (1954), Art. 85, in *Documents of the First National Congress of the People's Republic of China* (Beijing: Foreign Languages Press, 1955). Also see Pitman B. Potter, "Peng Zhen: Evolving Views on Party Organization and Law," in *China's Establishment Intellectuals,* ed. Carol Lee Hamrin and Timothy Cheek, (Armonk, N.Y.: M. E. Sharpe, 1986), 21.

39. See General Principles of Civil Law of the People's Republic of China (tr. William C. Jones), Article 3, in *Review of Socialist Law* 4 (1987): 357–86.

40. See General Principles of Civil Law, Art. III.

41. See, e.g., "Nongcun chengbao jingying hu qianding de chengbao jingying hetong, shou falu baohu" (A task management contract signed by a rural contractor receives legal safeguard), Case No. 70, in *Minshi jingji jinan anli jiesi* (Interpretation and analysis of difficult civil and economic cases), ed. Chen Youzun (Huhehaote: Inner Mongolia University Press, 1990), 119; "Hetong

Despite these developments, official doctrine on legal equality has been limited by policies aimed at preserving political inequality between the regime and its subjects. Beyond the formal statements on the primacy of the state[42] and the party,[43] regime doctrine entrenches political inequality through provisions on labor discipline[44] and work unit organization.[45] The presumptions about socioeconomic equality and attendant recognition of legal equality within society do not extend to relations between society and the party/state, where norms of inequality still govern.

Getihu Responses. The *getihu* responding to the questionnaire focused on notions about formal equality in institutional relationships and substantive equality in social relations. Equality in the application of formal rules was supported by notions about inherent equality in political and social relationships. In general, responses were consistently sup-

---

dangshiren yi fang you guocuo, bing zaocheng dui fang jingji sunshi de, yingdang chengdan minshi zeren" (Where one contract party is at fault and also causes economic losses to the other party, it should bear civil liability), Case No. 106, in *Minshi jingji jinan anli jiesi*, 187; "Lishi shang yiliu xialai de qi, qie dui zhangfu de yichan xiangyou pingdeng de jicheng chuanli" (A Wife and Concubine Left Over from History Have Equal Inheritance Rights Regarding the Legacy of the Husband), in *Minfa anli xuanbian* (Compilation of Civil Cases), ed. Shen Shaofang (Beijing: People's University Press, 1989), 222–24; and "Hefa you xiao de lizhu shou falu baohu" (A Legally Effective Will Received the Protection of Law), in *Minfa anli xuanbian*, 226–28.

42. For example, the constitutional grant of legal equality is qualified by the provision that the exercise of citizens' rights and freedoms cannot infringe on the interests of the state. See Constitution of the PRC (1982), Article 51.

43. The Four Basic Principles, which serve currently as the official political philosophy in Deng Xiaoping's China, include the duty to uphold the leadership of the party. See Deng Xiaoping, "Jianchi si xiang jiben yuanze" (Uphold the Four Basic Principles), in *Deng Xiaoping wenxuan* (Collected Writings of Deng Xiaoping) (Beijing: People's Press, 1983), 150–151.

44. The right to strike was deleted from the 1982 Chinese Constitution. Compare Constitution of the PRC (1978) (Beijing: New China News Agency, 1978), Article 45, with Constitution of the PRC (1982). In addition, penalties including fines, dismissal, or even criminal punishments may be imposed for "violating labor discipline." See "Qiye zhi gong jiang cheng tiaoli" (Regulations on Reward and Punishments for Enterprise Staff and Workers), Article 11, in *Zhonghua renmin gongheguo laodong fagui xuanbian* (Compilation of Labor Laws and Regulations of the PRC), ed. Laodong Renshi Bu Zhengce Yanjiu Shi (Policy Research Office of the Ministry of Labor and Personnel) (Beijing: Labor and Personnel Press, 1985), 310.

45. See Andrew G. Walder, *Communist Neo-Traditionalism: Work and Authority in Chinese Industry* (Berkeley and Los Angeles: University of California Press, 1986). Also see James A. Nelson and John A. Reeder, "Labor Relations in China," *California Management Review* 27, no. 4 (1985): 13.

portive of ideals about social equality. A majority of respondents (38/ 50, 76 percent) agreed that all members of society are equal and denied the notion of special legal rights depending on social, political, or family status. There was also significant support for gender equality: In response to the suggestions (1) that men should work and women look after the children, 44/50 disagreed or strongly disagreed; (2) that men and women are equally capable in business, professions, and government, 30/50 agreed or strongly agreed, and (3) that boys should have more chances to go to school than girls, 41/50 disagreed or strongly disagreed. These responses generally paralleled those of the general population surveyed.[46]

There were, however, a number of interesting disparities between the attitudes of male and female respondents from among the *getihu*. For example, in response to the proposition that men should work and women look after the children, male denials were somewhat less vigorous: 21/31 (67.7 percent) of the male respondents disagreed and 5/31 (16.1 percent) strongly disagreed, in contrast with 14/19 (73.7 percent) of the female respondents disagreeing and 4/19 (21.1 percent) strongly disagreeing. Women were less supportive of the suggestion that men and women are equally capable in business, the professions, and government: Male responses ran from 2/31 (6.5 percent) strongly disagreeing and 7/31 (22.6 percent) disagreeing to 22/31 (71 percent) agreeing and none strongly agreeing, while female responses ran from 1/19 (5.3 percent) strongly disagreeing and 6/19 (31.6 percent) disagreeing to 8/19 (42.1 percent) agreeing and 3/19 (15.8 percent) strongly agreeing. Gender disparity was also evident in the responses to the suggestion that boys should have more opportunities for school than girls. The proportion of men disagreeing or strongly disagreeing (24/31 = 77.5 percent total: 6/31 = 19.4 percent strongly disagreeing, 18/31 = 58.1 percent disagreeing) was significantly lower than among women respondents (17/19 = 89.5 percent total: 4/19 = 21.1 percent strongly disagreeing, 13/19 = 68.4 percent disagreeing), while more than twice the proportion of men (7/31 = 22.6 percent) than women (2/19 = 10.5 percent) agreed that boys should be favored in educational opportunity. These important gender differences aside, however, the *getihu* surveyed indicated strong support generally for the ideals of equality.

Yet this support for equality was qualified by responses indicating doubts as to whether these ideals were realized in fact. While a sub-

---

46. These results appear consistent with the views supporting ideals of equality discussed in Godwin C. Chu and Yanan Ju, *The Great Wall in Ruins: Communication and Cultural Change in China* (Albany: State University of New York Press, 1993), 239ff.

stantial majority of the *getihu* surveyed (37/50, 74 percent) agreed or strongly agreed with the suggestion that they have the same rights as wealthier people, these proportions were substantially lower than those in the general Jingan population, where 132/154 (85.7 percent) agreed or strongly agreed that they had the same rights as wealthier people. The *getihu* surveyed also appeared to have a clear appreciation of the substantive inequality in political relations. Only a minority of the *getihu* respondents (16/50, 32 percent) agreed that government officials are no different from ordinary people, while a majority (32/50, 64 percent) agreed that government officials were either more competent than ordinary people or required special treatment. Fully 20 percent of the *getihu* surveyed could not agree with the proposition that government officials were the same as common people. These views were compounded by doubts about whether the government officials must comply with legal requirements. In response to a question suggesting that government officials do not need as much as ordinary people to obey the law (*bu bi . . . zunshou fagui*), the proportion of *getihu* respondents disagreeing (34/50, 68 percent) was far lower than in the responses from the general Jingan population surveyed (150/154, 97 percent).

Two general trends appear from these data concerning *getihu* ideas about equality. First there was substantial support for the ideal of social equality, such that people were seen as equal regardless of political, social, or gender status. These views are broadly consistent with official doctrinal tenets of social equality and equality of legal treatment that stems from it. On the other hand there were significant indicators that the *getihu*, even more so than the general population, doubt whether these ideals of social equality are realized in practice, particularly in the political realm. The *getihu* respondents seem well aware of the real inequalities that surround them. Their expressed attitudes reflect agreement with the ideals embodied in the regime's official doctrines on equality but seem as well to demand a higher standard of performance than is currently in evidence.

Justice

Official Norms. Driven in part by state-centric notions of political inequality, but also influenced by ideas about legal equality, official doctrines about justice have tended to concentrate rather rigidly on compliance with legal rules. In the area of economic regulation, for example, judicial decisions have devoted great attention to formal rules and procedures with less regard for substantive fairness.[47] These conceptions of justice have been particularly acute in the context of political conflict, where compliance with law and regulation aimed at entrenching state power is the critical determinant.[48] Thus, doctrinal ideas about justice in post-Mao China have emphasized rigid interpretation and enforcement of law and policy in ways that support doctrinal presumptions about legal equality and political inequality. Relationships within society are considered just if they are in compliance with formal law, while substantive conditions and consequences are given less weight.

Getihu **Responses**. Responses to the questionnaire suggest that the *getihu* notions of justice derive in part from views about social equality. Particularly in the area of institutional behavior, justice was linked closely with ideas about equal treatment and procedural regularity. For example, in response to a question about fairness in governmental decisionmaking, the majority of *getihu* respondents focused on equality of application (59 percent) and adherence to formal procedure (34 percent) over issues about taking account of subjective circumstances

---

47. See "Mou xian shuini chang su mou diqu wujiaju an" (A Case Involving a Suit by a Certain County Cement Factory Against a Certain District Price Bureau," in *Zhong wai xingzheng anli xuanping*, ed. Ying Songnian and Hu Jiansen (Beijing: Politics and Law University Press, 1989), 133–137, where the court upheld penalties against a cement factory for violation of a price control regulation, despite the fact that the applicable regulation had been widely ignored and was to be retracted less than a year later. In another case, a court reviewing the validity of certain pricing arrangements focused mainly on the formal authority of the individuals involved rather than whether any substantive harm resulted from the pricing arrangements themselves. See "Mou fuzhuangchang bu fu Gong Shang wujia chufa an" (A Case Involving a Certain Clothing Factory Refusing to Comply With a Penalty Levied by the Price Penalty Imposed by the State Administration for Industry and Commerce), in *Xingzheng susong anli xuanbian*, ed. Gan Yusheng, Qiu Shi, and Yang Kaimin (Beijing: Chinese Economy Press, 1990), 203–204. Similarly, in a case involving findings by the State Administration for Industry and Commerce (SAIC) that private enterprises were engaging in illegal speculation (*tou ji dao ba*), the court focused on whether the SAIC had applied the proper regulations and declined to address whether the SAIC's intrusion in private business activities was fair or arbitrary. See, e.g., "Mou zhibu chang tou ji dao ba an" (A Speculation Case Involving a Certain Weaving Factory), in *Xingzheng susong anli xuanbian*, 173–77, 181–83.

48. For example, the trial of "Lin Biao-Jiang Qing clique" was deemed just simply because formal procedures were used, despite the existence of substantive biases against the defendants. See *A Great Trial in Chinese History* (Beijing: New World Press, 1981), 1–11, in which Fei Xiaotong concludes that the defendants received a just trial despite the fact that several of the judges, including Fei himself, had been persecuted by the defendants.

(7 percent). These were slightly at variance from the views of the general Jingan population surveyed, which gave significantly more weight to fairness based on subjective attention to circumstances (11 percent) and less to equality of application (55.5 percent). Similarly, in response to a question about fairness in judicial decisions, the majority of *getihu* respondents (66 percent) deemed fairness to depend on adherence to legal procedure and only 6 percent were concerned with whether the parties were satisfied. Respondents from the general Jingan population gave slightly less attention (63 percent) to the role of legal procedure in judicial fairness.

Despite these notions of justice as bound up with equality and procedural rigor, significant minority proportions of *getihu* respondents suggested that the operation of law ought to take into account the character of its subjects. The Chinese traditional norm of rewarding the good and punishing the bad was the focus of a substantial minority of *getihu* respondents (28 percent) in deciding whether a court judgment is fair. This approach was also evident in responses about law and virtue: In response to the suggestion that law should favor virtuous people, 19/50 (38 percent) indicated agreement. This percentage contrasted with the results of the Jingan general population survey in which only 27 percent agreed that the law should favor the virtuous, and suggested that the *getihu* surveyed take a somewhat subjective approach to determinations of justice.

The *getihu* respondents appeared to support notions about formal equality in the enforcement of legal rules. A clear majority (39/50, 78 percent) of the *getihu* surveyed agreed that people should not get special protection from the law. In response to a question about obedience to law, a significant majority (31/50, 62 percent) indicated that obedience should be without exception, even if the law is unjust or compliance harms a family relation or friend. Similarly there was significant agreement (32/50, 64 percent) that lawbreakers should be punished without exception, even if the law is unclear or unjust or there is a good reason for breaking the law. These responses paralleled those from the general population survey in Jingan, and suggested a willingness to accord broad authority to the enforcement of law.

On the other hand, when it came to government rules, the proportion of *getihu* respondents (38/50, 76 percent) who agreed with the proposition that people should obey government rules even if they disagreed with them was a far lower proportion than that derived from the general Jingan population survey (132 of 154 respondents agreed or strongly agreed with the proposition). While the majority of *getihu* respondents acceded to the authority of government rules,[49] the dispar-

---

49. See discussion of submission to authority in Chu and Ju, *The Great Wall in Ruins*, 233ff.

ity of views between *getihu* and general populace respondents suggests that the *getihu* distinguish more readily between "law" and "government rules" as legitimate sources of authority. Possibly reflecting their experience with the vagaries of bureaucratic regulators, the *getihu* surveyed seemed significantly less willing than the general population surveyed to take government rules at face value. Despite being well aware of the inequality in their relationships with officialdom, the Jingan *getihu* are not quite prepared to accept the regulatory products of such inequality as just. As economic actors routinely subjected to the whims of government officials, the *getihu* may have a more refined sense of the skepticism over the authority and behavior of the regulatory bureaucracy.

Such skepticism among the *getihu* respondents was also evident in expressions of uncertainty about the effect of law on behavior. Indeed, in response to the suggestion that in fact law does favor virtuous people, 26/50 (52 percent) of the *getihu* respondents disagreed but 21 (42 percent) agreed. *Getihu* responses to the suggestion that people make more of a difference than laws and rules were also mixed, as 22/50 disagreed and 20/50 agreed. This degree of uncertainty is underscored when contrasted with the survey results of the general Jingan population, whose certainty in the effect of laws and rules was indicated by their significant (63.4 percent) disagreement with the proposition that people make more of a difference than law. Doubts about the effectiveness of law were also evident in *getihu* responses to propositions concerning the motivators for people doing what is right, where a higher degree of certainty was accorded to the notion that the impetus comes from moral principles (72 percent) than law (68 percent).

On the other hand, law was not seen by the *getihu* respondents as completely without effect. In response to a suggestion that, if they had a friend in the government they need not worry about laws and regulations, the vast majority (45/50, 90 percent) either disagreed or strongly disagreed, a pattern repeated in the general Jingan population surveyed. This response suggests a view that the potential effect of law cannot be discounted, while implying a somewhat less than benign view of the potential application of law despite the availability of friendly bureaucratic intervenors. While law was not always seen as a determinant of behavior or as an assurance of justice, there remained a residual apprehension about the ongoing prospects for imposed legal sanctions.

Enforcement of Private Law Relations

Official Norms. Doctrine on private law relations reflects official ideas about equality and justice. In a reversal of Maoist policies, the economic reform policies enacted beginning in 1978 granted enterprises greater autonomy in decisionmaking and permitted increased diversity of economic actors and transactions.[50] Thus both the Economic Contract Law (ECL) and the General Principles of Civil Law (GPCL) supported expanding private property and contract relations by focusing on transactions conducted outside the confines of the state plan.[51] Although both the ECL and the GPCL require that private commercial transactions not conflict with state policies,[52] in the context of the market reform policies, private business activities were still permitted within quite broad parameters.

Reflecting doctrinal norms of justice as legal formalism, doctrine on enforcement of private law relations has given increased attention to formal procedures and institutions for dispute resolution.[53] Revisions to the Civil Procedure Law, for example, diluted long-standing provisions on mediation of civil disputes.[54] Legal formalism has also been

---

50. See generally, He Guanghui, "Continue to Deepen Reform by Centering on Economic Improvement and Rectification," *Zhongguo jingji tizhi gaige* (Reform of the Chinese Economic Structure), no. 2 (1990), translated in *FBIS Daily Report: China* (March 23, 1990): 21.

51. See Economic Contract Law of the PRC, Articles 2 and 5; and General Principles of Civil Law, Chapters 2 and 3 and Article 54. Also see Edward Epstein, "Tortious Liability for Defective Products in the People's Republic of China," *Journal of Chinese Law* 2 (1988): 285; Henry R. Zheng, *China's Civil and Commercial Law* (Singapore: Butterworth's Asia, 1988), 45ff.; and Pitman B. Potter, *The Economic Contract Law of China: Legitimation and Contract Autonomy in the PRC* (Seattle: University of Washington Press, 1992).

52. See Economic Contract Law of the PRC, Articles 1, 4, and 7; and General Principles of Civil Law, Article 6. Originally this principle extended to conflicts with the state plan, but references to the plan have been dropped of late in the course of accelerated reform. See "Final Version of 14th CPC National Congress Report,"*FBIS Daily Report-China* (October 21, 1992): 1–21, at 8; and "Decision of the CPC Central Committee on Issues Concerning the Establishment of a Socialist Market Economic Structure" (November 14, 1993), *China Economic News, 1993*, supplement no. 12 (November 29, 1993): 6–9. In keeping with these changes, the revised text of the Economic Contract Law issued in 1993 deleted references to state planning and replaced them with references to state policies. See Economic Contract Law of the PRC (1993).

53. See Gu Ming, "Guanyu 'Zhonghua renmin gongheguo jingji hetong fa caoan' de shuoming" (Explanation of the 'Draft Economic Contract Law of the PRC'), *Zhongguo fazhi bao* (Chinese Legal System Gazette), 13 (December 1981): 4. Also see "Zuigao renmin fayuan guanyu shenli jingji jiufen anjian juti shiyong 'Minshi susong fa (shixing)' de ruogan wenti de jieda" (Responses to Questions by the Supreme People's Court Concerning Several Issues in the Specific Use of the '(Draft) Civil Procedure Law' in Handling Economic Disputes) (July 21, 1987), in *Hetong fagui yu hetong shiyang huibian*, ed. Zhang Shouqiang (Harbin: Heilongjiang Science and Technology Press, 1988), 959–60.

54. See "Zhonghua renmin gongheguo minshi susong faw (Civil Procedure

evident in official doctrine on enforceability, which requires first that the requirements for formation be satisfied (including establishing the requisite capacity and authority of the parties).[55] Where performance is necessary to achieve policy goals (such as state plan requirements), specific performance may be ordered in addition to remedies of compensation and/or penalty payments.[56] Changes in the state plan may result in unenforceability of contracts, but parties whose non-performance results from mandated changes in state plan may still be required to bear liability.[57]

On the other hand, official doctrine permits significant flexibility in the granting of remedies where the interests of the state are not directly involved. Thus, courts have tried to minimize the size of private damage awards in an effort to control economic losses.[58] Courts have been

---

Law of the PRC), Chapter 8 in *Zhonghua renmin gongheguo xin fa gui huibian* (Compilation of New Laws and Regulations of the PRC) (Beijing: Law Publishers, 1991), vol. 2, 22.

55. See "Shourangfang jieshou jishu fuzhu shishi, bu dei chaoyue ziji jing Gong Shang Xingzheng Guanli Bumen hezhun dengji de shengchan jingying fanwei" (The Transferee Receives Technical Input, and Should Not Overstep Its Own Registered Scope of Production Management Received through Examination and Ratification by the Industrial and Commercial Administration Departments), in *Jingji fa anli xuan xi* (Compilation and Analysis of Economic Law Cases) ed. Dan You (Beijing: Law Publishers, 1990), 236, where the court held invalid a contract that was deemed to be outside the registered scope of business of one of the parties. Formalistic approaches to enforcement that focus on capacity also reinforce doctrinal requirements that obligations not conflict with state policies. See Economic Contract Law of the PRC, Articles 4 and 7, and General Principles of Civil Law of the PRC, Articles 55 and 58.

56. See Economic Contract Law, Article 35. Also see "Zui gao renmin fayuan guanyu guanche 'Jingji hetong fa' ruogan wenti de yijian," in *Hetong fagui yu hetong shiyang huibian*, ed. Zhang Shouqiang (Harbin: Heilongjiang Science and Technology Press, 1988), 934–941.

57. See Economic Contract Law, Article 27(b). Also see "Tantan dui jingji hetong jiufen anjian de shenli" (Discussion of Adjudication of Cases of Economic Contract Disputes), *Faxue zazhi* (Legal Studies Magazine), no. 6 (1982): 39; "Shanghai gangjichang peikuan er shi wan" (The Shanghai Harbour Machinery Factory Pays Indemnity of 200,000), *Jiefang ribao* (Liberation Daily), 4 March 1983, 1; and "Jingji anjian zhong de lushi huodong" (The Activities of Lawyers in Economic Cases), *Faxue yanjiu* (Studies in Law), no. 2 (1983): 44.

58. For example, in a case involving an automobile sales contract, the court held that the seller lacked legal capacity and imposed liability on two enterprises with which the contract seller was amalgamated in order to avoid losses to the purchaser. See "Faren chengli bixu fu hefa guiding de tiaojian" (The Creation of the Juridical Person Must Comply with the Conditions of Lawful Regulations), in *Shiyong anli shouce*, ed. Wang Suiqi, Liu Zhongya, Li Wanqin, Li Fengqin, Li Baoyue, Xiao Shengxi (Beijing: China Youth Press, 1990), 20–22. This decision was seen as preferable to declaring the contract void, as had been done under other circumstances where a party lacked proper capacity. See

willing to impose contract changes where strict enforcement of contract provisions would have resulted in severe losses to one of the contract parties.[59] Chinese courts have also emphasized the duty to mitigate damages resulting from non-performance, even where primary liability lay with the non-performing party,[60] or in cases of mistake.[61]

Getihu Responses. Responses of *getihu* operators to questions about enforcement of private law relations revealed the extent to which respondents had concerns over the enforcement of agreements through the formal legal system. Thus, the respondents appeared to remain wedded to informal mechanisms. On the matter of debt, the *getihu* respondents appeared to express a broader mix of human and institutional reasons for performance of obligations. In response to questions concerning enforcement of a loan agreement, the most common response (50 percent) to the debtor's refusal to pay was to seek a mutual friend to remind the debtor to perform. When asked under what circumstances would they go to court to enforce the loan agreement, the most common response (19/50) was that judicial action would be sought only after a mutual friend or family member had tried and failed to persuade the debtor to perform. The preference for this response over the one indicating that a suit would be filed only after the respondent had personally failed to persuade the debtor to perform suggests a lingering willingness to continue to use intervenors to resolve disputes before resorting to formal action.

"Gai faren meiyou zuzhuang he xiaoshou qiche de quanli nengli" (This Juridical Person Lacked the Authority and Capacity to Assemble and Sell Automobiles), in *Shiyong anli shouce*, 22–24.

59. See, e.g., "Nanjing shi jiangpu xian gongcheng suliao chang yu ben chang chengxing chejian chengbao hetong jiufen" (The Dispute Between the Engineering Plastics Factory of Jiangpu County in Nanjing Municipality and the Factory's Mould Shop Over a Responsibility Contract), *Zhonghua renmin gongheguo zui gao renmin fayuan gongbao* (PRC Supreme People's Court Reports), no. 1 (1985): 27–29.

60. See, e.g., "300 wan yuan ju'e susong an de shenli" (The Handling of a 3,000,000 Yuan Lawsuit), in *Shiyong anli shouce*, 142–147; and "Jiagong bianyaqi jufu jiakuan, ding zuofang yifa chang fu weiyuejin" (Upon the Manufacture of Transformers There Is a Refusal to Pay the Cost, Set the Penalty Payment to Be Made as Lawful Compensate by the Person Who Did So), in *Shiyong anli shouce*, 50–152.

61. See, e.g., "Bu dang de li yinggai tuihuan" (Unjust Enrichment Should Be Returned), in *Shiyong anli shouce*, 103–105; and "Yinhang dui qi gongzuo renyuan yin guocuo zaocheng ta ren sunhai ying chengdan minshi zeren" (The Bank Should Bear Liability for Harm to a Third Person Caused by Mistake by Its Employee) in *Shiyong anli shouce*, 127–28.

Yet there were also indications of increased support for the role of formal judicial mechanisms in dispute resolution. For example, a sizeable minority (41 percent) of the *getihu* respondents indicated they would ask a lawyer to arrange matters in the case of non-payment of the loan. While respondents from the general Jingan population respondents indicated similar views (38 percent indicated a willingness to seek a lawyer), when asked about the possibility of court action, nearly twice the proportion from the general Jingan populace indicated a strict aversion to litigation. Thus, there was evident an emerging willingness among the *getihu* respondents to use judicial institutions, its still embryonic nature explained perhaps by the fact that only six of the respondents had any actual experience with actual disputes, and these all concerned housing-related matters. Yet even of these, one had actually gone to court. Thus, the experience of the respondents with resolving disputes through friends and family contracts or through the work unit undoubtedly informed their responses yet also permitted an emerging capacity to view formal judicial institutions as a possible albeit untried mechanism for resolving disputes.

Summary

Attitudes expressed by the Jingan *getihu* about official norms of socialist legalism suggest that the regime may be unable to control the norms and ideologies of market actors. Respondent views about equality imposed a higher standard of substantive equality than is evident in the regime's formalistic doctrine. Similarly, support for justice as procedural fairness may hold official norms of formal justice to a more rigorous standard. As well, doubts emerged as to the prospects of realizing the ideals of equality and justice in practice. And while there was nascent support for formal dispute resolution, the general preferences for informal mechanisms serve as a counterpoint to regime norms requiring continued state control over the judiciary.

The responses of the Jingan *getihu* to regime doctrines of legal reform suggest the emergence of an "alienated legal culture" which stands in tension with the norms and institutions of the socialist legal system. Rather than uncritically subscribing to ideals and practices that are intended to perpetuate the state's hegemony, the respondents to this survey stand apart, cautiously using what is made available to them for their own purposes but not fully subscribing to the underlying norms or institutional arrangements. This finding has important implications for the efficacy of the regime's norms and institutions in preserving its hegemonic position, for the state is challenged by these private imaginings of ideals for social and economic relations that go well beyond the suggestions of formalized doctrines.

Conclusion

The link between market liberalization policies and democratization would appear to require the commitment of the state to withdraw from hegemony in social, economic, and political affairs. While China's economic reform policies have given considerable attention to market-oriented practices, the state's commitment to withdraw from hegemony does not appear strong—at least as far as the socialist legal system is concerned. Instead, the norms and institutions of the socialist legal system suggest that the regime is determined to retain a dominant role.

On the other hand, the small-scale business operators who are potential consumers of the legal rules and institutions established to support economic reform are significantly alienated from the system. Their normative standards of equality and justice appear more demanding of the regime than are the official norms. And they remain somewhat ambivalent about the implementation of the regime's norms and institutions, either in the abstract or in the specific context of enforcement of private law relations. Under circumstances where overt public challenges to regime norms remain unacceptable and dangerous, it is unlikely that the alienated legal culture of the *getihu* will find open expression. However, as the economic reform policies continue to create new sets of interests and as legal reforms begin to offer the prospect of realizing these interests, these important economic actors may yet elect to become legal actors and even political actors urging greater accommodation by the state.[62]

The disparity between official norms and the views of small-scale business operators presents a significant challenge to the Chinese regime to manage normative conflicts with market actors upon whom the regime's economic reform policies depend. Whether the Chinese regime will choose to co-opt market actors through greater concessions to popular norms of equality and justice, and by providing more effective institutions for enforcement of private law relations, remains to be seen. The state may opt for a path of coercion in an effort to compel compliance with its official norms. In any event, the existing normative

---

62. For a discussion of dispute resolution in Taiwan that reaches similar conclusions, see Michael J. Moser, *Law and Social Change in a Chinese Community: A Case Study from Rural Taiwan* (New York: Oceana, 1982).

and institutional supports for state hegemony in the socialist legal system suggest that the emergence of civil society or even the prospect of democratization must await a commitment from the state to accommodate popular norms and to permit institutions of civil society to emerge. As yet such a commitment seems a distant prospect indeed.

7

The Civil Society and Democratization in Mexico

Juan D. Lindau

O ver the last decade, scholars, social commentators, and pundits have argued that a civil society has emerged in Mexico. The civil society is defined here as the presence of independent associations that act on matters of concern to the state. Because of its association with political change and democratization, the notion of an awakened civil society has acquired almost mythic proportions. Opponents of the regime constantly refer and appeal to the civil society. Scholars have also focused on this issue, chronicling independent groups and movements and documenting the expansion in the number of organizations. These studies typically conclude that the presence of independent associations reveals the genesis of a civic culture and a more participatory population.[1]

In contrast, this chapter argues that these groups have less influence than is commonly supposed. The overwhelming majority of these associations have parochial concerns, frequently conflicting agendas, and relatively small memberships. For these reasons, despite their number, they remain divorced from the lives of most Mexicans. The eventual development of a more generalized civil society in Mexico is more likely to be a consequence, rather than a cause, of the democratization of the polity.

---

1. Notable examples of such studies include Carlos Monsivais's elegant essays on social groups, especially *Entrada libre: cronicas de la sociedad que se organiza* (México D.F.: Era, 1987). In addition, a particularly good collection containing several essays on the subject is *México el reclamo democrático*, ed. Rolando Cordera Campos, Raul Trejo Delarbre, and Juan Enrique Vega (México D.F.: Siglo Veintiuno Editores, 1988).

Over the last decade, the literature on the civil society in Mexico has largely failed to examine the continuing presence or absence, in strong or weak form, of the factors that acted against the growth of a civil society. If the civil society is a product, as many think, of economic modernization and greater modernity, it still confronts powerful "premodern" features of Mexican culture, society, and polity. As Octavio Paz wrote: "Most of our profound attitudes to love, death, friendship, food and festivals are not modern. Nor are our public morality, our family life, the cult of the Virgin, or our image of the president."[2]

This article examines these premodern factors and twentieth-century developments that militated against the emergence of a civil society. It also analyzes their contemporary reach and influence. The social and cultural nature of many of these factors requires a discussion of "Mexicanness," always a controversial task, given the danger of stereotype and cultural determinism. In addition, gross cultural and social generalizations miss and in fact disguise the presence of cultural differences and subcultures. Not surprisingly, relatively few authors have attempted this task. Notable Mexicans among them have included Samuel Ramos, Jose Vasconcelos, Antonio Caso, and Octavio Paz. Octavio Paz's work on the subject, because it was the most critical, has also been the most controversial, although it remains the most penetrating analysis of Mexicanness.[3]

While powerful social and cultural continuities persist in Mexico, these cultural and social arrangements are not static, determinative, or all-encompassing. The power of social arrangements and preferences and the commitment and preservation of cultural norms vary across any society. At the same time, cultural and social change is not seamless. Instead, it is a highly disjunctive process, transforming some portions of society, modifying others, and leaving many sectors largely untouched. More generally, socioeconomic, regional, urban-rural, and modern-traditional cleavages dividing Mexico increase the disjunctiveness of change.[4]

---

2. Octavio Paz, "The Philanthropic Ogre," in *The Labyrinth of Solitude and Other Writings* (New York: Grove Weidenfeld, 1985), 379–98, quote at 397.

3. Samuel Ramos, "Motivos para una investigacion del mexicano," *Examen* 1 (August 1932): 7–11, and *El perfil del hombre y la cultura en Mexico* (México D.F.: Imprenta Mundial, 1934); Jose Vasconcelos, *La raza cosmica* (Barcelona: Agencia Mundial de Libreria, 1925); Antonio Caso, *Obras completas*, 8 vols. (México D.F.: Universidad Nacional Autónoma de México, 1971–75); and Octavio Paz, "The Labyrinth of Solitude," in *The Labyrinth of Solitude and Other Writings*, 9–212.

4. The problems that these factors have posed for survey research are cogently analyzed in Ann L. Craig and Wayne A. Cornelius, "Political Culture in Mexico Continuities and Revisionist Interpretations," in *The Civic Culture Revisited*, ed. Gabriel A. Almond and Sidney Verba (Newberry Park, Calif.:

The extraordinarily contemporary nature of the subject enhances the difficulty of analysis. Given the immediacy of events, it is hard to separate surface from substance and to discern the durability and depth of apparent changes. This problem of perspective is especially acute in a polity where significant transformations are occurring. It is especially easy to underestimate the power and force of elements of continuity in the midst of change.

Definitions of the Civil Society

Historically, the concept of civil society has been broadly and variously defined in Western political thought. As Adam Seligman writes: "Originally posited in the eighteenth century as referring to the realm of social mutuality, in the nineteenth century it was used to characterize that aspect of social existence which existed beyond the realm of the State."[5] Andrew Arato notes this same transformation, writing that "differentiating what from the Greeks to the eighteenth century has been considered one, the political and the social dimensions that are united both in *politike koinonia* and *societas civilis*, the constitutive political symbolism of Western modernity, with important national and chronological differences, has been *institutionalized* as the duality of (political) state and civil society."[6]

This state-civil society duality became especially salient in the twentieth century with the vast expansion in the role and functions of the state. As Arato writes about western Europe, "the constitution of the state-civil society duality would have been unthinkable without the generating activity of the state, 'from above.' "[7] Through this generative activity, the state sought to mold portions of the polity— enormously increasing the power of the central government. In many cases, it effectively acquired virtual hegemony over the public sphere,

---

Sage Publications, 1989), 325–93. The depth of these differences has led scholars to argue that the country is composed of a variety of different Mexicos. Commonly, traditional rural Mexico is referred to as *"el México profundo"* (the deep Mexico) to distinguish it from modern, westernized urban Mexico. Another example of these views can be found in Jaime Castrejon Diez, *La política segun los mexicanos* (México D.F.: Oceano, 1995). He divides Mexico into a "primitive civilization," a "traditional civilization," a "modern civilization," and a "postmodern civilization" (89–94). These divisions correspond to the ethnic, regional, urban-rural, and class differences marking the country.

5. Adam Seligman, *The Idea of Civil Society* (New York: The Free Press, 1992).
6. Andrew Arato, *From Neo-Marxism to Democratic Theory* (Armonk, N.Y.: M. E. Sharpe, 1993), 173.
7. Ibid., 174.

absorbing or marginalizing other actors. By extension, the civil society is usually conceptualized as the presence of free associations, created at the grassroots level and existing independently of the state. Virtually all of the literature on Mexico reflects this view of the civil society. The mere presence of free associations, however, reveals nothing about their reach, depth, influence, and scope. While such groups can dot the political landscape, they may play a fairly small role in policy formulation and only aggregate a relatively small portion of the population. Under these conditions, independent associations may only be the first indication of a potential civil society.

The Civil Society and Democracy

Against the backdrop of an interventionist, generative state, the emergence of a civil society became a necessary condition for democratization. The generative activity of the state in some cases preempted or replaced independent associational activity. The associations, created "from above" by the state, often became the means to channel, control, and manage different groups and interests. Rather than checking and reducing the state's power, these associations enhanced the already overwhelming majesty of regimes. This enhancement had an enervating effect on political participation and reduced liberty because the individual lacked the organizational means to resist governmental power. A civil society reclaimed politics from the state and simultaneously reflected and encouraged increased political participation.

An apt example of these views can be found in *The Civic Culture* by Gabriel Almond and Sidney Verba. They write:

> Voluntary associations are the prime means by which the function of mediating between the individual and the state is performed. Through them the individual is able to relate himself effectively and meaningfully to the political system. These associations help him avoid the dilemma of being either a parochial, cut off from political influence, or an isolated and powerless individual, manipulated and mobilized by the mass institutions of politics and government. . . . If the citizen is a member of some voluntary organizations, he is involved in the broader social world but is less dependent upon and controlled by his political system. The association of which he is a member can represent his needs and demands before the government. It can make the government more chary of engaging in activities that would harm the individual.[8]

---

8. Gabriel Almond, and Sidney Verba, *The Civic Culture* (Boston: Little Brown and Co., 1965), 245.

Democratization can be carried out from above, involving a gradual opening and distension of the political arena as happened in Brazil during the 1970s and 1980s. It can also be marked by the internal reform of political institutions and practices, also carried out frequently from above. Change, however, can also be impelled from below. The difficulty of reforming ruling institutions and elite resistance often lead the advocates of democratization to see a remedy in grassroots changes, especially the emergence of a civil society.[9]

Critics of the Mexican regime initially pressed for change from above, focusing their demands on the reform of the ruling party and the establishment of other democratic procedures. Over time, however, especially by the late 1980s, a growing number of intellectuals and critics had come to see the ruling party (the PRI, Party of the Institutionalized Revolution) itself as an obsolete dinosaur. Their hope for democratization increasingly came to rest on change from below through the development of a civil society. More recent years have cemented these views. While substantial reforms have steadily democratized and opened up the electoral arena beginning with the presidential elections in 1994 and the mid-term elections in 1997, many other portions of the polity have retained both their institutional character and authoritarian features. The difficulty of reforming these institutions, including the ruling party and the executive and judicial branches, to mention just a few examples, has raised the saliency of grassroots change.

The Genesis of the Civil Society in Mexico

The literature on the civil society in Mexico was largely born after the 1985 earthquake which devastated Mexico City. The earthquake's massive destruction virtually paralyzed President Miguel de la Madrid's government (1982–88). Transfixed by the magnitude of the calamity, the government responded to the catastrophe in an extraordinarily disorganized and limited fashion, largely failing to mount an organized search for survivors in the damaged buildings or provide relief services for the tens of thousands of people left homeless by the earthquake.

In contrast, the population responded to the earthquake in a massive, spontaneous, and unprecedented civic fashion. Residents of affected areas of the city, as well as those outside these zones, organized themselves into rescue battalions, searching for survivors in the rubble of buildings, and providing food, water, clothing, and medicine to

---

9. Arato, *From Neo-Marxism*, 176–77.

those who had lost their homes. Given Mexico's long patrimonial, patriarchal tradition, in which citizen inactivity has been accompanied by the expectation of state action and remedies, this civic response was both startling and novel.

Despite this, evidence of the earthquake's longer-term influence on the creation of a civil society is at best ambiguous. In the earthquake's aftermath the government's inability to provide shelter to the thousands who had lost their homes led these same people to form an association seeking the resolution of housing shortages. The rise of this organization was part of a larger growth and expansion of urban popular movements pressing for the extension of a variety of services.[10] Other groups, notably a union of seamstresses whose workplaces were destroyed by the earthquake, also appeared during this period. These highly visible and vocal organizations, joined to citizen behavior during the earthquake, seemed to provide a clear indication of the emergence of a civil society. Many scholars interpreted this behavior as a profound sign that Mexican civic culture had changed dramatically and that the anomic lack of engagement in public matters had been replaced by voluntarism and participation. This transformation, in turn, was widely seen as one of the most important harbingers of democracy.[11] On the other hand, as Javier Elguea notes, in a study based on three hundred interviews with earthquake volunteers, "the dimensions of the aid movement were exaggerated . . . and the movement lacked the political characteristics attributed to it. . . . The most commonplace conjecture . . . [that the] aid movement was a manifestation of political participation . . . [is supported] by little empirical evidence."[12]

Both the movements spawned by the earthquake and citizen behav-

10. Paul Lawrence Haber, "El arte de la reestructuración y sus implicaciones politicas: el caso de los movimientos urbanos populares," in *Las dimensiones politicas de la reestructuración economica*, ed. Maria Lorena Cook, Kevin J. Middlebrook, and Juan Molinar Horcasitas (México D.F.: Cal y Arena, 1996), 337.

11. See, for example, Alvaro Arreola, Jose Georgette, Matilde Luna, and Ricardo Tirado, "Memoria de los primeros ocho dias," *Revista Mexicana de Sociologia* XLVIII, no. 2 (1986). Articles published on the subject in magazines by prominent Mexican intellectuals include Octavio Paz, "Escombros y semillas," *Vuelta* 9, no. 180 (1985): 8–10; Enrique Krauze, "Revelaciones entre ruinas," *Vuelta* 9, no. 180 (1985): 11–14. This view has also been echoed in more recent works. See, for example, Federico Reyes Heroles, *Sondear a México* (México D.F.: Oceano, 1995), 195; and Haber, "El arte de la reestructuración y sus implicaciones politicas: el caso de los movimientos urbanos populares," 333–70.

12. Javier Elguea, "Los sismos de 1985 y el comportamiento de ayuda entre los mexicanos: mitos y realidades," in *México Auge, Crisis y Ajuste*, ed. Carlos Bazdresch, Nisso Bucay, Nora Lustig, and Soledad Loaeza (México D.F.: Fondo de Cultura Economica, 1992), 151–66, quote at 155.

ior during the calamity fueled myths and assumptions about an awakening civil society and led scholars and social commentators to examine other grassroots civic associations. Since the early 1980s the number of these groups rose from a few hundred to over 1,300 by the mid-1990s, according to the government's Directory of Civic Associations. In fact, however, because many groups are not registered, the total number of civic associations may exceed 5,000.[13] The greatest share of these organizations, not surprisingly, are concentrated in Mexico City, the most modern area of the country.

Rural areas and smaller provincial cities, by comparison, typically contain fewer, smaller, and more weakly organized independent groups and associations. By extension, these groups are often much less articulate and effective than their counterparts in major urban areas. In addition to their isolation and the generally less politically active nature of Mexico's rural population, independent organizations have been hampered by the government's much greater willingness to use repression in the countryside. While important independent peasant and indigenous groups exist in a number of rural areas, notably in Oaxaca and more recently in the state of Chiapas, they remain the exception rather than the rule.

The most dramatic growth in independent associational activity has occurred in issue areas, including the environment. Although Mexico's first environmental laws date from the early 1970s, the issue did not receive much government attention or spawn much associational activity until the early 1980s. Since then, however, the extraordinary degradation of Mexico's environment, epitomized most dramatically by the terrible conditions prevailing in Mexico City, has galvanized the creation of literally hundreds of environmental groups around the country. The most notable are the Movimiento Ecologista Mexicano (Mexican Ecologist Movement, MEM), and the Group of 100, named after one hundred prominent intellectuals and led by the poet Homero Aridjis. There are also small local environmental associations in a substantial number of the country's provincial cities and towns. International environmental organizations like the World Wildlife Fund have also established a presence in the country and a Green Party exists. Most environmental activism, however, has focused on local issues and on seeking larger remedies from the executive branch. Environmental issues still play a relatively minor role in political campaigns, including the 1994 and 1997 elections, and are rarely discussed by the major political parties.

---

13. Andrés Oppenheimer, *Bordering on Chaos* (Boston: Little, Brown & Co., 1996), 170–71.

Associational activity has also grown dramatically in the human rights area. These groups, led by lawyers and community activists, have sought to document and restrain the river of judicial abuses, including illegal detention, torture, extrajudicial killings, and disappearances that routinely occur throughout Mexico. On occasion, notably in the case of Norma Corona, a lawyer and human rights activist who was assassinated for her activities by the Federal Judicial Police in the state of Sinaloa in 1990, these activists have lost their lives.

Independent organizations have also arisen in the last few years to press for clean elections. These organizations monitor elections as poll watchers and independent observers trying to prevent fraud. The most important of these groups is Alianza Civica (Civic Alliance), an umbrella organization that has coordinated the activities of independent observers during the recent elections. Alianza Civica, which aggregates more than four hundred small groups scattered around the country, placed independent observers at 5,000 of the country's 96,415 polling places in the 1994 elections. It also played an important role in monitoring the 1997 elections.

Associations have also arisen around the abortion issue, although much less dramatically than in the United States. Pro-life groups include Pro Vida (Pro Life), and there are a number of pro-choice organizations. All of these groups, however, are far smaller, less active, and less influential than quasi-independent population control associations (such as MexFam) which stress contraception over abortion. Because these latter groups reflect government policy, they enjoy substantially more support than groups lined up on either side of the abortion question. Indeed, abortion is still an almost completely dormant political issue. Despite the extent of population pressure in Mexico, the legalization of abortion remains unlikely given the power of the Catholic Church and the influence of Opus Dei among the business community and portions of the political elite. On the other hand, especially in southwestern Mexico, there has been substantial growth in independent religious organizations. In particular, a plethora of community organizing efforts have been produced by the dramatic spread of evangelical Protestantism.

Independent labor unions, long a feature of the political landscape, continue to appear. These unions, however, have always played a fairly insignificant role in the labor movement, given the power and reach of the official trade unions linked to the ruling party. Independent unions have an important presence in certain industries and have aggregated and articulated the interests of workers who were not part of the official labor movement. However, despite the relatively large number of these organizations, their influence remains fairly confined. The official labor unions, because of patronage and government support, although they are weakening, have an important organizational advantage. More important, the extreme looseness of Mexico's labor market, especially in unskilled trades, joined to the activities of the government and employers, impedes the ability of all unions to establish a more important presence.

Independent peasant organizations have also existed for a long time, seeking to preserve or acquire land. These organizations, born out of poverty and desperation, face levels of repression unthinkable in urban areas. The terrible struggle for land in rural Mexico, often lost by peasant communities despite the enactment of land reform in the 1930s, has taken on an increasingly desperate character, especially in southern Mexico. The Salinas administration's (1988–94) changes in the land tenure regime—opening up communal lands to private ownership, joined to the agricultural provisions of NAFTA—have had devastating effects on many peasants' way of life. These events helped produce the Chiapas uprising that exploded in 1994 when rebels seized several cities around the state. Most important, perhaps, fairly weak and marginalized indigenous organizations throughout southern Mexico have become much more visible since the Chiapas uprising.

Groups of squatters are an urban equivalent of independent peasant organizations. Squatter settlements have sprouted over the last forty years in all of Mexico's cities, especially in the capital. Using Mexico's usufruct laws, these squatters have pressed for titles to the land they occupy and, subsequently, for the extension of city services.

Other associations have arisen at the grassroots level in cities to press for a variety of demands. Many of these associations have appeared in slum areas, seeking the resolution of acute, chronic problems, especially housing shortages. Notable examples of such movements include the Asamblea de Barrios (Assembly of Neighborhoods) in Mexico City and the Comite de Defensa Popular (Committee for Popular Defense) in the city of Durango. Other urban groups, whose membership is typically more middle class, have come into existence, pushing everything from neighborhood beautification to historic preservation.

Finally, a relatively new entrant onto the political scene is a group called El Barzon. The economic crisis experienced by the country over much of the last fifteen years, but especially after the collapse of the Mexican currency following the devaluation in December 1994, led to an extraordinary rise in the number of debtors. These debtors formed El Barzon, a huge association, given the number of debtors, to press the government, banks, and other financial institutions for less punitive treatment of people who defaulted on business, mortgage, and consumer loans.

Despite the number of independent associations, their influence and social reach have to be carefully evaluated. At first glance, the plethora of groups mentioned above seem to indicate the emergence of a civil society. Some groups have quite substantial memberships, particularly certain popular urban movements, electoral watchdog organizations, specific peasant and labor associations, and especially El Barzon. The overwhelming majority of independent associations, however, are marked by very small memberships, rarely exceeding a few hundred committed activists. Although data on their size is often limited and frequently contradictory, survey research indicates that overall participation in such groups remains quite low, despite substantial increases over the years. Indeed, a poll indicated that only 4 percent of Mexicans were members of independent political organizations at the beginning of the 1990s.[14] The relatively static quality of many of these groups also suggests that their mobilizational capacity remains quite limited. Indeed, expanded participation in civic organizations over the last decade has been marked more by the appearance of new groups than the growth of existing independent organizations.

On the other hand, it is unquestionably true that participation, understood more generally, has expanded over the years. Significantly, more than 81,000 people participated as voluntary poll watchers during the 1994 presidential elections.[15] The same elections were also marked by unprecedentedly high levels of voter turnout (77 percent). In addition, similar levels of engagement marked the mid-term 1997 elections when electoral participation reached levels equivalent to the 1997 elections. This expanded participation, although an important indication of democratization, must still be interpreted cautiously, for this change in behavior has still not been accompanied by an equally clear shift in political culture.[16] Moreover, a number of other factors continue to militate against broader civic engagement.

Factors Attenuating the Political Influence and Social Penetration of Independent Associations

Several factors have impeded the development of independent associations and preserved their distance from the lives of most Mexicans.

14. *Los Angeles Times*, August 1989.
15. Rafael Segovia, "Una cultura política inmovil," *Nexos*, July 1996, 58.
16. Ibid., 57–62.

These factors include preemptive actions by the state; the historical, centrifugal attraction of the government; the weak legitimacy of law and the power of custom; a long history of exclusion; the power of society and the concomitant distinction between public and private spheres; the hardness of class divisions; a highly personalistic tradition; and fragmentation within and across issues.

Associational Independence and Preemptive Actions by the State

In Mexico, the constitution of a state occurred before the expansion of political participation or the appearance of a significant number of intermediary organizations created from below. In part, as a result, the state was the generative force behind the development of most associations, creating these organizations from above. The Mexican Revolution and the postrevolutionary regime effectively destroyed most features of Mexico's feudal nineteenth-century society. At the same time, the state created in the aftermath of the revolution prevented the development of independent political associations by creating groups linked to the regime before the expansion of political participation.

The associations created from above by the state permitted the regime to preemptively and segmentally incorporate different groups. In the late 1930s the ruling party was organized along corporatist lines. The PRI's corporatist sectors aggregated peasant, labor, and certain middle-class groups. With memberships numbering in the millions, these sectors incorporated a significant portion of the organized working population. While this strategy enhanced political stability by maximizing state control, it had an enervating effect on participation and on associational activity. Stripped of their function as vehicles of interest articulation and representation, associations became formalistic shells with passive rather than active memberships. Inclusion in these associations did not breed participation. Indeed, if anything, these organizations had a demobilizational effect, strengthening political apathy and inertia. Because these groups received state backing, patronage, and other favors in return for their support and quiescence, they exerted virtually monopolistic control over substantial spheres of associational activity.

In addition, beyond the corporatist sectors of the ruling party, the state also used mobilizational tactics to create different groups. Paradoxically, environmental groups, now among the most vibrant independent associations, originally received much of their impetus from the state. Part of the de la Madrid administration's strategy to combat environmental degradation was to promote popular mobilization.[17] As Mumme, Bath, and Assetto write, "Prior to 1980, the few existing interest groups were largely confined to professional associations, but by 1984, several hundred interest groups were focusing on environmental themes. . . . While many of these groups formed 'spontaneously' after 1982, others were a direct outgrowth of the government's popular mobilization program."[18] Though these groups, in many cases, subsequently became independent of the government and consistent critics of the regime, the state impetus behind their formation and growth powerfully reveals the weakness of spontaneous civic mobilization and organization.

While the state still exercises a generative role, the efficacy of the original corporatist sectors linked to the PRI has steadily declined. Although these organizations continue to have substantial power, conferred by their link to the regime and by inertia and longevity, their captive status and the corruption of their leadership undermine their legitimacy. Moreover, the PRI and its official sectors suffer from increasing obsolescence. The functional scheme informing the corporatist organization of the ruling party has become less and less reflective of the complexity accompanying an increasingly modern and diverse society. The PRI's corporatist structure cannot accommodate new groups, especially issue interests spawned by decades of economic growth and change. This, in part, explains the expansion in the number of independent associations that, despite their much smaller size, fill a social need. On the other hand, the relative marginalization of these groups also continues to attenuate their appeal. This same factor, of course, also helps to sustain the organizations linked to the PRI, despite their decreased legitimacy and efficacy.

The Historical, Centrifugal Attraction of the State

The efficacy and durability of independent groups have also been hurt by another phenomenon. A long paternalistic tradition in Mexico has led individuals and groups to seek remedies from the state. The state not only seized power over the public sphere, but was granted this authority by the population. As such, it acquired, by both initiative and default, the sole capacity to deal with public issues and problems.

---

17. Stephen P. Mumme, Richard C. Bath, and Valerie J. Assetto, "Political Development and Environmental Policy in Mexico," *Latin American Research Review* 23, no. 1 (1988): 7–34, 18–21.

18. Ibid., 20.

The pull toward the state has consistently undermined the independence of new associations. Rather than trying to organize local remedies to problems, these groups have habitually sought state action. This tendency turned them into captives of the state, since the government determined their effectiveness and, by extension, their legitimacy. In addition, the regime consistently used its resources to divide, manipulate, and co-opt groups. Conferring benefits to some while denying it to others has divided groups from each other and often created cleavages within the membership of associations.

An apt example of this strategy was President Salinas's use of a massive anti-poverty program established during his administration. This program, called PRONASOL, or National Solidarity Program, was ostensibly designed to alleviate poverty. In return for materials and advice provided by the state, neighborhoods and communities donated their labor to construct roads and other civic improvements. However, a highly political calculus guided the provision of the billions of dollars a year spent by the program during the Salinas administration. The poorest and most marginalized communities typically did not receive these funds. Instead, money was directed toward areas that had supported the opposition in previous elections and was clearly designed to erode this support. Simultaneously, as Paul Haber notes, in order to counteract the increasing obsolescence and lack of efficacy of the ruling party's corporatist sectors, President Salinas initiated a policy of "*concertacion social*," or social concertation, with groups such as urban popular movements outside the party.[19] This policy involved the signing of agreements between individual groups and the president over the provision of funds under the Solidarity Program. Some groups chose to participate, while others did not. Those that did received extensive economic benefits but at a cost to their autonomy. Moreover, they were inevitably perceived as having sold out by those who chose not to receive the government's funds and remain in opposition. These latter organizations, in turn, because they were bereft of resources, were much less able to address their members' needs than those that had accepted the government's largesse. As a consequence, they often suffered a significant decline in membership. An apt example of this decline was the Asamblea de Barrios in Mexico City, whose membership declined during the Salinas administration from 50,000 to 10,000.[20] Not surprisingly, this political use of government funds also

19. Haber, "El arte de la reestructuración y sus implicaciones políticas: el caso de los movimientos urbanos populares," 333–70.
20. Ibid., 368.

helped to engender divisions within and resentments between associations.[21]

Clientelism also facilitates co-optation. While new, independent groups continue to appear on the political stage, many succumb to this statist, clientelistic urge. By conferring benefits on groups, the government makes them dependent on state policy.

The lack of a tradition of independent voluntarism and charitable giving reinforces the attraction toward the state. While some voluntary charitable organizations exist, including the Red Cross, their reach is still quite limited. In addition, the Catholic Church and other religious groups have always performed important social welfare functions. Nonetheless, voluntarism remains the exception rather than the rule.

The absence of voluntarism has serious consequences for the development of a civil society. Voluntarism reflects and creates a climate that encourages association, aggregation, and participation. It also provides an alternative to state activity. On the negative side, charitable organizations frequently provide an alibi and rationale for government inactivity, since their presence presumably makes such action unnecessary.

Though extensive, the state's social welfare activities have been very inadequate. This inadequacy has reflected both the government's developmental and budgetary priorities and the magnitude of social ills confronted by the country. Nonetheless, the state has seen itself, and has been perceived by the population, as the primary agent responsible for creating larger institutions designed to address social problems.[22] Orphanages, old age homes, and other social institutions, whose reach is still hopelessly insufficient, have been largely created and run by the state.

Philanthropy in Mexico is also extremely weak. The historical absence of charitable giving, with the exception of donations to the Catholic Church, has long been reinforced by the tax code. The tax structure, until relatively recent modifications, did not encourage or reward philanthropy. Moreover, weak enforcement, which only became somewhat more vigorous during the 1990s, eviscerated the few provisions designed to encourage philanthropy. The country, despite

---

21. The discussion presented here about the use of the Solidarity Program and its impact on groups, especially urban popular movements, owes much to Paul Haber's excellent analysis in "El arte de la reestructuracion y sus implicaciones politicas el caso de los movimientos urbanos populares."

22. This perception still exists today. In a recent survey, Ulises Beltran et al., *Los mexicanos de los noventa* (Mexico D.F.: Instituto de Investigaciones Sociales, UNAM, 1996), 52 percent of Mexicans believed that the state was solely responsible for attending to these needs.

the presence of huge personal fortunes, has relatively few domestic foundations and other independent philanthropic institutions. The few existing foundations typically have narrow, ideologically conservative agendas and have tended to fund groups and institutions reflecting their views. This practice has hurt the development of other associations and independent institutions because non-government sources of financing have been limited, fragile, and haphazard. While financing is available from international sources, including foundations, these funds remain quite limited, although foundations and international non-governmental organizations (NGOs) have supported local groups in important ways. Financial weakness undoubtedly strengthens the already deep tradition of clientelism and the attraction toward the state.

Interest Groups, Regulation, and Law and Custom

Paradoxically, a deep cynicism about state action and the efficacy of regulation and law accompanies the attraction toward the state. Interest groups, almost by definition, focus their attention on the policy, regulatory, and legal arenas because they usually seek to change and occasionally preserve government practices. For a variety of reasons, however, these areas remain part of the surface rather than the substance in Mexico. Discretionary application and haphazard enforcement, colored by corruption and frequent change, have undermined laws and regulations. The weak legitimacy of these areas and their distance from the lives of most Mexicans hurts associational activity. Put simply, laws and regulations have historically played a weak role in governing human behavior. Consequently, the changes in these areas frequently sought by interest groups do not excite engagement or passion in the mass of the population. This trivializes associational activity, inhibiting the ability of independent organizations to expand their memberships.

The rule of law has been attenuated by a number of powerful, long-standing factors. With many other Latin Americans, Mexicans share a faith in formalism and the codification of norms. This faith, however, coexists with an equally powerful and contrary belief that the tonalities of human nature resist these rules. As a result, laws become moral exhortations, lodestars defining an ideal, but not conforming to daily life. By extension, legal formalism and the belief in codification have led to the enactment of laws without possibility of implementation. Enacting laws that cannot be implemented weakens the daily vitality and meaning of law, increasing the perception that law is contingent and part of the surface rather than the substance.

State-society relations also partially explain attitudes about the rule of law. The strength of society and custom weakens the legitimacy of government by making it into a man-made epiphenomenon, whose rules and injunctions do not have the depth and reach of traditional societal customs and norms existing "under the skin." Not surprisingly, the rules emanating from government under these circumstances are perceived with a great degree of skepticism.

The tradition informing this view of law dates from Mexico's colonial period. The viceroys in the colonies had the power to resist and ignore the laws, decrees, and regulations emanating from the Spanish crown. This practice, known as *obedezco pero no cumplo* (I obey but do not comply), opened up a substantial gap between law and implementation. In addition, deep historical problems of implementation running from independence to the present reduced the legitimacy of law as a guide to human behavior. Differential standards and treatment have existed for different groups. Corporate rights and privileges running from the colonial period through the first half of the nineteenth century effectively meant that different groups were governed by distinct legal regimes. Even after the abolition of corporate privileges during the second half of the nineteenth century, law continued to be applied in an extraordinarily uneven fashion. Indeed, to this day, the poor and especially the indigenous poor receive treatment from the judicial system that is unimaginable for rich Mexicans. Differential treatment extends from the likelihood and form of arrest and detention through trial procedures and even incarceration. While many, if not most, of these problems exist in other countries' judicial systems, they are especially profound and acute in Mexico.

Arbitrary practices increase these problems. Arrest and detention often occur randomly, torture is routinely used, and everybody from the policeman on the beat to judges is subornable. Moreover, the judicial branch has been a captive of the executive, acquiring little independent prestige.

Regulatory enforcement has suffered from similar problems. Graft and the power of connections have led to the discretionary, uneven application of regulations. Against this backdrop, avoidance and evasion, rather than compliance, became the common response to the legal and regulatory regime.

The public policy arena has been hurt by other factors. Policies have often been grandiose and consequently prone to dramatic failure. This produced an enormous gap between policy and reality, deepening cynicism and weakening participation. In addition, policy formulation and decisionmaking are among the most closed and authoritarian features of the polity. In Mexico, policy initiatives often flow from the top down, and consultation occurs in an *a posteriori* rather than an *a priori* fashion. In this regard, many interest groups in Mexico are still largely confined to the reactive role first noted by Susan Kaufman Purcell twenty years ago.[23] While exceptions exist, interest groups have been notably unsuccessful in initiating policy or in moving issues up the political agenda. Moreover, their successes have only tended to come when a confluence of other factors, including international pressures, have raised the saliency of the issue for the government.

The traditional authoritarianism of decisionmaking was most dramatically demonstrated by President Salinas's declaration in 1989 that he intended to pursue a free trade agreement with the United States. This decision was made entirely at the pinnacle of the executive branch. There was no *a priori* public discussion about this dramatic policy change despite its impact on the population. Other equally far-reaching decisions, notably the Salinas administration's transformation of the land tenure regime in rural Mexico, were also determined at the top of the regime, while those affected by the change—millions of peasants working communal land-holdings—were hardly consulted.

Moreover, the government did not even make an attempt to seek public ratification of these decisions, except through the formalistic means of a largely captive legislature. Opponents were confined to a reactive role, whose inefficacy was ensured from the outset, given the absence of any institutional means to resist the will of the president. Thus, these policies were a *fait accompli* in Mexico from the day of their announcement. More recent presidential initiatives evidence many of these same traits, although the opposition's majority in the Chamber of Deputies after 1997 offers hope for change.

The difficulty of influencing the government has also been evident in other areas, including human rights. While the government has elevated the importance of the human rights issue, manifested most importantly by the Salinas administration's creation of a National Commission on Human Rights (CNDH) to investigate reports of abuses, this policy change was almost entirely a product of international pressure and not the activities of local groups. Indeed, it was a highly critical report by Americas Watch in 1991 about the human rights situation in Mexico that prompted this change.[24] The government is highly sensitive about its image abroad, a sensitivity heightened in the early 1990s by the desire to secure U. S. approval of the

---

23. Susan Kaufman Purcell, *The Mexican Profit Sharing Decision* (Berkeley: University of California Press, 1976).

24. "Human Rights in Mexico," *Americas Watch* (1991).

North American Free Trade Agreement. Not surprisingly, against this
backdrop, independent associations and other opponents of the regime, given their inability to effect change domestically, often sought
international forums for their grievances, notably the U.S. Congress
and press, seeking to bring outside pressure to bear on the government.

While outside pressure has occasionally prompted policy change, its
influence should not be exaggerated. The government has often sought
to placate and attenuate this criticism through symbolic changes, ren-
dered moot by the conscious weakness of the policy and ineffective
implementation. These elements have been notably present in the
human rights arena. The CNDH, whose establishment was announced
with much fanfare by the government, has only relatively limited
power. In part, as a consequence, the CNDH has had a quite limited
impact on the incidence of human rights abuses in Mexico, as recent
reports by Amnesty International continue to indicate.[25] The power,
scope, and independence of the police still produce a torrent of human
rights abuses, including the continuing use of torture, illegal deten-
tions, and other unsavory practices. In addition, the government's initial, savage repression of the indigenous, peasant uprising in the state
of Chiapas in early 1994, including the use of "disappearances," torture, and summary executions, tellingly revealed the regime's continuing willingness to use these practices as an instrument of policy. In
fact, the international outcry over the brutality of this response was
one of the primary factors that led the government to desist from these
tactics and seek a negotiated solution with the rebels.

Not surprisingly, the futility of opposition on most policy questions
had an enervating effect on independent associations and their memberships. Rather than seeking changes in policy, their activity has often
been confined to seeking particularistic remedies from the state. This
powerlessness, especially at the policy formulation stage, also reduced
the desire to meaningfully participate in the public policy arena. While
some groups, especially powerful business interests, have influenced
policy and have been consulted by the government on policy questions, most associations have not possessed this power. In sum, all of
the factors weakening the legitimacy of the public policy arena fundamentally undermined many associations, helping to explain their
small size.

---

25. See sections on Mexico in the 1992, 1993, 1994, 1995, and 1996 *Amnesty
International Reports* (London: Amnesty International).

Mexican Society, the State, and the Distinction Between the Private and Public Spheres

According to the traditional scholarly consensus on Mexico, one of the fundamental problems of the polity was the lack of a distinction between the private and public spheres. The existence of the patrimonial state most powerfully characterized the supposed fusion between the two spheres. Octavio Paz, for example, argues that the insertion of the private into the public sphere contributes to many of Mexico's political ills. He says about the Mexican state:

> In many aspects, especially in its dealings with the public and its manner of conducting business, it continues to be patrimonialist. In a regime of this sort the head of government—be it prince or president—considers the state his personal patrimony. . . . Patrimonialism, in essence, is the incrustation of private upon public life. The ministers are the intimates and servants of the king. . . . People irreproachable in their private behavior, shining lights of morality on their home ground, have no scruples about disposing of public goods as if they were their own property. The issue is less one of immorality than of the unconscious operation of another set of morals in the patrimonial regime [where] the frontiers between public and private spheres, family and state are rather vague and fluctuating. If everyone is king of his house, the kingdom is like the house and the nation is like the family. If the state is the king's patrimony, how can it not also be the patrimony of his relations, friends, servants and favorites?[26]

However, the traditional argument suffers from an inherent contradiction. If people are irreproachable in their private life and if the Mexican state is the "incrustation of private upon public life," why do not these private virtues manifest themselves in the public sphere? The answer, of course, is that a profound distinction has existed in Mexico, reminiscent of Machiavelli, between public and private virtues and vices. Miguel Basañez also makes this argument, asserting that Mexicans, as a product of their Catholic, Iberian heritage, possess a double code of conduct: one code is valid for one's circle of intimates, including family and friends, while the other code applies to one's external life.[27] Moreover, while Mexican politicians may indeed treat the state's budget as if it were their private pocketbook, one of the hallmarks of the patrimonial state and of the "incrustation of private upon public

---

26. Paz, "The Philanthropic Ogre," 387–388, 397.

27. Miguel Basanez, *El pulso de los sexenios: 20 anos de crisis en México* (México D.F.: Siglo XXI, 1991), 310–17.

life," this does not mean that the two spheres are fused. Indeed, the public, political realm has been much more unregulated in Mexico than the private world, since it has lacked the strong norms and customs governing private actions. This distinction has contributed to public behavior that would have been privately intolerable.

In addition, the mass of the population remains largely removed from the public sphere. Historical developments, conjoined to powerful social and cultural features of Mexico, led to a society turned inward toward the private realm and away from public engagements. Most importantly, perhaps, the futility of such engagements and, for many, the outright exclusion from the public sphere strengthened the focus on the inner, private social world. In turn, the strength of this private sphere cannot be exaggerated. The historical lack of a civil society is not indicative of a weak society. In fact, Mexican society is extremely powerful. Paradoxically, its very strength, joined to its inner focus, has attenuated participation in the public sphere. This internal focus created great order in private spaces but much less regulation in the public sphere.

To this day, most Mexican activities, loyalties, and interests are largely focused inward, toward the family. The Mexican family has undergone enormous changes over the last several decades, moving from an extended to an ever-more-nuclear form. It also has faced the stresses produced by modernization and migration, including a dramatic expansion in single-parent homes. Nonetheless, it remains the focus of intense, almost mythological loyalties. The inward nature of Mexican society, epitomized most dramatically by attitudes about the family, reflects a larger, central duality between the inner and the outer that is one of the defining features of Mexico. The power of the inner world can be found everywhere in the country. Houses face inward toward a courtyard or garden rather than outward. The disorder of the street accompanies the meticulous cleanliness, formality, and order of inner spaces. Rudeness toward strangers shifts to exquisite courtesy once a human connection has been established.

In contrast to this argument, the family has often been seen as a support for the civil society. For example, Polish intellectuals seeking to reform the Polish regime during the 1980s believed that "circles of family and friends represent the protection of the private sphere from an administered and controlled public one. They are means that permit the defense of a given society, its customs, mentalities, its national and local identities. The reconstruction of society is possible in such countries because the foundations are there; social ties as such do not have to be reconstituted, only their more complex forms."[28] However, family

---

28. Arato, *From Neo-Marxism*, 180.

ties and social networks can command such deep loyalties and attach-ments that they prevent the establishment of ties with others outside of these circles.[29]

The natural, cultural reliance on the inner, private sphere has been strengthened historically by the uncertainty of public life and the in-ability of institutions other than the family to provide much sustenance and support for the individual. In practical terms, despite attitudes about state responsibility, the family has long been the primary pro-vider of social welfare in Mexico. Indeed, its activities in this area have been so extensive that it has facilitated neglect of this area by other social actors and created both the fact and the illusion of a social safety net. In return, the family has demanded, and received, loyalties and commitments that impeded the establishment of larger connections. Moreover, the state's historical inability to provide for the needs of enormous sectors of the population not only produced alienation from public life but also enhanced the individual's reliance on the family. The uncertainties and failures of the public sphere contributed to a larger social distrust and enhanced the general unwillingness to partic-ipate in public organizations. While these factors made many families extraordinarily strong, they also prevented the development of a civic culture and sense of civic responsibility. Thus, in Mexico, great order and formality continue to mark private relationships, while public re-lations often exhibit a high degree of atomization.

The nature of social networks further strengthens the inward focus of the society. Despite the modernization of Mexico, school continues to be the primary place where social connections are established. In politics, business, and other social spheres, the networks that bring people together are often created during childhood, adolescence, and at the university. The strength and relative impenetrability of these networks, given their basis in lifelong associations, contribute further to this inward dynamic, attenuating the development of strong cross-cutting allegiances. The depth and reach of these ties, whose power can inhibit the establishment of connections on other, creedal grounds, hurt civic organizations and interest groups, since their development depends on allegiances cemented by shared convictions. However, the massification of Mexico may be gradually eroding this insularity.

The uncertainties of the public sphere and the concomitant lack of civic behavior have contributed importantly to a lack of general social

---

29. For other discussions of the impact of familism or associational activity, see Edward Banfield, *The Moral Basis of a Backward Society* (New York: The Free Press, 1958), and Glen Caudill Dealy, *The Latin Americans: Spirit and Ethos* (Boulder, Colo.: Westview, 1992), 179.

trust. Thirty years ago Gabriel Almond and Sidney Verba asserted, in an argument with continuing relevance, "In [Italy, Germany, and Mexico] the absence of a cooperative, group-forming political style appears to be related, not only to the lower frequency of expression of general social trust, but also to the fact that even the trust which is expressed does not increase the probability that an individual will think of working with others in trying to influence the government."[30] These findings were echoed by other surveys at the time.[31] Despite the passage of thirty years, recent surveys have continued to indicate a lack of social trust.[32]

The lack of social trust also reflects the power of the closed, inner features of Mexican society and culture. As Octavio Paz wrote: "Hermeticism is one of the several recourses of our suspicion and distrust. . . . This predominance of the closed over the open manifests itself . . . as impassivity and distrust, irony and suspicion."[33] Grassroots independent associations, in particular, are weakened by the relative distrust of strangers accompanying the dual focus on the family and long-established social networks, since these groups, especially at the outset, need to bring strangers together around a common issue or problem.

At present, the still extant fear of a continuing anarchic strain lurking just below the surface of political life most powerfully manifests the lack of social trust. Although this fear is much less strong in young Mexicans, it still exists in portions of the population. While the endless instability of the nineteenth century and the violence and destructiveness of the Mexican Revolution provided ample historical substance for this view, seventy years of political stability and the emergence of a country vastly different from the one existing before and during the revolution have not totally managed to erase this fear, although the passage of time has clearly made it much less powerful, as Linda Stevenson and Mitchell Seligson have observed.[34] The residual concerns about anarchy continue to fuel desires for, and to legitimize, strong government capable of restraining these tendencies and ensuring stability. Rising crime also nurtures these views. To this day, concerns

30. Almond and Verba, *The Civic Culture*, 228–30.

31. See, for example, Joseph F. Kahl, *The Measurement of Modernism* (Austin: University of Texas Press, 1968), 82.

32. See, for example, Beltran, *Los mexicanos de los noventa*.

33. Paz, *The Labyrinth of Solitude and Other Writings*, 30, 31.

34. Linda Stevenson and Mitchell Seligson, "Fading Memories of the Revolution: Is Stability Eroding in Mexico?" in *Polling for Democracy: Public Opinion and Political Liberalization in Mexico*, ed. Roderic Ai Camp (Wilmington, Del.: Scholarly Resources, 1996).

about "social peace" animate support for the PRI among certain sectors of the population. This view is also manifested in the notion that the postrevolutionary regime has been a reflection of Mexican "idiosyncrasies," whose containment has required the regime's authoritarian institutions and ruling practices. By extension, this fear has nurtured the belief, especially within portions of the political elite, that democracy would both create and inflame political cleavages, increasing the likelihood of political violence.

Ironically, however, while Mexicans have lived under authoritarian regimes throughout most of their history and have often believed in and desired strong government, the dichotomy between the public and the private sphere de-legitimized the state. Despite its size and apparent reach, the state has remained an artifice, with neither the depth nor reach of a society and culture existing independently of political arrangements. During seventy years of rule, the postrevolutionary regime was unable to solve this legitimacy problem and extend its roots deeper into the soil. Instead, its legitimacy remained tied to a set of gradually less evocative revolutionary myths and to its efficacy. This last factor, because of its contingency, made legitimacy ever more fragile, brittle, and dependent on immediate performance. Over time, this manifested itself in ever lower regard for government institutions. By the mid-1990s, according to a survey, 70 percent of Mexicans had little or no confidence in the political system.[35]

On the other hand, the distinction between the private and the public world has been used and dignified by the Mexican government. Indeed, its respect for this distinction has contributed, in no small measure, to its longevity. By and large, the regime sought to control and order the public realm not through law but through a ruling style and set of practices governed (not always successfully) by political pragmatism. At the same time, it was typically careful not to intrude upon the private, social world. The silences of the state in this area created very substantial spaces of liberty. As a consequence, private liberties in Mexico were much broader than public, political ones.[36]

The distinction between the private and public spheres has had an especially strong effect on the efficacy and reach of associations seeking change that extends beyond government actions to individual consciousness and behavior. Environmental groups face this problem to a

---

35. Reyes Heroles, *Sondear a México,* 148.
36. A good discussion of this distinction can be found in Gabriel Szekely and Daniel Levy, *Mexico: Paradoxes of Stability and Change* (Boulder, Colo.: Westview Press, 1987), 87–104.

special degree. While a broad, general consciousness of environmental problems has been growing in Mexico over the last decade, individual behavior remains almost entirely divorced from this awareness. To this day, many Mexicans, except for indigenous groups, do not have a sense of a commons. Everybody from industrialists to people on the streets exhibits behavior patterns that do not evidence a desire to preserve and protect public spaces. Inconvenient environmental regulations like the Hoy No Circula program in Mexico City—which forced drivers not to use their cars one day a week—have been circumvented by the purchase of additional vehicles. Garbage is dumped indiscriminately on hillsides, and people litter public spaces. Most fundamentally, this behavior reflects a continuing lack of connection with or sense of responsibility for the public realm. This same lack of connection, in turn, militates against participation and the concomitant expansion of independent associations. Mexico's paradox is that it has both a strong and weak society—internally strong but civically weak—and a strong and weak state—still dominant in the public sphere, but without deeper roots into the society.

Exclusion, Alienation, and Participation

Civic, community participation has also been hurt by centuries of exclusion, powerlessness, and voicelessness. Exclusion and voicelessness were imposed by the Spanish on the indigenous population from the outset of the colonial period. The peasantry, despite composing the overwhelming majority of the population, remained effectively marginalized from political life. During the colonial period the political arena was largely restricted to "peninsular" Spaniards serving as the Crown's representatives. Though the indigenous population had little voice, the paternalistic, tutelary behavior of the Church and Crown provided some measure of protection to native communities. After independence, however, these protections gradually fell away, especially after the triumph of the Liberals in the War of the Reform in the 1850s. The Liberals, reflecting their belief in the market and private property, drastically changed the land tenure regime in rural Mexico, opening up communal lands to private ownership. This immiserated the largely indigenous peasantry whose lands were seized by a small group of speculators and landowners. The process of marginalization and immiseration continued during the dictatorship of Porfirio Díaz (1874–1910). Although the dictatorship produced spectacular economic growth, the expansion of agricultural enterprises placed further pressure on indigenous and village lands, driving even more of the peasantry into sharecropping and debt peonage.

The growing misery of the indigenous population, especially during the latter half of the nineteenth century, was accompanied by their complete exclusion from political life. After independence, politics remained confined to a small elite. This period was marked by the struggle for power between leaders called *caudillos*. The primary channel into politics was the army, whose officer class was largely composed of *criollos* (whites) and *mestizos* (those with Spanish and Indian origins). The indigenous and peasant population provided the foot soldiers and cannon fodder for individual *caudillos*. These same oligarchical, exclusionary elements marked politics during the Porfirian dictatorship. Although the revolution opened up politics to a broader group of Mexicans, especially the nascent middle class, large portions of the population remained effectively excluded and marginalized from political life. While land reform in the 1930s temporarily improved the living standards of many peasants, the authoritarian nature of the political system continued the long tradition of exclusion. This was aggravated by the pragmatic, necessitarian calculus guiding the regime's responsiveness to the population. The regime typically responded to groups based on their importance as either potential supporters or opponents. Most benefits were devoted to these groups, excluding those who lacked political significance. This exclusion was especially dramatic in the southwestern states of Guerrero, Oaxaca, and Chiapas, whose indigenous and peasant population continues to live in conditions of unspeakable penury, subject to the rapaciousness of local political bosses and landowners (both linked to the PRI). Indeed, their world has been hardly touched by either economic modernization or the changes produced by the revolution.

While the indigenous and peasant population has been the most excluded group, other Mexicans have historically not enjoyed much of a voice in government, despite the economic development experienced by the country since the 1940s. The authoritarian nature of the political system, marked by closed, hierarchical decisionmaking and formalistic inclusion designed to control demand articulation, left most of the population without much influence or voice. However, exclusion, or attenuated citizenship, did not breed mass opposition, but instead promoted widespread political apathy.

In sum, exclusion, joined to a long clientelistic tradition, effectively turned civic life into an abstraction foreclosed to many and conceded by others to a relatively small group of politically engaged individuals. This tradition left the state as the sole occupant of the public sphere. Not surprisingly, in a feedback loop, state dominance reinforced clientelism and the pull toward the state, impeded the development of a civic culture, and increased the sense of exclusion and voicelessness. All of these factors, in turn, inhibited the development of a participatory tradition. Surveys over the years consistently documented the weakness of non-electoral participation.[37] Although participation has grown, formidable barriers born of this history still reduce non-electoral civic behavior.

The "Hardness" of Class Divisions

The expansion of independent, crosscutting interest groups has also been somewhat inhibited by the continuing strength of class divisions. Although Mexico is gradually becoming a less class-conscious and hierarchical society, class divisions remain strong. The depth of these divisions hurts the development of a civil society in a number of ways. Class differences restrict encounters across classes. More important, class distinctions act against the formation of cross-class groups. These divisions also reinforce parochialism and fragmentation. Groups' frequent difficulty extending beyond their class base restricts their appeal, limits their membership, and makes them especially prone to reflect only narrow class interests.

The presence of class divisions does not mean, however, that only educated, middle- to upper-class individuals have a propensity to form independent groups. The plethora of lower-class groups organized around housing, neighborhood, and indigenous issues strongly attests to this fact. This continues to reflect a pattern discussed thirty years ago by Gabriel Almond and Sidney Verba. They found that "most other significant political attitudes and behavior—interest in politics, political discussion, voting, knowledge of politics, and general sense of competence to influence the government—were found to vary strongly with an individual's educational attainment or his socioeconomic status. . . . But unlike the political attitudes and behavior that seem heavily dependent on social position within a nation, the strategy of using informal groups as a means of influencing government seems to be relatively independent of social position."[38] On the other hand, while interest groups may appear in any social class, this does not mean that their membership cuts across Mexico's social structure.

Naturally enough, squatter groups and peasant and labor organizations will have a class basis. More notably, social class also conditions and forms the membership and agenda of issue groups. Environmental groups exhibit this characteristic to an especially pronounced degree. By and large, though certainly not exclusively, environmental

---

37. See, for example, Richard R. Fagen and William S. Tuohy, *Politics and Privilege in a Mexican City* (Stanford, Calif.: Stanford University Press, 1972), 116.

38. Almond and Verba, *The Civic Culture*, 218.

activism remains confined to the middle and upper classes, who have the luxury to involve themselves in the issue.

Intellectuals, who mostly come from quite privileged social backgrounds, typically play a prominent role in a number of independent associations. However, the political efficacy of the intelligentsia in part depends upon its ability to establish connections with other groups. Despite the ubiquity of intellectuals among critics of the postrevolutionary regime, it remains unclear how effectively they have established these sorts of connections. In addition, despite their prominence, it is also hard to gauge how much their discourse touches and reflects the political desires and demands of most Mexicans.

Moreover, the very prominence of intellectuals tends to diminish and marginalize other groups. In several areas, associations consisting primarily of intellectuals and artists quickly acquire the greatest visibility. In the environmental area, the Group of 100, despite its small size, quickly became the most frequently cited organization in the media. Among organizations pressing for electoral reform and democratization, the Group of San Angel, formed before the 1994 presidential elections by eighty prominent individuals, including figures like Lorenzo Meyer, Jorge Castaneda, and Carlos Fuentes, almost immediately became one of the most prominent groups on the issue.

Although these associations have strong moral authority, they remain essentially elite organizations. The visibility and prominence of their members, who often belong to more than one independent association, exaggerate their social depth and reach. In addition, the presence of the same individuals across a number of groups makes this portion of the civil society even more of an elite phenomenon. The relatively small size of the intellectual community in Mexico—and the even smaller size of the community of prominent intellectual political activists—thrusts these individuals into constant encounters with the government, the press, the international community, and each other. Not surprisingly, given the centrality of these activities to the lives of these individuals, they come to believe that the rest of society shares their preoccupations. The problem, of course, is that while these activities may be important to a few, they may remain largely divorced from the lives of the many.

Personalism and Fragmentation

Throughout Mexican history, political currents, movements, and groups have tended to form around charismatic individuals. *Caudillismo* still has a powerful impact on political activity and on associational structure and behavior. Despite bureaucratization, Weberian charismatic leadership is still commonplace. The focus on this type of leadership reinforces hierarchy and can also encourage fragmentation. To this day, groups in Mexico, rather than being identified by their political affiliation or title, receive the name of their leader, for example, the *zedillistas*, the *cardenistas*.

Independent associations have rightly criticized the hierarchy and personalism of the official groups linked to the PRI. The epitome of this personalism in the PRI was Fidel Velazquez, who led the CTM (the Mexican Workers Confederation), the largest labor organization in Mexico, for roughly sixty years until his death in 1997. The CTM is the core of the PRI's labor sector. Fidel Velazquez retained iron control of the organization, delivering its unconditional support to the government while turning the CTM into his personal fiefdom. In consonance with practices across the regime, decisionmaking in the CTM was highly authoritarian and restricted to the top of the organization. This leadership, in turn, took its cues from the president. Ironically, however, independent unions have often exhibited precisely these same traits. While vigorously opposing the CTM and deploring its hierarchy and its personalism, many independent labor organizations originally were, or became, political vehicles for individual leaders.

This same phenomenon can be found elsewhere. Environmental groups, for example, a relatively new entrant into the political scene, have often exhibited the same *caudillista* propensities. By and large, these groups tend to be organized around individual activists. Personality differences and distinct and conflicting priorities encourage fragmentation, markedly reducing the political reach and efficacy of these groups. Grassroots community activists in urban areas often exhibit the same traits. Much has been made, for example, of the *Superbarrio* phenomenon in Mexico City. *Superbarrio* is a community activist who dresses up like a masked wrestler and presses the demands of slum dwellers for housing and other necessities. Although *Superbarrio* has acquired national prominence, becoming a virtual folk hero, the movement he heads remains entirely focused around his figure.

Some of the same *caudillista* elements have surrounded *Subcomandante* Marcos, the leader of the peasant army in Chiapas, the EZLN (Zapatista National Liberation Army). Marcos's compelling verbal and written skills and the mystery and drama surrounding his figure produced a virtual personality cult until he almost dwarfed the *Zapatista* movement.

For all of these reasons, independent associations are still often plagued by the same problem that historically limited the efficacy of Mexico's political opposition—namely, the inability to establish effective and lasting alliances. There are some exceptions to this rule, notably the so-called *Coordinadoras,* regional umbrella organizations that have joined associations pressing for similar demands such as popular urban movements. *Coordinadoras* have also linked certain peasant and labor groups. In addition, alliances of human rights groups have appeared, and umbrella organizations like Alianza Civica have united electoral watchdog associations. However, many of these alliances are quite short-lived and succumb to conflicting agendas, priorities, and state manipulation.

The lack of cooperation trivializes individual groups, limiting their capacity to recruit new members. Indeed, the membership of many associations is quite static, never extending beyond the original group of committed supporters who founded the organization. An apt example of this fragmentation can be found among environmental groups. An *Ecological Directory* published by the Friedrich Ebert Stiftung in 1988 already listed fifty environmental associations in Mexico City alone.[39] This number has grown even larger in subsequent years. The vast majority of these groups are tiny, often containing only a dozen active members, and are riven by conflicting priorities and agendas.

The groups formed after the earthquake in 1985 also epitomize the constraining effects on civic behavior imposed by personalism and fragmentation. As Javier Elguea notes:

> The majority of those interviewed in our study perceived a great disorganization among the aid groups, including redundancy of functions, conflicts over decision-making, lack of internal information, an absence of clear priorities . . . , conflicts of interest, and conflicts over leadership. . . . These attitudes are highly dysfunctional in rescue activities where collective, concerted work is decisive to success. . . . The evidence suggests that the . . . aid groups must have functioned with a considerable degree of inefficiency and disorganization, and explains, in substantial measure, why they tended to disappear over time, victims of messianic individualism.[40]

In addition to their impact on the growth of a civil society, these factors facilitated the government's co-optive measures against opposition groups and independent associations. Both co-optive and repressive measures could be quite narrowly focused, since the successful control of the leader often ended a group's independent existence. In most cases, the state's hegemony was maintained and opposition managed at a relatively low cost.

Finally, the government, using a time-honored practice, has encour-

---

39. *Directorio Ecológico* (México D.F.: Friedrich Ebert Stiftung, 1988).
40. Elguea, "Los sismos de 1985 y el comportamiento de ayuda," 162.

aged fragmentation by subsidizing counter-groups on the same issues. This practice divided movements and opposition groups, ruptured the coherence of their agendas, and enabled the government to partially appropriate their demands. Typically, as was noted about the use of the Solidarity Program, the government dignified some groups and not others, further rupturing their ability to maintain broader alliances and demands.

Conclusion

Clearly, one of the most powerful, long-term sustenances for democracy in Mexico would be the development of a real civil society. While a host of grassroots and neighborhood organizations have arisen in Mexico over the last decade, it remains unclear if these organizations really represent the maturation of a civil society. Despite their number, these groups are typically small and atomized. Their frequently common dislike of the regime does not translate into a coherent opposition or political agenda, even on narrow policy questions.

Most important, perhaps, the presence of independent associations does not necessarily mean that they play a vital, significant role in the public sphere. In this regard, the literature on civil society in Mexico reflects the same tendency noted by Timothy Cheek about China. As he writes:

> Thus, the concept of civil society turns out to have two components: the basic, what Canadian political thinker Charles Taylor calls the "minimal" sense of civil society, where free associations not under state control exist, and the public sphere (which Taylor calls the "strong" sense of civil society), where those associations structure themselves independently of the state while addressing issues of concern to the state. Applications of this in Chinese studies tend to conflate the two senses of civil society or, rather, see in examples of possible civil society organizations (in the weak sense) necessary promise of the strong sense, or politically active public sphere life.[41]

The presence of these groups clearly indicates the presence of the "minimal sense of the civil society." An "active public sphere life," however, remains much more confined. Although evident, such activity still engages a relatively small portion of the population.

In addition to all of the factors discussed throughout this chapter,

---

41. Timothy Cheek, "From Market to Democracy in China: Gaps in the Civil Society Model," chapter 8 (p. 222) in this volume.

the profound cleavages dividing Mexico also reduce the reach of the civil society while producing very fragmented political change. The enormous gulf between northern and southern Mexico, between the rich and the poor, and between Mexicans who participate in the global economy and those who are still tied to traditional activities fractures the country. This heterogeneity truncates the appeal of associations. Moreover, extraordinarily uneven rates of change continually widen these cleavages, creating a country where modern, politically articulate sectors of the population coexist with more traditional elements. By extension, only a concerted and still not discernible attempt to reduce these cleavages, especially the gap between rich and poor, would create a more fertile terrain for a civil society.

Despite its relative weakness, the civil society remains a powerfully emotive, indeed mythic, construct. The civil society's mythical force stems from many sources. Most important, perhaps, its development represents a natural, almost organic movement toward democracy. The appeal of the civil society also derives from its emancipatory promise, since independent associations presumably enable individuals to have greater power over the decisions that affect their lives. In addition, the participation underlying independent associational activity shrinks the need and desire for state paternalism, as people engage themselves in the public sphere and increasingly pursue autonomous, local remedies. Moreover, as a grassroots process, the awakening of a civil society presumably has an irresistible force, creating pressures for reform and providing the underpinnings for democracy. The civil society seizes some of the initiative for reform and creates a context where resistances to democracy can be more easily overcome. A civil society also naturally disperses power, counteracting the centralization and elitism that accompany authoritarianism.

In Mexico, the notion of an awakened civil society resonates across the ideological spectrum, appealing to opponents of the post-revolutionary regime on both the right and the left. The right, opposed to state intervention and paternalism, sees the civil society as a restraint to the state. At the same time, the civil society appeals even more powerfully to the left, embodying older themes drawn from Marxism and liberation theology. This latter group, including intellectuals and grassroots activists, is especially drawn to the civil society's emancipatory and liberating themes. Even Subcomandante Marcos saw the most powerful hope for democracy in the emergence of a New Civic Mexican.[42] By extension, widespread independent associational activity marks the end of political apathy and further sustenance for change.

---

42. "Marcos: Las elecciones no se van a resolver en Gobernación, sino en las calles o en las montanas," *Proceso*, no. 924 (July 18, 1994): 32.

Advocates of democratization have also been drawn to the concept of a civil society because it provides additional refutation of the historical argument that Mexican social reality precluded democracy. Proponents of centralized, authoritarian arrangements—including the conservatives in the nineteenth century, the ideologues of the Porfiriato, and the architects and supporters of the postrevolutionary regime—grounded their arguments in realism and pragmatism. Democrats, despite the moral virtue of their arguments, always labored to free themselves from the belief that they were utopian idealists, whose political formulations did not fit the country's circumstances. The emergence of a civil society totally shifts this terrain, turning the democrats into pragmatists whose advocacy of reform is grounded on both idealism and the desire to construct a political system that reflects Mexico's modern social reality. At the same time, those who desire the perpetuation of the current system become unrealistic dinosaurs, desperately seeking to hold on to an increasingly obsolete regime.

Nonetheless, despite its appeal, the civil society remains suspect. Even the leadership of the EZLN, which once saw the civil society as its most formidable ally and source of support, increasingly came to perceive its weakness. No mass, civic outpouring occurred which could have sustained the EZLN. Indeed, the weakness of the response of the civil society was one of the reasons why the EZLN decided to give up its armed struggle in 1996 and pursue a peace agreement with the government.

To conclude, a host of factors continue to inhibit non-electoral political participation and nurture disassociation from the public sphere. Despite the emergence of independent associations over the last decade, the vast majority of Mexicans have not become engaged in outward, civic activity and remain focused on the inner, private social sphere. The emergence of a nascent electoral democracy is still not accompanied by equivalent, deeper change in other civic behavior, although the democratization of the polity may itself encourage a more extensive civil society. Most encouraging, the July 1997 elections may promote just this trend.

8

From Market to Democracy in China: Gaps in the Civil Society Model

Timothy Cheek

L ike Mexico, the People's Republic of China (PRC) has vigorously pursued economic liberalization and reform over the past decade and a half. The results have been impressive: China's GDP grew by 8.7 percent in 1996 (achieving the planned-for "soft landing" after recent years of overheated growth peaking with 13.6 percent GDP growth in 1992) and that rate is likely to remain moderate at 9.5 percent in 1997.[1] Agriculture has been de-collectivized and industry has moved away from the state monopoly of the Maoist period. A decade ago 78 percent of China's industrial output came from state-owned enterprises, with only 21 percent coming from collective-owned enterprises and 1 percent from the private sector. Now state-owned production is down to 53 percent and collective and private production up to 36 percent and 11 percent, respectively.[2] This economic liberalization extends to greater foreign contact and international investment. China

I would like to thank the members of the 1994 conference on Mexico and China at Colorado College, as well as colleagues at the Australian Defense Force Academy, Sydney University, and the Australian National University, who listened to and commented on this paper. Special thanks are due to David Kelly and the Political Science Department at the Australian Defense Force Academy for hosting me in June 1995 while pursuing this research.

1. Economist Intelligence Unit, *China: Country Report* (3rd Quarter, 1996) (London, 1996), 9.
2. Elizabeth J. Perry, "China in 1992: An Experiment in Neo-Authoritarianism," *Asian Survey* 33, no. 1 (January 1993): 15.

wants to play by world rules; it wants to join the World Trade Organization. Economic reform has certainly led to economic development. However, economic liberalization in China has not led to political democratization. The brutal military crackdown around Tiananmen Square in June 1989 is but the most extreme example of a consistent effort by the Chinese Communist Party (CCP) to maintain a Leninist one-party state and the CCP's control of that system. Every year since 1989 has seen the punishment or imprisonment of dissidents, democrats, or any who question the party's supreme right to rule.[3] Thus, China (despite its different political structure) resembles Mexico: economic liberalization without political reform, or at least without political democratization.[4]

In the case of China, the point has been the subject of much research and debate. Scholarly analysis of the relationship between economic and political reform in China has most often been cast in terms of civil society. The assumed general linkage between economic marketization and political democratization has been cast in terms of Habermas's model—both "civil society" and "public sphere"—of this process for western European societies over the past three hundred years. Civil society has come to stand for a sort of reified or de-cultured version of modernization theory: that societies outside the Euro-American orbit would—or ideally should—eventually, through the mechanism of economic development, become liberal states. Scholars have argued that China does have a civil society, that it doesn't; or that it did in the past and that it didn't; but most have assumed that at some point in the future China will have a civil society in terms recognizable to the Habermas model.[5]

These debates are extremely well researched and theoretically sophisticated, but they leave fundamental questions begging and distract our understanding of Chinese political economy from conceptualizations more useful to cross-cultural comparison. This chapter reviews that literature and suggests some alternative approaches to the question of the link between economic and political reform. My proposed

3. John Bryan Starr, "China in 1995: Mounting Problems, Waning Capacity," *Asian Survey* 36, no. 1 (January 1996): esp. 21–22.
4. The very great differences between Mexico and China are considered carefully in the first chapter of this volume.
5. In fairness to Professor Habermas, he has never claimed that his model of civil society or public sphere has such general, cross-cultural application. It remains an interesting question in intellectual history why we in China studies have found these categories so attractive in our analysis of current and past Chinese political economy. I suspect we found Habermasian civil society a handy alternative to Marxism after the general collapse of state socialism in 1989 as well as an alternative to modernization theory.

solutions are not so much novel as a re-deployment of tools already in the literature. I will argue (a) that it is a better resolution of the eternal tension in theoretical approaches between "universals" and "relativism" to announce our pragmatic concerns without the deceptive dressing of social science theory; (b) that the Gramscian functional conception of civil society is a better model than Habermasian developmental/teleological conception for the analysis of economic and political reform in China (and perhaps Mexico); and (c) that the analytical perspective of political culture can helpfully articulate a concrete analysis of the relationship between changes in the economy and in the polity of China. I will raise four examples to explore this analytical approach: the role of the party, the function of business associations, the values of Chinese entrepreneurs, and the place of intellectuals. And I offer my assessment: Market forces mediated by current Chinese political culture are producing not a liberal democratic polity with independent entrepreneurs (or even very promising signs of this) but rather nomenklatura capitalism or socialist corporatism at the local level, "Janus-faced" business associations that serve as a bridge between state and social interests, and an intellectual climate of dependent co-option rather than independent adversarial litigation. I see no necessary teleology in these developments; there is no systemic impetus for things necessarily to get worse or better. However, it is quite possible that undemocratic corporatist cooperation between local business and state interests may produce many of the goals we associate with civil society: restraints on government power, defacto pluralism, social peace, and sensible economic growth.

I am not suggesting that I have definitive answers that my colleagues under review here have failed to find. Rather, this chapter is a plea for a theoretically informed and methodologically explicit comparative history rather than grand theory building and procrustean application of such theory across time and cultures.

Civil Society and China: A Review of the Literature

The discussion over civil society and China rests on the equation "Δ polity = Δ economy" or more precisely, "Δ democracy = Δ market." Through some set of mechanisms, agents, processes, recombination of social forces, etc., we expect economic liberalization to lead to political democratization, as it has in western European experience. This is why we are surprised by the cases of Mexico and China. Habermas's civil society articulates the presumed mechanisms of this expression of the economic base in the political superstructure by suggesting reified versions of early modern European experience: the development of a public sphere, autonomous legal systems that put constraints on governments, legitimate and safe means of public expression and interest group articulation, and democratic elections. The social space created by bourgeois economic activity creates a civil society that becomes filled with a "public sphere" of citizen opinion and criticism of the state.

Thus, the concept of civil society turns out to have two components: the basic, what Canadian political thinker Charles Taylor calls the "minimal" sense of civil society, where free associations not under state control exist, and the public sphere (which Taylor calls the "strong" sense of civil society), where those institutions structure themselves independently of the state while publicly addressing issues of state concern.[6] Applications of this in Chinese studies tend to conflate the two senses of civil society or, rather, see in examples of possible civil society organizations (in the weak sense) necessary promise of the strong sense—politically active life in the public sphere.

Regardless of Habermas's caution about applying his model beyond Europe, we carry important implications of his model. For example, civil society is the private sphere of citizens acting independently of the state, but they inevitably challenge the state and that transforms civil society into the public sphere. Habermas says,

> The state authorities evoked a resonance leading the *publicum,* the abstract counterpart of public authority, into an awareness of itself *as the latter's opponent,* that is, as the public of the now emerging public sphere of civil society.[7]

Over time, for Habermas himself, the public sphere has garnered a more general meaning, as the core of what makes liberal democratic society:

> By "public sphere" we mean first of all a domain of our social life in which such a thing as public opinion can be formed. Access to the public sphere is open in principle to all citizens. A portion of the public sphere is constituted in every conversation in which private persons come together to form a public. They are then acting neither as business or professional people conducting their private affairs, nor as legal consociates subject to the legal regulations of a state bureaucracy and obligated to

---

6. Charles Taylor, "Modes of Civil Society," *Public Culture* 3, no. 1 (Fall 1990): 98.

7. Jurgen Habermas, *The Structural Transformation of the Public Sphere: An Inquiry into a Category of Bourgeois Society* (Cambridge: MIT Press, 1989), 23; emphasis mine.

obedience. Citizens act as a public when they deal with the guarantee that they may assemble and unite freely, and express and publicize their opinions freely.[8]

There are three assumptions in this model that cause problems for Chinese scholars: the concept of "public," the concept of "citizen," and the presumption that the public sphere must be in opposition to the state (the "opponent" I emphasized in the first quote). By reifying bourgeois European experience of the seventeenth and eighteenth centuries into a structural model, proponents of civil society and public sphere have neglected culture. Key components of the model, we shall see, become transformed in the Chinese context so much that the attempt to use Habermas's definition of civil society as an explanatory model has raised much debate among sinologists.

The best reviews of the civil society debate in Chinese studies are by Gu Xin (1993–94), Frederick Wakeman (1993), Philip Huang (1991), and William Rowe (1990); indeed, these four articles nicely trace the rise and current contention of the civil society approach.[9] Philip Huang, the editor of *Modern China*, has suggested that the attractiveness of Habermas's concept derives from the paradigm crisis in Western modern China studies: old models of totalitarianism, modernization, or political culture have failed us.[10] The two major

---

8. Jurgen Habermas, "The Public Sphere," in *Jürgen Habermas on Society and Politics: A Reader*, ed. Steven Seidman (Boston: Beacon Press, 1989), 231.

9. By far the fullest review is by Gu Xin, "A Civil Society and Public Sphere in Post-Mao China? An Overview of Western Publications," *China Information* (Leiden) 8, no. 3 (Winter 1993–94): 1–14. See also Frederick Wakeman, Jr., "The Civil Society and Public Sphere Debate: Western Reflections on Chinese Political Culture," *Modern China* (UCLA) 19, no. 2 (April 1993): 108–38, which is part of a special issue of that journal devoted to the question. Philip C. C. Huang, "The Paradigmatic Crisis in Chinese Studies," *Modern China* 17, no. 3 (July 1991): 299–341, puts the question in broader context. William T. Rowe, "The Public Sphere in Modern China," *Modern China* 16, no. 3 (July 1990): 309–29, sounded a clarion call to use the concept. A good review of the limited debate about "civil society" (as *shimin shehui*, "townspeople society") among Chinese in the PRC and in exile is given in Shu-Yun Ma, "The Chinese Discourse on Civil Society," *The China Quarterly*, no. 137 (March 1994): 180–93.

10. Elizabeth Perry gives the best brief sociology of knowledge account of postwar political theories in "Chinese Political Culture Revisited," in *Popular Protest and Political Culture in Modern China: Learning from 1989*, ed. Jeffrey N. Wasserstrom and Elizabeth Perry (Boulder, Colo.: Westview Press, 1994), 1–3. Harry Harding gives a comprehensive and thoughtful review of political science trends in Chinese studies in "The Evolution of American Scholarship on Contemporary China," in *American Studies of Contemporary China*, ed. David Shambaugh (Armonk, N.Y.: M. E. Sharpe/Woodrow Wilson Press, 1993), 14–40.

trends of analysis in recent years, it seems to me, have been structural—with either bureaucratic interest cum rational actor studies or
civil society cum economic determinism models dominant—or cultural—with neotraditional models or political cultural studies drawing
more on recent historiography of the French Revolution (i.e., Furet,
Lynn Hunt, etc.) than on Freud or Lucian Pye.[11] Whatever their problems, studies of China using the civil society perspective have added
greatly to our knowledge and understanding of Chinese politics and
history. We can review these studies under two topics: studies of pre-
1949 China and studies of post-Mao China.

"Roots": Civil Society in Pre-1949 China

William T. Rowe's work on Hankou, the major city on the mid-
Yangzi River, traces the search for civil society roots back into the eighteenth century. Rowe's project in his 1984 book was to refute Weber's
depiction of Chinese society as stagnant or lacking the pressures that
brought modernization in Europe. Thus, Rowe sought to demonstrate
the dynamic features of Chinese urban society before Western contact,
especially the degree of de facto autonomy achieved by *shimin*—urban
residents and their various public associations.[12] There was little government intervention in the city's business, and much of the local level
administration was in the hands of gentry managers. Rowe sees this
as a trend toward social and economic pluralism which by the years
following the great Taiping rebellion (of 1850–62, which engulfed the
city) produced a world of commerce that began to look much like the
Western image of a preindustrial, urban, capitalist society. According
to Rowe, Hankou had a great deal "in common with early modern
European cities," including "the steady development of organized,
corporate-style civic action and the proliferation of a wide range of
philanthropic and public-service institutions, designed to meet unprecedented and specifically urban social problems faced by cities in the
early modern period."[13] While Rowe's conclusions about the civil soci-

---

11. An intelligent defense of rational actor analysis is given by Daniel Little,
"Rational-Choice Models and Asian Studies," *Journal of Asian Studies* 50 (February 1991): 53–66. Examples of the "new" political culture approach, with an
articulate theoretical exposition by Elizabeth Perry in the introduction, can be
found in Wasserstrom and Perry, *Popular Protest and Political Culture.*

12. William T. Rowe, *Hankow: Commerce and Society in a Chinese City, 1796–
1889* (Stanford, Calif.: Stanford University Press, 1984); continued in *Hankow:
Conflict and Community in a Chinese City, 1796–1985* (Stanford, Calif.: Stanford
University Press, 1989).

13. Rowe, *Hankow: Commerce and Society*, 3–5.

ety nature of Hankou in the nineteenth century have been subject to severe criticism (see Wakeman, below), his two volumes stand as the finest original research on the social history of a Chinese city, rich with detail for comparative study. He also lays to rest the Marxist/Weberian image of at least urban Chinese society in the late imperial period as in any way stagnant or lacking growth and change.

Mary B. Rankin has charted the changes among local elites from the late sixteenth century and the development of a public sphere in China. She sees a broad pattern, a sort of rise and fall of the public sphere from the seventeenth to the twentieth centuries.[14] First, in the late sixteenth century—just the period communist Chinese historians look for Marxian "sprouts of capitalism"—a public sphere emerged in the voluntary management of aspects of local affairs outside the bureaucratic framework by men of local standing and wealth. This sort of local management was confined to the Lower Yangzi and Canton delta areas and particularly in the Qing Dynasty (1644–1911) occurred under considerable official supervision. Still, the Qing state's refusal to fund local administration sufficiently to run schools, famine relief, and other services compelled that state to solicit and support efforts by local elites in these areas. Rankin concludes this managerial public sphere was real, though she concedes, "Management rather than open public discussion was its central characteristic. Relations between officials and elites active in local public affairs were generally consensual rather than confrontational, and elites did not try to define rights against the state or set formal limits on state power."[15] Second, this limited public sphere broadened enormously with the concessions the Qing state gave to local authorities in order to quell the Taiping rebellion in the mid-nineteenth century. A semblance of public opinion on national affairs emerged with the Qing's ignoble defeat by the Japanese in Korea in 1895 and the Qing's own efforts at reform which legalized local associations (*fatuan*), such as chambers of commerce and provincial representative assemblies in the early years of the twentieth cen-

---

14. Mary B. Rankin, *Elite Activism and Political Transformation in China: Zhejiang Province 1865–1911* (Stanford, Calif.: Stanford University Press, 1986); "The Origins of a Chinese Public Sphere: Local Community Affairs in the Late-Imperial Period," *Études Chinoises* 2, no. 2 (Autumn 1990): 13–60; and "Some Observations on a Chinese Public Sphere," *Modern China*, 19, no. 2 (April 1993): 158–82. See, Gu Xin's account of these in his review, "A Civil Society and Public Sphere in Post-Mao China?" 6–8. This approach to the study of local elites has been richly extended with case studies into the mid-twentieth century in Joseph W. Esherick and Mary B. Rankin, eds., *Chinese Local Elites and Patterns of Dominance* (Berkeley: University of California Press, 1990).
15. Rankin, "Some Observations," 160–161.

tury.[16] At some times in some places, unofficial Chinese elites in public organizations—chambers of commerce, lawyers' guilds, bankers' associations—managed public affairs and expressed themselves with some authority on issues of public concern. The third stage, however, is characterized by the weakness of civil society during the Republican period (1911–49) and its virtual demise under the new Communist national government after 1949. During the former period the government was not stable enough to support the growth of civil institutions, and in the latter period the CCP preempted that social space with its massive Leninist organization.

The application of civil society to early modern Chinese history has been severely criticized. Philip Huang denounces it as a kind of reductionist and teleological exercise searching for "sprouts of democracy" in a manner parallel to Communist Chinese historians' search for "sprouts of capitalism." This implies there is, or should be, only one model of history, leading to European liberal democracies.[17] Frederick Wakeman has made an empirical critique, turning Rowe's own rich data against him—arguing case by case that Rowe (and Rankin and Strand) exaggerate the similarities between certain Chinese phenomena and the development in the West of preindustrial, urban, capitalist society.[18] Wakeman chides these authors for neglecting important cultural realities—inter-ethnic (or sub-ethnic) rivalries, elite-bureaucratic cooperation, and the role of outsiders (especially Western influence from the International settlement in Shanghai via, for example, the "Hankou" newspaper *Shenbao*, which was published by an Englishman in Shanghai).

"Buds": Civil Society in Post-Mao China

The critique of the civil society approach in historical studies really became clear in Chinese studies in 1993. Before then, and especially in response to the post-Mao reforms and the spectacular events of 1989, civil society dominated sociological and political studies of contemporary China. Scholars first suggested the student and popular demonstrations in Beijing in spring 1989 constituted either "buds of civil society" or signs of a growing public sphere.[19] Certainly, aspects of

16. The social impact of these developments on the residents of Beijing is carefully studied by David Strand in his *Rickshaw Beijing: City People and Politics in 1920s China* (Berkeley: University of California Press, 1989).

17. Huang, "The Paradigmatic Crisis."

18. Wakeman, "The Civil Society and Public Sphere Debate," 128–33.

19. According to Gu Xin, "A Civil Society and Public Sphere in Post-Mao China," 2, the first scholar to do this was the Danish scholar Clemens Stubbe

what we might consider a public sphere appeared: students met in small groups, particularly in Beijing's coffee houses and salons, throughout the spring to discuss "China's fate"; a public forum of sorts existed via the international media that reported back to China on the VOA and BBC World Service and through the new use of international telephones and fax—all out of control of the government and cleverly used by the protesting students; and international culture had influenced university teachers and professional researchers who were beginning to apply Western social theory and literary criticism to a very independent reassessment of key ideas and symbols of China's revolutionary heritage and Chinese traditional culture. In retrospect, this seems more of a "Treaty Port civil society" supported by extrasocialist international business and press interests than a reflection of something deeply rooted in contemporary Chinese society.[20] Nonetheless, at the time and for a number of China scholars since, Tiananmen was the tip of the civil society iceberg.

Thomas B. Gold suggests that "the remarkable events of April and May 1989 revealed the degree to which civil society has *re-emerged* in Communist China." While he thus draws from the Rankin–Rowe–Strand scholarship on pre-1949 civil society, Gold notes that the bloody suppression of June 1989 shows the degree to which the CCP remains unwilling to accept a nascent civil society in China.[21]

David Strand goes further, seeing a real public sphere in the strong sense of a civil society where social autonomy is becoming a reality in economic, political, and intellectual life. He points to the human rights petition in Beijing in early 1989, the salons at various universities, the willingness of established intellectuals to serve as mediators between the demonstrating students and the government, and the financial involvement of quasi-private enterprises like the Stone Corporation (a Chinese computer firm in Beijing). Strand makes a sophisticated argument. Many people, including workers, teachers, civil servants, and even party cadres, traveled to Tiananmen Square in May 1989 with banners proclaiming their unit identity, that is, the name of their *danwei* (work units). Strand concludes:

> Now, elements of the state, broadly conceived to include state-controlled institutions like universities, newspapers, and factories, have developed

Østergaard in his "Citizens, Groups and a Nascent Civil Society in China: Towards an Understanding of the 1989 Student Demonstration," *China Information*, 4, no. 2 (Autumn 1989): 28.

20. Indeed, this is the theme of Wasserstrom and Perry, *Popular Protest and Political Culture*.

21. Thomas B. Gold, "The Resurgence of Civil Society in China," *Journal of Democracy* 1, no. 1 (Winter 1990): 18–31, quote on 18; emphasis mine.

an independent social identity. They can attack the state by creating a
Chinese version of the East European strategy of "social self-defense."
In the past, this ambiguity between state and society redounded to the
advantage of the regime in its quest for political and social control. But
now, the state's increasing difficulty to control itself can trigger a sudden
enlargement of society, as we have witnessed last year. As was indicated
by defecting journalists from the official media, workers in state enterprises, researchers, and office personnel in 1989, the state, or portions of
it, could form the social basis of protest against the regime itself.[22]

Finally, Martin K. Whyte traces the emergence of a civil society in
China to the Cultural Revolution (1966–76) and the late Maoist era. The
antibureaucratic thrust of Mao's assault on the party in the Cultural
Revolution, the immobilization then of most official organs (aside from
the army), and the traumatic personal trials of Red Guard student
activists during the Cultural Revolution, not to mention those they
tormented, all threw doubt on the "infallibility" of the party and suggested the legitimacy of criticizing the government. To these are added
the resentments and loss of faith of those who suffered under Mao's
mass movements. Post-Mao reforms and leadership squabbles have
only strengthened this civil society.[23] This is a common theme, with
much factual basis, in China studies: Red Guard ultra-Maoists survive
to become post-Mao democracy wall advocates and dissidents.[24]

China scholars have naturally turned to broader social indicators
than the famous Beijing demonstrations. Mayfair Mei-hui Yang has
studied a small, collectively owned printing factory in Beijing and concludes that economic corporate groups such as this provide one of the
mechanisms for an emerging civil society. In China, society and the
state depend on work units not only to produce their stated good or
service but to carry out many social functions, such as housing, insurance, schooling, and more. This dependency has encouraged the tendency in corporate groups to develop their own interests, even when

22. David Strand, "Protest from Beijing: Civil Society and Public Sphere in
China," *Problems of Communism* 39, no. 3 (May–June 1990): 1–19, quote on 18.
Another who would largely agree with this is Lawrence R. Sullivan, "The
Emergence of Civil Society in China, Spring 1989," in *The Chinese People's Move-
ment: Perspectives on Spring 1989*, ed. Tony Saich (Armonk, N.Y.: M. E. Sharpe,
1990), 126–44.

23. Martin K. Whyte, "Urban China: A Civil Society in the Making?" in *State
and Society in China: The Consequences of Reform*, ed. Arthur Lewis Rosenbaum
(Boulder, Colo.: Westview Press, 1992), 85–94.

24. A point first made by Peter R. Moody, *Opposition and Dissent in Contemporary China* (Stanford, Calif.: Hoover Institution Press, 1977).

these do not coincide with the state's interests. "Thus," concludes Yang, "the horizontal integration of civil society is enhanced in the economic sphere, and civil society begins to detach itself from the state."[25]

Gu Xin aptly questions whether Yang's example is not rather an example of the rise of "institutional pluralism," which some scholars felt characterized the political economy of the late Soviet Union.[26] Dorothy J. Solinger flatly rejects Yang's civil society conclusions. Based on her study of business entrepreneurs who have, indeed, been created by the post-Mao reforms, Solinger sees that "the essential economic monolith of the old party-state now shapes official and merchant alike; both have become dependent, mutually interpenetrated semi-classes. . . . agents of the plan and practitioners in the market are, respectively, no longer fully bureaucrats nor yet true merchants operating autonomously."[27] In short, local officials need businesspeople to make money to show success under Deng Xiaoping's reforms, and local entrepreneurs need the "contacts," or *guanxi*, of such officials for everything from raw materials to preferential tax treatment to protection.

New institutions have emerged in the economic reforms that encourage this symbiosis between officials and entrepreneurs. First, there are institutions to regulate the private sector. These include associations of private entrepreneurs and other kinds of business guilds. Second, there are associations that merchants themselves have set up, albeit with state approval and support, mainly technological development corporations and centers. A third sort includes trading "companies" set up by bureaucrats. "All three of these kinds of institutions," says Solinger, "draw either merchant or bureaucrat into the transition to the market economy and create vested interests that prolong that transition."[28] The question is, what are those vested interests? Lewis Rosenbaum introduces the volume that includes Solinger's essay by pointing out that "a fundamental change in the organization and operation of state

---

25. Mayfair Mei-hui Yang, "Between State and Society: The Construction of Corporations in a Chinese Socialist Factory," *The Australian Journal of Chinese Affairs*, no. 22 (July 1989): 31–60, quote on 59. Yang extends this analysis via the concept of *guanxixue* (the science of personal relations in China) in her book *Gifts, Favors, and Banquets: The Art of Social Relations in China* (Ithaca, N.Y.: Cornell University Press, 1994).

26. Gu Xin, "A Civil Society and Public Sphere in Post-Mao China," 10. See also Robert V. Daniels, "Soviet Politics since Khrushchev," in *The Soviet Union under Brezhnev and Kosygin*, ed. John W. Strong (New York: Van Norstran-Reinhold Co., 1971), 22–23.

27. Dorothy J. Solinger, "Urban Entrepreneurs and the State: The Merger of State and Society," in Rosenbaum, *State and Society in China*, 121–22.

28. Solinger, "Urban Entrepreneurs and the State," 130–36.

power in China most likely will facilitate greater autonomy, but does not necessarily mean the acceptance and institutionalization of civil society."[29]

In addition to the theoretical and empirical questions raised, all these sophisticated models of civil society applied to China leave some fundamental questions begging. Who cares if China has such a civil society? Why does it matter to us? The pragmatic concern behind the civil society debate for China is the significance of civil society to Western academics. I see two fundamental value assumptions disguised as social theory in the current use of civil society: (1) the search for a moral/just society for the country of study as a good in and of itself; and (2) a concern for the national interest of the researcher's country, i.e., what changes in the country of study are best for my country or "the world"? The concept of civil society currently used answers these concerns for most Anglo/Western scholars by positing a pseudo-objective standard: dignity of the individual and reasonable economic development along current international capitalist standards, let's say along World Bank/IMF lines. But the current usage badly conflates universal categories for comparative analysis—"sense of self" or "economic interest"—with particular, and therefore relative, values—"individualism" or "capitalism."[30] I personally embrace these values, but we must find a way to keep them clearly separate or maintain our awareness of their distinctiveness when trying to make sense of China.

The effort should, however, protect us from the unaddressed teleological presumptions of the Habermas civil society model and the attendant moral imperialism that William McNeill sees in American popular and foreign policy: our desire to make other societies act like ours.[31] It is a matter of amazement to me that we—and I include myself—took the civil society model and ran with it for so many years. A bit of postmodern "reflexivity" hardly seems an idle precaution at this point. Tim Brook has revived civil society through careful consider-

---

29. Rosenbaum, *State and Society in China*, 3.

30. If indeed we can even accept the possibility of universal categories of analysis beyond each culture. I am unable to think of how to proceed if we despair of the possibility of such comparable categories, at least at a functional/approximate level. A valuable articulation of this problem and three research papers exploring it may be found in David D. Buck, ed., "Forum on Universalism and Relativism in Asian Studies," *Journal of Asian Studies*, 50, no. 1 (February 1991): 29–83, esp. 29–30.

31. William H. McNeill, "Decline of the West?" *The New York Review of Books*, 9 January 1997, 18. I agree with McNeill's characterization that "Americans have liked to think of themselves as showing other peoples how to bring public affairs into harmony with [our] eighteenth-century conceptions of universal human rights."

ation of "auto-organization" in Chinese society, suggesting that these concepts have helped scholars "confront our conceptual habits as well as to rethink the constraints and possibilities in the state-society relationship in China."[32] While Brook defends a normative use of civil society that avoids many of the pitfalls of the Habermas model, I suggest there is a more functional definition of civil society available in Western theory, with fewer teleological presumptions, that might be useful within an explicit framework of political culture analysis.

Political Culture as an Approach

Political culture has been a dirty word in contemporary Chinese studies. Borrowing from modernization theorists of the 1960s interested in "political socialization" and "secularization" (i.e., "the process whereby men become increasingly rational, analytical, and empirical in their political actions"), some China scholars used "political culture" to explain the "irrationalities" (or failure to conform to the modernization/development paradigm) of the Cultural Revolution.[33] Elizabeth Perry gives a succinct account of this "old political culture" approach and its limitations. Unable to conduct field research, these scholars resorted to a mixture of personal impressions (presented as psychocultural analysis) and small-scale surveys in Taiwan or Hong Kong, plus quick reviews of classical philosophical texts and historical events, "so as to cobble together a portrait of Chinese political culture that proved unconvincing to many in the sinological and social science camps alike."[34] The relatively stable years of the 1980s encouraged a return to "structuralist" models of comparative analysis, only to be beset, once again, by the unexpected: Tiananmen 1989.[35]

---

32. Timothy Brook and B. Michael Frolic, eds., *Civil Society in China* (Armonk, N.Y.: M. E. Sharpe, 1997), "Introduction," 4.

33. The standard version of political culture then as "attitudes, beliefs, values and skills which are current in an entire population, as well as those especial propensities and patterns which may be found within separate parts of that population" appears in Gabriel A. Almond and G. Bingham Powell, Jr., *Comparative Politics: A Developmental Approach* (Boston: Little, Brown, 1966), 23. The most noted examples of the "old political culture studies" of China are Lucien W. Pye, *The Spirit of Chinese Politics* (Cambridge: MIT Press, 1968); and Richard Solomon, *Mao's Revolution and Chinese Political Culture* (Berkeley: University of California Press, 1971).

34. Perry, "Introduction," in Wasserstrom and Perry, *Popular Protest and Political Culture*, 2–3.

35. This development is well captured in Paul A. Cohen, *Discovering History in China: American Historical Writings on the Recent Chinese Past* (New York: Columbia University Press, 1984); and Harding, "The Evolution of American Scholarship."

One response to our failure—and the relative uselessness of structuralist approaches—to predict or explain very well the events of 1989 in
China has been an effort by some scholars to tackle China's political
culture again. Perry gives the defense to the reasonable doubt: Is this
neoculturalist perspective any better than the old political culture studies? She notes that both historians and political scientists are exploring
this approach, moderating "the eccentricities of antiquarianism, on the
one hand, and paradigm faddism, on the other, to which each of these
branches of learning—if left to its own devices—was often prone."[36]
This stems in large part from the access to fieldwork and previously
unavailable sources that came with the post-Mao reforms.

The result of these new scholarly circumstances has been an aversion
to static or total pictures of Chinese culture. This has led to an appreciation of what we might call "political cultures" in China. Perry sums
up the challenge and our response:

> Differences in time period, social status, and geographical location were,
> we now realize, characterized by important distinctions in belief and be-
> havior. As a consequence, the challenge is to *discover which of a multitude
> of available cultural repertoires is being drawn upon.*[37]

The assumption here is that behavior cannot be understood outside of
the context of history and locality and that actors must act with the
tools they have, but that "the fluidity and flexibility of cultural practice
alerts the analyst to the possibility of innovation and originality."
Equally, and here we draw from recent scholarship on the French Revolution and especially the work of Lynn Hunt, the new political cul-
ture(s) approach sees political culture "as an arena of *conflict* as well as
consensus—rooted in, yet not reducible to, the social context."[38] The
preferred methodology of neocultural studies is not socialization but
language, symbolism, and ritual—the "loci of confrontation and contestation among social actors."

In all, the conception of political culture in these new studies is as a
fully independent variable interacting with other variables in the social
equation of change. We cannot understand the dynamics of Chinese
political economy without it, yet political culture only makes sense in
concrete social context. The approach gives "'equal time' for cultural

36. Perry, "Introduction," in Wasserstrom and Perry, *Popular Protest and Political Culture*, 4.
37. Perry, "Introduction," 4–5. Emphasis added.
38. Perry, "Introduction,"4–5, characterizing Lynn Hunt, ed., *The New Cultural History* (Berkeley: University of California Press, 1989).

practice and social structure."[39] It is an excellent tool for the comparative contextual analysis.

Another object of this approach has been articulately summarized by David D. Buck, as editor of the *Journal of Asian Studies*:

> Political culture is best understood as the conceptual framework within a society that provides operating principles by which goals are identified and efforts made to achieve those goals.[40]

This takes us fully into the realm of psychology—affect, consciousness, even subconscious forces. As far as I am concerned, this simply constitutes a further ramification, at the individual level, of "cultural practice." It is appropriate for us to attend to the conceptual frameworks that inform the experience of and responses to economic and political events among Chinese actors. Equally, broadly shared conceptual frameworks should be apparent in popular culture, traditional literature, current ideologies, religious practices.

How does the political culture approach work out in actual research? Clearly it can address a wide spectrum of realms in social experience. Our interest, however, is with economic and political change. We are to look for the "multitude of available cultural repertoires being drawn upon" by our subjects and deduce the operation of their "conceptual frames" in their cultural practices as part of an expanded equation that represents the role of culture: "Δ polity $= f$ (political culture) Δ economy." But can we narrow the range of investigation to something we could possibly hope to cover? Here Antonio Gramsci's notion of civil society as a functional part of the polity might help.

Gramsci's Conception of Civil Society

Gramsci's conception of civil society is less used than Habermas's, but it holds promise for a more useful analysis of Chinese political economy.[41] In essence, Gramsci posits civil society as a functional category or arena in the polity, alongside its counterpart, political society, the mechanisms of political domination. Political society, in Gramsci's image, comprises the means of coercion of the ruling class, while civil society holds their persuasive or hegemonic means of convincing other

---

39. Ibid.

40. Buck, "Forum on Universalism," 31. He is actually summarizing the essay by Richard W. Wilson (53–66), but I could not find Wilson's point so succinctly expressed in his own words.

41. A useful review and caution about Gramsci's version is given by Kjeld Eric Broodsgarad, *Copenhagen Papers* 1 (1991).

classes to serve the elite's interests. Together the institutions of force and consent, what he calls "dictatorship and hegemony," make up the superstructure of society (what he generally calls the "state" in the broad sense). The key to Gramsci's sense of civil society is what goes on there—hegemony. If the public sphere (and Habermas's German term is more properly translated as "publicity") is the significant action in Habermas's conception of civil society, then hegemony is the significant operation taking place in Gramsci's civil society.[42]

Gramsci defines civil society as the ensemble of educational, religious, and associational institutions of society that shape the cognitive and affective structures whereby people perceive and evaluate problematic social reality.[43] The process that "shapes the cognitive and affective structures" that are the tools of social actors is hegemony. He defines hegemony as an order in which a common social and moral language is spoken, in which one concept of reality is dominant, informing with its spirit all modes of thought and behavior.[44] The ensemble of institutions of civil society and the cultural order of hegemony are, for Gramsci, not meaningful outside of a specific context: the concept of superstructure that is made up of a duality—political society and civil society. Both, in addition, must have economic roots: The force and hegemony of the elite in the superstructure must be matched by economic power in the base. Gramsci's model, therefore, is an attempt to conceptualize the workings of the social superstructure in a neo-Marxist model that does not assume the reductive supremacy of the economic base (i.e., that the organization of the means and mode of production determine the nature of the superstructure).[45] For us, Gramsci's civil society can serve as a useful model of how social power is deployed by the economic and political elite and thus suggest the mechanisms to look for in explaining our troubled "Δ polity $=$ Δ economy" question.

A key point of Gramsci's conception of civil society is that it is part

---

42. The primary source of Gramsci's political theories is his less than fully systematic prison notes. See Antonio Gramsci, *Selections from the Prison Notebooks, 1929–1935*, ed. Quintin Hoare and Geoffrey Nowell Smith (London: Lawrence & Wishart, 1971); and Gramsci, *The Modern Prince and Other Writings* (New York: International Publishers, 1957). I rely heavily on the analysis and contextual interpretations of Gramsci given by Joseph V. Femia in *Gramsci's Political Thought: Hegemony, Consciousness, and Revolutionary Process* (New York: Oxford University Press, 1981).

43. This definition is the paraphrase by Femia based on the Italian original of Gramsci's. Femia, *Gramsci's Political Thought*, 24.

44. Ibid. This definition is the paraphrase by Femia based on the Italian original of Gramsci's.

45. Ibid., 1–3.

of the state, where the state is broadly conceived as the social institutions supporting an elite. This conception breaks the state-society dichotomy assumed in the Habermas model of state-civil society. Instead of the prime agent of force alienated from society, the state is part of a package of domination by a coalition of elites over everyone else. This is a useful reconceptualization of political economy in China, where most serious analysts (such as Solinger, above) note the interpenetration of "state" and "society."[46] Gramsci's model of political force and ideological consent in the service of a social elite fruitfully requires us to recast our questions about how China's political economy works: We can now meaningfully ask, "How do various social forms, public beliefs, or social groups work to sustain or contest the current power relations in Chinese society to divvy out the goods to some folks but not others?" His categories give greater specificity to the broad mandate of the new political culture(s) approach.

Like Habermas's conception of civil society and public sphere, Gramsci's political/civil society duality and hegemony carry conceptual baggage. Habermas was interested in explaining the rise of liberal democracy and has the pragmatic concern to defend it against modern and postmodern assaults. Gramsci was interested in explaining why the spontaneous collapse of capitalism predicted by Marx had not occurred by the 1920s and had the pragmatic concern of promoting a class revolution on behalf of industrial workers. Gramsci was a Communist and revered Lenin. In addition to the Marxist analytical assumptions of economic base and political superstructure, Gramsci carried the embedded value orientation of Marxist analysis: revolutionary praxis in class warfare.

If we let go of Gramsci's conception of the social elite (or its coalition) as a simple Marxian economic class, then we can ask: What acts "like" his "class" elite?[47] It may be an unusual or unexpected coalition of social actors or forces. Indeed, we shall suggest just such an odd coalition at the local level in China between Leninist cadres and capitalist entrepreneurs in a new "socialist corporatist" elite. Gramsci's conception of the orders of social control and the attention he gives to consensus, as well as force, suggest useful questions to ask of the state-society nexus in China. This seems to me a useful perspective, a handy heuristic device that focuses our attention on how particular Chinese

---

46. See also the idea of "institutional amphibiousness" connecting state and society in China in Xueliang Ding, *The Decline of Communism in China: Legitimacy Crisis, 1977–1989* (Cambridge: Cambridge University Press, 1994).

47. In any event, we should be able to use, or test, Gramsci's analytical categories separate from his intended use of them—we can steal their truth-finding usefulness for our own agendas.

actors interpret the "Δ polity = Δeconomy" equation. That is, we insert a moderating variable, or more accurately, a transformational function in the equation: "Δ polity = ƒ (political culture) Δ economy."[48] In short, Gramsci's conception of civil society encourages us to ask, What is the hegemonic order in Chinese political culture as we can empirically observe it among various discrete actors, and how is this order subject to contention and change?

A Political Culture(s) View of Current Developments in China

Now we turn to a brief test of this approach to see if it might help us explain what is going on in China, suggest what might be likely in the near future, and provide some basis for productive comparison with Mexico.

The basic assumptions, practices, and beliefs of current Chinese political culture(s) as they affect the expression of economic change in the political arena can be seen in four specific aspects of the political economy: in the role of the party in the Chinese polity, in the organization of business through public associations, in the working values of Chinese entrepreneurs and managers, and in the function of the intellectual elite. This is not meant to be an exhaustive analysis in terms of either categories or data, but I hope to throw some light on the issues of how economic liberalization relates to democracy.

The CCP: "*Dang*" as "*Gong*" in the Chinese Polity

What is the role of the CCP in the Chinese polity? In most civil society analyses of contemporary China, it is equated with the state in the model of state vs. society. From the political culture perspective using Gramsci's political/civil society categories of social dominance, how might we conceive the role of the party? Joseph Fewsmith, based on careful research on the political economy of the Republican period, suggests the "party" (*dang*) fills the conceptual space of the "public" (*gong*) in Chinese conceptions of state and society.[49] Drawing from re-

---

48. This mathematical metaphor, of course, is merely heuristic. Each of the complex elements in reality slowly change the nature of each other in a way the simple equation cannot represent.

49. Joseph Fewsmith, "The Dengist Reforms in Historical Perspective," in *Contemporary Chinese Politics in Historical Perspective*, ed. Brantly Womack (Cambridge: Cambridge University Press, 1991), 23–52, especially the last few pages of this essay. Fewsmith's argument draws from his detailed study, *Party, State, and Local Elites in Republican China* (Honolulu: University of Hawaii Press, 1985).

search on the Chinese polity from the late nineteenth century by Rankin and others, Fewsmith reviews late imperial Chinese conceptions of the polity.[50] Three realms are conceptualized by Chinese thinkers and are deducible from Chinese practice: *guan*, or the official realm of designated agents (employees) of the state; *si*, or the private realm of individuals and family concerns; and *gong*, or the public realm in which issues of general concern but beyond the strict concerns of the administration or private individuals are negotiated. Under the Qing Dynasty, a variety of social actors operated in the *gong* realm—local elites, religious institutions, various voluntary associations (all covered in valuable detail, for example, in the Esherick and Rankin volume). But the key was a viable state, a clear and legitimate occupant of the *guan* domain which made the "conversation" between official and private concerns produce a coherent public realm.

Two important points derive from this Chinese cultural construction of the *publicum*: It is a relational field between two others, not an independently conceived abstraction, and it historically operated more by agreed rules of co-option than by opposition. Officials co-opted local elites to perform administrative functions (such as tax collection, famine relief, local education, and even commercial supervision) which the Confucian state chose not to administer directly, and local elites drew upon the political and status resources of the state to prop up their dominance over resources in local society. There were naturally tensions between the occupants of official and private interests, but the legitimate public language of Confucian politics required the contest not to be cast in adversarial terms.

This dynamic but relatively stable triad fell apart with the demise of the Qing state over the half-century before its complete collapse in 1911. In the Republic, there was no clear and legitimate *guan* in practice in most areas of China. Thus, Fewsmith implies, the articulation of the *gong*, or the Chinese version of the public sphere, was frustrated. He suggests that the Leninist party, *dang* in Chinese, filled the social space of *gong* in the absence of the possibility of a sensible "coopting conversation" between official and private realms.

This is a most promising suggestion. It can be extended in the PRC since 1949: the party *is* civil society and its propaganda system (the *xuanjiao xitong*) is the public sphere (in Habermas's sense). Together they are the articulation of the *gong* realm in the form of a "directed public sphere" that is closer to Gramsci's idea of a civil society but-

---

50. Fewsmith's use of Rankin's research and articulation of *guan-gong-si* highlights my point that the research on Chinese civil society is much richer and broadly useful than the strengths and weakness of the Habermas model.

tressing the political society of the current elite than Habermas's oppositional public sphere inside the legally independent institutions of his
civil society. The institutions of civility and social publicity are organized and controlled in China in the *xuanjiao xitong*.[51] That system includes the current newspaper and media systems, as well as internal
reporting systems, the Chinese Academy of Social Sciences, and all
universities and research institutes. It was born in the revolutionary
base areas run by the CCP during World War II and has continued into
the post-Mao period. The concept of "directed culture" comes from
Victor Serge's depiction of the Stalin period in which the state controls
art, ethics, and ideas "for the good of the people."[52] Because the propaganda and education *xitong* in China includes the arts and universities,
writers, professors, and researchers as well as journalists belong to that
web which is under the direct control of the Propaganda Department
of the CCP. In Mao's China there was no other "space" in which to
speak. This was the "directed public sphere" of socialist China.[53] The
reforms of post-Mao China have only fitfully changed that monolith.
There is more latitude and more market pressure, but the residual
strength of the institutions of China's propaganda state confound a
simple model of marketization = intellectual freedom. We shall see in
the fourth example below, on intellectuals, that much of their culture
supports a statist rather than independent approach to change.

51. *Xuanjiao xitong*, literally "the propaganda and education system." This
is one of the six major integrated administrative systems of the PRC that are
common knowledge to Chinese officials but little studied, so far, outside
China. The best summary presentation of this integrated social information
system is in Kenneth Lieberthal, *Governing China: From Revolution Through Re-
form* (New York: W. W. Norton, 1995), 192–99. For more detail, see Yan Huai,
"Organizational Hierarchy and the Cadre Management System," in *Decision
Making in Deng's China*, ed. Carol Hamrin and Suisheng Zhao, (Armonk, N.Y.:
M. E. Sharpe, 1995), 39–50. A useful chart of the range of activities covered in
the propaganda and publicity aspects of this *xitong* in the 1950s appears in
Julian Chang, "The Mechanics of State Propaganda: The People's Republic of
China and the Soviet Union in the 1950s," in *New Perspectives on State Socialism
in China*, ed. Timothy Cheek and Tony Saich (Armonk, N.Y.: M. E. Sharpe,
1997), 81. See also Alan P. L. Liu, *Communications and National Integration in
Communist China* (Berkeley: University of California Press, 1975), 36–38.
    52. Miklós Haraszti has shown the appeal of directed culture for intellectu-
als under state socialism in Hungary. In his ironic novel *The Velvet Prison*, Haraszti's cynical censor concludes, "Socialism, contrary to appearances, does not
suppress artistic Nietzchean desires but satisfies them. . . . The state prevents
my art from becoming a commodity, and it guarantees my status as a teacher
of the nation." Miklós Haraszti, *The Velvet Prison: Artists under State Socialism*
(New York: Basic Books, 1986), 24, 94.
    53. This is a central theme of Timothy Cheek, *Propaganda and Culture in
Mao's China: Deng Tuo and the Intelligentsia* (Oxford: Clarendon Press, 1997),
esp. 13–18.

The history of the CCP is key to understanding likely current developments of this directed public sphere and the party itself. Here the model suggested by Philip Kuhn for understanding the social function of the Taiping rebels' ideology in mid-nineteenth-century China is helpful.[54] Kuhn sees the twisted version of hellfire Protestant Christianity adopted by Hakka minorities in the southwest province of Guanxi as answering a social need—ethnic conflict—and providing a way of understanding it, articulating it, and acting upon it (through the militant "God Worshipping Society") that was inexpressible in Confucian political discourse. In a similar fashion the Maoist variant of the Bolshevik party was a conceptual frame and social organization as alien to Chinese political culture as the monotheism and women's militias of the Taipings, but it took root in Chinese society because it, too, answered an urgent social need—in this case a means of representing and organizing the *gong* in the absence of a clear and legitimate official realm in the turbulent world of the 1930s and 1940s. And, following Kuhn's explanation of the disappearance of the Taiping vision so quickly after it took over nearly half of China, the CCP vision of *dang* as the instantiation of *gong* has faded with the change of social experience since 1950: there is now a clear and legitimate *guan*, the PRC state (ironically, for the party, its own creation). Thus, we might better conceive of the crisis of faith and loss of legitimacy of the Leninist party in contemporary China as the search by the current incumbents of that institution to find a new role for their *dang* now that its repressive organization of the *gong*—through party control of all public associations and the media through the directed public sphere of the *xuanjiao xitong*—increasingly does not "speak to" the social experience of Chinese actors in the public arena.

The Habermasian civil society is not necessarily emerging, and most commentators cannot find empirical evidence for the civility and legal protections associated with it—beyond Potter's carefully delimited model of the *getihu* entrepreneurs in chapter 6 (one should consider Tim Brook's arguments concerning the traditions of "auto-organization" in China over the past four centuries as well). Rather we can see the reconstitution of a transformed co-optive conversation between the official and private realms of China's economic and social elites that draws upon Chinese historical experience in the late Qing and early Republican periods.

The party may be able to revive its role as the instantiation of the

---

54. Philip A. Kuhn, "Origins of the Taiping Vision: Cross-Cultural Dimensions of a Chinese Rebellion," *Comparative Studies in History & Society* 19, no. 3 (1977): 350–66.

gong realm, as well as the *guan* (state) role, or at least as the leading
institution in these realms, by co-opting new economic elites—rural
entrepreneurs—and serving as the forum for co-optive conversation
between those private interests and the formal state administration.
James Williams has fruitfully compared this effort by the CCP to those
of Mexico's Party of the Institutionalized Revolution (PRI). Both parties
have designed economic institutions to promote economic growth in
the world capitalist/market system which are nonetheless amenable to
continued party power. In this, the tasks confronting the CCP and its
actual solutions resemble those of the PRI:

> The PRI is not a Leninist party, and Mexico's current neoliberal restruc-
> turing was brought on by a debt crisis rather than the Cultural Revolu-
> tion. Despite these enormous differences the tasks confronted by the PRI
> and the CCP—to create an expanding niche in the world economy, to
> divert a restive public from democratization demands into money-mak-
> ing, and to create a social-economic basis for ongoing political monop-
> oly—are quite similar.[55]

The PRI of Salinas, suggests Williams, sought to transform the role of
its basic-level cadres from grassroots political mobilizers to efficient
technocrats. This has caused friction within the PRI and has entailed
co-opting of essential social groups. The key link in this co-option has
been the PRI's ability to funnel resources to those groups. The CCP's
strategy seems similar. It, too, has sought to transform its powerful
constituency of some fifty-seven million party members (as of 1996)
into technocratic managers. Indeed, the composition of the 13th, 14th,
and 15th Party Congresses (in 1987, 1992, and 1996) shows an absolute
majority of members with college-level education in economics or engineering. The party has thus devised a system for co-opting the new
wealth generated by economic liberalization (and thus frustrating our
equation of that with political democratization). "The key to this," says
Williams (in concert with much recent empirical research by Solinger
and others), "lies in the system of ownership and control of economic
enterprises—the contract responsibility system."[56] Most scholars treat
this as "privatization,"[57] but it is not. The lion's share of the new form
of ownership is "collective ownership," which in reality is still in pub-

---

55. James H. Williams, "Reforms and the Future of China's Environment,"
manuscript (1993).

56. Ibid., 9–10.

57. See, for example, Elizabeth Perry's summary of economic performance,
which declares that 47 percent of economic production in China in 1992 was
outside state hands. Perry, "China in 1992," 15.

lic or, more precisely, local bureaucratic hands. The mechanism of ownership does not give property rights to individuals and relies, ultimately, on the good will of local party cadres, whether they are actual co-owners of enterprises or not.

These suggestions have been substantiated by recent field research. Andrew Watson addresses the changing nature of government and administration in rural China. He stresses the unpredictable results of the devolution of economic decisionmaking under the decentralizing reforms of the 1980s. Cadres and entrepreneurs, he finds, have developed a new sense of *local* economic identity that cuts across putative state vs. society or communist vs. capitalist divides. He notes the unpredictability of these changes and calls on us to look at specific new economic groups and their interests as the likely driving forces in China's changing political economy.[58] More recent field research in Yunnan province by Xiaolin Guo confirms this picture and offers some tentative answers. She compares two townships with different political statuses—one as a "minority" area and the other not. The complex realities of economic reform in these two villages nonetheless confirm that there is no simple equation between economic liberalization and democratization. The local joke she heard was "the market (*shichang*) cannot over-ride the mayor (*shizhang*)" (a near-pun in Chinese).[59] Indeed, her study of property rights shows that "formal and informal constraints exerted by the government still effectively regulate the market economy." She concludes with a useful refocusing of our attention to the middle levels of the PRC economy:

> Decentralization has created a structure which is "small at both ends and big in the middle." This structure reflects the relatively insignificant roles played by the central state and individuals in contrast to the powerful role assumed by the government at local levels.[60]

The vertical downloading of economic incentive and responsibility to managers below the central government level has not produced incentives for political autonomy or Habermasian civil society. Rather, party domination is now local and dispersed rather than central and

---

58. Andrew Watson, ed., *Economic Reform and Social Change in China* (London: Routledge, 1992), 5, 14, 178–201, and conclusion.

59. Xiaolin Guo, "Local Practices of Property Rights in Land and Township Enterprises: An Analysis of Incentive Structures," in *Property Rights in Transitional Economies: Insights from Research on China*, ed. Jean Oi and Andrew G. Walder (Cambridge: Harvard University Press, forthcoming). Quotation is from manuscript, 31.

60. Ibid., 30, 32.

monolithic. We should not mistake decentralization of party bureaucratic control for democratization of decisionmaking among a significantly broader spectrum of the citizenry.

Party dominance at the local level thus serves economic liberalization and, Williams cautions, a fierce mercantilist competitiveness that
lacks all concern for long-term costs, such as environmental degradation. Williams calls this "cadre capitalism." Tony Saich describes this
phenomenon as "Nomenklatura capitalism."[61] Cheng Li and David
Bachman stress the dire implications of this "economic localism" for
the future of the central party because local actors can, in effect, "write
their own laws" without regard to national goals.[62] Whether for the
party itself or for the "good life," in China the prospects of this new
market-driven hegemony are not bright. Margaret Pearson develops
this in a model of "socialist corporatism." Let us turn our gaze, then,
from the party's perspective to those who organize China's economic
boom.

Business Associations and Socialist Corporatism

If the power relations of local level cadres and capitalists have
formed a new hegemony that precludes democratization, how are
these interests articulated in the polity? Post-Mao society has seen the
revitalization of the role of associations (*xiehui*) of economic groups.
Such merchant associations are often seen as the building blocks of the
Habermasian conception of civil society, giving political expression to
economic interests separate from the state. In China this turns out not
to be the case. Margaret Pearson's study of associations in the foreign-
capital-invested industrial sector (including equity joint ventures, con-
tractual joint ventures, and wholly foreign-owned enterprises) suggests such associations operate in a pattern that can be called "socialist
corporatism."[63] That is, they continue the conversational and co-opting

---

61. Tony Saich, "The Fourteenth Congress of the CCP," *The China Quarterly*
(1993).

62. Cheng Li and David Bachman, "Localism, Elitism, and Immobilism:
Elite Formation and Social Change in Post-Mao China," *World Politics* 45, no. 1
(1992): 85.

63. Margaret M. Pearson, "The Janus Face of Business Associations in
China: Socialist Corporatism in Foreign Enterprises," *The Australian Journal of
Chinese Affairs*, no. 31 (January 1994): 25–46; and Pearson, *China's New Business
Elite* (Berkeley: University of California Press, 1997). Her views on incorpora-
tion of entrepreneurial interests into the party-state are confirmed and ex-
tended to the concept of "citizenship" in Kristen Parris, "Private
Entrepreneurs as Citizens: from Leninism to Corporatism," *China Information*
10, nos. 3–4 (Winter 1995/Spring 1996): 1–28.

role of Qing period merchant associations that represented official and private interests simultaneously.[64] As such, from our political culture perspective, we can see such associations joining the party as institutions in the *gong* public realm. As the *dang* serves to articulate the needs and interests of the political elite in the CCP, so too do the *xiehui* articulate the needs and interests of the new economic elite in China's reformed economy. Both social institutions co-opt members of the other, mediate disputes, and form a self-sustaining pact that can guarantee economic development for local consumption and international trade needs. *Dang* and *xiehui* act as specific instances of the political/civil society domination of Chinese society by these elites. In their coercive, legal arms they are part of Gramsci's political society; in their "moral and intellectual leadership" roles, which present their activities as for the public good, they perform the functions of hegemony in the civil society.

Like Fewsmith in his analysis of the role of the party, Pearson also draws from the research of Mary Rankin et al. to trace the role of professional guilds and associations (*huiguan, hanghui, gongsuo*) in the late Qing and Republic. They are a special case of the general pattern of local elite co-option and coordination with state interests we have seen above. Because of the low status of merchants and business in Confucian ideology, merchant guilds buttressed their public image by performing public (*gong*) acts such as upkeep of canals, fire fighting, or town planning on behalf of the state. The late Qing reforms legalized and formalized guilds that had in any event always been tied to the state. The collapse of the state saw a golden age of increasingly independent merchant associations in the 1910s and 1920s, but this came to an end in the major cities with the reassertion of government control by the Nationalist Party (Kuomintang, KMT) government set up in Nanjing in 1927. The PRC in the 1950s converted the old "conversation" of private and official interests in the associations into a monologue delivered by party cadres to cowed (and often ideologically attacked) business leaders. Yet, Pearson gives four compelling reasons

---

64. Jonathan Ungar and Anita Chan show that the corporatist pattern also draws from broader East Asian models of successful economic development in "Corporatism in China: A Developmental State in an East Asian Context," in *China after Socialism: In the Footsteps of Eastern Europe or East Asia?* ed. J. Unger and Barrett McCormick (Armonk, N.Y.: M. E. Sharpe, 1996), 95–129. Like many analyses, they note that the "direction" of corporatist organization could lead to more democracy or more authoritarian rule; note their useful typologies of various forms of corporatism in China, particularly "state-corporatist" and "societal corporatist" modes of aggregation. *China's New Business Elite* stresses the differences between Chinese and East Asian corporatism that seem to explain China's current non-democratization.

why the Janus-faced (simultaneously oriented toward state and society) legacy of business associations should be compelling in post-Mao China—that is, in our terms, why it should be part of the repertoire available in China's political culture. First, both late Qing and Nationalist regimes and the post-Mao reformers "recognize the same functional need to harness the resources and skills of the business elite." Second, there is some continuity between pre- and post-1949 institutions (such as particular associations), giving the possibility of institutional memory. Third, contemporary Chinese scholars and political advisors are reexamining Qing and Republican merchant experience with an eye to productive models for today. Finally, Pearson notes "an enduring cultural and intellectual context" over the decades.[65]

Her empirical data on the China Association for Enterprises with Foreign Investment (CAEFI) seeks to demonstrate that this model survives and that it extends to other business associations, such as the Individual Business Association (*getihu laodongzhe xiehui*).[66] But, as with the new political culture approach, Pearson is not suggesting a mechanical, unchanging continuity. She sees the novel transformation of the old Qing official-merchant associations as socialist corporatism. This gives considerable specificity to her analysis of the structure and function of *xiehui*. She explicitly draws from Philippe Schmitter's model of state corporatism in which corporatist structures are foisted upon society by the state where the state retains ultimate authority while allowing some autonomy within functional realms.[67] For Pearson, socialist corporatism captures some key distinctions and it acknowledges the different social context of socialist and post-socialist states relative to Schmitter's examples of late, dependent capitalist countries. Thus, instead of substituting a weak bourgeois with repression of subordinate class interests, socialist regimes act to preempt the

---

65. Pearson, "The Janus Face," 31.

66. Ibid., 37–45. See Chapter 6, by Pitman Potter, on the legal culture of individual entrepreneurs.

67. Pearson, "The Janus Face," 32. This is a subset of Schmitter's generic definition of corporatism: "a system of interest representation in which the constituent units are organized into a limited number of singular, compulsory, noncompetitive, hierarchically ordered and functionally differentiated categories, recognized or licensed (if not created) by the state and granted a deliberate representational monopoly within their respective categories in exchange for observing certain controls on their selection of leaders and articulation of demands and supports." See Philippe Schmitter, "Still the Century of Corporatism?" in *The New Corporatism: Social-Political Structures in the Iberian World*, ed. Frederick B. Pike and Thomas Stritch (Notre Dame, Ind.: University of Notre Dame Press, 1974), 93–94

emergence of autonomous groups. Second, instead of gathering in existing social forces through corporatism, socialist corporatism seeks to devolve some of the state's power (overcentralized from the Stalinist model) to stimulate national production. Finally, socialist corporatism takes account of the parallel party-state structure of communist regimes, which differ from the unitary state structure of authoritarian regimes.[68] This seems to me a productive model for assessing the roughly 2,000 associations, chambers of commerce, federations, societies, research units, foundations, cooperatives, and "privately run" (*minjian*) research institutes formed by 1989 and, since 1989, registered with the Social Organizations Department of the Ministry of Civil Affairs.[69]

We have looked in some detail at the role of the party and business organizations. We should equally look at the level of individual motivations and "conceptual frames" of actors in the polity. Two obvious examples are entrepreneurs and high-level intellectuals. Here we should see the experience of economic interest and the expression of "moral and intellectual leadership," respectively. In both arenas we can see values, habits, and historically functional patterns of behavior that support the higher-level (i.e., group) expressions of *dang* and *xiehui* as co-opting and conversational mechanisms of hegemony supporting a renewed pact between China's current political elite and emerging entrepreneurial elites.

Entrepreneurs and Managers: The Spirit of Chinese Capitalism

Can we get a sense of the values that animate economic activity at the level of individual entrepreneurs? Study of this topic in the PRC is in its infancy, and Potter's chapter on the legal culture of small entrepreneurs in Shanghai is pathbreaking work. Potter shows us promising "sprouts of autonomy" in the instrumental values held by this low-status but economically dynamic and needed group. Tim Brook also traces "consistent patterns of associative behavior based on volunary cooperation" in Shanghai over the past four centuries that include occupation groups (guilds, trade associations, etc.), as well as groups based on locality, fellowship (religious groups, academies), and common cause. Brook suggests that such "auto-organization . . . testifies to the presence within Chinese society of horizontal integration" that

68. Pearson, "The Janus Face," 33.
69. Data from ibid., 34–35.

constitute cultural resources for indigenous civil society in China.[70] Susan Young's study of attitudes toward private business in the 1980s, however, underlines the fragility of these "sprouts."[71] While independent entrepreneurs do, indeed, long for institutional and legal orders which will protect their work, neither the legal regime nor the administrative *habitus* to protect businesspeople exists in China. Rather than pushing for these liberal democratic protections, Young finds her entrepreneurs adopting strategies for self-protection that are reminiscent of the Qing and Republican case: they disguise themselves as collectives or attach themselves to a state industry; they support social welfare charities to show they are not exploitive; they submit to party pressures to conform to current policy and ultimately engage in corruption to survive. They also adopt a short-term horizon that plays into the lack of economic rationalism and unfortunate environmental degradation noted by Williams (see Cheek and Lindau, "Introduction," this volume).

Research on Chinese manager-owners outside mainland China confirms in greater detail the cautions raised by Young. Gordon Redding in *The Spirit of Chinese Capitalism* turns to the crux of Weber's classic *The Protestant Ethic and the Spirit of Capitalism*—the explanation of how people came to be "rational economic actors" in Europe, that is, the analysis of the entrepreneurial class.[72] Redding sets out to describe the development of Chinese entrepreneurs among the 43 million overseas Chinese whose economic power extends across the Asia–Pacific region. His approach is explicitly cultural, as he believes Weber's was. It is a careful study, based on extended interviews with some seventy-two Chinese chief executives in Hong Kong, Taiwan, and Southeast Asia, of the relationship between societal values and economic activity. Redding adopts the framework of "economic culture" (as promoted by Peter Berger at Boston University, at whose institute Redding did some of his work for the book)[73] both to define overseas Chinese as a

---

70. Timothy Brook, "Auto-Organization in Chinese Society," in Brook and Frolic, *Civil Society in China*, 23–5, 22, 45. Readers should consult this thoroughly researched and cogently argued essay and the following essay in that book by B. Michael Frolic, "State-Led Civil Society," 47–67 that argues a position closer to the one which I take on the limits of civil society in China.

71. Susan Young, "Wealth but Not Security: Attitudes Towards Private Business in the 1980s," in Watson, *Economic Reform and Social Change in China*, 63–87. These attitudes are similarly present in the business leaders Pearson studied in *China's New Business Elite*.

72. Gordon S. Redding, *The Spirit of Chinese Capitalism* (Berlin: Walter de Gruyter, 1990), 8.

73. Redding's working definition of "economic culture" is: "There are, within a certain geographical boundary, sufficient connections between socio-

distinct group and to analyze how their managers, enterprises, and relations with society work. The book is built around this core analytical matrix that defines the spirit of Chinese capitalism as derived from the legacies of Chinese social history. These values and behavior patterns are defined as paternalism, personalism, and insecurity among owner-managers, which he pursues in terms of individual perceptions and behavior in the realms of self, kinship and business relations, enterprise organization, and role in society.[74] The point for our analysis is: These habits, and the social institutions they represent, among Chinese entrepreneurs get the economic job done while maintaining political relationships inimical to liberal democracy.

Work on Chinese "secret societies" (the so-called *mimi hui*) connects the themes of individual motivation and social organization raised by the case of business association and entrepreneurial values in China. David Ownby has shown that *hui* (the usual Chinese name for these brotherhoods, such as the Triads) have had a varied life over the past three centuries—sometimes as self-help groups at the village level, sometimes as entrepreneurs in rural violence, sometimes as gangs running drugs and prostitution, but sometimes as legal business associations (*gongsi*).[75] Like the model of official-merchant cooperation drawn from the Qing, the cultural tools of the *hui* bequeathed to current Chinese entrepreneurs suggest precisely the approaches, assumptions, and habits outlined in Redding's picture of fundamental values of Chinese capitalism.

Redding's conclusions are not controversial, but neither are they guilty of the methodological sloppiness of the old political culture studies of the past. Chinese businesses run themselves along family lines and seek a low profile in public and accommodation with political authorities, rather than pushing for legal rights. The work ethic comes from a family sense of obligation and political insecurity in host countries (including Chinese administrations in Hong Kong and Taiwan). These findings further weaken the simple "Δ market = Δ democracy" assumptions of current civil society-style analyses and strengthen the political culture perspective suggested here.

---

cultural values and economic behavior to make for a distinctive and unique constellation of features, identifiable both by particular economic characteristics and results and by overlapping social values." Ibid., 7. Redding is drawing from Peter Berger, *The Capitalist Revolution* (New York: Basic Books, 1986).

74. See chart in Redding, *The Spirit of Chinese Capitalism*, 83, and his analysis.

75. David Ownby, "Mutual Benefit Societies in Chinese History," in *Social Security Mutualism: The Comparative History of Mutual Benefit Societies*, ed. Marcel van der Linden (Bern: Peter Lang, 1996), 529–53; and Ownby, *Brotherhoods and Secret Societies in Early and Mid-Qing China: The Formation of a Tradition* (Stanford, Calif.: Stanford University Press, 1996).

Intellectuals: Agents of Hegemony for the State

If capitalists are unlikely to take the lead in democratization, what of intellectual leadership? What are the prospects of China's intellectuals leading her politically apathetic capitalists and careerist cadres toward liberal democracy? Not very promising, because I do not think all that many Chinese intellectuals intend to take the Euro–American political road. Indeed, the history of Chinese thought on constitutional issues since the early nineteenth century suggests a continued strain of bureaucratic authoritarianism among influential "establishment intellectuals" in China.[76] My own research on Chinese intellectuals at the national and metropolitan levels has sought to understand the role of such "establishment intellectuals."[77] Even the reform-oriented intellectuals of the 1980s and early 1990s operated more in the mode of "priest-rentiers serving the cosmic state (Confucian or Leninist)" than "professionals salaried in a bourgeois society" who might articulate values and interests in opposition to the state.[78] Such high-level intellectuals remain an artifact of the CCP party-state, employed by state institutions in the propaganda and education *xitong* (including research institutes and universities) and able to express themselves only through official media.[79] This has changed in the past ten years, but such changes remain (for reasons outlined in the case of *xiehui* above) matters of degree and not kind. The root causes for intellectuals' continuing focus on the state rather than on independent association are a lack of a conception of intellectual autonomy and weak social support for autonomous activities. This is not to say there are no Chinese intellectuals interested in liberal democratic reforms. David Kelly, He Baogang, and Barrett McCormick make a strong case for the significance of freedom and limits on authoritarianism among some leading Chinese thinkers.[80] However, most Chinese intellectuals maintain a value orien-

76. See Philip Kuhn, "Ideas behind China's Modern State," *Harvard Journal of Asiatic Studies* 55, no. 2 (1995): 295–337. Kuhn's analysis is all the more challenging as his key examples are Wei Yuan and Feng Guifen, who have been admired by Western scholars as forward-thinking reformers.

77. Cheek, *Propaganda and Culture in Mao's China*. Some of this work and the concept of "establishment intellectuals" in the PRC are presented in Carol Hamrin and Timothy Cheek, *China's Establishment Intellectuals* (Armonk, N.Y.: M. E. Sharpe, 1986), especially our introduction.

78. Timothy Cheek, "From Priests to Professionals: Intellectuals and the State Under the CCP," in Wasserstrom and Perry, *Popular Protest and Political Culture*, 125.

79. David Kelly, "Chinese Intellectuals in the 1989 Democracy Movement," in *The Broken Mirror: China After Tiananmen*, ed. George Hicks (London: Longman, 1990), 46–47.

80. David Kelly and He Baogang, "Emergent Civil Society and the Intellec-

tation that seeks to negotiate with and improve the state, in the end to serve or be part of the state, rather than improve governance by challenging the state in some adversarial role. As Gu Xin shows, even the famous entrepreneuer-activists of Tiananmen in 1989, Wang Juntao and Chen Ziming, *intended* to be establishment intellectuals and only turned to independent criticism after failing to make bureaucratic links with party and government leaders.[81]

There are positive reasons, as well, in the cultural tools handed down to Chinese intellectuals from historical experience. Propaganda on behalf of the ideals of the state is an honorable vocation in Chinese culture as well as an explicit expectation of the current party-state. The assumptions and social practices behind propaganda in contemporary China can be seen in the eighteenth-century *xuanjiang*, the lectures propagandizing the sacred edicts of the Kangxi Emperor which were to be given in villages all around China in the Qing period, and in the "community compact" (*xiangyue*) tradition in Neo-Confucian writings from which they drew.[82] Central to this tradition was the injunction from the ancient *Rites of Zhou* "to transform the common people through ritual" (*yi li jiao min*). The audience for these Confucian propaganda lectures is passive and in need of moral reformation (sometimes simply to survive the vicissitudes of rural life and sometimes to avoid and turn back from banditry or litigiousness—as in Wang Yangming's sixteenth-century *xiangyue*). The audience is both literate (overlapping with potential and actual practitioners) and illiterate (the farmer-ma-

tuals in China," in *The Developments of Civil Society in Communist Systems*, ed. Robert Miller (North Sydney: Allen & Unwin, 1992), 24–39; Barrett McCormick and David Kelly, "The Limits of Anti-Liberalism," *The Journal of Asian Studies* 53, no. 3 (August 1994): 804–831; and David Kelly, ed., *Asian Freedoms: The Idea of Freedom in East and Southeast Asia* (New York: Cambridge University Press, 1988).

81. Gu Xin, "The Structural Transformation of the Intellectual Public Sphere in Socialist China (1979–1989)," Ph.d. dissertation, Leiden University, 1997, chapter 9.

82. Hsiao Kung-ch'üan, *Rural China: Imperial Control in the 19th Century* (Seattle: University of Washington Press, 1960), 184–85; Philip Kuhn gives the most succinct review of Zhu Xi's and Lü Kun's models in "Local Self-Government under the Republic: Problems of Control, Autonomy, and Mobilization," in *Conflict and Control in Late Imperial China*, ed. Frederic Wakeman and Carolyn Grant (Berkeley: University of California Press, 1975), 261. See also Victor Mair's chapter on "Sacred Edict Lectures," in *Popular Culture in Late Imperial China*, ed. David Johnson et al. (Berkeley: University of California Press, 1985); and Monika Übelhör, "The Community Compact (*Hsiang-yüeh*) of the Sung and Its Educational Significance," in *Neo-Confucian Education: The Formative Stage*, ed. Wm. Theodore de Bary and John W. Chaffe (Berkeley: University of California Press, 1989), 371–88.

jority). They are also homogeneous, at least in their role as recipients of the cultural education the propaganda lectures provided. In Li Lai-zhang's *Explanations of the Sacred Edict Lectures* of 1705 the audience is divided between commoners and local scholars.[83] This distinction between the commoner and the highly educated audience extends into CCP documents on propaganda in the internal (*neibu*) materials for cadre study and the public (*gongkai*) materials for general and foreign readers.[84] In this whole cultural repertoire, intellectuals are privileged as transcendent speakers for the general public, not as republican representatives or co-equal discussants.

Chinese intellectuals' attitudes about their relationship to political power further reinforce the co-optive and "conversational" organizations of *dang* and *xiehui* and do not fit the adversarial model of *publicum* in Habermas's model of civil society. Chinese intellectuals' attitudes toward that state have been characterized by a fierce patriotism; their behavior with superiors, peers, and subordinates reflects an acceptance of vertical patronage; and their self-expressions reflect a profound elitism and sense of paternalism (which we see echoed in the political culture of Chinese entrepreneurs, according to Redding).[85]

These values have supported an unwritten deal between the CCP and intellectuals in the PRC: in return for obedient service to the party, establishment intellectuals are promised the opportunity to serve China and to engage in intellectual pursuits at a reasonable standard of living. It is clear from the activities and writings of a number of the founding generation of establishment intellectuals between the 1930s and early 1960s that they found this deal to be a desirable revision of the old "contract" between intellectuals and the state that had collapsed with the fall of the empire. Under this deal with the CCP, the educated elite gave up claims to the wealth and political power of their

---

83. *Li Shanyuan quanji* (preface dated 1705; edited by Wei Xiang), "Shengyu xuanjian xiang-bao tiaoyue" [Regulations for Community Security (Xiang & Bao) Sacred Edict Lectures]. Marvelous illustrations for the setup of these lectures appear in this collection.

84. See Ching-chen Hsiao and Timothy Cheek, "Open and Closed Media: External and Internal Newspapers in the Propaganda System," in Hamrin and Zhao, *Decision Making in Deng's China*, 76–90.

85. This analysis is pursued in Timothy Cheek, "Habits of the Heart: Intellectual Assumptions Reflected by Chinese Reformers from Deng Tuo to Fang Lizhi," in *Changes in China: Party, State, and Society*, ed. Shao-chuan Leng (Lanham, Md.: University Press of America, 1989), 117–43. Studies of lower-level institutions, or factories, suggest similar understandings (about expressions of patriotism, loyalty to the party, and patronage) extend to the working classes. See Andrew G. Walder, *Chinese Neotraditionalism* (Berkeley: University of California Press, 1986).

scholar-gentry ancestors to serve what they felt was a more egalitarian and socially just government. They rejected the status of landlord and scholar-elite (*shenshi*) and accepted the status of intellectual (*zhishifenzi*) and cadre (*ganbu*). They honored the common people as never before in history and gave of their talents to raise the cultural and economic level of every Chinese—by serving in the party-state.[86]

This model has changed with the repercussions of the post-Mao reforms. There have been periods when sharp criticism, not to mention sullen silence, from intellectuals has been tolerated by the CCP. Yet, down to the present, the CCP has continually reasserted its prerogative to silence and punish any critics.[87] We can certainly see examples of intellectuals who tried, valiantly, to extend the realm of intellectual autonomy, to find a fulcrum outside party dogma on which to leverage the party in the direction they felt best. But the point remains: all were interested in improving the party. Even Fang Lizhi, the famous astrophysicist turned gadfly who had to shelter in the U.S. embassy in Beijing following the crackdown of June 1989, spent his time trying to work with the party until it tossed him out of the country.[88] There are certainly Chinese intellectuals, particularly now among the post-Tiananmen diaspora, who seek liberal democratic institutions for China. But I do not see them in China, nor do I see their influence among most Chinese intellectuals. The discourse of positive rights, limited government, and antagonistic public contention remains alien to Chinese intellectuals in general.[89] Clever maneuvering, tactful negotiating, and a pragmatic sense of finding the best dollar for one's skills, how-

86. See the examples in Hamrin and Cheek, *China's Establishment Intellectuals*, and Cheek, *Propaganda Culture in Mao's China*. An example among the so-called democratic parties of China is given for the case of the historian Wu Han in Mary Mazur, "The United Front Redefined for the Party-State: A Case Study of Transition and Legitimation," in Cheek and Saich, *New Perspectives on State Socialism in China*, 51–75.

87. For recent examples, see Perry, "China in 1992," 14, and Starr, "China in 1995," 21. A vivid account of recent battles between China's "counter elite" and the post-Mao state is given in Bill Brugger and David Kelly, *Chinese Marxism in the Post-Mao Era* (Stanford, Calif.: Stanford University Press, 1990); and Merle Goldman, *Sowing the Seeds of Democracy in China: Political Reform in the Deng Xiaoping Era* (Cambridge: Harvard University Press, 1994). Participant analysis by Chinese who left after 1989 appears in Hamrin and Zhao, *Decision-Making in Deng's China*.

88. James H. Williams, "The Expanding Universe of Fang Lizhi," *The China Quarterly*, no. 23 (1990): 458–83.

89. See Gu Xin, "The Structural Transformation." For the contrary view that sees more hope for precisely these democratic values among contemporary Chinese intellectuals inside the PRC, see McCormick and Kelly, "The Limits of Anti-Liberalism," *Journal of Asian Studies*, and Brook, "Auto-organization."

ever, are more common among Chinese intellectuals. Thus, high-level intellectuals are unlikely to act as a major force for democratization. However, they can easily fit into the institutions of *dang* and *xiehui* in a way that will promote liberalization. Opportunities for intellectuals in the 1990s are greater by *xiahai*, descending into the sea of commerce, where they will likely contribute to the official-private negotiations that will determine some limits on state rule, than by remaining in their priestly positions as Olympian interpreters trying to democratize a party that is changing its role from church to corporate hegemon.

Conclusion

There is an important distinction raised by F. A. Hayek and nicely applied to the current Chinese case by Arrow Augerot: Democracy determines who rules; liberalism reflects the amount of constraint on whoever rules.[90] The developing patterns in China's political culture—represented by a technocratic party, co-opted business associations, and the mutual benefit in local enterprises for entrepreneurs and state cadres—will very likely produce liberal constraints on the exercise of both political and civil power to serve the interests of a newly emerging entrepreneurial class. They will want predictability in economic relations, but it might be possible to achieve that without the democratic strictures of an independent judiciary and political democracy. Just as possible is the revived co-option and conversation between political and economic elites through the *dang* and *xiehui*.

Conversely, what we see of real autonomy at the local level, in the case of nomenklatura capitalism or economic localism, looks less like the sprouts of Habermasian-style civil society and more like social anarchy. All the signs we see of "autonomy" and "separation from the state" can as easily provide the social space for equivalents of the hateful ethnonationalism we see destroying the former Yugoslavia and the slash-and-burn industrial anomie that now pollutes the former Soviet Union. It is possible that the neocorporatist political culture of post-Mao China with its lack of democracy but corporately negotiated liberal constraints may in fact contribute to a better life for the Chinese and a better partner for America than democratic articulation of harshly mercantilist local economic interests.

---

90. F. A. Hayek, *Studies in Philosophy, Politics and Economics* (New York: Simon & Schuster, 1967), 160. See also Arrow Augerot, "Will China Return to the Center of the Universe?" manuscript, February 1994, 5ff.

Part IV

EXTENDING THE ANALYSIS

9

Constructive Engagement and Economic Sanctions: The Debate over Intervention for Democracy

David Hendrickson

The promotion of democracy and human rights through economic sanctions has become one of the most important projects of contemporary U.S. foreign policy. For two decades—since the congressional legislation of the mid-1970s—the U.S. government has imposed economic sanctions on states whose governments violate human rights, including the right to live under a democratically elected government. The enlargement of democracy, the Clinton administration said on coming to office, ought to replace the containment of communism as our foremost foreign policy objective. Economic sanctions—imposed against a number of countries, threatened against many others—are an important aspect of that quest.

It is not, however, the only aspect. A competing perspective holds that the maintenance of economic ties with authoritarian states, especially if paired with market liberalization, will over time promote various forms of political liberalization—including, but not limited to, the institution of democratic forms of government. Indeed, U.S. foreign policy in the last twenty years has been continually confronted with the question of how to deal with governments whose institutions or practices we find distasteful. Should the United States "engage" these

Portions of this chapter originally appeared as "The Democratist Crusade," *World Policy Journal* 11, no. 4 (Winter 1994/5). Reprinted by permission.

regimes through "trade, contact and communication" or attempt to "asphyxiate" them through "sanctions, boycott and breach"?[1]

Both approaches concern the relationship, broadly conceived, between society and state. Proponents of economic sanctions typically argue that the maintenance of trading relations strengthens the coercive apparatus of an oppressive state or otherwise confers legitimacy on its regime. If we trade with repressive regimes, in other words, we strengthen their ability to maintain their control over their own societies and become complicit in the exercise of despotic authority. In this view, trade is the enemy of reform. The opposing view holds that, over time, the existence or expansion of commercial contacts, especially if paired with moves toward market liberalization in the "engaged" country, strengthens the society against the state. It expands the domain of civil society—the arena of economic, social, and cultural life that exists independently of the state, and it lays the foundation for the greater realization of human rights and, ultimately, points toward democratization. Trade, in this view, is the ally of reform.

The chapters in this volume have shown that the relationship between market liberalization and political democratization is highly complex, though no consensus has been reached (either here or in the larger scholarly literature) on the precise character of the relationship. While both Jorge Domínguez and Robert Packenham are favorably disposed to the proposition that market liberalization will promote a degree of political liberalization, Lorenzo Meyer, Juan Lindau, and Timothy Cheek all write in a far more skeptical vein. Whichever perspective is deemed most persuasive, it would, at a minimum, seem helpful to examine the obverse side of the question—asking not simply whether trade and the economic liberalization often associated with it contribute to political liberalization, but whether the closure of trade or other forms of economic sanctions do so. The problem needs to be addressed from a more normative standpoint as well. To what extent is it legitimate for another state to attempt to effect far-reaching changes in the internal government of another? Do economic sanctions that have as their purpose the transition to democracy or the protection of human rights constitute a "dictatorial interference" in the internal affairs of another state?

Both of these questions will be taken up in the course of this chapter.

---

1. See Franklin L. Lavin, "Asphyxiation or Oxygen? The Sanctions Dilemma," *Foreign Policy*, no. 104 (Fall 1996): 139–53; and John Chettle, "The American Way: Or How the Chaos, Unpredictability, Contradictions, Complexity, and Example of Our System Undid Communism and Apartheid," *The National Interest*, no. 41 (Fall 1995): 3–18, at 7.

A few caveats, however, are in order before proceeding. The first is that the kind of activities associated with "engagement"—the maintenance of trade relations, student and cultural exchanges, tourism—are related to, but not identical with, the extent of market liberalization in the "engaged" society. The United States has maintained a high level of trade relations with the oil-producing states of the Persian Gulf; but arguably it has been the extreme concentration of wealth in the hands of the state that has exacerbated the extreme imbalance between state and civil society in those states and made some of those regimes among the most repressive in the world. Here the connection between trade and either market or political liberalization has been noticeably absent. So, too, the trade relations the West began developing in the 1970s with the Eastern bloc, under the rubric of detente, were with state-controlled companies and had nothing to do with market liberalization. The increasing contact between East and West that occurred in the 1970s and 1980s did exercise a corrosive effect on the legitimacy of communist regimes. The vast gap that developed between the prosperity of the West and the penury of the East, together with the stark contrast between the cultural vibrancy of the one and the stale conformity of the other, contributed substantially to destroying the last vestiges of legitimacy those regimes commanded. But whatever causal effect is attributed to "engagement" in accelerating these processes and in placing these societies on the road to both market liberalization and political democratization, it was clearly not market liberalization as such that produced the change.

A second caveat is that the promotion of human rights and democracy, even if deemed legitimate, is but one of the questions with which U.S. foreign policy must concern itself. This observation seems particularly apposite with respect to both Mexico and China, the two countries that have received the most sustained attention in this volume. Mexico's proximity to the United States, the enormous economic and social problems it confronts, its ominous demographic profile (with approximately half of its rapidly growing population under the age of seventeen), the manifold problems that would ensue for the United States were the Mexican government to collapse in chaos or otherwise fail in raising the standard of living of its people—all these considerations argue for a strong U.S. interest in ensuring political stability and economic development in Mexico. At the same time, the historical sensitivity of Mexicans to U.S. intervention in their internal affairs makes the choice of policy instruments a highly delicate one. Though some prominent Mexican democratizers, like Lorenzo Meyer and Jorge Castañeda, have broken from the traditional consensus against U.S. intervention and have come to look favorably upon the exercise of pressure on behalf of democratization, the risks of excessive U.S. interference in Mexican affairs remain substantial. Geographical proximity, together with the inequality of power between the two states, makes U.S. influence a permanent feature of the relations between the two states; but Mexico remains, as Delal Baer has recently noted, "tough terrain for the exercise of Wilsonian dreams"[2]—as Woodrow Wilson himself had occasion to discover.

The United States' China policy, too, presents special characteristics. The awakening of China may prove to be the most significant event in world politics in the coming century. If a centralized state can survive the centrifugal forces that tear at it, and if China's economy can surmount the larger regional economic crisis and keep growing rapidly, the implications for the distribution of power in East Asia and the Pacific cannot fail to be profound. The history of international politics is replete with examples of how the uneven growth of power is a natural incubator of state rivalry. The delegitimization of communist ideology has, moreover, induced a vacuum into which a powerful sense of nationalism has moved, making the Chinese ever more sensitive to manifestations of U.S. dictation. With the collapse of Soviet power, the common fear that bound the United States and China in uneasy partnership in the 1970s and 1980s no longer exists; indeed, there was scarcely any aspect of their relationship in the first half of the 1990s that was not roiled by controversy. Menacing Chinese demonstrations over the status of Taiwan, the existence of far-reaching Chinese claims over islands in the East China and South China seas, U.S. suspicions that China is sabotaging antiproliferation efforts, the growth of trade imbalances (with China in 1996 surpassing Japan in some months as the country with the largest bilateral trade surplus with the United States)—all these irritants suggest that preserving a cooperative relationship with China will prove very difficult at best. The Sino-U.S. relationship was never free from difficulty, even in the 1980s; but the common strategic interests of the two states, together with the sense that China was moving toward freer institutions, made for generally positive relations during much of that decade. Tiananmen put an end to the expectation of progress toward political liberalization; the collapse of the Soviet Union virtually eliminated the basis for their strategic cooperation. The specter of war does not yet hang over the relationship between the two countries; but rumors of war begin to rumble in the distance. It unfortunately takes no flight of super-heated imagination to imagine the circumstances in which the two sides might

---

2. M. Delal Baer, "The New Order and Disorder in U.S.-Mexican Relations," in *A New North America: Cooperation and Enhanced Interdependence*, ed. Charles F. Foran and Alvin Paul Drischler (Westport, Conn.: Praeger, 1996), 23.

be brought to the brink of war, and this despite the settled understanding on both sides that war would be profoundly contrary to the interests of each country.

Advocates for imposing sanctions to promote democracy and human rights share the belief that the universal appeal and intrinsic justice of their objectives serve to override the traditional legal prohibition against interference in the internal affairs of other states, but there are still significant internal tensions within the broader movement.[3] Human rights activists came largely out of the political left. Protesting against "counterrevolutionary America," they called in the 1970s for a rupture of U.S. relations with rightist authoritarian regimes such as South Vietnam, Cambodia, South Korea, Iran, Nicaragua, and South Africa. The Carter administration placed far greater emphasis on human rights than on democratization. The democratist project was more an innovation of the Reagan administration, whose object initially was the support of insurgent groups against communist regimes (Afghanistan, Nicaragua, Angola). By the late 1980s, however, a certain junction had been effected that bridged the older ideological divide. The Reagan administration withdrew support from rightist regimes in the Philippines and Haiti and voted against loans to Chile during the last phases of the Pinochet dictatorship; the Democratic left harshly condemned Chinese repression at Tiananmen. Success, moreover, gave a fillip to the enterprise. The "third wave" of democratization, which began in 1974 and brought near its crest the breakup of the Soviet Union and the adoption of democratic institutions in South Africa, coincided in large part with the shift of American policy in the mid-1970s and seemed to dramatically attest to the wisdom of an activist pro-democracy policy.[4]

Just as there are differing priorities among those who wish to actively enlarge the domain of democracy and human rights, so too there are a wide variety of actions imprecisely though conventionally identified with economic sanctions. Sanctions may include restrictions on travel and financial remittances, cutoffs in military or export aid, adverse changes in trade status (e.g., the elimination of the sugar quota or the denial of most favored nation status), prohibitions on loans from private banks or international financial institutions, or restrictions on investment by United States–based companies.[5] "Engagement," too,

---

3. For an assessment of the differing priorities of democratists and human rights activists, see Thomas Carothers, "Democracy and Human Rights: Policy Allies or Rivals," *The Washington Quarterly* 17, no. 3 (Summer 1994): 109–20.

4. See Samuel P. Huntington, *The Third Wave: Democratization in the Late Twentieth Century* (Norman: University of Oklahoma Press, 1991).

5. This list is not exhaustive. Recent additions to the menu of economic sanctions include restrictions on investment by foreign-based companies, such as

has a diverse array of meanings. The kind of far-reaching engagement symbolized by the North American Free Trade Agreement is quite distinct from a decision to maintain most favored nation trading status with China and other regimes.

Significantly, acts customarily identified with sanctions range from measures such as the withdrawal of military aid—which are clearly within the moral and legal discretion of the sanctioning government and are not owed to anyone—to steps that involve the active destabilization of the target regime, up to and including measures such as economic blockades that were once considered acts of war. Acts conventionally identified with economic sanctions, in other words, occur on both sides of the legal barrier traditionally distinguishing peace from war, just as they fall on both sides of the moral barrier distinguishing the withdrawal of aid from the infliction of injury. Recovering the significance of those distinctions is an important purpose of this chapter.

The Problem of Intervention

Perhaps the most striking feature of the democratist project is its illegality under the traditional standards of international law. That law forbade intervention in the internal affairs of states. According to that older conception, which prevailed during the greater part of the Westphalian system (1648–1945), the members of international society consisted of states, not of individuals. Individual rights entered into the fabric of the law of nations only insofar as a state might take umbrage at an offense done one of its subjects or citizens. In that system, as the legal scholar W. E. Hall wrote, every state had the right "to live its life in its own way, so long as it [kept] rigidly to itself, and refrain[ed] from interfering with the equal right of other states to live their life in the manner which commend[ed] itself to them."[6]

In the light of our contemporary policies, it is ironic to recall that it

---

were featured in the 1996 Helms-Burton Act. For a thorough review of the effectiveness of economic sanctions, together with a valuable compendium of case studies since 1918, see Gary Clyde Hufbauer, Jeffrey J. Schott, and Kimberly Ann Elliott, *Economic Sanctions Reconsidered*, 2nd ed. (Washington, D.C.: Institute for International Economics, 1990). For a legal analysis of the instruments available, see Barry E. Carter, *International Economic Sanctions: Improving the Haphazard U.S. Legal Regime* (Cambridge: Cambridge University Press, 1988).

6. William Edward Hall, *A Treatise on International Law*, 6th ed., ed. J. B. Atlay (Oxford: Oxford University Press, 1909), 43–44.

was the U.S. government that did most to establish the primacy of this rule in the nineteenth-century law of nations, a practice that changed only with Woodrow Wilson's Mexican policy in 1913. Summarizing that doctrine in 1852, Daniel Webster noted that "from President Washington's time down to the present day it has been a principle, always acknowledged by the United States, that every nation possesses a right to govern itself according to its own will, to change institutions at discretion, and to transact its business through whatever agents it may think proper to employ. This cardinal point in our policy has been strongly illustrated by recognizing the many forms of political power which have been successively adopted by France in the series of revolutions with which that country has been visited."[7] That traditional understanding was restated by John Bassett Moore, then legal counselor of the Department of State, at precisely the moment that Wilson was moving to overturn it: "The Government of the United States having originally set itself up by revolution has always acted upon the de facto principle. We regard governments as existing or as not existing. We do not require them to be chosen by popular vote. We look simply to the fact of the existence of the government and to its ability and inclination to discharge the national obligations." The reason for this policy, as Moore explained, was that we could not "become the censors of the morals or conduct of other nations and make our approval or disapproval of their methods the test of our recognition without intervening in their affairs. The government of the United States once boasted that the Pope, the Emperor of Russia and President Jackson were the only rulers that ever recognized Don Miguel as King of Portugal. This action on the part of President Jackson was ascribed to 'our sacred regard for the independence of nations.' "[8]

The United States has frequently departed from this standard in the twentieth century, the departures having grown far more frequent in recent decades; nevertheless, the nonintervention principle underlying this doctrine of recognition continues to find expression in contemporary treaties and agreements. Prohibitions against intervention in the internal affairs of states are reaffirmed, often in the strongest terms, in all the governing charters and declarations of contemporary international law. At the same time, there has grown up alongside the traditional prohibition against internal intervention a body of human rights

---

7. Cited in John Bassett Moore, ed., *A Digest of International Law* (Washington, D.C.: GPO, 1906), I, 126.

8. Arthur S. Link et al., "The Mexican Situation," May 14, 1913, *The Papers of Woodrow Wilson* (Princeton: Princeton University Press), 1966–1993, vol. 17, 437–38.

law that strongly affirms the rights of individuals, declarations that increasingly contain statements of the democratic entitlement. It is often held that the United States and its allies have secured widespread agreement to the proposition that the norms commanding the observance of democracy and human rights have entirely displaced the traditional prohibition against intervention, thereby virtually obliterating the substantive content of "domestic jurisdiction." According to legal scholar Thomas Franck, a "democratic entitlement" has emerged in recent years that enjoys a "high degree of legitimacy" within international society.[9] But this view is highly questionable for three reasons.

First, the fact that these contradictory norms appear side by side in international legal documents may more plausibly be read as indicating a state of confusion rather than of consensus within contemporary international law. Secondly, nowhere in the charters and declarations that ostensibly speak for all mankind (as opposed to those with a merely regional significance) is authorization given to employ either economic or military coercion to fulfill the rights proclaimed. Indeed, many such declarations clearly deny any such inference.[10] There is a striking contrast, finally, between the purported near-universal agreement on these norms and the reality of profound dissensus among actually existing nations and regimes. According to Freedom House, the number of free governments (seventy-four) remained outnumbered by partly free (sixty-two) and unfree (fifty-five) regimes at the end of 1993.[11] Without examining in detail the reservations and stipulations that attend state adherence to these agreements, it is surely a curious fact that many partly free or unfree states have signed international declarations that, on the predominant Western reading, have badly undermined their legitimacy and that authorize the coercion of the "international community" against them. It is no doubt the case that the cumulative weight of international legal norms gives outside states a right of comment (or, as the case may be, of denunciation) in the case of human rights abuses. It is far more difficult to tease

---

9. Thomas M. Franck, "The Emerging Right to Democratic Governance," *American Journal of International Law* 86 (January 1992): 90–91. Franck anticipates the day when "compliance with the democratic entitlement" would be "linked to a right of representation in international organs, to international fiscal, trade, and development benefits, and to the protection of UN and regional collective security measures." To similar effect, see Morton H. Halperin, "Guaranteeing Democracy," *Foreign Policy* 91 (Summer 1993): 105–122.

10. See the documents in Michael Krinsky and David Golove, eds., *United States Economic Measures Against Cuba: Proceedings in the United Nations and International Law Issues* (Northampton, Mass.: Aletheia Press, 1993).

11. "Despots and Democrats," *The Economist*, 27 August 1994: 16.

out of this body of law the authority to undertake coercive internal interventions.

The case for observing the nonintervention norm need not rest on its legal standing. More impressive are the prudential reasons that support nonintervention, above all the contribution its observance makes toward peace. Nonintervention is one of the central devices by which the society of states has traditionally managed differences and accommodated itself to humankind's plural and heterogeneous character. Coercive democratization, by contrast, is dangerous precisely because it aims for a degree of homogeneity in the political organization of humankind that has never existed and that, in all probability, will never exist. It is a revolutionary enterprise. It not only divides the international system between democratic and non-democratic states, but proposes hostile measures that are intended to force authoritarian states into the democratic camp or punish them severely if they do not give in. It proposes no policy of peaceful coexistence; it propounds no ethic of "live and let live."

That this policy is justified in the name of peace is perfectly understandable. All such homogenizing projects in international history— whether of the revolutionary variety associated with Jacobinism and Bolshevism or the counter-revolutionary variety associated with the Counter-Reformation and the Holy Alliance—have rested upon the same justification. Because democracies do generally maintain pacific relations with one another, moreover, the democracy equals peace argument commands widespread assent. Insofar as the experience among democracies is made to justify aggressive measures against non-democracies, however, the argument is a non sequitur. Because democracies do not fight each other, we are urged to undertake war or war-like measures against non-democratic states, the ultimate goal of perpetual peace forming the ground for the commencement of economic sanctions and possibly of war. The pacific relationship that democracies tend to have with one another provides no justification for any such policy.[12]

It may be objected, of course, that intervention for democracy is not really intervention. When there exists, as there may well exist, a sharp disjunction between state and society, between the apparatus of coercive control and the mass of humanity that groans beneath it, identify-

12. A similar qualification, though on somewhat different grounds, is made by Michael Doyle, one of the first scholars to develop the thesis that democracies almost never go to war with one another. See "An International Liberal Community," in *Rethinking America's Security: Beyond Cold War to New World Order*, ed. Graham Allison and Gregory F. Treverton (New York: W. W. Norton & Co., 1992), 307–33, esp. 311, 318–19.

ing the state as the representative of the community seems obtuse. This argument has appeal in two quite distinct situations—one in which the society is identified with a suppressed "nation" seeking autonomy, self-determination, or statehood; the other when an authoritarian or totalitarian regime refuses to obtain popular legitimation through elections, but in which there is no expectation that a change of government will also mean a change of borders.[13]

It may be doubted, however, whether active external intervention is justified even in those cases where a clear disjunction between state and society exists. Secession has an unenviable track record of being closely associated with civil war; as a general remedy for the problems of nationalism and ethnicity, it seems highly toxic in its effects and utterly frightening if carried to its logical conclusion—a vast splintering of the globe into ethnically or linguistically based states.[14] No people can be denied a right of revolution, if the oppression is unbearable and every other mode of resistance is unavailing. To recognize such claims before their achievement, however, can only serve to encourage a fracturing of territorial integrity that would menace political stability in many areas of the world.

In the other case—that of supporting a people in its struggle against a native tyranny—the classic liberal justification for nonintervention was provided by John Stuart Mill. Mill held, in Michael Walzer's paraphrase, that "the members of a political community must seek their own freedom, just as the individual must cultivate his own virtue. They cannot be set free, as he cannot be made virtuous, by any external force."[15] We know that that proposition is not exactly true: the reconstruction of Germany and Japan after World War II shows that states and individuals can be set free and made virtuous by external forces. It is striking, however, that the most notable examples of that happening occur in the aftermath of crushing military defeat and occupation. That experience is perfectly irrelevant to the question we are here considering: the use of economic sanctions and embargoes to effect such change. It is far more instructive to look, as Tony Smith has done, at U.S. efforts to implant democracy through less draconian means.[16]

---

13. See the discussion in Terry Nardin, "Sovereignty, Self-Determination, and International Intervention," in *Morals and Might*, ed. G. Lopez and D. Christiansen (Boulder, Colo.: Westview Press, 1993).

14. For further consideration of the problem of self-determination and secession, see Robert W. Tucker and David C. Hendrickson, "America and Bosnia," *The National Interest*, Fall 1993.

15. Michael Walzer, *Just and Unjust Wars: A Moral Argument with Historical Illustrations* (New York: Basic Books, 1977), 87.

16. Tony Smith, *America's Mission: The United States and the Worldwide Struggle for Democracy in the Twentieth Century* (Princeton, N.J.: Princeton University Press, 1994).

Smith argues that U.S. efforts to promote democracy failed because they were not thorough enough and thus failed to reach the social and economic underpinnings of authoritarian governments. That's why Reconstruction in the South failed, why democratic institutions failed to take root in the Philippines after the U.S. occupation, why the Alliance for Progress lost its way—an experience that largely confirms Mill's intuition. It may well be that external pressure for democracy, particularly by the United States, made a clear difference in giving the "third wave" of democratization a higher crest than it would otherwise have had. Still, the larger experience of history seems clearly to show that a little intervention does not go a long way and that it is only really successful when it is an outgrowth of total war.

The questionable authority to undertake coercive democratization is only slightly improved by the support it receives from the United Nations or other international organizations. It is true that multilateral authorization corresponds broadly to intuitive notions of international legitimacy. The broader the scope of concerted action, the more it seems the action has the sponsorship of international society as a whole. Multilateralism may constitute insurance against the pursuit of purely selfish interests and provide a valuable source of restraint.

Without denying the value of acting in concert with the UN or regional security organizations, one may still note a few oddities in what exactly is happening when we speak of action by the "international community." The role of U.S. leadership, in the first place, clearly seems to be crucial; the effectiveness of interventions conducted by the "international community" has been heavily dependent on U.S. initiative, financing, logistical support, or military power. In the cases where the so-called international community has taken action in recent years (e.g., Iraq, Somalia, Haiti), it has usually done so at the behest of this country. Normally, the consensus is achieved through U.S. pressure, and it often happens that states swallow real misgivings over the wisdom of U.S. action so as not to prejudice their relations with this country. It is doubtful that "consensus" is the right term to describe what is happening; in its basic characteristics, it seems rather to be an elevated exercise in ward heeling.

A second oddity has to do with the authority of international organizations to undertake the democratist project. In the case of Haiti, both the United Nations Security Council and the Organization of American States (OAS) authorized economic embargoes that had the restoration of democracy as their object; and the Security Council (but not, significantly, the OAS) authorized the use of U.S. military power to accomplish that objective as well. Still, one searches in vain through the UN or OAS charters for the authority to do so. Whether wisely or not, these organizations were erected squarely on the foundation of the equal sovereignty of states. They contain no guarantee of a republican form of government, such as exists in the United States Constitution.[17]

But let us waive these objections for the moment—conceding that the "constitution" of international society can undergo growth, and that to bind it too closely to the original understanding is to deprive it of its capacity to adapt to the changing needs of the international society it is meant to serve. Let us also concede that the movement for democracy and human rights is part of the warp and woof of international politics today, and that this movement has support from voices all over the world, in every civilizational time zone. Having noted the objections to the journey, let us go ahead and set sail on this mission to make every state a liberal democracy. What do we find when this objective is paired with the instrument of economic sanctions?

Economic Sanctions: Unintended Consequences and Innocent Bystanders

The image of embarking on a voyage is not inappropriate, for the principal forerunner of today's trade embargo is the naval blockade. In strategic thought, economic sanctions exemplify the strategy of attrition, that is, the attempt to wear down the enemy by striking at the whole of its economic life, which is ultimately the basis of its military power. In the classic economic boycott, like the airtight naval blockade, sanctions move toward the total elimination of economic and diplomatic intercourse with the target state, of the sort described by Woodrow Wilson in 1919 in characterizing the measures that would be taken against aggressors under the League of Nations: "We absolutely boycott them. . . . There shall be no communication even between them and the rest of the world. They shall receive no goods; they shall ship

---

17. It may be argued that the UN charter does not and cannot confine the Security Council in a defined ambit of authority and that the council's discretion is in fact unlimited save by the requirements of its voting provisions. It is doubtful, however, if its unlimited discretion in matters relating to "international peace and security" reaches so far as to obliterate the domestic jurisdiction of the state. The Security Council, at least, appears to acknowledge that its actions must be founded in the charter and do not reflect simply its unlimited discretion. Thus, in justifying the American-led intervention in Haiti, the council thought it necessary to justify its authority in relation to Article VII and its cognizance of the Security Council's jurisdiction over "international peace and security." What was not apparent from Resolutions 917 and 940 was the relationship that the Haitian crisis posed in fact to "international peace and security."

no goods. They shall receive no telegraphic messages; they shall send none. They shall receive no mail; no mail will be received from them."[18] Such a strategy represents an attempt to punish the enemy so badly that it has no choice—on any rational calculation of costs and benefits—but to submit.

Attrition's main competitor in strategic thought is a strategy of forcible disarmament, in which military operations are aimed, as the phrase suggests, at forcibly disarming the military power of the adversary. The great promise of the economic blockade is that it allows you to harm the enemy without hurting yourself. Unlike military operations aimed at forcibly disarming the adversary, you need not risk your soldiers. In the most favorable circumstances, this kind of operation against the enemy's economy is capable of establishing a radical asymmetry between what you pay and what the adversary suffers. That is why it is so attractive.

A condition of what political economists call asymmetrical interdependence will not always apply, and where it does not apply, economic sanctions will begin to appear much less attractive.[19] But even when this condition does apply—when, that is, we can inflict a lot of pain on the other guy without suffering too much ourselves—there are problems to be encountered.

Historically, two great liabilities have attended this strategic concept, both of which are relevant to the contemporary policy of spreading democracy through economic sanctions. The first is that this kind of long-term squeeze is normally incapable of achieving a decision, a liability that is exacerbated in proportion to the scale of the objectives sought. If, as is often the case today, the objective is the removal of the enemy government from power—which an insistence on democratic procedures will normally require—the ability of economic sanctions to achieve a decision is highly doubtful.

That failure, in turn, normally raises again the question of whether it is advisable to do directly what you had previously tried to do indirectly. Though economic sanctions have normally been conceived as an alternative to war—certainly they were by Jefferson and Wilson— the total boycott or embargo tends historically to be associated closely with military action, either because military force is necessary to enforce the thoroughgoing blockade or because the situation produced by sanctions may produce strong incentives to go to war. The trade

---

18. Link, *The Papers of Woodrow Wilson*, vol. 63, 68.
19. On "asymmetrical interdependence," see Klaus Knorr, *The Power of Nations: The Political Economy of International Relations* (New York: Basic Books, 1975), 207–38.

embargo against Panama in 1988 and 1989 displayed this dynamic; the embargo against Haiti did the same. They are only the latest instances of a frequently recurring phenomenon.[20]

The pressure to go to war—to move toward a strategy of forcible disarmament—that often ensues from the failure of draconian economic sanctions is related to the second liability that attends the economic squeeze, which is its indiscriminate character. Unlike military operations directed at the enemy's military power, sanctions inflict punishment on the entire economy and society. This distinction between discriminate military operations aimed at forcibly disarming the enemy's armed forces and a strategy of attrition that inflicts punishment on the entire economy and society may, of course, break down in practice. Under conditions of modern warfare, a strategy of forcible disarmament will often mean the intensification rather than relaxation of such indiscriminate punishment, especially if "military necessity" is given a broad definition; the saving grace of such a strategy is that it offers the promise of a rapid decision and a quicker return to peace.

Three particular disadvantages are associated with the economic embargo. It badly hurts the most vulnerable sections of society, the sick, the young, and the aged. Given the circumstances in which it is applied, it can have no result but that. Yet acts that inflict foreseeable suffering on the civilian population have always been considered the most objectionable feature of interstate conflicts; international law has always been intent on minimizing such action to the degree compatible with military effectiveness. In deference to such objections, nearly all the recent embargoes—such as those against Iraq, Serbia, and Haiti—have exempted food and medical supplies from their terms.[21] Concerned states and non-governmental organizations, moreover, usually mount compensating efforts to supply food and medicine. Despite these efforts, sanctions always reach in practice items critical to the well-being of the civilian population; the general destruction of economic life that is the avowed purpose of such embargoes swamps the half-hearted compensating efforts that accompany them. However emphatic we are in insisting on the humanitarian exemption, therefore, it cannot be taken seriously as a description of existing practice.

A second liability is that the sectors of the economy that suffer most from external sanctions are those that have the most intercourse with

20. Examples in U.S. history in which economic coercion played a crucial role in accelerating the drift to war include the two wars with Great Britain in 1775–83 and 1812–15, and the oil embargo against Japan in 1941.

21. An exception to this general stance is the Cuban Democracy Act, which bans any shipments to Cuba, including food, from U.S. subsidiaries and which imposes highly restrictive rules on the donation of medical supplies.

the rest of the world and tend to be more amenable to its influence. Such was the case in South Africa; it remains the case today in Cuba. This baneful effect is exacerbated by the near total blackout in embargoed societies of information from printed sources.

Finally, economic sanctions may hurt neighboring economies in whose well-being we have a stake. The revocation of most favored nation status for China would deal a serious blow to the economies of Hong Kong, Taiwan, and other Southeast Asian economies which have developed close ties with China. The trade embargo against Yugoslavia, though employed as a measure of collective security against Serbian aggression in Bosnia-Herzegovina and not as part of the democratist project, had a ruinous effect on the economies of surrounding states. Despite the effects on neighboring economies, the international community or the Western powers have not provided a commensurate level of financial compensation to states injured by recent economic sanctions. A particularly unfortunate side effect of sanctions is that economic activities come to be dominated by criminal organizations, a stranglehold they are not likely to easily yield when the conditions that gave rise to them are no longer present.

The consequences for innocent bystanders may not be intended, but they are foreseeable. It seems wholly implausible to allow refuge in the justification that because good consequences were intended we can wash our hands of responsibility for the evil consequences that in fact occur. The justification for this project, if there be one, must be on the theory that it is permissible to do evil so that good may come, that the norm against harming the innocent must be overridden by the greater good of ensuring liberal democratic government.

Economic Engagement: The Chinese Case

In contrast to the disadvantages associated with sanctions, the maintenance of economic ties with undemocratic or otherwise oppressive regimes at least has the advantage of improving the material condition of their people or, conversely, of not making them more miserable than they already are. It is useful to consider this question, in the first instance, not in relation to civil and political rights but to the provision of "basic human needs."[22] There are many countries—Indonesia and China, for example—whose regimes have plenty of blood on their hands but who have nevertheless performed admirably in raising the

---

22. See R. J. Vincent, *Human Rights and International Relations* (Cambridge: Cambridge University Press, 1986).

material condition of their people. In Indonesia, the number of people living in absolute poverty has dropped, according to the World Bank, from 60 percent of the population two decades ago to 15 percent in 1995. There has been a comparable change in China. Millions of people are entering "middleclassdom," ensuring a greater measure of economic security for themselves and their families. Though the vast satisfaction of basic human needs that it has brought and will bring is a good in itself, not dependent on whether it leads to benign consequences in the political realm, this great Asiatic transformation probably will have benign consequences in several respects.

In assessing the significance of this epochal change, some historical perspective is necessary. For much of this century, not only was East Asia an exporter of war (we fought, after all, three wars there from 1941 to 1975); the whole region underwent a Joy Luck's club of internal catastrophes—Korea and Indochina flattened by civil wars and outside intervention, mass murder in Indonesia against the Chinese minority, all the insanities of the Cultural Revolution in China, genocide in Cambodia. Against this background, the fact that the weightiest of Asian societies—China—has turned toward economic development as its primary objective is a highly welcome change. The elevation of economic calculation over ideological fanaticism (or, to employ an older terminology, of interest over passion) signifies a profound and auspicious civilizational turn.

This change is likely, in the first place, to promote a pacific bearing in external relations stemming from the realization that material well-being depends on peace. It would be absurd to conclude that this effect, by itself, is capable of swamping all the other motives that lead states to make war. There are many features of the emerging Asian system—extensive territorial disputes, uneven rates of economic and military growth, and nationalist attachments far more powerful than those existing in western Europe—that make hazardous any expectation of prolonged stability.[23] Nevertheless, the early theorists of capitalism were right, I think, in expecting that the pursuit of wealth—what an earlier generation had termed avarice—would operate to diminish the weight in human personality of the demonic forces that normally lead mankind to pursue its bloody wars and revolutions.[24] We have, in

---

23. For two thorough analyses, see Aaron L. Friedberg, "Ripe for Rivalry: Prospects for Peace in a Multipolar Asia," *International Security* 18 (Winter 1993/94): 5–33; and Richard K. Betts, "Wealth, Power, and Instability: East Asia and the United States after the Cold War," 34–77.

24. See Albert O. Hirschman, *The Passions and the Interests: Political Arguments for Capitalism before Its Triumph* (Princeton, N.J.: Princeton University Press, 1977).

any case, every reason for thinking that a concerted U.S. strategy to prevent economic development in China (either because such development will over time threaten U.S. preeminence in Asia, or because the Chinese regime is undemocratic and illiberal) would exacerbate, rather than mitigate, the tensions arising from unequal growth.

Second, the continuance of economic contacts seems likely to moderate the authoritarian mold of the Chinese regime. This is, admittedly, a highly complex process, and probably it should be acknowledged by all sides in the debate that the effect of external actions on the evolution of a state and society so large, and so different from our own, is far more likely to be marginal than decisive. It should probably also be acknowledged that the effect of a strategy of engagement will almost certainly be double-edged. The party and the state may gain in power and legitimacy from the satisfactions brought by trade; it is, in any case, difficult to see why the party leadership should have embarked on its new economic strategy unless it had a certain confidence—even if a misplaced confidence—that its consequences for the regime could be controlled. But still the effects that work toward moderating the authoritarian mold of the Chinese regime should not be discounted. One is the awakening to the external world of ever-widening circles of people. Trade allows them a window on the world; it also allows the world a window on them. Over time, the advance of communications that insinuates itself into this dense network of economic contacts seems likely to weaken the capacity of the state to control the structure of social reality.

The penetration of capitalist techniques weakens the power of authoritarian and totalitarian states in a second way. To prosper, the state must make its peace with the power of the market. Governments that are otherwise arbitrary will find it in their interest to institute many of the legal protections of a liberal regime. Partly this is because doing so is a condition for participation in international trade agreements, though it stems as well from the need to create a legal environment that seems sufficiently secure for foreign investors to risk their money. As more economic transactions are governed by the rule of law, there may emerge modest spillover effects on other sectors of the economy and polity. As the Asian economic crisis that began in the summer of 1997 has vividly demonstrated (no doubt to the extreme discomfort of China's rulers), dependence on international trade and credit may beget far-reaching demands for internal transformation that are extremely difficult to resist if the confidence of investors is to be restored.

Finally, market economies tend to produce growing numbers of people who enjoy means of support independent of the state bureaucracy and who occupy increasingly important cogs in the machinery of wealth creation. The expectation seems justified that at some point their political power will grow accordingly. But even if this does not occur, the emergence of a situation in which individuals and families no longer depend on the state for the necessities and amenities of life makes for a far greater degree of individual freedom.[25]

Market liberalization in China has already produced a greater degree of personal freedom, and there is a sense in which the two processes are inseparable and virtually identical. At the same time, the hypothesis that it will produce democracy, Western-style, is far more problematic, and it would take a giant leap of faith to make U.S. foreign policy dependent on the veracity of the hypothesis. It is equally true, however, that there is no reason to think that a strategy of "sanctions, boycott, and breach" would produce such democratization, or even contribute to a greater respect for human rights. China's rulers clearly see such Western demands as being a fundamental challenge to the legitimacy of the regime; standing up to such demands may even heighten the regime's nationalist credentials. On the basis of these considerations, it would seem prudent to base the United States' China policy on factors other than the contribution it may make to the realization of human rights and democracy in China. "Engagement" has a more positive effect than sanctions on the extent of personal freedom in China and it may contribute marginally toward democratization, but neither engagement nor sanctions are likely to have far-reaching effects on China's internal evolution. It would thus seem best to rest U.S. policy on the management of China's external behavior. In the absence of a more discriminating strategy, the danger that these relations will spiral out of control and lock the two states in dangerous hostility should not be discounted.[26]

The Hemispheric Conundrum

It is in the Western Hemisphere—more particularly, the Caribbean and Central America—that the democratist project has been most vigor-

---

25. Under Mao, as Elizabeth J. Perry notes, "the provision, via one's work or residential unit, of everything from grain rations to theater tickets afforded the state inordinate leverage over the personal and political lives of city dwellers." China's market reforms have profoundly altered this dependence. See Perry's "China in 1992: An Experiment in Neo-Authoritarianism," *Asian Survey* 33, no. 1 (January 1993): 15. For a classic statement on this point, see Milton Friedman, *Capitalism and Freedom* (Chicago: University of Chicago Press, 1962).

26. For a more developed argument along these lines, see Kenneth Lieberthal, "A New China Strategy," *Foreign Affairs* 74, no. 6 (November/December 1995): 35–49.

ously pursued in the recent past and where it promises to be of critical importance in the future. Given the inherent disparity of power between the United States and the small states of the Caribbean and Central America, the conditions for successfully pursuing economic sanctions are better satisfied here than anywhere else. As is noted by the authors of the most comprehensive study of the effectiveness of economic sanctions, such methods are most successful when they "pick on the weak and helpless."[27]

In this hemisphere, to return to our earlier terminology, the interdependence is truly asymmetrical. The only retaliation of which target states are capable comes in the form of refugee crises; so long as we are sufficiently hard-hearted, that danger can presumably be contained. In this hemisphere, too, the Organization of American States has given its imprimatur to the imposition of economic sanctions against nondemocratic states. The kind of objections that might be raised against this project in the Confucian or Islamic worlds—whose governments seem uniformly to regard it as an arrogant assertion of Western values—do not apply in this hemisphere with anywhere near the same force. Finally, the movement toward democratic institutions that occurred throughout Latin America in the 1980s remains shaky in some instances. As President Clinton emphasized in his address justifying intervention in Haiti, the failure to act against coup-makers in this hemisphere may render more precarious the durability of this historic move to democratic institutions.

Of all the justifications for the democratist project, it is probably the last that carries the greatest weight. When Franklin Roosevelt proclaimed the Good Neighbor Policy in 1933, bringing to an end the U.S. interventions of the preceding era, an increase in authoritarian governments did follow in its wake. When the Johnson administration proclaimed the Mann Doctrine in 1964, retreating from the democratic tendencies of the Alliance for Progress, the same result occurred. During the Cold War, to be sure, the United States often gave active support to authoritarian governments in Latin America, a reflection of the fear that the practical alternative to authoritarianism was not democracy but communism; the end of the Cold War has happily brought that reflex under control.[28] Even in the absence of U.S. support for authoritarians, however, it might still be argued that a failure to aggres-

---

27. Hufbauer, Schott, and Elliott, *Economic Sanctions Reconsidered*, I, 114.

28. Expert considerations of the U.S. record include Abraham F. Lowenthal, ed., *Exporting Democracy: The United States and Latin America*, 2 vols. (Baltimore: Johns Hopkins University Press: 1991); and Gaddis Smith, *The Last Years of the Monroe Doctrine 1945–1993* (New York: Hill and Wang, 1994).

sively move against authoritarian governments would weaken the ability of other democratic regimes within the hemisphere to sustain themselves against their internal enemies.

In the end, however, that consideration seems inadequate to justify a guarantee of a democratic form of government in this hemisphere, especially a guarantee that is to be brought about through the economic embargo. As the experience in Haiti shows, even weak and unpopular governments can hold out for a very long time against trade embargoes. A combination of factors—apparent not only in Haiti but also from previous interventions, such as Panama—makes it difficult not to move to military intervention. The credibility and prestige of the U.S. president is called increasingly into question; the suffering among the civilian population caused by the breakdown of economic life, together with refugee crises exacerbated by the embargo, makes it seem imperative to do *something*. At that point, military intervention is about all there is left to do.

Strangely enough, however, there is almost no support within the hemisphere for U.S.-led military interventions to restore democracy. In the Haitian crisis, our sister republics did us the favor of supporting every step along the way toward military intervention—save of course the occupation itself. The Clinton administration refused to take the matter to the OAS for the same reason it refused to get authorization from Congress: the votes in either place would almost certainly have failed.

From this experience, one can only conclude that the multilateral declarations the OAS has issued in recent years in favor of representative democracy—most prominently the Santiago Declaration of 1991—do not mean what they seem to mean. They clearly do not betoken support for a military guarantee of democratic government. Nor may they necessarily be understood as indicating support for economic embargoes; predominant opinion among hemispheric states, though it favored sanctions in the case of Haiti, is decidedly opposed to similar measures in the case of Cuba. This general attitude, one suspects, is most unlikely to change. The attachment of the Latin American republics to the nonintervention norm is too deeply rooted in their historical experience, where it has served as a shield against the well-meaning officiousness of the Colossus to the North, for it to be easily surrendered, even if it subjects them to the criticism of willing the end (democracy) but not the means.

A policy of nonintervention toward Haiti after the coup d'état against Aristide in 1991, one must acknowledge, would have left his prospects of returning very remote indeed. The U.S. military occupation of Haiti, moreover, surely represented a more honorable course of action than the perpetual maintenance of an inhumane embargo; having arrived at that measure, to have backed away from it and instituted a different and less coercive policy would have cost the president dearly in credibility and prestige. The fears that opponents of the intervention expressed at the time, finally, have proven to be exaggerated. Haiti has not transformed itself into a model democracy, but economic and political conditions are much better there than they were in the years of the coup and the embargo. These considerations must surely qualify any harsh condemnation of the Haitian intervention, and they perhaps go far toward supporting the judgment that, in the circumstances, it was the wisest course among disagreeable alternatives. Even if this judgment is accepted, however, the course of events would seem to demonstrate that economic sanctions are seldom sufficient by themselves to produce democratization, and it would be prudent to digest the lesson that they will often lead to the use of military force.

Will policy toward Cuba follow the same trajectory as that toward Haiti and Panama? The danger that it may do so ought surely to prompt a reconsideration of the thirty-five-year-old embargo. Whatever the weight of its initial justification, to persist in it and even move more aggressively toward its tightening, as the Clinton administration has done in league with the Republican Congress, is a policy that seems seriously wrongheaded. The sole remaining legitimating principle of the Castro regime is its repeated insistence that its failures stem from U.S. aggression. We may well conclude that this charge is, in fundamental respects, mistaken, and that the failures of the Cuban model are to be attributed, above all, to the regime's attachment to Marxist principles, which do not work because they cannot work. It is nevertheless distinctly unlikely that any Caribbean state, even if its political and economic institutions had been designed by James Madison and Adam Smith, could have succeeded economically in the face of our relentless opposition. By all accounts, in any case, our hostile measures have exacerbated those failures and made the material condition of the Cuban people much worse than it would otherwise have been.

A different policy would aim to open up the island to U.S. trade, tourism, and communications; would drop the hostile measures we have undertaken for over a generation; and would end the state of virtual war that now exists between the two countries. Its objective would be to prepare for the day—which is surely coming—when the transition to democracy takes place, contributing to the likelihood that it occurs peacefully rather than violently. A peaceful transition is a consummation devoutly to be desired; current U.S. policy works decisively against it. One is tempted to rest this change of policy solely on the ground, with Jefferson, that the "exchange of surpluses and wants between neighbor nations is both a right and a duty under the moral law."[29] But it does nevertheless seem likely that a U.S. initiative toward a more normal relationship would hasten rather than delay Cuba's move toward economic and political liberalization.[30]

If relations with Cuba constitute an extreme form of the strategy of inducing democratization and respect for human rights through sanctions and boycott, relations with Mexico constitute an equally extreme form of "engagement." The thoroughgoing integration of legal procedures and standards called for in the North American Free Trade Agreement goes far beyond what is normally signified by engagement. To critics such as Jorge Castañeda, indeed, the measures that the United States has taken in recent years to engage Mexico—above all, the 1993 free trade agreement and the 1995 peso rescue—appear as bailouts that have "allowed Mexico's authorities to fail miserably yet remain in power," locking in misguided policies and stunting the emergence of new leadership.[31] These criticisms probably contain a considerable degree of merit. Despite the Zedillo reforms announced in 1996, economic growth remains slow and uncertain, while the judiciary lacks independence from the executive and is generally regarded as corrupt. U.S. aid, whether in the form of an opening of markets or the provision of a large rescue package to salvage Mexico's plunging currency, lessens the urgency of the far-reaching reforms for which democratizers contend.

But though these criticisms have considerable force, it is difficult to see that the United States has much of an alternative to pursuing policies fostering Mexican economic development and stability. To deliberately exacerbate the enormous political and economic problems confronting Mexico would seem, on the face of it, to be highly imprudent. The kind of sweeping changes in the Mexican political system for which Casteñada has called—and which are implicit as well in Lorenzo Meyer's contribution to this volume—are of a character so intimate that a concerted effort to impose them from Washington seems almost certain to misfire. We can have very little assurance that precipitating a breakdown in the Mexican regime—whether through cutting off access to the American market or making a new political bargain in Mexico a condition for the support of Mexico's floundering peso—

---

29. Jefferson to William Short, July 28, 1791, in Paul Ford, ed., *The Writings of Thomas Jefferson*, V (New York: G. P. Putnam's Sons: 1892–99), 10 vols., 364.

30. For an extended and persuasive analysis of this issue, see Owen Harries, "An Offer Castro Couldn't Refuse—or Survive," *The National Interest*, no. 44 (Summer 1996): 126–28.

31. Jorge G. Castañeda, "Mexico's Circle of Misery," *Foreign Affairs* 75, no. 4 (July/August 1996): 92–105, at 104.

would really produce the thoroughgoing reforms that Mexico undoubtedly needs. As in the Chinese case, the skeptics have shown that
neither market liberalization nor economic engagement constitutes a
miracle cure for the travails of authoritarian regimes; there is certainly
no direct and inescapable logic between either and democratization.
We must, alas, take the world as it is, not as we would like it to be. The
converse proposition—that sanctions, boycott, and breach will produce desirable changes in fostering greater respect for human rights
and democratization—is, it seems to me, even more entitled to skeptical deconstruction.

Conclusion

Economic sanctions and war are the two primary coercive instruments
to which states resort in order to achieve their goals. Just as one can
draw attention to the moral and prudential liabilities that attend the
latter without being a pacifist, so one can draw attention to the costs of
economic sanctions without categorically forbidding their use in diplomacy. Given the role they have come to play in American diplomacy,
such a conclusion would in any case be somewhat absurd. The practical question is not whether the United States should or will cease em-
ploying economic sanctions, but whether some limits can be placed on
its readiness to do so.

When paired with the goals of democratization or human rights,
draconian economic sanctions are particularly suspect. They can only
have effect by wreaking serious damage on a broad range of civil activities, yet they are normally incapable of inflicting sufficient deprivation
on the holders of power to make them relent. The maintenance of economic contacts, by contrast, will normally promote certain forms of
political liberalization. These effects are admittedly modest; market liberalism and bureaucratic authoritarianism may exist together, even if
uneasily, for protracted periods. Still, the case for engagement need
not rest on the limited contribution it makes toward democratization,
but on a cluster of other considerations: the relationship between market reforms and greater personal freedom, the contribution it makes
toward the provision of "basic human needs," its greater conformity
with the rule proscribing intervention in the internal affairs of other
states, and a range of prudential considerations deriving from the danger that a crisis in U.S. relations with large and important states (like
Mexico and China) would adversely affect U.S. interests while serving
no positive purpose.

A policy of engagement with authoritarian regimes does not require the United States to cease distinguishing between the free and unfree worlds. The distinction between the two, in my view, ought to be at the center of our understanding of U.S. purposes in the world. Though the area of the free world is not coterminous with the area embraced in U.S. security commitments, there is a genuine connection between the two. Through asylum, economic aid, publicity, or practical help in the way of institution-building, the United States can and should take steps to bolster the cause of free government. We should clearly not aim, in our stance toward the unfree world, for anything approaching the degree of cooperation and mutual concordance that should be our objective within the democratic zone of peace. The question is how far our hostility should extend toward states that are not within the zone; and here the United States has tended to place a greater confidence in economic sanctions than is warranted by either their legitimacy or their effectiveness.

The great fear associated with the adoption of a less hostile policy is that it will encourage the forces of despotism in the world, producing a sharp contraction in the number of free governments. On this interesting question in philosophical history, I confess to having a greater degree of confidence than the pessimists in the appeal of free institutions. The ideals and institutions underlying U.S. constitutionalism— representative government, freedom of speech and of opinion, the separation of church and state, the judicial protection of private property and individual rights, a stable currency—have often succeeded, in cultures vastly different from our own, in bringing prosperity and freedom within the framework of law. That is a very impressive achievement, especially given the far greater liabilities associated with all the available alternatives in politics and economics. The practical advantages offered by free institutions in delivering the goods that people want gives them an insufficiently appreciated strength. If we could learn to act on that idea, we could afford to dispense with the often ineffective and normally inhumane embargoes and sanctions to which U.S. policy still often remains wedded.

10

Market Liberalization and Democratic Politics: Perspectives from the Russian Experience

David D. Finley

This chapter explores the relationship of market liberalization to democratizing political processes and values, with reference to ongoing changes in Russia over the past decade. More specifically, it will use the Soviet/Russian experience to interpret some hypotheses that emerge from the focus of this volume on comparable changes in China and Mexico.

The late 1980s disintegration of the Soviet empire and the collapse of communist regimes in eastern Europe coincided with a proliferation of more or less democratic transitions around the world.[1] The apparent global tide of democratic political transition reinforced Western hopes that post-Soviet Russia too would move toward liberal democracy. Discrediting the Soviet economic model seemed to validate expectations there and abroad that the natural economic future of Russia lay in a capitalist market.[2] The "end of history" school envisioned market lib-

---

1. See Samuel P. Huntington, *The Third Wave: Democratization in the Late Twentieth Century* (Norman: University of Oklahoma Press, 1992); and Doh Chull Shin, "On the Third Wave of Democratization," *World Politics* 47 (October 1994): 135–70.
2. See Daniel Yergin and Thane Gustafson, *Russia 2010 and What It Means for the World* (New York: Random House, 1993), who argue that absent unpredictable interventions all reasonably foreseeable paths of Russian economic development lead to "capitalism Russian style" by 2010.

eralism and democratic politics as codetermined consequences of the Western scientific revolution.[3]

But in the 1990s most scholars have backed away from the more deterministic theories of direct causation between market economies and democratic politics. That the two are often compatible and could be mutually reinforcing is not at issue, but most of the empirical studies of this volume emphasize the agency of strategic choice acting within political culture rather than institutional determinism in the transition of societies either way between command and market economies, authoritarian and democratic political orders.[4]

Gaye Christoffersen, addressing this question in chapter 4, explores four alternative hypotheses: structural determinism, strategic choice, state-society negotiation, and international influence, concluding that the latter two are more helpful for explaining changes in East Asia, including the Russian Far East. The thrust of my interpretation of a dramatic Soviet/Russian decade of change is to confirm a predominant role for strategic choice and state-society negotiation in this elusive relationship.

The Soviet Union's disintegration, followed by efforts to reinvent post-Soviet Russia, provides two analytically separable historical sequences in which to examine the relationship of market liberalization to democratization of political process and values. The first stage—authoritarian collapse from 1986 through 1991—might be considered phase one of democratization in Doh Chull Shin's scheme,[5] although that implies the teleological presumption of Western "transitologists," which seems premature at best for Russia.[6] January 1992 to the present may be regarded as a separate stage and should prompt a second inquiry—this time into the relationship during a period of conscious reconstruction. We are still in that second stage; no one can responsibly conclude its outcome. But Russia today is a long way from consolidat-

---

3. Francis Fukuyama, *The End of History and the Last Man* (New York: The Free Press, 1992).

4. Shin, "On the Third Wave," 138–41. For a strong argument for the importance of strategic choice and state-interest group negotiation in Russian privatization up to 1994, see Michael McFaul, "State Power, Institutional Change, and the Politics of Privatization in Russia," *World Politics* 47 (January 1995): 210–43.

5. Shin, "On the Third Wave," 142–43.

6. See Peter Rutland, "On the Road to Capitalism? Reflections on East Europe and the Global Economy" (Paper for the International Studies Association, Chicago, 24 February 1995). Also, Philippe C. Schmitter and Terry Lynn Karl, "The Conceptual Travels of Transitologists and Consolidologists: How Far to the East Should They Attempt to Go?" *Slavic Review* 53:1 (Spring 1994): 173–85.

ing either political democracy or a predominantly market-driven economy.

The First Case: Soviet Reforms, 1986–91

The years 1986–91 witnessed Gorbachev's perestroika as the failed effort to rescue a Soviet system which in its prime had been the antithesis of market liberalism and political democracy. Here is a summary of what happened with respect to our marketization-democratization focus.

The specter of economic stagnation and paralysis had intensified over the long twilight of the Brezhnev era. The anachronistic Stalinist economic model revealed its shortcomings most vividly in the early 1980s when challenged from outside by the West, particularly the United States and more specifically the apparent U.S. determination to carry the superpower arms race into space via President Reagan's SDI project. The drain of global military competition also accentuated woeful systemic shortcomings at home. The cumbersome command model that had served effectively (if inefficiently) to mobilize economic modernization and growth while supporting the autocratic party-state now maintained less and less respect and evoked pervasive cynicism.[7]

Gorbachev's answer was perestroika: a cautious incorporation of market demand and decentralized production decisions to replace central planning and a command economy. Few would contest the primacy of economic motivation when the new secretary general contemplated reform. Whether referring to Soviet or external estimates, one finds steady decline in the rate of Soviet output growth from 1960 through the mid-1980s: from about 4.5 percent to essentially no growth across the board and negative growth in some sectors.[8] During the same twenty-five-year period, factor productivity steadily declined; capital productivity in particular was increasingly negative.[9] Contrary to the bright prospects for "overtaking the leading capitalist countries by 1980" assayed by Khrushchev at the 22nd CPSU Congress in 1961, relative per capita Soviet consumption actually fell further behind. In

---

7. For a trenchant critique of the Brezhnev years, see Martin Malia, *The Soviet Tragedy* (New York: The Free Press, 1994), Chapter 10.

8. See Dmitri Steinberg, *The Soviet Economy 1970–1990: A Statistical Analysis* (San Francisco: International Trade Press, 1990), and Central Intelligence Agency, Directorate of Intelligence, *Revisiting Soviet Economic Performance under Glasnost: Implications for CIA Estimates* (Washington, D.C.: CIA, 1988).

9. CIA, Directorate of Intelligence, *Handbook of Economic Statistics, 1991* (Washington. D.C.: CIA, 1991), tables 35–36.

1985 the Soviet consumption level was less than 30 percent of that in the United States, well behind France and only slightly ahead of Turkey.[10] The social correlates of economic stagnation included seeping corruption from both the bottom and the top of Soviet society, draining the vestiges of Leninist conviction.

But Soviet context, as Gorbachev was painfully aware, interposed a huge political obstacle to economic reform. Economic rationalization confronted the theoretical and practical foundations of the Communist Party's political power. The precedent of Khrushchev's failure a generation earlier to significantly reconfigure the Stalinist economic model warned him of the pitfalls.[11] There was no doubt that economic priority precipitated Gorbachev's venturesome policies. But preparing the political setting had to come first, and that task preoccupied Gorbachev and ultimately defeated him. It was Gorbachev's political choices, taken at the summit of party-state power, that startled the world and began rapid Soviet change.

Limited "democratization" came first, undertaken to thwart the self-interested resistance of powerful bureaucracies to fundamental economic change. Glasnost sought the constraint of transparency; competitive elections, initially still circumscribed by party oversight, sought more accountability.[12] The increments of political and economic policy came piecemeal, the initiatives of a pragmatic secretary-general and his reformist cadres boring *within* the unreceptive power structure of the Soviet party-state—not as a plot to destroy the socialist vision but desperate measures to revitalize it in the face of two decades of systemic decline, decay, demoralization, and drift. The agent of change was the secretary general himself, whose role was the only one that could introduce such abrupt departures. Gorbachev chose glasnost and democratization to pave the way for economic perestroika. The surprise with which his actions struck the world stems from just this fact: he imposed radical change on an intransigent organization from the only point at which it could be done swiftly.

Ultimately, the social pressures unleashed by Gorbachev's reform policies overtook the imperfect vision of their implementors. They prompted uncertainty and temporizing. In late 1990 Gorbachev tried

---

10. Abram Bergson, "The USSR before the Fall: How Poor and Why?" *Journal of Economic Perspectives* 5:4 (Fall 1991): Table 1.

11. See Ronald J. Hill, "Khrushchev, Gorbachev, and the Party," in *The Sons of Sergei, Khrushchev and Gorbachev as Reformers,* ed. D. Kelley and S. Davis (New York: Praeger, 1992), 5–26.

12. Stephen White, *After Gorbachev,* 4th ed. (New York: Cambridge University Press, 1993), chapter 7.

to rein in the pace of change, incurring the wrath of both those who felt he had sown the wind and those who felt he had reneged on his promise. In short order the abortive elite reaction of the August 1991 putsch rose and fell; and that in turn precipitated sudden institutional collapse.[13]

Market reform and democratic reform thus were related parts of these dynamics. What the Soviet political elite perceived as intolerable economic shortfalls of the old regime precipitated a search for economic reform. Political reforms, although independently popular among certain elite sectors, came principally to pave the way for the economic reforms—to remove intransigent obstacles to systemic change that had paralyzed significant economic reform since Khrushchev's first efforts in the early 1960s. There were independent political motives too. But these stemmed from the epiphenomena of Soviet socialism after the long Brezhnev decay: the entrenched, insulated, arrogant bureaucracies self-vested in the status quo, the gnawing corruption high and low that had sapped the last remnants of utopian morality.

Both the economic and political reforms Gorbachev undertook contained pluralist, populist tendencies. They ran head-on against the premises of "democratic-centralism" upon which the party-state was erected and its claims to legitimacy established. In terms of cause and effect, it was economic conditions that led first to a strategy of political openness and limited pluralism, then to small moves in the direction of economic decentralization and economic pluralism, toward a "socialist market." Before the latter were fully in place, the political changes got out of control. Real politics was heady stuff; union republics began proclaiming independence.

To sum up, the changes in Russian society from 1986 to 1991 were economically inspired. But they were initiated within and from the top of a monolithic state as conscious strategies. They were not manifestations of group pressures from below, and there is little to suggest the timing was inevitable. They created neither political democracy nor market capitalism. Rather they stimulated a tearing apart of the Soviet order, discrediting its rationale for authority and thus releasing both a reactionary backlash from its defenders and opportunistic centrifugal disintegration in its ethnic periphery. Market capitalism and political democratization were only two possible scenarios for what might come next.

---

13. The best of many accounts is Jack F. Matlock, Jr., *Autopsy on an Empire* (New York: Random House, 1995). See particularly chapters 16–18.

The Second Case: Russian Reconstruction, 1992–96

The post-1991 period of the Soviet Russian experience presents a second case. This latter half of a dramatic decade has witnessed convulsive efforts to build and integrate new political and economic institutions and to graft them onto the buffeted society left in the wreckage of discredited Soviet socialism. The formal institutional arena for these efforts now resembles a parliamentary democratic state. As in the spring of 1917 when power was in the streets, new organizing principles were again imported. This time, it was said, they came on a plane from Washington rather than a train from Zurich.[14]

Since Gorbachev's resignation, we have seen two Russian parliamentary elections and one presidential, all vigorously contested among a plethora of self-styled political parties. The 1993 constitution provides for a presidential republic, distributing powers among legislative, executive, and judicial branches at the national level and between the central government and some eighty-nine regional and republican governments of the Russian Federation. No less than forty-seven constitutional articles affirm an array of civil rights and liberties even broader than those that appeared in the old Soviet constitution. This time, however, there is also explicit provision for ideological pluralism, and the powers of the state are ultimately attributed to the people.[15]

Formally too, 70–80 percent of the former Soviet state economy has been privatized. Prices have been liberalized, and wages in the private sector are similarly free to follow the market. After four years of devastating inflation, the ruble has been relatively stable over 1995–96, with domestic inflation for 1996 below 40 percent. Overall production dropped at an annual rate of about 20 percent from 1992 through 1994, but that too appears to be bottoming out with a decline of less than 10 percent in 1995, expectations of a further 5–6 percent reduction when the final figures for 1996 are in, but credible projections of modest growth in 1997.[16]

---

14. Rutland, "On the Road to Capitalism?" p. 3. See also his chapter, "Has Democracy Failed Russia?" in *Democracy and Development*, ed. Adrian Leftwich (New York: Oxford University Press, 1995).

15. *Constitutions of the Russian Federation* (Washington, D.C.: Embassy of the Russian Federation, 1994), Ch. 2, Articles 17–63; Ch. 1, Articles 3, 13.

16. Richard E. Ericson, "The Russian Economy Since Independence," in *The New Russia*, ed. G. Lapidus (Boulder, Colo.: Westview Press, 1995), 37–77; Lynn D. Nelson and Irina Y. Kuzes, "Privatisation and the New Business Class," in *Russia in Transition*, ed. David Lane (London: Longman, 1995), 119–41; Peter Rutland, "An Economy Running on Empty," in *Building Democracy: The OMRI Annual Survey of Eastern Europe and the Former Soviet Union 1995* (New York: M. E. Sharpe, 1996), 190–97; and Keith Bush, "The Russian Economy in Febru-

An undeniable measure of contest, participation, and private owner-ship attests that the institutional forms have brought a primitive liber-alism and democratic process to Russia. What they do not show is the toll on quality of Russian life the economic decline of these first five post-Soviet years has taken and its consequence for the political cul-ture. Despite the unreliability of much survey research in Russia, cau-tious Western analysts conclude that support for democratic values has been broad but shallow, stronger in the abstract. People approve of a free press, protected dissent, and other individual rights and liberties, but little admiration is evident for compromise or tolerant respect toward political adversaries. Support for competitive elections and a multiparty system is fragile.[17] Most parties, except for the communists, have lacked constituent infrastructure, and their leaders have shunned grassroots organizing of the electorate.

James Millar reports a Russian survey in September 1993 in which a 29 percent plurality of respondents identified economic prosperity as the single most important characteristic of a democracy. Competitive parties, freedom to criticize the government, protection of minority rights, and even the opportunity to choose the government through free elections trailed far behind.[18] One careful study based on winter 1993 surveys showed a strong positive correlation among education level and elite status and liberal political attitudes. It found a similar correlation in the general public between the attractions of markets and of liberal political values.[19] In spite of uncertainties, increased voter

ary 1996" (Research memorandum, Center for Strategic and International Studies, 27 February 1996).

17. James L. Gibson, "The Resilience of Mass Support for Democratic Insti-tutions and Processes in the Nascent Russian and Ukrainian Democracies," in *Political Culture and Civil Society in Russia and the New States of Eurasia*, ed. Vla-dimir Tismaneanu (New York: M. E. Sharpe, 1995), 53–111. But note the con-clusions of Jeffrey Hahn, whose study of attitudes in Yaroslavl in 1990 and 1993 shows a deterioration of support for democratic values associated with the economic decline, though insufficient to turn prevalent opinion to the sup-port of authoritarian values. Jeffrey W. Hahn, "Contemporary Russian Political Culture," in Tismaneanu, *Political Culture and Civil Society*, 112–36. Cf. Ada Finifter and Ellen Mickiewicz, "Redefining the Political System of the USSR: Mass Support for Political Change," *American Political Science Review* 86 (De-cember 1992): 857–74.

18. James Millar, "From Utopian Socialism to Utopian Capitalism," *Prob-lems of Post-Communism*, May–June 1995.

19. William Zimmerman, "Synoptic Thinking and Political Culture in Post-Soviet Russia," *Slavic Review* 54:3 (Fall 1995): 630–41. Cf. Gibson, "The Resil-ience of Mass Support"; and R. J. Shiller, M. Boyko, and V. Korobov, "Popular Attitudes Toward Free Markets: The Soviet Union and the United States Com-pared," *American Economic Review* 81 (1991): 385–400.

turnout between the 1993 and 1995 Duma elections (barely 50 percent to about 65 percent nationally) and nearly 70 percent participation in both rounds of the 1996 presidential election show a persistent will to participate despite continuing material privation.

But the radical shift from an institutional structure erected on Leninist premises to one professing liberal assumptions about "political man" tempt one to neglect the substantial carry-overs from the Soviet era. As Juan Lindau noted in chapter 7, rapid change obscures simultaneous continuities.

The material building blocks remain rich in Russia: unmatched natural resources including extensive energy reserves; the physical infrastructure of an urban industrial society, including a highly developed military-industrial complex; a well-educated social elite and well-trained and disciplined workforce; the foundation for unexcelled scientific and technological creativity; and advantageous geopolitical size and location—all the components of a materially prosperous society and a great international power.

Continuities also emerged amid the tumultuous efforts to change the economy. The short-lived tenure of Yegor Gaidar as Yeltsin's prime minister serves as an example of what has happened over the five years' effort to transform. Captivated by the bold imported vision of "shock therapy" as a quick fix for the Russian economy (the acute pain would soon be eclipsed by the new Western-style prosperity it would spawn), Gaidar became the lightning rod of dislocations visited on post-Soviet Russia. The shock was deep and persistent, the therapy unavailing from the vantage point of most ordinary Russians. Liberalized prices preceded liberalized wages, and rampant inflation destroyed savings and reduced state workers to penury. Voucher privatization, misunderstood by the uninformed public, transferred an appreciable part of the economy into private hands quickly. But those new hands turned out to belong to the more nimble elements of the old nomenklatura managerial elite.[20]

Yeltsin quickly cut Prime Minister Gaidar loose before 1992 ended and retreated to the pragmatic caution of Viktor Chernomyrdin, epitome of the retreaded old Soviet managers and a personal beneficiary of privatization in *Gazprom*, the giant natural gas combine. Political necessity reasserted itself in a society where the old political order had collapsed, and economic rationality therefore yielded to reconstructing

---

20. Ericson, "The Russian Economy Since Independence"; Nelson and Kuzes, "Privatisation and the New Business Class"; also Simon Clarke and Veronika Kabalina, "Privatisation and the Struggle for Control of the Enterprise," in Lane, *Russia in Transition*, 142–58.

an authoritative political order capable of enforcing painful economic decisions.

But Yeltsin temporized with state reconstruction. The Congress of People's Deputies and Supreme Soviet had acquired some legitimacy as a result of the August 1991 confrontation. At that time they represented a relatively popular voice raised against the old Soviet order. It was that Supreme Soviet that had first given Yeltsin his platform to oppose Gorbachev and later conceded him broad decree powers. So instead of calling new elections quickly, which likely would have eliminated the old CPSU contingent of the Congress and returned him a solid liberal majority, Yeltsin put adoption of a new constitution on hold and left the old legislature in place, seeking quick economic transformation through decrees and relying on his own charisma to bridge the indeterminate period of painful dislocation.[21]

The result was a weak and increasingly divided state, as the Supreme Soviet lost faith in shock therapy while privations deepened and the naive promises of quick capitalist prosperity dissolved.[22] Through the first half of 1993 a chasm divided the president and his technocratic advisers on one side from an uncomfortable combination of democratic purists and increasingly nostalgic Communists on the other.

Market liberalism and democratic political institutions, though possessed of a superficial appeal against the backdrop of a failed Leninist experiment, presented essentially suspect foreign formulations to the givens of Russian society and political culture. There is very little cultural memory (even if we jump back over three generations of Soviet socialism) of a liberal economy or democratic processes in Russia. There is even less cultural memory of success associated with them.

Their credibility is thus limited to the material prosperity Russians associate with them abroad. The social values that undergird the instrumental success of market capitalism and pluralist democracy are scarce in the Russian heritage. And unlike postwar Germany and Japan, there was no external victor in 1992 to impose unfamiliar institutions in Russia under the authority of occupation. The privations of a disrupted society added to the humiliation of domestic and imperial collapse, not defeat.

The stalemate between president and Parliament came to a head in September 1993, as Yeltsin, emboldened by popular support in an April referendum on his leadership, determined to rid himself of this drag against reform. Failing to dissolve a truculent Parliament by de-

---

21. Rutland, "Has Democracy Failed Russia?" 213–16.
22. See McFaul, "State Power," 238–43.

cree, he resorted to force. Reluctantly, the army turned tank guns on the Parliament building in October, etching a graphic picture of near civil war before the eyes of a bewildered, increasingly disillusioned Russian people.[23]

Just over two months later, his parliamentary adversaries temporarily neutralized, Yeltsin conducted elections for a new legislature. They followed the provisions of his new draft constitution, which was put to popular referendum simultaneously. Although the national turnout was low, the electoral commission reported that the constitution had been ratified. With it came a strong presidential republic in which Yeltsin's position was fortified by emergency powers, dissolution powers, and the right to appoint and keep a government chiefly accountable to the president.[24]

The electoral outcome in December 1993, however, did not relieve Yeltsin of the legislative obstacle to his freedom of action. A combination of resentment toward his high-handed disdain of the old Parliament, regional resistance to centralized government power in Moscow, and widespread disillusion with market liberalism's apparent material failure led to a new Duma composed of a strong Left (Communist) and a strong Right (Nationalist) opposition but weak in the center.[25] This center is where marketization finds its strongest advocates. Thus the incorporation of a broader spectrum of political opinion into democratic participation, one measure of the progress of democratization, began to dilute political support for marketization. Rather than accelerate marketization, then, democracy may have retarded it.[26]

When the second Duma elections were held in December 1995, the balance of the protest vote against the government shifted from Nationalists to Communists, but the result was to further weaken the president in the liberal center.[27]

---

23. See Dimitri Simes, "The Return of Russian History," *Foreign Affairs* 73:1 (January/February 1994): 67–82; and Stephen Sestanovich, "Russia Turns the Corner," *Foreign Affairs* 73:1 (January/February 1994): 83–98.

24. *Constitution of the Russian Federation*, Ch. 4, Articles 80–93.

25. See Commission on Security and Cooperation in Europe, *Russia's Parliamentary Election and Constitutional Referendum, December 12, 1993* (Washington, D.C.: CSCE, January 1994); also reports by Serge Schmemann, Celestine Bohlen, and Steven Erlanger in *New York Times*, 13–16 December 1993; and *RFE/RL Daily Report*, 10–20 December 1993.

26. David S. Mason, "Attitudes toward the Market and Political Participation in the Postcommunist State," *Slavic Review* 54:2 (Summer 1995): 385–406. See just this prospect suggested by Cheek and Lindau in chapter 1 of this volume.

27. Laura Belin and Robert W. Orttung, "On Political Front, Slow Progress Toward Democracy," in Rutland, *Building Democracy*, 210–20.

Thus market liberalization and democratization now confront each other in rebuilding Russian political culture. They are simultaneously pitted together against neo-communist apologias for the old regime, when material conditions of life were better. They have begun to face nationalist appeals too, to the unique character of Russia, whose historic glories might offer resources of vitality preferable to alien imports. The new institutions must fight both identification with economic failure and the image of alien imports unsuited to Russian exceptionalism.[28]

In this competition to put together a new system all at once, liberalism, democracy, and their instrumental manifestations play related parts. What has emerged is a significantly marketized and privatized economy with some very Russian elements: agricultural land still largely collectively or state-owned and industry capitalized by the "mafia." What has emerged also bears some of the instrumental characteristics of a democratic polity (though the curve is jagged, as the October 1993 events testify): plural economic elites based on wealth replacing old Communist elites that were based on party loyalty. The new plural elites are reflected in the process and composition of the polity as well as the economy. In the 1992–96 period, political reconstruction—the effort of various groups to establish or consolidate political power—generally drove economic policies. A rudimentary system of new/old political elites replaced the beheaded CPSU. They are now competing to reconstruct Russia in self-serving ways. Continuing marketization flows from the efforts of the economic reformers now ascendant around Yeltsin to consolidate their political base against other elites more effectively entrenched in the Parliament and the regions. The raw power struggle fascinated the world when its intrigues burst into view during Yeltsin's illness and surgery, reminiscent of the restless boyars around the tsar of an earlier Russia.

Mexico and China

From this snapshot orientation to the Russian scene, let us turn to some hypotheses about the relationship between market liberalization and democratic processes and values that arise in the discussions of China and Mexico in foregoing chapters of this volume. What observations of China and Mexico resonate in the Russian experience? Do the Russian cases contribute anything to our mutual effort to generalize about marketization-democratization connections?

---

28. See *Economist*, 15 June 1966, 19–21

Meyer's summary of contemporary Mexican political obstacles to democratization[29] mirrors the counterpart Russian situation:

> The very negative effects of economic depression on all social classes, the
> weakness of political parties and social organizations, the widening of the
> gap between rich and poor, the Chiapas guerrillas and finally, the lack of
> a democratic tradition.

Each of these five obstacles finds a strong Russian parallel. One need
only substitute "Chechen" for "Chiapas" to fit the list verbatim to Russia. Collectively it also establishes the domestic agenda for the Russian
polity.

Despite the obvious differences between the two countries, the challenges bear a remarkable resemblance. In neither Mexico nor China
has the old order collapsed abruptly. China now boasts the world's
most rapid economic growth, and separatism in Tibet or Sinkiang as
yet does not compare to Chechnya or Chiapas. But "contestation and
participation" ferment in all three.

Cheek and Lindau invoke Schumpeter at the outset of chapter 1 to
identify "contestation" and "participation" as defining characteristics
of democratic politics.[30] By that rudimentary criterion, Russian politics,
like those of Mexico and even China at some levels, have indeed become more democratic over the past decade. Russian contestation has
spread from the covert struggle among elements of a narrow power-
elite, typical during the Soviet period, to include a new entrepreneurial
class, regional voices, and more articulated sub-interests throughout
society—legitimated by constitutional affirmation of pluralism in place
of the hegemonic dogma of the Communist party-state. A generally
free and fractious press mirrors a high level of political conflict. "Participation," heretofore a hollow exercise associated almost exclusively with political socialization, now has taken on significant political
agency by virtue of competitive elections as the effective mode of leadership recruitment. Elections were critical for demonstrating the party's loss of legitimacy, and thus for ending CPSU control. Since 1991,
however grudgingly, plural elites increasingly acknowledge the obligation to secure popular elective mandate for office and exert their
energies to elicit that mandate.

But if we go beyond such a rudimentary standard of democracy, to
the question of democratic values in Russia, evidence is murky at best.
We cited a poll above that suggests economic prosperity is viewed as

29. Meyer, chapter 5 in this volume.
30. Cheek and Lindau, chapter 1 in this volume.

a more important "characteristic of a democracy" than free elections or individual rights. One is reminded that even as optimistic a champion of market democratization as Lipset judged prosperity a necessary premise for limited government and deconcentration of political power. The embourgeoisement of the population was an intermediate step on the road to democracy.[31] Similarly, Robert Packenham, in chapter 3, predicates his optimism for eventual democratic political evolution in Latin America on the expectation that market liberalization will achieve a higher standard of living first.[32] If democratic values in Russia depend upon material prosperity, their status is currently very fragile.

The chapters in Part III all address the issue of civil society and political democracy, generally agreeing that democratic institutions require the support of a civil culture to become resilient and self-perpetuating in either China or Mexico. Cheek invokes the Habermas and Gramsci views of civil society to assess prospects in China. These theories may assist thinking about the same question in the Russian case. Habermas emphasizes the production of a public sphere open to all citizens and existing in tension with the state. An autonomous legal system constrains government and legitimates public expression, interest group articulation, and democratic elections. The public sphere thus gives politics its content.[33] Gramsci envisions civil society as a parallel arena, in which political culture is shaped. It is composed of the educational, religious, and associational institutions that shape the cognitive and affective structures of popular perception and evaluation.[34]

Looking at Russia over the past decade, we may say that before the collapse of the Soviet state a nascent public sphere struggled in restricted circumstances to generate a politics that aspired to replace the moribund official order. After 1991, however, the new "third sector" associations—the *neformaly* of 1986–91, many of which represented the democratic dissident movement—were eclipsed by a new pluralism in which the entrepreneurial class and the redefined managerial and governmental elites became the principal actors. The latter have approached the formal democratic order as an arena in which to fight for power and advantage, appropriating democratic forms where useful or necessary to that end. It was the *neformaly*, pre-1991, that began to propagate democratic values. Today both these associations and their values are in remission. In Gramscian terms, the old nomenklatura tie,

---

31. Domínguez, chapter 2 in this volume.
32. Packenham, chapter 3 in this volume.
33. Cheek, chapter 8 in this volume.
34. As summarized in ibid.

common across much of the new entrepreneur class as well as the re-created managers and the old/new government bureaucrats, preserves many of the values of Soviet political culture.

Gaye Christofferson identifies "nomenklatura capitalism" in eastern Siberia as representative of state-society negotiation that shapes political and economic change in East Asia.[35] Her analysis suggests a dominant role for elite negotiations, which are nevertheless constrained by a growing need to appeal for the approval of the "ordinarily quiescent citizen." That assessment fits into the broader conclusions one may draw from the post-Soviet Russian experience: The economic failure of the Soviet economic model stimulated Gorbachev's strategic gamble with democratic political reforms aimed at economic recovery. Its political consequences brought on the Soviet collapse. The social, political, and economic consequences of the collapse yielded the current dynamics of political-economic interaction. The nomenklatura class are the surviving cadres of the old state, now intermingled with the new entrepreneurial elite to negotiate their interests with the surviving elements of the old state, such as military and security bureaucracies, in the arena of a weak new state, and in the face of a sort of popular-veto mass politics.[36]

Let us look briefly at the character of both the "new elites" and the "new masses" of Russia. Do they and their interplay have counterparts in China or Mexico?

The power-elite of Soviet Russia manifested a limited pluralism. Post-1991 that pluralism has fractured further—among firms as well as sectors of elite. But the scope of elite influence has not enlarged as much as one might suppose the possibilities of entrepreneurship would support. That is because the mechanisms of privatization (mainly vouchers and managerial prerogative) were manipulated by the old elite to keep power in their hands. Some of the old nomenklatura have been excluded because they were not agile enough to appropriate the new sources of power when the old disintegrated. Disgruntled, these people have often moved into the opposition groups

35. Christoffersen, chapter 4 in this volume.

36. Interest group pluralism of course existed in Soviet politics and helped explain the public policies of the post-Stalin era. It was limited, muted pluralism, however, necessarily disavowed officially and generally relegated to intra-party struggle at a high level. See H. G. Skilling and F. Griffiths, eds., *Interest Groups in Soviet Politics* (Princeton, N.J.: Princeton University Press, 1971); and Jerry Hough, *Soviet Leadership in Transition* (Washington, D.C.: The Brookings Institution, 1980). The old as well as new interest groups, some interpenetrated, compose the field of the new liberally sanctioned pluralism of contemporary Russia.

of extreme nationalism or reactionary communism. Some of them also compose the new service sector of private security (KGB, military, and police), and some have swelled the robust ranks of organized crime.

The old currency of power in Soviet society was political position. Material perquisites were its byproduct. The later Soviet era insinuated financial advantage too. Post-1991, it is increasingly financial wealth itself that carries political influence as its byproduct. Vladimir Potanin, president of *Oneksimbank*, became first deputy prime minister for economy after raising the funds for Yeltsin's victory. Boris Berezovskii, another prosperous banker who massively supported Yeltsin's campaign, served as deputy secretary of the National Security Council. The new pattern is part of the imported paraphernalia from Western market-democratic practice.

Because the old-new nomenklatura remains the ownership class, it maintains its accustomed arrogance. The opportunistic new beneficiaries of entrepreneurship readily adopt the same sense of entitlement. Thus, though pluralism has become more complex in Russia, and the state far weaker, not much mutual deference or respect has been generated—which might be considered necessary to the growth of civil society as found in the West. One simply recognizes power and makes the necessary concessions to it; one does not concede legitimacy to the voice of democracy. Thus, in Russia, it does not necessarily follow that the forms of democratic political practice lead directly to democratic values. Ironically, as we saw in the 1996 presidential campaign, the imported electioneering apparatus of Western democracy may not encourage the growth of democratic values in Russia but may be adapted to the power struggle among competing, very undemocratically inclined elites.

But turning to China, Potter's observations in Shanghai also resonate for the Soviet Union after 1985 and then in post-1991 Russia: "the emerging attitudes of the Shanghai *getihu* concerning ideals of equality, justice, and civil law relations suggest that changing regulatory and ideological forms have had an effect on ideas and behavior." Here too "the regime attempted to prevent economic reform from giving rise to political liberalization." But "certain unintended consequences" derived from the reform process: "The Leninist party system, which derive[d] its purpose and legitimacy from assumptions about class struggle and the need for a vanguard party . . . [was] undermined further by the spread of popular ideals about social equality."[37] Potter concludes that "what may be unfolding in China is a process whereby economic reform engenders new attitudes about legal and ultimately

---

37. Potter, chapter 6 in this volume.

political relations." And finally, "Herein may lie the foundations for lasting political change." Gorbachev tried to limit the political liberalization to what his conception of the party-state of Soviet socialism could assimilate. But unintended consequences gutted the fragile remaining authority of the CPSU. Post-1991 Russian economic reform may be nurturing attitudes about legal and ultimately political relations that will provide the foundations of lasting political change. But, as in China, that is still an open question. Meanwhile, the current relationship of democratization and market liberalism is not yet driven by such new sprouts in the political culture. They grow in the background of strategic choices and tacit negotiation of interests among competing elites and between a weak state and a turbulent society.

Lindau and Cheek note that many scholars have speculated that economic liberalization may release individual and corporate initiative, that spills over from the pursuit of strictly economic self-interests into voices which seek political protection to support economic opportunities and reclaim public space from the state.[38] That has happened in the new Russian polity as competing economic elites stake out political turf in the arena of governing institutions at the national and regional levels, building coalitions of mutual interest and harnessing the assets of parliamentary, partisan, bureaucratic, and federal institutions to their causes.

Cutting against this tendency in Russia, however (as Lindau observes in Mexico and Cheek in China), is the consequent disruption of order that the cacophony of self-seeking new voices creates. The "new masses" of post-Soviet Russia may yet evoke suppression of the new pluralism, conceivably by using their new democratic empowerment on behalf of an aspiring demagogue. The survey literature shows that a fear of chaos predisposes a large part of the Russian population to accept fatalistically the idea of "strong leadership." It is as though the yearning for "a strong tsar, who knows best what his people need" coexists uneasily with a rebellious libertarian yearning in Russian political culture. The latter resonates to rights, liberties, and the democratic authority of the people. But the former keeps those affirmations abstract and erratic.

There is no doubt that a frontier mentality pervades much of urban Russian society today. The disorder and uncertainty of the new pluralism encourage an each-for-oneself environment in which individual initiative untrammeled by either the old (discredited) morality or any other morality is not subject to self-restraint. Absent a functioning legal order, not only is the most outrageous corruption rampant but its very

38. Cheek and Lindau, chapter 1.

definition is hopelessly vague. And the scope of organized crime has become notorious. Thus three more scenarios common to China and Mexico can also be traced in post-Soviet Russia.

"Participation" faces other challenges in post-Soviet Russia that have Chinese or Mexican counterparts. At one level it was always recognized as a legitimator of the Soviet order: "voting yes" genuflected to the party line. Hence the expense lavished on frequent election campaigns and near unanimous endorsements. So there is some popular cynicism about making the voting franchise an active agency of popular choice. Does it really make a difference now? And there is probably a hangover of the old ritualized Soviet elections that encourages the old-new elite to think of contemporary electoral exercises as socialization by competitive propaganda rather than expressions of popular will. The imported techniques of Western campaigning may, ironically, reinforce this tendency.[39]

The intelligentsia of Russia never conceded much authority to the "masses." Nor did Lenin. Nor have the socioeconomic elite of Mexico or the post–Cultural Revolution Chinese leadership. The failure of a reformist "Go to the People" movement in the 1870s pushed pre-1917 Russia toward a bipolar revolutionary and reactionary society and away from compromise liberalism. Thus there is little grassroots populism or "town-meeting" democratic tradition to encourage the new party politics of post-1991 Russia.[40] Time spent persuading the masses is at best put up with as an ancillary obligation to the central task of figuring out what the real interest of society is or should be. There is not much patience to be found among the programmatic reformers of Russia, even those who adhere strongly to the symbols of abstract democracy, such as the late Andrei Sakharov or the young economist politicians led by Chubais, Nemtsov, or Yavlinsky.

Last, another deterrent to the growth of civil society well described in Lindau's assessment of Mexican political culture finds a strong parallel in Russia. In Mexico, Lindau identifies a recurrent inclination of the social elite to affirm its formative values from a traditional, conservative private order, parallel to but unpenetrated by the unstable polity. Thus, the face of liberalism gives a deceptive appearance to Mexican society without controlling its fundamental relationships, and the enduring private order undercuts constitutional democracy.[41]

---

39. See Michael Kramer in *Time*, 15 July 1996, 29–37.

40. But for a recent qualification of the traditional view on this issue, see Nicolai N. Petro, *The Rebirth of Russian Democracy: An Interpretation of Political Culture* (Cambridge: Harvard University Press, 1995).

41. Lindau, chapter 7.

So too in Russia. Once the shiny appeal of Marxist ideology had been discredited by the Leninist and then Stalinist evolution after 1917, an individual had two options. One could accommodate reality and follow opportunities for recognition within the system, sensing the political wind and seeking a niche in a favored part of the new privileged class. Or one could try to keep the storm of building Soviet socialism at arm's length and live primarily in a private world, by cultivating a few genuine personal ties and interests while observing the obligatory rituals of public life. Whatever way one chose to adapt to Soviet norms, now, in the rootless uncertainty of Russia, it still seems a rash gamble to commit oneself fully to the premises of liberalism or democracy. Made doubly cautious by the painful failures of Soviet socialism, Russians should not be expected to grasp an unproven civic alternative easily. But that discourages a genuinely democratic political culture—which needs enough fusion of private and public cultures to make citizenship vital.

Conclusions

We return to Christoffersen's four hypotheses to summarize some conclusions indicated by this short exploration of Russia in comparison to China and Mexico.

First, the structural argument: We find no evidence in either case that there is a direct deterministic link between economic liberalization and the growth of democratic processes. Liberalization may include a wide variety of changes, some of which undoubtedly nurture too many voices to silence effectively. Other interests newly delineated into contesting political groups may nurture pluralism without significantly expanding popular political participation or impact. In fact, these groups may find it in their interest to curtail the scope of pluralism to a competition of elites, especially in a case where a weak state is unwilling or unable to assert its legal writ to protect popular opportunity. The collapse of the Soviet party-state was not followed by the establishment of a new rule of law; power devolved to regional satrapies. Nomenklatura capitalists created a new corporate pluralism in Russia that is only beginning to feel the stirring of constitutional restraints from the Russian people.

We certainly may not say liberal marketization is dependent upon widespread growth of democratic processes or values. In Russia since 1991, such market liberalization as has evolved is the product of strategic government choices modified by state-society negotiated limits that reflect de facto power distribution. Thus privatization stops short of agricultural land ownership and short of permitting the collapse of parasitic state industrial concerns. The large nomenklatura capitalist enterprises, such as *Gazprom* and *Lukneft* in the gas and oil sector, enjoy the benefits of close state support and vice versa.

Nor may we conclude that democratic processes necessarily accelerate liberal marketization. Both the Duma elections of December 1995 and the presidential election of June and July 1996 demonstrate that these processes, as heartening as they may seem intrinsically, may raise to influence either liberal reformers or determined opponents of liberalization. The processes themselves did not stand in the way of Zhirinovsky's misnamed Liberal Democrats in December 1993. They did not deter Yeltsin's unconstitutional dismissal of the Duma by force in October 1993. They served Zyuganov's anti-liberal Communist victory in the Duma elections of December 1995. It was not these democratic processes that decided the struggle between Yeltsin and Zyuganov for the presidency. Yet the outcomes of these competitions for political power have been far more decisive for the fate of liberalization in Russia over the past five years than any interest group influences spawned by the processes themselves.

But both these Russian cases confirm that economic liberalization and democratic processes do generate sociological consequences. Just as the rhetoric of the old party-state long helped legitimate Communist authority, now the procedures of democracy are called upon to legitimate the new distribution of political power. However, democracy, like economic liberalization, should be regarded as an aggregate concept, containing potentially discordant elements.[42] It is not clear whether President Yeltsin would have turned over the reins of power to Zyuganov peacefully, had the July 3rd runoff election given Zyuganov a plurality of votes. The fragile myth of democratic authority was not put to such a problematic test.[43] But it is highly probable that, should Yeltsin die or become too incapacitated to remain in office, democratic procedures—however distorted—will again shape the arena of competition for succession. Russian political culture has by no means accepted the customary deference to democratic practices that many generations have instilled in some Western societies. But given the discrediting of authoritarian alternatives, some democratic forms show widespread acceptance.[44]

---

42. Packenham, chapter 3 in this volume.

43. David Remnick, "The War for the Kremlin," *The New Yorker*, 22 July 1996, 48–57, argues that the Yeltsin administration would have failed the test in 1996.

44. See *OMRI Daily Digest*, 2 August 1996, for an indication of supportive public opinion after the presidential election.

What must be emphasized is that the sociological consequences of democratic and liberal institutions, though visible, cannot be expected to prevail against sudden storms of high politics. They have not transformed the fabric of Soviet society into something strong enough to resist transgression by a powerful leader (witness October 1993). Nor can they be expected to survive indefinitely the association with popular material immiseration. Time and eventually association with material success, popular freedoms, and security may weave such a social fabric. It would be fatuous to proclaim its achievement or imminent arrival in today's Russia.

The reverse coin of the structural modernization hypothesis is strategic choice and individual agency. Certainly both the first case of Soviet collapse and the second case of subsequent transformation show the critical role of conscious leadership choices. Our widespread surprise and subsequent handwringing about our inability to predict occur because we did not suspect that the role of preeminent Soviet power would itself be used to give the *coup de grace* to the party-state. Gorbachev's choices were both decisive and contextually unnecessary. There were alternatives, and who can doubt that, say, Grigorii Romanov of Leningrad would have chosen differently to different immediate effect? Six years later the irresolute choice of the coup makers of August 1991 precipitated the final collapse of the Soviet order, a sequence of events that though probable in the longer term was not inevitable at that moment.

Individual agency has been demonstrably important since 1991 as well as before. Yeltsin chose to disregard the legal strictures of executive-legislative relations in October 1993, to break the stalemate by disbanding the Congress of Deputies, and to mobilize a reluctant military to make his choice effective with tank guns against the burning facade of the Russian White House. Thus, paradoxically, some continuity toward institutionalizing market liberalization and democratic political procedures was maintained by highly autocratic means.

"High politics" are the occasions for individual human agency in the affairs of societies and states. The background conditions molded by accretions of institutional behavior provide the setting and limit the possibilities of high politics, but no observer of the jagged curve of Russia in the past decade could responsibly attribute its departures to impersonal forces alone.

The Soviet collapse shattered an economic, political, and social order, but it did not atomize the component units of Soviet society, not even the formally dissolved and discredited Communist Party. It was the architecture that configured these component units into a functioning system that was shattered and discredited: the organs remained, the skeleton disappeared. In the enterprise of reassembly, many of the units gained independent power as a function of chaos. Thus the transformation of the state-society relationship over the past five years has been largely a product of negotiations among these surviving units of the *ancien régime*, each maximizing its assets for influence and testing its relative power in a changed arena.

Fourth, what does the Russian case say to the hypothesis of external influence as a change agent in the relationship of market liberalization and democratization? Christoffersen finds that channel of influence powerful in East Asia. Meyer and Lindau trace its unintended effects in Mexico. Our own observation of Russia suggests that example has had an enormous impact. Thus the blurred image of a liberal democratic alternative to the old Soviet order played a large role in the image democratic reformers had of a new Russian future. Such images often provide the vocabulary and abstract goals of institutional behavior, conditioning the terms of pragmatic policy-making. In that fashion Western images of market liberalism and democratic politics have no doubt channeled the choices and set the context of struggle among the residual power units of post-Soviet Russia.

Beyond that largely heuristic role, we note the matrix of governmental and non-governmental organizational connections that have provided multifarious channels of external influence at a micro- as well as a macro-level in Russian society. From the impact of technical assistance, IMF loans and their baggage of restrictions, and the prospects of NATO and EU expansion eastward (at the macro-level), to the vicissitudes of religious movements and private foundations operating across borders (at the micro-level),[45] Russia's transformation has been steadily abetted and contaminated from abroad—by groups proceeding from an equally diverse set of motives. The neo-Slavophile and Eurasian movements of Russian nationalism compete against the new economic permeability of all frontiers to contain these influences.

Finally, one may come back to come back to Meyer's description of Mexico's obstacles to democratization and reiterate that overcoming them is also the formidable challenge of democratic reformers in Russia. The outcome is indeterminate, and the resources for success must come primarily from within Russia. The gradual building of a resilient new political culture to sustain democratic processes with democratic values will be a long development and will depend in the near term on associating liberalization and democracy with material and moral success in the newly empowered public mind. The burden of the pre-

---

45. See M. Holt Ruffin et al., eds., *The Post-Soviet Handbook* (Seattle: University of Washington Press, 1996), 164–262.

ceding chapters has been to define the roles of all four hypotheses, not to exclude but to dissuade us of the independent sufficiency of each. Both Russian cases reinforce that conclusion.

Early in this volume Jorge Domínguez, having reviewed the scholarship of Lipset, Moore, and Guillermo O'Donnell, synthesizes a hypothetical pattern of the partnership between market liberalization and political democratization which I would summarize as follows: Without market liberalism, no democracy. With market liberalism, *maybe* democracy—depending on three conditions: liberty preserved by constitutional and political culture, prosperity credibly attributable to the market economy, and absence of powerful social coalitions mobilized to suppress democracy.[46] These are very challenging conditions for Russian democrats, or Chinese or Mexican, to achieve. But the relative success or failure of their strategies will probably define the future of political economy in all three societies.

---

46. Domínguez, chapter 2.

Bibliography

Aberbach, Joel, David Dollar, and Kenneth Sokoloff, eds. *The Role of the State in Taiwan's Development*. Armonk, N.Y.: M. E. Sharpe, Inc., 1994.

Aldunate, Arturo Fontaine. *Los economistas y el presidente Pinochet*. Santiago: Zig-Zag, 1988.

Almond, Gabriel A., and G. Bingham Powell, Jr. *Comparative Politics: A Developmental Approach*. Boston: Little, Brown and Co., 1966.

Almond, Gabriel, and Sidney Verba. *The Civic Culture*. Boston: Little, Brown and Co., 1965.

Amnesty International Reports, 1992, 1993, 1994, 1995, and 1996. London: Amnesty International.

Amsden, Alice. "The Specter of Anglo-Saxonization Is Haunting South Korea." In *Korea's Political Economy: An Institutional Perspective*, edited by Lee-Jay Cho and Yoon Hyung Kim (Boulder, Colo.: Westview Press, 1994).

Apter, David E. *The Politics of Modernization*. Chicago: University of Chicago Press, 1965.

Arato, Andrew. *From Neo-Marxism to Democratic Theory*. Armonk, N.Y.: M. E. Sharpe, 1993.

Arreola, Alvaro, Jose Georgette, Matilde Luna, and Ricardo Tirado. "Memoria de los primeros ocho dias." *Revista Mexicana de Sociologia* 158, no. 2 (April–June 1986).

Asia Pacific Foundation of Canada. *Canada Asia Review 1997*. 1997.

The Asia Society. *U.S.-Japan Policy Dialogue on China: Economic Issues*. (A report.) Washington, D.C., 18–19 December 1991.

Asian Development Bank. *Law and Development at the Asian Development Bank*. 1997.

"Asia's Ailing State Enterprises: China." *Far Eastern Economic Review*, 23 February 1995.

Aslund, Anders. "The Case for Radical Reform." *Journal of Democracy* 5, no. 4 (October 1994).

Augerot, Arrow. "Will China Return to the Center of the Universe?" Colorado College, Manuscript, February 1994.

Aziz, Alberto, and Jacqueline Peschard, coordinators. *Las elecciones federales de 1991*. México: National University of México and Porrúa, 1992.

Aziz Nassif, Alberto. "Chihuahua: historia de una alternativa." *México: La Jor-nada-CIESAS* (1994).

Baer, M. Delal. "The New Order and Disorder in U.S.–Mexican Relations." In *A New North America: Cooperation and Enhanced Interdependence*, edited by Charles F. Doran and Alvin Paul Drischler. Westport, Conn.: Praeger, 1996.

Banfield, Edward. *The Moral Basis of a Backward Society*. New York: The Free Press, 1958.

Barberán, José, et al. *Radiografica del fraude. Análisis de los datos oficiales del 6 de julio*. México: Nuestro Tiempo, 1988.

Barro, Robert J. "Democracy and Growth." *Working Paper*, no. 4909. Cambridge, Mass.: National Bureau of Economic Research, October 1994.

Basanez, Miguel. *El pulso de los sexenios: 20 anos de crisis en México*. Mexico, D.F.: Siglo XXI, 1991.

Bazdresch, Carlos, et al. *México. Auge, crisis y ajuste*, 2 vols. México: Fondo de Cultura Económica, 1992.

Belin, Laura, and Robert W. Orttung, "On the Political Front, Slow Progress toward Democracy." In *Building Democracy: The OMRI Annual Survey of Eastern Europe and the Former Soviet Union 1995*. New York: M. E. Sharp, 1996.

Bell, Michael, Hoe Ee Khor, and Kalpana Kochhar. *China at the Threshold of a Market Economy*. Washington, D.C.: International Monetary Fund, September 1993.

Beltran, Ulisses, et al. *Los mexicanos de los noventa*. México, D.F.: Instituto de Investigaciones Sociales, UNAM, 1996.

Benjamin, Thomas. *A Rich Land, a Poor People: Politics and Society in Modern Chiapas*. Albuquerque: University of New Mexico Press, 1989.

Berger, Peter. *The Capitalist Revolution*. New York: Basic Books, 1986.

Berger, Suzanne, ed. *Organizing Interests in Western Europe*. Cambridge: Cambridge University Press, 1981.

Bergson, Abram. "The USSR before the Fall: How Poor and Why?" *Journal of Economic Perspectives* 5, no. 4, (Fall 1991).

Betts, Richard K. "Wealth, Power, and Instability: East Asia and the United States after the Cold War." *International Security*. (Winter 1993/94).

Bodde, Derk, and Clarence Morris. *Law in Imperial China*. Philadelphia: University of Pennsylvania Press, 1967.

Bonfil, Guillermo. *México profundo. Una civilización negada*. México: Secretaría de Educación Pública, 1987.

Bosworth, Barry P., Rudiger Dornbusch, and Raul Laban, eds. *The Chilean Economy: Policy Lessons and Challenges*. Washington, D.C.: Brookings Institution, 1994.

Brading, David. *Orbe indiano. De la monarquía católica a la república criolla*. México: Fondo de Cultura Económica, 1991.

Brandenburg, Frank. *The Making of Modern Mexico*. Englewood Cliffs, N.J.: Prentice-Hall. 1964.

Broodsgarad, Kjeld Eric. *Copenhagen Papers*, 1. 1991.

Brook, Timothy, and B. Michael Frolic, eds. *Civil Society in China*. Armonk, New York: M. E. Sharpe, 1997.

Brown, Ken. "Having Left Campus for the Arena, Winner in Brazil Shifts to the Right." *New York Times*, 11 November 1994.

Brugger, Bill, and David Kelly. *Chinese Marxism in the Post-Mao Era*. Stanford: Stanford University Press, 1990.

Buck, David D., ed. "Forum on Universalism and Relativism in Asian Studies." *Journal of Asian Studies*, 50, no. 1. (February 1991).

Burkholder, Mark, and Diaz Chandler. *From Impotence to Authority: The Spanish Crown and the American Audiencias, 1687–1808*. New York: Columbia University Press, 1977.

Bush, Keith. "The Russian Economy in February 1996," Research Memorandum, Center for Strategic and International Studies, 27 February 1996.

Cabanellas, Guillermo. *Diccionario enciclopédico de derecho usual*. Buenos Aires: Editorial Helestia, 1986.

Calva, José Luis. *El Financiero*. 18 November 1994.

Camín, Héctor Aguilar, and Lorenzo Meyer. In *The Shadow of the Mexican Revolution: Contemporary Mexican History, 1910–1989*. Austin: University of Texas Press, 1993.

Campos, Julieta. *¿Qué hacemos con los pobres? La reiterada querella por la nación*. México: Aguilar, 1995.

Campos, Rolando Cordera, Raul Trejo Delarbre, and Juan Enrique Vega, eds. *Mexico el reclamo democrático*. México D.F.: Siglo Veintiuno Editores, 1988.

Canadian International Development Agency. *China: Country Development Policy Framework*. (Toronto: 1994).

Cardoso, Fernando Henrique. "Surprises and Challenges for Democracy in Latin America." Panel on Prospects for the Hemisphere in Symposium on Global Peace and Development: Prospects for the Future. Notre Dame, Ind.: Kellogg Institute, 13 September 1991.

Cardoso, Fernando Henrique, and Enzo Faletto. *Dependency and Development in Latin America*. Berkeley and Los Angeles: University of California Press, 1979.

Carothers, Thomas. "Democracy and Human Rights: Policy Allies or Rivals." *The Washington Quarterly* 17, no. 3 (Summer 1994).

Carpizo, Jorge. *El presidencialismo mexicano*. México: Siglo Veintiuno, 1978.

Carter, Barry E. *International Economic Sanctions: Improving the Haphazard U.S. Legal Regime*. Cambridge: Cambridge University Press, 1988.

Caso, Antonio. *Obras completas*, 8 vols. México D.F.: Universidad Nacional Autonoma de México, 1971–1975.

Castañeda, Jorge G. "Mexico's Circle of Misery." *Foreign Affairs* 75, no. 4 (July/August 1996).

Castrejon Diez, Jaime. *La política segun los mexicanos*. México D.F.: Oceano, 1995.

Caudill Dealy, Glen. *The Latin Americans' Spirit and Ethos*. Boulder, Colo.: Westview, 1992.

Centeno, Miguel Angel. *Democracy Within Reason: Technocratic Revolution in Mexico*. University Park: The Pennsylvania State University Press, 1994.

Central Intelligence Agency, Directorate of Intelligence. *Revisiting Soviet Economic Performance under Glasnost: Implications for CIA Estimates*. Washington, D.C.: CIA, 1988.

Central Intelligence Agency, Directorate of Intelligence. *Handbook of Economic Statistics, 1991*. Washington, D.C.: CIA, 1991.

CEPAL. *Panorama Economico de America Latina 1995*. Santiago de Chile: United Nations, September 1995.

CEPAL. *Panorama Economico de America Latina 1996*. Santiago de Chile: United Nations, September 1996.

CEPAL. *Balance Preliminar de la Economica de America Latina y el Caribe 1996*. Santiago de Chile: United Nations, December 1996.

Chai, Sun-ki. *A Cognitive Approach to Rational Action*. Ann Arbor: University of Michigan Press. Forthcoming.

Chang, Da-kuang. "The Making of the Chinese Bankruptcy Law: A Study in the Chinese Legislative Process." *Harvard International Law Journal* 28 (1987).

Chang, Hsia-ching, and Timothy Cheek. "Open and Closed Media." In *Decision-Making in Deng's China: Perspectives from Insiders*, edited by Carol Lee Hamrin and Suisheng Zhao. Armonk, New York: M. E. Sharpe, 1995.

Chang, Julian. "The Mechanics of State Propaganda: The People's Republic of China and the Soviet Union in the 1950s." In *New Perspectives on State Socialism in China*, edited by Timothy Cheek and Tony Saich. Armonk, New York: M. E. Sharpe, 1997.

Chao, Linda, and Ramon H. Myers. "The First Chinese Democracy: Political Development of the Republic of China on Taiwan, 1986–1994." *Asian Survey* 34, no. 3 (March 1994).

Cheek, Timothy. "Habits of the Heart: Intellectual Assumptions Reflected by Chinese Reformers from Deng Tuo to Fang Lizhi." In *Changes in China: Party, State, and Society*, edited by Shao-chuan Leng. Lanham, Md.: University Press of America, 1989.

Cheek, Timothy. "From Priests to Professionals: Intellectuals and the State Under the CCP." In *Popular Protest and Political Culture in China: Learning from 1989*, edited by Jeffrey Wasserstrom and Elizabeth J. Perry. Boulder, Colo.: Westview Press, 1992 and 1994.

Cheek, Timothy. *Propaganda and Culture in Mao's China: Deng Two and the Intelligentsia*. Oxford: Clarendon Press, 1997.

Cheek, Timothy, and Tony Saich, eds. *New Perspectives on State Socialism in China* (Armonk, N.Y.: M. E. Sharpe, 1997).

Chen, Albert H. Y. *An Introduction to the Legal System of the PRC*. Hong Kong: Butterworth's, 1993.

Chen, Youzun, ed. *Minshi jingji jinan anli jiesi* (Interpretation and analysis of difficult civil and economic cases). Huhehaote: Inner Mongolia University Press, 1990.

Chettle, John. "The American Way: Or How the Chaos, Unpredictability, Contradictions, Complexity, and Example of Our System Undid Communism and Apartheid." *The National Interest*, no. 41 (Fall 1995).

Cho, Lee-Jay, and Yoon Hyuang Kim, eds. *Korea's Political Economy: An Institutional Perspective*. Boulder, Colo.: Westview Press, 1994.

Chu, Godwiin C., and Yanan Ju. *The Great Wall in Ruins: Communication and Cultural Change in China*. Albany: State University of New York Press, 1993.

Clarke, Donald C. "Dispute Resolution in China." *Journal of Chinese Law* 5 (1991).

Clarke, Simon, and Veronika Kabalina. "Privatisation and the Struggle for Control of the Enterprise." In *Russia in Transition*, edited by David Lane. London: Longman, 1995.

Coates, Austin. *Myself a Mandarin*. London: Frederick Muller, 1968.

Coble, Parks. *The Shanghai Capitalists and the Nationalist Government, 1927–1937*. Cambridge: Harvard Council on East Asian Studies, 1980.

Cockcroft, James D. *Intellectual Precursors of the Mexican Revolution, 1900–1913*. Austin: University of Texas Press, 1968.

Cohen, Paul A. *Between Tradition and Modernity: Wang T'ao and Late Qing Reform*. Cambridge: Harvard University Press, 1974.

Cohen, Paul A. *Discovering History in China: American Historical Writings on the Recent Chinese Past*. New York: Columbia University Press, 1984.

Collier, Ruth Berins, and David Collier. "Inducements versus Constraints: Disaggregating Corporatism." *American Political Science Review* 73 (December 1979).

Commission on Security and Cooperation in Europe. *Russia's Parliamentary Election and Constitutional Referendum, December 12, 1993*. Washington: CSCE, January 1994.

Conaghan, Catherine M., and James M. Malloy. *Unsettling Statecraft: Democracy and Neoliberalism in the Central Andes*. Pittsburgh: University of Pittsburgh Press, 1994.

Conner, Alison W. "To Get Rich is Precarious: Regulation of Private Enterprise in the People's Republic of China." *Journal of Chinese Law* 5 (1991).

Constitution of the People's Republic of China. 1954. Documents of the First National Congress of the People's Republic of China. Beijing: Foreign Languages Press, 1955.

Constitution of the PRC. 1982. Beijing: New China News Agency, 1982.

Constitution of the PRC. 1978. Beijing: New China News Agency, 1978. "Final Version of 14th CPC National Congress Report." *FBIS Daily Report-China*. 21 October 1992.

Constitution of the Russian Federation, Ch. 2, Articles 17–63; Ch. 1, Articles 3, 13. *Economist*, 15 June 1966.

Cook, Maria Lorena, Kevin J. Middlebrook, and Juan Molinar Horcasitas. "Introducción." In *Las dimensiones políticas de la reestructuración económica*, edited by Maria Loren Cook, Kevin J. Middlebrook, and Juan Molinar Horcasitas. México D.F.: Cal y Arena, 1996.

Cook, Sherburne F., and Woodrow Borah. *Essays in Population Study*, 2 vols. Berkeley and Los Angeles: University of California Press, 1971 and 1973.

Cooper, George. "The Avoidance Dynamic: A Tale of Tax Planning, Tax Ethics, and Tax Reform." *Columbia Law Review* 80 (1980).

Corbo, V., J. De Melo, and J. Tybout. "What Went Wrong with the Recent Reforms in the Southern Cone." *Economic Development and Cultural Change* 34, no. 3 (April 1986): 607–37.

Cordoba, Jose. "Mexico." In *The Political Economy of Policy Reform*, edited by

John Williamson. Washington, D.C.: Institute for International Economics, January 1994.

Cornelius, Wayne, Ann Craig, and Jonathan Fox. "Mexico's National Solidarity Program: An Overview." In *Transforming State-Society Relations in Mexico: The National Strategy,* edited by Wayne C. Cornelius, Ann L. Craig, and Jonathan Fox. San Diego: Center for U.S.-Mexican Studies, 1994.

Corrales, Javier. "Why Argentines Follow Cavallo: A Technopol Between Democracy and Economic Reform," In *Technopols: Freeing Politics and Markets in Latin America in the 1990s,* edited by Jorge I. Domínguez. University Park: Pennsylvania State University Press, 1996.

Craig, Ann L., and Wayne A. Cornelius. "Political Culture in Mexico Continuities and Revisionist Interpretations." In *The Civic Culture Revisited,* edited by Gabriel A. Almond and Sidney Verba. Newberry Park, Calif.: Sage Publications, 1989.

Croan, Melvin, ed. "Is Latin America the Future of Eastern Europe?" *Problems of Communism* 61, no. 3. (May 1992).

Cumings, Bruce. "The Origins and Development of the Northeast Asian Political Economy: Industrial Sectors, Product Cycles, and Political Consequences." In *the Political Economy of the New Asian Industrialism,* edited by Frederic C. Deyo. Ithaca: Cornell University Press, 1987.

Dahl, Robert A., ed. *Political Oppositions in Western Democracies.* New Haven: Yale University Press, 1966.

Dahl, Robert A. *Polyarchy: Participation and Opposition.* New Haven: Yale University Press, 1971.

Dahl, Robert, and Charles E. Lindbloom. *Politics, Economics and Welfare.* New York: Harper and Row, 1953.

Dakolias, Maria. *The Judicial Sector in Latin America and the Caribbean: Elements of Reform.* Washington, D.C.: World Bank Technical Paper No. 319, June 1996.

Daniels, Robert V. "Soviet Politics since Khrushchev." In *The Soviet Union under Brezhnev and Kosygin,* edited by John W. Strong. New York: Van Norstran-Reinhold Co., 1971.

de Tocqueville, Alexis. *Democracy in America.* Richard D. Hefner, ed. New York: Vintage Books, 1945; Mentor, 1956.

"Decision of the CPC Central Committee on Issues Concerning the Establishment of a Socialist Market Economic Structure." 14 November 1993. *China Economic News.* 1993 Supplement, no. 12 (29 November 1993).

Deng, Xiaoping. "Jianchi si xiang jiben yuanze" (Uphold the Four Basic Principles). In *Deng Xiaoping wenxuan* (Collected Writings of Deng Xiaoping). Beijing: People's Press, 1983.

"Despots and Democrats." *The Economist,* 27 August 1994.

Díaz, Carlos Tello. *La rebelión de las cañadas.* México: Cal y Arena, 1995.

Ding, Xueliang. *The Decline of Communism in China: Legitimacy Crisis, 1977–1989.* Hong Kong: Cambridge University Press, 1994.

Directorio Ecologico. México D.F.: Friedrich Ebert Stiftung, 1988.

Domes, Jurgen. "Taiwan in 1992: On the Verge of Democracy." *Asian Survey* 33, no. 1 (January 1993).

Domínguez, Jorge I., and James McCann. *Democratizing Mexico: Public Opinion and Electoral Choices.* Baltimore: The Johns Hopkins University Press, 1996.

Dornbusch, Rudiger, and Sebastian Edwards. "Macroeconomic Populism." *Journal of Development Economics* 32 (1990).

Doyle, Michael. "An International Liberal Community." In *Rethinking America's Security: Beyond Cold War to New World Order,* edited by Graham Allison and Gregory F. Treverton. New York: W. W. Norton & Co., 1992.

Dresser, Denise. *Neopopulist Solutions to Neoliberal Problems: Mexico's National Solidarity Program.* La Jolla, Calif.: Current Issue Brief Series, no. 3, Center for U.S.-Mexican Studies Center, University of California, 1991.

Dresser, Denise. "Bringing the Poor Back In: National Solidarity as a Strategy of Regime Legitimation." In *Transforming State-Society Relations in Mexico: The National Strategy,* edited by Wayne C. Cornelius, Ann L. Craig, and Jonathan Fox. San Diego: Center for U.S.-Mexican Studies, 1994.

Dutton, Michael. *Policing and Punishment in China: From Patriarchy to "The People."* Hong Kong: Oxford University Press, 1992.

ECLAC. *Balance preliminar de la economía de América Latína y el Caribe 1993.* Documento informativo. Santiago: ECLAC, 17 de diciembre 1993.

ECLAC. *Economic Panorama of Latin America 1994.* U.N. Doc. LC/G. 1369/1994. Santiago: ECLAC, September 1994.

ECLAC. *Social Panorama of Latin America: 1994 Edition.* LC/G. 1844. Santiago: ECLAC, Statistics and Economic Projects Division and Social Development Division, November 1994.

Economic Contract Law 1993. *China Law and Practice.* December 1993.

Economist Intelligence Unit. *China: Country Report* (3rd Quarter, 1996). London, 1969.

Edwards, Sebastian. "Stabilization with Liberalization: An Evaluation of Ten Years of Chile's Experiment with Free-Market Policies, 1973–1983. *Economic Development and Cultural Change* 33 (1985).

Edwards, Sebastian. *Crisis and Reform in Latin America: From Despair to Hope.* New York: Oxford University Press, 1995.

Edwards, Sebastian. "Latin America's Underperformance." *Foreign Affairs* 76, no. 2 (March/April 1997).

El Financiero, 24 May 1994.

El Financiero, 25 October 1994.

Elguea, Javier. "Los sismos de 1985 y el comportamiento de ayuda entre los mexicanos: mitos y realidades." In *México Auge, Crisis y Ajuste,* edited by Carlos Bazdresch, Nisso Bucay, Nora Lustig, and Soledad Loaeza. México D.F.: Fondo de Cultura Económica, 1992.

Epstein, Edward. "Tortious Liability for Defective Products in the People's Republic of China." *Journal of Chinese Law* 2 (1988).

Epstein, Edward J., and Ye Lin. "Individual Enterprise in Contemporary Urban China: A Legal Analysis of Status and Regulation." *The International Lawyer* 21 (1987).

Epstein, Jack. "Land Grabbers Under Fire in Brazil." *San Francisco Chronicle,* 28 June 1997.

Ericson, Richard E. "The Russian Economy Since Independence." In *The New Russia*, G. Lapidus, ed. Boulder, Colo.: Westview Press, 1995.

Esherick, Joseph W., and Mary B. Rankin, eds. *Chinese Local Elites and Patterns of Dominance*. Berkeley: University of California Press, 1990.

Evans, Peter B., Dietrich Rueschemeyer, and Theda Skocpol, eds. *Bringing the State Back In*. Cambridge: Cambridge University Press, 1985.

Fagen, Richard R., and William S. Tuohy. *Politics and Privilege in a Mexican City*. Stanford: Stanford University Press, 1972.

"Fayuan caijue peichang sunshi" (The Court Decides That Losses Should Be Compensated). *Sichuan ribao* (Sichuan Daily), 18 April 1984.

Fei, Xiaotong. *A Great Trial in Chinese History*. Beijing: New World Press, 1981.

Feinerman, James, "Economic and Legal Reform in China, 1978–91," *Problems of Communism* (September–October, 1991).

Femia, Joseph V. *Gramsci's Political Thought: Hegemony, Consciousness, and Revolutionary Process*. New York: Oxford University Press, 1981.

Fewsmith, Joseph. *Party, State, and Local Elites in Republican China*. Honolulu: University of Hawaii Press, 1985.

Fewsmith, Joseph. "The Dengist Reforms in Historical Perspective." In *Contemporary Chinese Politics in Historical Perspective*, edited by Brantly Womack. Cambridge: Cambridge University Press, 1991.

Fewsmith, Joseph. *Dilemmas of Reform in China: Political Conflict and Economic Debate*. Armonk, New York: M. E. Sharpe, 1994.

Finifter, Ada, and Ellen Mickiewicz. "Redefining the Political System of the USSR: Mass Support for Political Change." *American Political Science Review* 86 (December 1992).

Fishlow, Albert. "The State of Latin American Economics." In *Changing Perspectives in Latin American Studies*, edited by Christopher Mitchell. Stanford: Stanford University Press, 1988.

Fix Fierro, Héctor, ed. *A la puerta de la ley. El Estado de derecho en México*. México: Cal y Arena, 1994.

Florescano, Enrique. *Memoria mexicana*. 2nd ed. México: Fondo de Cultura Económica, 1994.

Flynn, Peter. "Brazil: The Politics of the 'Plano Real.' " *Third World Quarterly* 17, no. 3 (September 1996).

Ford, Paul, ed. "Jefferson to William Short," July 28, 1791. In *The Writings of Thomas Jefferson*, v. 364. New York: C.P. Putnam's Sons, 1892–99, 10 vols.

Foxley, Alejandro. *Latin American Experiments in Neoconservative Economics*. Berkeley: University of California Press, 1983.

Foxley, Alejandro. *Economia politica de la transicion: El camino del dialogo*. Santiago: Dolmen, 1993.

Franck, Thomas M. "The Emerging Right to Democratic Governance." *American Journal of International Law* 86 (January 1992).

Friedberg, Aaron L. "Ripe for Rivalry: Prospects for Peace in a Multipolar Asia." *International Security*. (Winter 1993/94).

Frieden, Jeffry A. *Debt, Development, and Democracy: Modern Political Economy and Latin America, 1965–1985*. Princeton: Princeton University Press, 1991.

Friedman, Edward. "Is Democracy a Universal Ethical Standard?" In *National Identity and Democratic Prospects in Socialist China*. Armonk, New York: M. E. Sharpe, 1995.

Friedman, Edward, ed. *The Politics of Democratization: Generalizing the East Asian Experience*. Boulder, Colo.: Westview Press, 1994.

Friedman, Lawrence M. *The Legal System: A Social Science Perspective*. Englewood Cliffs, N.J.: Prentice-Hall, 1975.

Friedman, Milton. *Capitalism and Freedom*. Chicago: University of Chicago Press, 1962.

Fu, Dedi, ed. *Nan chaoxian jingji de jueqi* (The South Korean Economy's Rise). Beijing: Zhongguo guoji rencai kaifa yanjiusuo yanjiu fazhanbu, June 1990.

Fukuyama, Francis. *The End of History and the Last Man*. New York: The Free Press, 1992.

Fukuyama, Francis. "Virtue and Prosperity." *The National Interest*, no. 40 (Summer 1995).

Gallagher, David. "Chile: la revolución pendiente." In *El Desafío Neoliberal: El fin del tercermundismo en America Latina*, edited by Barry B. Levine. Bogotá: Grupo Editorial Norma, 1992.

Gan, Yusheng, Qui Shi, and Yang Kaimin, eds. "Mou fuzhuangchang bu fu Gong Shang wujia chufa an" (A Case Involving a Certain Clothing Factory Refusing to Comply With a Penalty Levied by the Price Penalty Imposed by the State Administration for Industry and Commerce). In *Xingzhen susong anli xuanbian*. Beijing: Chinese Economy Press, 1990.

Gan, Yusheng, Qui Shi, and Yang Kaimin, eds. "Mou zhibu chang tou ji dao ba an" (A Speculation Case Involving a Certain Weaving Factory). In *Xingzheng susong anli xuanbian*. Beijing: Chinese Economy Press, 1990.

Gang, Zhang. "Government Intervention vs Marketization in China's Rural Industries: The Role of Local Governments." *China Information* 8, nos. 1–2. (1993).

Garrido, Luis Javier. *El partido de la revolución institucionalizada: medio siglo de poder en México. La formación del nuevo estado (1928–1945)*. México: Siglo XXI, 1982.

Garrido, Luis Javier. *La ruptura. La corriente democrática del PRI*. México: Grijalbo, 1993.

Gervasoni, Carlos H. "El Impacto Electoral de las Politicas de Estabilización y Reforma Estructural en America Latina." *Journal of Latin American Affairs* 3, no. 1 (Spring/Summer 1995).

Gibson, James L. "The Resilience of Mass Support for Democratic Institutions and Processes in the Nascent Russian and Ukrainian Democracies." In *Political Culture and Civil Society in Russia and the New States of Eurasia*, edited by Vladimir Tismaneanu. New York: M. E. Sharpe, 1995.

Giraldo, Jeanne Kinney, "Development and Democracy in Chile: Finance Minister Alejandro Foxley and the Concertación's Project for the 90s." In *Technopols: Freeing Politics and Markets in Latin America in the 1990s*, edited by Jorge I. Domínguez. University Park: Pennsylvania State University Press, 1996.

Gold, Thomas B. *State and Society in the Taiwan Miracle*. Armonk, N.Y.: M. E. Sharpe, Inc. 1986.

Gold, Thomas B. "Guerilla Interviewing Among the *Getihu.*" In *Unofficial China: Popular Culture and Thought in the People's Republic*, edited by Perry Link, Richard Madsen, and Paul G. Pickowicz. Boulder, London: Westview, 1989.

Gold, Thomas B. "The Resurgence of Civil Society in China." *Journal of Democracy* 1, no. 1 (Winter 1990).

"The Golden Ghetto of Individual Businesses." *China News Analysis,* no. 1476 (1 January 1993).

Goldman, Merle. *Sowing the Seeds of Democracy in China.* Cambridge: Harvard University Press, 1994.

Goldstone, Jack A. *Revolution and Rebellion in the Early Modern World.* Berkeley: University of California Press, 1991.

"Gongya xian fayuan caijue yi qi hetong jiufen" (The Gongya County Court Arbitrates a Contract Dispute). *Sichuan ribao* (Sichuan Daily), 10 April 1984.

González Casanova, Pablo, coordinator. *Segundo informe sobre la democracia: México el 6 de julio de 1988.* México: Siglo XXI-UNAM, 1990.

Graham, Carol. *Safety Nets, Politics, and the Poor: Transitions to Market Economies.* Washington, D.C.: Brookings Institution, 1994.

Gramsci, Antonio. *The Modern Prince and Other Writings.* New York: International Publishers, 1957.

Gramsci, Antonio. *Selections from the Prison Notebooks.* Edited and translated by Quintin Hoare and Geoffrey Nowell Smith. New York: International Publishers, 1971.

Greenway, Gregory. "Democratization, Economic Liberalization, and Social Policy: The Case of Mexico's National Solidarity Program." Seminar Presentation, Stanford University, 22 February 1995.

Grey, Thomas C. "Langdell's Orthodoxy." *University of Pittsburgh Law Review* 45, no. 1 (1983).

Gu, Ming. "Guanyu 'Zhonghua renmin gongheguo jingji hetong fa caoan' de shuoming" (Explanation of the 'Draft Economic Contract Law of the PRC'). *Zhongguo fazhi bao* (Chinese Legal System Gazette), 13 December 1981.

Gu, Xin. "A Civil Society and Public Sphere in Post-Mao China? An Overview of Western Publications." *China Information* 8, no. 3 (Winter 1993–94).

Gu, Xin. "The Structural Transformation of the Intellectual Public Sphere in Socialist China (1979–1989), Ph.D. dissertation, Leiden University, 1997.

Guerra, Francis-Xavier. *México: del antiguo régimen a la régimen a la revolución.* México: Fondo de Cultura Económica, 1988.

Guo, Xiaolin. "Local Practices of Property Rights in Land and Township Enterprises: An Analysis of Incentive Structures." In *Property Rights in Transitional Economies: Insights from Research on China,* edited by Jean Oi and Andrew G. Walder. Cambridge: Harvard University Press, forthcoming.

Gwartney, James, Robert Lawson, and Walter Block. *Economic Freedom of the Work: 1975–1995.* Vancouver: Fraser Institute, 1996.

Haber, Paul Lawrence. "El arte de la reestructuración y sus implicaciones políticas: el caso de los movimientos urbanos populares." In *Las dimensiones políticas de la reestructuración económica,* edited by Maria Lorena Cook, Kevin J. Middlebrook, and Juan Molinar Horcasitas. México D.F.: Cal y Arena, 1996.

Habermas, Jurgen. "The Public Sphere." In *Jürgen Habermas on Society and Politics: A Reader,* edited by Steven Seidman. Boston: Beacon Press, 1989.

Habermas, Jurgen. *The Structural Transformation of the Public Sphere: An Inquiry into a Category of Bourgeois Society.* Cambridge: MIT Press, 1989.

Haggard, Stephan, and Robert F. Kaufman. "Economic Adjustments and the Prospects for Democracy." In *The Politics of Economic Adjustment,* edited by Stephan Haggard and Robert R. Kaufman. Princeton: Princeton University Press, 1992.

Haggard, Stephan. *Pathways from the Periphery: The Politics of Growth in the Newly Industrializing Countries.* Ithaca: Cornell University Press, 1990.

Hahn, Jeffery W. "Contemporary Russian Political Culture," In *Political Culture and Civil Society in Russia and the New States of Eurasia,* edited by Vladimir Tismaneanu. New York: M. E. Sharpe, 1995.

Hale, Charles. *Mexican Liberalism in the Age of Mora 1821–1853.* New Haven: Yale University Press, 1968.

Hale, Charles. *The Transformation of Liberalism in Nineteenth Century Mexico.* Princeton, N.J.: Princeton University Press, 1989.

Hall, William Edward. *A Treatise on International Law,* edited by J. B. Atlay. Oxford: Oxford University Press, 1909, 6th ed.

Halperin, Morton H. "Guaranteeing Democracy." *Foreign Policy,* no. 91 (Summer, 1993).

Hamill, Hugh M. *The Hidalgo Revolt. Prelude to Mexican Independence.* Gainesville: University of Florida Press, 1966.

Hamrin, Carol Lee. *China and the Challenge of the Future Changing Political Patterns.* Boulder, Colo.: Westview Press, 1990.

Hamrin, Carol, and Timothy Cheek. *China's Establishment Intellectuals.* Armonk, New York: M. E. Sharpe, 1986.

Hanna, Alfred Jackson, and Kathryn Abbey Hanna. *Napoleon III and Mexico.* Chapel Hill: University of North Carolina Press, 1971.

Hansen, Roger D. *The Politics of Mexican Development.* Baltimore, MD.: The Johns Hopkins University Press, 1971.

Hao, Wang. "The Ruling Party and the Transition to Democracy: The Case of the Chinese Nationalist Party (KIT) on Taiwan." Ph.D. dissertation, University of British Columbia, 1996.

Haraszti, Miklós. *The Velvet Prison: Artists Under State Socialism.* New York: Basic Books, 1986.

Harding, Harry. "The Evolution of American Scholarship on Contemporary China." In *American Studies of Contemporary China,* edited by David Shambaugh. Armonk, New York: M. E. Sharpe/Woodrow Wilson Press, 1993.

Harries, Owen. "An Offer Castro Couldn't Refuse—or Survive." *The National Interest,* no. 44 (Summer 1996).

Harrold, Peter, and Rajiv Lall. *China: Reform and Development in 1992–93.* World Bank Discussion Paper, no. 215. Washington, D.C.: World Bank, 1993.

Hayek, F. A. *Studies in Philosophy, Politics and Economics.* New York: Simon & Schuster, 1967.

He, Guanghui. "Continue to Deepen Reform by Centering on Economic Improvement and Rectification." *Zhongguo jingji tizhhi gaige* (Reform of the Chinese Economic Structure), no. 2 (1990), translated in *FBIS Daily Report: China,* 23 March 1990.

Held, David. "Pluralism, Corporate Capitalism and the State." In *Models of Democracy,* edited by David Held. Stanford: Stanford University Press, 1987.

Hibbs, Douglas A., Jr. *The Political Economy of Industrial Democracies.* Cambridge: Harvard University Press, 1987.

Hill, Ronald J. "Khrushchev, Gorbachev, and the Party." In *The Sons of Sergei, Khrushchev and Gorbachev as Reformers,* edited by D. Kelley and S. Davis. New York: Praeger, 1992.

Hirschman, Albert O. *Exit, Voice, and Loyalty: Responses to Decline in Firms, Organizations, and States.* Cambridge: Harvard University Press, 1970.

Hirschman, Albert O. *The Passions and the Interests: Political Arguments for Capitalism before its Triumph.* Princeton: Princeton University Press, 1977.

Hobbes, Thomas. *Leviathan.* Michael Oakeshott, ed. New York: Collier, 1962. See especially chapter 22, "Of Systems Subject, Political, and Private."

Hough, Jerry. *Soviet Leadership in Transition.* Washington, D.C.: The Brookings Institution, 1980.

Hsiao, Ching-chen, and Timothy Cheek, "Open and Closed Media: External and Internal Newspapers in the Propaganda System." In *Decision-Making in Deng's China Perspectives from Insiders,* edited by Carol Lee Hamrin and Suisheng Zhao. Armonk, New York: M. E. Sharpe, 1995.

Huang, Philip C. C. "The Paradigmatic Crisis in Chinese Studies." *Modern China* 17, no. 3 (July 1991).

Huang, Yanming. "Mediation in the Settlement of Business Disputes." *Journal of International Arbitration* 8, no. 4 (1991).

Huang, Yanming. "The Stylization and Regularization of the Management and Operation of the Chinese Arbitration Institute." *Journal of International Arbitration* 11, no. 2 (1994).

Huang, Yanming. "The Ethics of Arbitrators in CIETAC Arbitration." *Journal of International Arbitration* 12, no. 2 (1995).

Huber, Evelyne, Dietrich Rusechemeyer, and John D. Stephens. "The Paradoxes of Contemporary Democracy: Formal, Participatory and Social Democracy." In *Comparative Politics* 29, no. 3 (1997).

Hufbauer, Gary Clyde, Jeffrey J. Schott, and Kimberly Ann Elliott. *Economic Sanctions Reconsidered,* 2nd ed. Washington, D.C.: Institute for International Economics, 1990.

"Human Rights in Mexico." *Americas Watch* (1991).

Human Rights Watch. "Commerce Kills China Criticism Says Human Rights Watch." 3 April 1997.

Hunt, Alan. *Explorations in Law and Society: Toward a Constitutive Theory of Law.* New York: Routledge, 1993.

Hunt, Lynn, *The New Cultural History.* Berkeley: University of California Press, 1989.

Huntington, Samuel. "Will More Countries Become Democratic?" *Political Science Quarterly* 99, no. 2 (Summer 1984).

Huntington, Samuel P. *The Third Wave: Democratization in the Late Twentieth Century*. Norman: University of Oklahoma Press, 1991, 1992.

Iglesias, Enrique. "Economic Reform: A View From Latin America." In *The Political Economy of Policy Reform*, edited by John Williamson. Washington, D.C.: Institute for International Economics, January 1994.

Inglehart, Ronald. *Modernization and Postmodernization: Cultural, Economic and Political Change in 43 Societies*. Princeton: Princeton University Press, 1997.

Ishihara, Kyoichi. *China's Conversion to a Market Economy*. Tokyo: Institute of Developing Economics, 1993.

"Jingji anjian zhong de luchi huodong" (The Activities of Lawyers in Economic Cases). *Faxue yanjiu* (Studies in Law), no. 2 (1983).

Johnson, Bryan T., and Thomas P. Sheehy. *The Index of Economic Freedom*. Washington, D.C.: The Heritage Foundation, 1995.

Johnson, Chalmers, and E. B. Keehn. "A Disaster in the Making: Rational Choice and Asian Studies." *The National Interest*, no. 36 (Summer 1994).

Jones, William C., trans. "General Principles of Civil Law of the People's Republic of China." *Review of Socialist Law* 4 (1987).

La Jornada, 4 July 1994.

La Jornada, 15 to 19 June 1995.

La Jornada, 18 July 1995.

Joseph, Richard. "Democratization in Africa after 1989: Comparative and Theoretical Perspectives." *Comparative Politics* 29, no. 3 (1997).

Kahl, Joseph F. *The Measurement of Modernism*. Austin: University of Texas Press, 1968.

Kairys, David, ed. "Edward Greer, Antonio Gramsci and 'Legal Hegemony.' " In *The Politics of Law*. New York: Pantheon, 1982.

Kanayama, Hisahiro. *The Marketization of China and Japan's Response: Prospects for the Future*. Tokyo: Institute for International Policy Studies, 1993.

Kaufman Purcell, Susan. *The Mexican Profit Sharing Decision*. Berkeley: University of California Press, 1976.

Keddie, Nikki R., ed. *Debating Revolutions*. New York: New York University Press, 1995.

Keith, Ronald C. *China's Struggle for the Rule of Law*. New York: St. Martin's Press, 1994.

Kelly, David. "Chinese Intellectuals in the 1989 Democracy Movement." In *The Broken Mirror: China After Tiananmen*, edited by George Hicks. London: Longman, 1990.

Kelly, David, ed. *Asian Freedoms: The Idea of Freedom in East and Southeast Asia* (New York: Cambridge University Press, 1998).

Kelly, David, and He Baogang. "Emergent Civil Society and the Intellectuals in China." In *The Developments of Civil Society in Communist Systems*, edited by Robert Miller. North Sydney: Allen & Unwin, 1992.

Kenez, Peter. *The Birth of the Propaganda State Soviet Methods of Mass Mobilization, 1917–1929*. Cambridge: Cambridge University Press, 1985.

Kennedy, Duncan, and Frank Michelman. "Are Property and Contract Efficient." *Hofstra Law Review* 8 (1980).

Knorr, Klaus. *The Power of Nations: The Political Economy of International Relations.* New York: Basic Books, 1975.

Kojima, Sueo. "Japan-China Economic Interchange and Enterprise Reform." *China Newsletter,* no. 40 (September–October 1982).

Koo, Hagen. "Introduction: Beyond State-Market Relations." In *State and Society in Contemporary Korea,* edited by Hagen Koo. Ithaca: Cornell University Press, 1993.

Kramer, Michael, *Time,* 15 July 1996.

Krauze, Enrique. "Revelaciones entre ruinas." *Vuelta* 9, no. 180 (1985).

Krauze, Enrique. "Old Paradigms and New Openings in Latin America." *Journal of Democracy* 3, no. 1 (January 1992).

Krauze, Enrique. *La presidencia imperial. Ascenso y caída del sistema político mexicano, 1940–1996.* México: Tusquets, 1997.

Krinsky, Michael, and David Golove, eds. *United States Economic Measures Against Cuba: Proceedings in the United Nations and International Law Issues.* Northhampton, Mass.: Aletheia Press, 1993.

Kuhn, Philip. "Ideas behind China's Modern State." *Harvard Journal of Asiatic Studies* 55, no. 2 (1995): 295–337.

Kuhn, Philip A. "Origins of the Taiping Vision: Cross-Cultural Dimensions of a Chinese Rebellion." *Comparative Studies in History & Society* 19, no. 3 (1977).

Kuhn, Philip. "Local Self-Government Under the Republic: Problems of Control, Autonomy, and Mobilization." In Frederic Wakeman and Carolyn Grant, eds., *Conflict and Control in Late Imperial China.* Berkeley: University of California Press, 1975.

Kung-ch'üan, Hsiao. *Rural China: Imperial Control in the 19th Century.* Seattle: University of Washington Press, 1960.

Lange, Peter, and Geoffrey Garrett. "The Politics of Growth: Strategic Interaction and Economic Performance in Advanced Industrial Democracies, 1974–1980." *Journal of Politics* 47 (1985).

Laodong Renshi Bu Zhengce Yanjiu (Policy Research Office of the Ministry of Labor and Personnel), ed. "Qiye zhi gong jiang chen tiaoli" (Regulations on Reward and Punishments for Enterprise Staff and Workers), Article 11. In *Zhonghua renmin gongheguo laodong fagui xuanbian* (Compilation of Labor Laws and Regulations of the PRC). Beijing: Labor and Personnel Press, 1985.

Lavin, Franklin L. "Asphyxiation or Oxygen? The Sanctions Dilemma." *Foreign Policy,* no. 104 (Fall 1996).

Lee, Kuo-wei. "The Road to Democracy: Taiwan Experience." *Asian Profile* 19, no. 6 (December 1991).

Leng, Shao-chuan, and Cheng-yi Lin. "Political Change on Taiwan: Transition to Democracy?" *China Quarterly,* no. 136 (December 1993).

Levenson, Joseph. *Confucian China and Its Modern Fate.* Berkeley: University of California Press, 1958.

Levy, Daniel, and Gabriel Szekely. *Mexico: Paradoxes of Stability and Change.* Boulder, Colo.: Westview, 1987.

Leys, Colin. *The Rise and Fall of Development Theory.* Bloomington: Indiana University Press, 1996.

Li, Cheng, and David Bachman. "Localism, Elitism, and Immobilism: Elite Formation and Social Change in Post-Mao China." *World Politics* 45, no. 1 (1992).

Li, Lanqing. "Foreign Trade Enterprises Should Rapidly Change Their Operational Mechanisms." *Guoji shangbao*, 3 December 1992. In *Foreign Broadcast Information Service*-CHI-93–004. 7 January 1993.

Li Shanyuan quanji. (The Complete Works of Li Shanyuan) Preface dated 1705; edited by Wei Xiang. "Shengyu xuanjian xiang-bao tiaoyue" (Regulations for Community Security [Xiang & Bao] Sacred Edict Lectures).

Li, Victor H. "The Evolution and Development of the Chinese Legal System." In *CHINA: Management of a Revolutionary Society*, edited by John Lindbeck. Seattle: University of Washington Press, 1970.

Lieberthal, Kenneth. *Governing China: From Revolution through Reform*. New York: W. W. Norton, 1995.

Lieberthal, Kenneth. "A New China Strategy." *Foreign Affairs* 74, no. 6 (November/December 1995).

Lin, Zili. *China: Going toward the Market*. Translated and edited by Joseph Fewsmith. *Chinese Economic Studies* 27, no. 1–2 (January-February/March-April 1994).

Lindau, Juan. *La elite gobernante mexicana*. México, D.F.: Joaquin Mortiz, 1993.

Link, Arthur S., et al. "The Mexican Situation," May 14, 1913. In *The Papers of Woodrow Wilson*. XVII. Princeton: Princeton University Press. 1966–1993.

Link, Arthur S., ed. *The Papers of Woodrow Wilson*. Princeton: Princeton University Press, 1990.

Linz, Juan. "An Authoritarian Regime: Spain." In *Cleavages, Ideologies and Party Systems: Contributions to Comparative Political Sociology*, edited by Erik Allardt and Yrje Littunen. Transactions of the Westermarck Society, 1964.

Linz, Juan. "The Future of an Authoritarian Situation or the Institutionalization of an Authoritarian Regime: The Case of Brazil." In *Authoritarian Brazil*, edited by Alfred Stepan. New Haven: Yale University Press, 1973.

Linz, Juan L. "Totalitarian and Authoritarian Regimes." In *Handbook of Political Science*, vol. 3, edited by F. I. Greenstein and N. W. Polsby. Reading, Mass.: Addison-Wesley, 1975.

Lipset, Seymour Martin, *Political Man*. New York: Doubleday, 1960.

Lipset, Seymour Martin, and Stein Rokkan. "Cleavage Structures, Party Systems, and Voter Alignments." In *Party Systems and Voter Alignments*, edited by S. M. Lipset and Stein Rokkan. New York: The Free Press, 1967.

Little, Daniel. "Rational-Choice Models and Asian Studies," *Journal of Asian Studies* 50, no. 1. (February 1991).

Liu, Alan P. L. *Communications and National Integration in Communist China*. Berkeley: University of California Press, 1975.

Liu, Zeyuan. "Zhong han ri jingji fazhan bijiao yanjiu" (Comparative Research on the Economic Development of China, Korea, and Japan). *Dongbei ya*, no. 4 (1993).

Locke, John. "An Essay Concerning the True Original, Extent and End of Civil Government." In *Treatise of Civil Government and A Letter Concerning Toleration*, edited by Charles L. Sherman. New York: Appleton-Century-Crofts, 1937.

Long, Simon. "Taiwan's National Assembly Elections." *China Quarterly*, no. 129 (March 1992).

Love, Joseph. "Economic Ideas and Ideologies in Latin America Since 1930." In *The Cambridge History of Latin America*, Vol. 6, edited by Leslie Bethell. Cambridge: Cambridge University Press, 1994.

Lowenthal, Abraham F., ed. *Exporting Democracy: The United States and Latin America*, 2 vols. Baltimore: Johns Hopkins University Press, 1991.

Lu, Jiarui. "Lun shehui zhuyi kuaguo gongsi" (On the Socialist Transnational Corporation). *Xuexi yu tansu*, no. 4 (1990).

Lu, Shengliang, "Shilun waimao jingying jituanhua" (On the Grouping of Foreign Trade Enterprises). *Guoji maoyi wenti*, no. 5 (1991).

Lubman, Stanley. "Studying Contemporary Chinese Law: Limits, Possibilities and Strategy." *American Journal of Comparative Law* 36 (1991).

Lubman, Stanley B. "Methodological Problems in Studying Chinese Communist 'Civil' Law." In *Contemporary Chinese Law: Research Problems and Perspectives*, edited by Jerome A. Cohen. Cambridge: Harvard University Press, 1970.

Lubman, Stanley B. "Emerging Functions of Formal Legal Institutions in China's Modernization." In *China under the Four Modernizations*, edited by Joint Economic Committee of U.S. Congress. Washington, D.C.: U.S. Government Printing Office, 1994.

Lubman, Stanley B. "Introduction." In *Domestic Law Reform in Post-Mao China*, edited by Pitman B. Potter. Armonk, N.Y.: M. E. Sharpe, 1994.

Lubman, Stanley B. "Setback for the China-Wide Rule of Law." *Far Eastern Economic Review*, 17 November 1996.

Lustig, Nora. *Mexico: The Remaking of the Economy*. Washington, D.C.: The Brookings Institution, 1992.

Lustig, Nora. "Solidarity as a Strategy of Poverty Alleviation." In *Transforming State-Society Relations in Mexico: The National Strategy*, edited by Wayne C. Cornelius, Ann L. Craig, and Jonathan Fox. San Diego: Center for U.S.-Mexican Studies, 1994.

Ma, Shu-Yun. "The Chinese Discourse on Civil Society." *The China Quarterly*, no. 137 (March 1994).

Mahon, R. "Regulatory Agencies: Captive agents or hegemonic apparatuses?" In *Class, State Ideology and Change: Marxist Perspectives on Canada*, edited by P. Grayson. Toronto: Holt, Rinehart and Winston, 1980.

Malia, Martin. *The Soviet Tragedy*. New York: The Free Press, 1994.

Mao, Zedong. "On the People's Democratic Dictatorship." In *Selected Works of Mao Zedong*. Peking: Foreign Languages Press, 1969.

Marcel, Mario, and Andres Solimano. "The Distribution of Income and Economic Adjustment." In *The Chilean Economy*, ed. Barry Bosworth, et al. Washington, D.C.: The Brookings Institution, 1994.

"Marcos: Las elecciones no se van a resolver en Gobernación, sino en las calles o en las montañas," *Proceso*, no. 924 (18 July 1994).

Marx, Karl. *The Eighteenth Brumaire of Louis Bonaparte*. New York: International Publishers, 1963.

Marx, Karl. *Class Struggles in France, 1848–1850.* New York: International Publishers, 1964.

Marx, Karl, and Friedrich Engels. "Manifesto of the Communist Party." In *Marx and Engels,* edited by Lewis S. Feuer. New York: Anchor, 1959. First published in 1848.

Mason, David S. "Attitudes toward the Market and Political Participation in the Postcommunist States." *Slavic Review* 54, no. 2 (Summer 1995).

Matlock, Jack F., Jr. *Autopsy on an Empire.* New York: Random House, 1995.

Matsumoto, Morio. "China's Industrial Policy and Participation in the GATT." *China Newsletter,* no. 112 (September–October 1994).

McCormick, Barrett, and David Kelly, "The Limits of Anti-Liberalism," *The Journal of Asian Studies* 53, no. 3 (August 1994).

McEwen, Susan. "New Kids on the Block." *The China Business Review* 21, no. 3 (May–June 1994).

McFaul, Michael. "State Power, Institutional Change, and the Politics of Privatization in Russia." *World Politics* 47, no. 2 (January 1995).

McKinnon, Ronald. *The Order of Economic Liberalization.* Baltimore: Johns Hopkins University Press, 1992.

McNeill, William H. "Decline of the West?" *The New York Review of Books,* 9 January 1997.

Medina Peña, Luis. *Hacia el nuevo estado. México, 1920–1993.* México: Fondo de Cultura Económica, 1994.

Meyer, Lorenzo, "Historical Roots of the Authoritarian State in Mexico." In *Authoritarianism in Mexico,* edited by J. L. Reyna and R. S. Weinert. Philadelphia: Institute for the Study of Human Issues, 1977.

Meyer, Lorenzo. "Aquí, Perestroika sin Glasnost." In *Excelsior.* Mexico, December 13, 1989.

Mill, John Stuart. *On Liberty.* Trans. by Currin Shields. New York: The Liberal Arts Press, 1956.

Mill, John Stuart. *Considerations on Representative Government.* London: Longman, Green, and Co., 1991.

Millar, James, "From Utopian Socialism to Utopian Capitalism," *Problems of Post-Communism,* May–June 1995.

Minami, Ryoshi. *The Economic Development of China: A Comparison with the Japanese Experience.* New York: St. Martin's Press, 1994.

Miranda, Jose. *Las ideas y las instituciones políticas mexicanas.* México: Universidad Nacional Autónoma de México, 1978.

Molina, Isabel. *Un sexenio de violencia política.* México: Congreso de la Unión, Grupo Parlamentario del PRD, 1993.

Molinar, Juan. *El tiempo de la legitimidad. Elecciones, autoritarismo y democracia en México.* México: Cal y Arena, 1991.

Monsivais, Carlos. *Entrada libre: cronicas de la sociedad que se organiza.* México D.F.: Era, 1987.

Montemayor, Carlos. *Guerra en el paraíso.* México: Diana, 1991.

Montesquieu, *The Spirit of the Laws.* Trans. by Thomas Nugent. New York: Hafner, 1966.

Moody, Peter R. *Opposition and Dissent in Contemporary China*. Stanford: Hoover Institution Press, 1977.

Moore, Barrington, Jr. *The Social Origins of Dictatorship and Democracy*. Boston: Beacon Press, 1966.

Moore, John Bassett, ed. *A Digest of International Law*. Washington, D.C.: GPO, 1906.

Morley, Samuel A. *Poverty and Inequality in Latin America: Past Evidence, Future Prospects*, Policy Essay No. 3. Washington, D.C.: Overseas Development Council, 1994.

Morris, Stephen D. *Corruption and Politics in Contemporary Mexico*. Tuscaloosa: The University of Alabama Press, 1991.

Moser, Michael J. *Law and Social Change in a Chinese Community: A Case Study From Rural Taiwan*. New York: Oceana, 1982.

Mumme, Stephen P., Richard C. Bath, and Valerie J. Assetto. "Political Development and Environmental Policy in Mexico." *Latin American Research Review* 23, no. 1 (1988).

Naim, Moises. "Latin America: The Second Stage of Reform." *Journal of Democracy* 5, no. 4 (1994).

"Nanjing shi jiangpu xian gongchen suliao chang yu ben chang chengxing chejian chengbao hetong jiufen" (The Dispute Between the Engineering Plastics Factory of Jiangpu County in Nanjing Municipality and the Factory's Mould Shop Over a Responsibility Contract). *Zhonghua renmin gongheguo zui gai renmin fayuan gongbao* (PRC Supreme People's Court Reports), no. 1 (1985).

"Nanjing zhong j I fayuan renzhen zuo hao jingji shenpan gongzuo" (The Nanjing Middle Level Court Conscientiously Does a Good Job in Economic Adjudication Work). *Renmin Ribao* (People's Daily), 24 June 1984.

Nardin, Terry. "Sovereignty, Self-Determination, and International Intervention." In *Morals and Might*, edited by G. Lopez and D. Christiansen. Boulder, Colo.: Westview, 1993.

Nathan, Andrew J., and Helena V. S. Ho. "Chiang ching-kuo's Decision for Political Reform." In *Chiang Ching-kuo's Leadership in the Development of the Republic of China on Taiwan*. Lanham, Md.: University Press of America, 1993.

Nelson, James A., and John A. Reeder. "Labor Relations in China." *California Management Review* 27, no. 4 (1985).

Nelson, Joan, ed. *Economic Crisis and Policy Choice: The Politics of Adjustment in the Third World*. Princeton: Princeton University Press 1990.

Nelson, Lynn D., and Irina Y. Kuzes. "Privatisation and the New Business Class." In *Russia in Transition*, edited by David Lane. London: Longman, 1995.

Niu, Jingtao, and Cai Xingyang. "Riben guanting zhudao xia de shichang jingji yunzuo ji qi qishi" (Operation of a Market-oriented Economy under the Guidance of the Japanese Government and its Inspiration). *Dongbeiya luntan*, no. 2 (1993).

North, Douglass. *Institutions, Institutional Change and Development*. Cambridge: Cambridge University Press, 1990.

O'Brien, Kevin. "China's National People's Congress: Reform and Its Limits." *Legislative Studies Quarterly*, no. 3 (1988).

O'Brien, Kevin. *Reform Without Liberalization: The National People's Congress and the Politics of Institutional Change*. New York: Cambridge University Press, 1990.

O'Donnell, Guillermo. *Modernization and Bureaucratic-Authoritarianism*. Berkeley: Institute of International Studies, University of California, 1973.

Offe, Claus. "Competitive Party Democracies and the Keynesian Welfare State." *Policy Sciences* 15 (1983). Reprinted in Offe, *Contradictions of the Welfare State*. Cambridge: MIT Press, 1984.

Offe, Claus, and Wiesenthal Helmut. "Two Logics of Collective Action: Theoretical Notes on Social Class and Organizational Form." In *Contradictions of the Welfare State*, edited by Claus Offe. Cambridge: MIT Press, 1984.

Oi, Jean C. "Fiscal Reform and the Economic Foundations of Local State Corporatism in China." *World Politics* 45 (October 1992).

Okimoto, Daniel I. *Between MITI and the Market: Japanese Industrial Policy for High Technology*. Stanford: Stanford University Press, 1989.

Oksenberg, Michael, Pitman B. Potter, and William B. Abnett. "Advancing Intellectual Property Rights: Information Technologies and the Course of Economic Development in China." Seattle: National Bureau of Asian Research, 1996.

Olson, Mancur. *The Rise and Decline of Nations*. New Haven: Yale University Press, 1982.

OMRI Daily Digest, 2 August 1996, 20 September 1996.

Oppenheimer, Andres. *Bordering on Chaos: Guerrillas, Stockbrokers, Politicians, and Mexico's Road to Prosperity*. New York: Little, Brown, 1996.

Organization for Economic Cooperation and Development. *OECD Economic Surveys, Mexico*. Paris: OECD 1992.

"The Origins of a Chinese Public Sphere: Local Community Affairs in the Late-Imperial Period." *Études Chinoises* 2, no. 2 (Autumn 1990).

Orme, William A. "NAFTA: Myths versus Facts." *Foreign Affairs* 72, no. 5 (Nov./Dec. 1993).

Østergaard, Clemens Stubbe. "Citizens, Groups and a Nascent Civil Society in China: Towards an Understanding of the 1989 Student Demonstration." *China Information* 4, no. 2. (Autumn 1989).

Ownby, David. *Brotherhoods and Secret Societies in Early and Mid-Qing China: The Formation of a Tradition*. Stanford: Stanford University Press, 1996.

Ownby, David. "Mutual Benefit Societies in Chinese History." In *Social Security Mutualism: The Comparative History of Mutual Benefit Societies*, edited by Marcel van der Linden. Bern: Peter Lang, 1996.

Packenham, Robert. *The Dependency Movement; Scholarship and Politics in Development Studies*. Cambridge: Harvard University Press, 1992.

Packenham, Robert A. "The Politics of Economic Liberalization: Argentina and Brazil in Comparative Perspective." *Working Paper* no. 206. Notre Dame, Ind.: Kellogg Institute, April 1994.

La palabra de los armados de verdad y fuego, 2 vols. México: Editorial Fuenteovejuna, 1994–1995.

Pang, Chien-kuo. *The State and Economic Transformation: The Taiwan Case*. New York: Garland Publishing, Inc., 1992.

Parris, Kristen. "Local Initiative and National Reform: The Wenzhou Model of Development." *The China Quarterly* 34 (June 1993).

Parris, Kristen. "Private Entrepreneurs as Citizens: From Leninism to Corporatism." *China Information* 10, nos. 3–4. (Winter 1995/Spring 1996).

Pastor, Robert A. *Integration with Mexico. Options for U.S. Policy*. New York: The Twentieth Century Fund Press, 1993.

Paz, Octavio. "Escombros y semillas." *Vuelta* 9, no. 180 (1985).

Paz, Octavio. "The Labyrinth of Solitude" and "The Philanthropic Ogre." In *The Labyrinth of Solitude and Other Writings*. New York: Grove Weidenfeld, 1985.

Pearson, Margaret. *China's New Business Elite: The Political Consequences of Economic Reform*. Berkeley: University of California Press, 1997.

Pearson, Margaret M. "The Janus Face of Business Associations in China: Socialist Corporatism in Foreign Enterprises." *The Australian Journal of Chinese Affairs*, no. 31 (January 1994).

Peng, Zhen. "Guanyu qi ge falu caian de shuoming" (Explanation of seven draft laws). In *Lun xin shiqi de shehuizhu minzhu yu fazhi jianshe* (One the establishment of socialist democracy and legal system in the new period). Beijing: Central Digest Publishers, 1989.

Perkins, Dwight, ed. *China's Modern Economy in Historical Perspective*. Stanford: Stanford University Press, 1975.

Perkins, Dwight H. "Summary: Why is Reforming State Owned Enterprises so Difficult?" *China Economic Review* 4, no. 2 (1993).

Perry, Elizabeth J. "China in 1992: An Experiment in Neo-Authoritarianism." *Asian Survey* 33, no. 1 (January 1993).

Perry, Elizabeth J. "Chinese Political Culture Revisited." In *Popular Protest and Political Culture in Modern China: Learning from 1989*, edited by Jeffrey N. Wasserstrom and Elizabeth Perry. Boulder, Colo.: Westview Press, 1994.

Petro, Nicolai N. *The Rebirth of Russian Democracy: An Interpretation of Political Culture*. Cambridge: Harvard University Press, 1995.

Pike, Frederick B., and Thomas Stritch, eds. *The New Corporatism: Social-Political Structures in the Iberian World*. Notre Dame: University of Notre Dame Press, 1974.

Potter, Pitman B. "Peng Zhen: Evolving Views on Party Organization and Law." In *China's Establishment Intellectuals*, edited by Carol Lee Hamrin and Timothy Cheek. Armonk, N.Y.: M. E. Sharpe, 1986.

Potter, Pitman B. *The Economic Contract Law of China: Legitimation and Contract Autonomy in the PRC*. Seattle: University of Washington Press, 1992.

Potter, Pitman B. "Judicial Review and Bureaucratic Reform: The Administrative Litigation Law of the PRC." In *Domestic Law Reforms in Post-Mao China*, edited by Pitman B. Potter. Armonk, N.Y.: M. E. Sharpe, 1994.

Potter, Pitman B. "Riding the Tiger: Legitimacy and Legal Reform in Post-Mao China." *The China Quarterly* 138 (June 1994).

Potter, Pitman B. "Socialist Legality and Legal Culture in Shanghai: A Survey of the *Getihu*." *Canadian Journal of Law and Society* 9, no. 2. 1994.

Przeworksi, Adam. *Capitalism and Social Democracy*. Cambridge: Cambridge University Press, 1985.

Przeworski, Adam. *Democracy and the Market: Political and Economic Reforms in Eastern Europe and Latin America*. New York: Cambridge University Press, 1991.

Purcell, Susan Kaufman, and Riordan Roett, eds. *Brazil under Cardoso*. Boulder, Colo.: Lynne Rienner Publishers, 1997.

Pye, Lucien W. *The Spirit of Chinese Politics*. Cambridge: MIT Press, 1968.

Rae, Douglas. *The Political Consequences of Electoral Laws*. New Haven: Yale University Press, 1971.

Ramos, Alejandro, coordinator. *Sucesión pactada. La ingeniería política del salinismo*. México: Plaza y Valdés, 1993.

Ramos, Joseph. *Neoconservative Economics in the Southern Cone of Latin America, 1973–1983*. Baltimore: Johns Hopkins University Press, 1986.

Ramos, Samuel. "Motivos para una investigación del mexicano." *Examen* 1 (August 1932).

Ramos, Samuel. *El perfil del hombre y la cultura en México*. México, D.F.: Imprenta Mundial, 1934.

Rankin, Mary B. *Elite Activism and Political Transformation in China: Zhejiang Province 1865–1911*. Stanford: Stanford University Press, 1986.

Rawski, Thomas G. "Progress without Privatization: The Reform of China's State Industries." In *Changing Political Economies: Privitization in Post-Communist and Reforming Communist States*, ed. Vedat Milor (Boulder, Colo.: Lynne Rienner Publishers, 1994), 53–66.

Redding, Gordon S. *The Spirit of Chinese Capitalism*. Berlin: Walter de Gruyter, 1990.

Remnick, David. "The War for the Kremlin." *The New Yorker*, 22 July 1996.

Resende-Santos, Joao, "Fernando Henrique Cardoso: Social and Institutional Rebuilding in Brazil," In *Technopols: Freeing Politics and Markets in Latin America in the 1990s*, edited by Jorge I. Domínguez. University Park: Pennsylvania State University Press, 1996.

Reyes, Heroles Federico. *Sondear a Mexico*. México D.F.: Oceano, 1995.

Reynolds, Clark W. *The Mexican Economy: Twentieth-Century Structure and Growth*. New Haven, Conn.: Yale University Press, 1970.

Roeder, Ralph. *Juárez and His Mexico*, 2 vols. New York: Viking Press, 1947.

Ros, Jaime, "La crisis económica: un análisis general." In *México ante la crisis*, edited by Pablo González Casanova and Héctor Aguilar Camín. México: Siglo XXI, 1985.

Rostow, W. W. *The Stages of Economic Growth: A Non-Communist Manifesto*. Cambridge: Cambridge University Press, 1960.

Rowe, William T. *Hankow: Commerce and Society in a Chinese City, 1796–1889*. Stanford: Stanford University Press, 1984.

Rowe, William T., *Hankow: Conflict and Community in a Chinese City, 1796–1985*. Stanford: Stanford University Press, 1989.

Rowe, William T. "The Public Sphere in Modern China." *Modern China* 16. no. 3 (July 1990).

Rowen, Harry. "World Wealth Expanding." In *Growth and Development*, edited by Ralph Landau, Gavin Wright, and Timothy Taylor. Stanford: Stanford University Press, forthcoming.

Ruffin, M. Holt, et al., eds. *The Post-Soviet Handbook*. Seattle: University of Washington Press, 1996.

Ruiz, Ramón Eduardo. "La guerra de 1847 y el fracaso de los criollos." In *De la rebelión de Texas a la guerra del 47*, edited by Josefina Zoraida Vázquez. México: Nueva Imagen, 1994.

Rutland, Peter. "Has Democracy Failed Russia?" In *Democracy and Development*, edited by Adrian Leftwich. New York: Oxford University Press, 1995.

Rutland, Peter. "On the Road to Capitalism? Reflections on East Europe and the Global Economy." Paper for the International Studies Association, Chicago, 24 February 1995.

Rutland, Peter. "An Economy Running on Empty." In *Building Democracy: The OMRI Annual Survey of Eastern Europe and the Former Soviet Union 1995*. New York: M. E. Sharpe, 1996.

Sabel, Charles F., and David Stark. "Planning, Politics, and Shop-Floor Power: Hidden Forms of Bargaining in Soviet-Imposed State-Socialist Societies." *Politics and Society* 11, no. 4 (1982).

Saich, Tony. "The Fourteenth Congress of the CCP." *The China Quarterly* (1993).

Saich, Tony. "The Search for Civil Society and Democracy in China." *Current History*, September 1994.

Schettino, Macario. *Para reconstruir México*. México: Océano, 1996.

Schmemann, Serge, Celestine Bohlen, and Steven Erlanger, *The New York Times*, 13–16 December 1993; and *RFE/RL Daily Report*, 10–20 December 1993.

Schmitter, Philippe C., and Terry Lynn Karl. "The Conceptual Travels of Transitologists and Consolidologists: How Far to the East Should They Attempt to Go?" *Slavic Review* 53, no. 1 (Spring 1994).

Schmitter, Philippe, and Gerhard Lehmbruch, eds. *Trends Toward Corporatist Intermediation*. Beverly Hills: Sage Publications, 1979.

Schumpeter, Joseph. *Capitalism, Socialism, and Democracy*. 2nd ed. New York: Harper and Bros., 1947.

Schwartz, Benjamin I. *Chinese Communism and the Rise of Mao*. Cambridge: Harvard University Press, 1951.

Segovia, Rafael. "Una cultura política inmovil." *Nexos*. July 1996.

Seligman, Adam. *The Idea of Civil Society*. New York: The Free Press, 1992.

Sestanovich, Stephen, "Russia Turns the Corner." *Foreign Affairs* 73, no. 1 (January/February 1994).

"Shanghai gangjichang peikuan er shi wan" (The Shanghai Harbour Machinery Factory Pays Indemnity of 2000,000). *Jiefang ribao* (Liberation Daily), 4 March 1983.

Shen, Shaofang, ed. *Minfa anli xuanbian* (Compilation of Civil Cases). Beijing: People's University Press, 1989.

Shiller, R. J., M. Boycko, and V. Korobov. "Popular Attitudes toward Free Markets: The Soviet Union and the United States Compared," *American Economic Review* 81 (1991).

Shin, Doh Chull. "On the Third Wave of Democratization: A Synthesis and Evaluation of Recent Theory and Research." *World Politics* 47, no. 1 (October 1994).

Shirk, Susan L. *The Political Logic of Economic Reform in China*. Berkeley: University of California Press, 1993.

Silva, Eduardo. "Capitalist Coalitions, the State, and Neoliberal Economic Restructuring: Chile, 1973–1988." *World Politics* 45, no. 4 (July 1993).

Simes, Dimitri. "The Return of Russian History." *Foreign Affairs* 73, no. 1 (January/February 1994).

Skilling, H. G., and F. Griffiths, eds. *Interest Groups in Soviet Politics*. Princeton: Princeton University Press, 1971.

Skocpol, Theda. *States and Social Revolution: A Comparative Analysis of France, Russia, and China*. Cambridge: Cambridge University Press, 1979.

Smith, Gaddis. *The Last Years of the Monroe Doctrine 1945–1993*. New York, 1994.

Smith, Peter. *Labyrinth of Power*. Princeton: Princeton University Press, 1979.

Smith, Peter H. "The State and Development in Historical Perspective." In *Americas: New Interpretive Essays*, edited by Alfred Stepan. New York: Oxford University Press, 1992.

Smith, Tony. *America's Mission: The United States and the Worldwide Struggle for Democracy in the Twentieth Century*. Princeton: Princeton University Press, 1994.

Solinger, Dorothy J. "Urban Entrepreneurs and the State: the Merger of State and Society." In *State and Society in China: The Consequences of Reform*, edited by Arthur Lewis Rosenbaum. Boulder, Colo.: Westview Press, 1992.

Solomon, Richard. *Mao's Revolution and Chinese Political Culture*. Berkeley: University of California Press, 1971.

Solow, Robert M. "Dollars and Democracy." *The New Republic*, 15 and 22 September 1986.

"Some Observations on a Chinese Public Sphere." *Modern China* 19, no. 2 (April 1993).

Spence, Jonathan. *In Search of Modern China*. New York: Norton, 1990.

Starr, John Bryan. "China in 1995: Mountain Problems, Waning Capacity." *Asian Survey* 36, no. 1 (January 1996).

Steinberg, Dmitri. *The Soviet Economy 1970–1990: A Statistical Analysis*. San Francisco: International Trade Press, 1990.

Stevens. Evelyn P., ed. *Protest and Response in Mexico*, Cambridge: MIT Press, 1974.

Stevenson, Linda, and Mitchell Seligson. "Fading Memories of the Revolution: Is Stability Eroding in Mexico?" In *Polling for Democracy: Public Opinion and Political Liberalization in Mexico*, edited by Roderic Ai Camp. Wilmington, Del: Scholarly Resources, 1996.

Strand, David. *Rickshaw Beijing: City People and Politics in 1920s China*. Berkeley: University of California Press, 1989.

Strand, David. "Protest from Beijing: Civil Society and Public Sphere in China." *Problems of Communism* 39, no. 3 (May–June 1990).

Sullivan, Lawrence R. "The Emergence of Civil Society in China, Spring 1989."

In *The Chinese People's Movement: Perspectives on Spring 1989*, edited by Tony Saich. Armonk, New York: M. E. Sharpe, 1990.

"A Survey of South Africa." *The Economist*. 20 March 1983.

Sustaining Rapid Development in East Asia and the Pacific. Washington, D.C.: The World Bank, 1993.

Swenson, Peter. "Bringing Capital Back In, or Social Democracy Reconsidered: Employer Power, Cross-Class Alliances, and Centralization of Industrial Relations in Denmark and Sweden." *World Politics* 43, no. 4 (July 1991).

Szekely, Gabriel, and Daniel Levy. *Mexico: Paradoxes of Stability and Change*. Boulder, Colo.: Westview Press, 1987.

Tanner, Murray Scot. "Organizations and Politics in China's Post-Mao Law-Making System." In *Domestic Law Reforms in Post-Mao China*, edited by Pitman B. Potter. Armonk, N.Y.: M. E. Sharpe, 1994.

Tanner, Murray Scot. "How a Bill Becomes Law in China: Stages and Processes in Lawmaking." *The China Quarterly*, no. 141 (1995).

"Tantan dui jingji hetong jiufen anjian de shenli" (Discussion of Adjudication of Cases of Economic Contracts Disputes). *Faxue zazhi* (Legal Studies Magazine), no. 6 (1982).

Taylor, Charles. "Modes of Civil Society." *Public Culture* 3, no. 1 (Fall 1990).

Theodore de Bary, Wm., and John W. Chaffe, eds. *Neo-Confucian Education: The Formative Stage*. Berkeley: University of California Press, 1989.

Thurston, Anne F. (in collaboration with Li Zhisui). *The Private Life of Chairman Mao: The Memoirs of Mao's Personal Physician*. New York: Random House, 1994.

Tobler, Hanz Werner. *La revolución mexicana. Transformación social y cambio político 1876–1940*. México: Alianza Editorial, 1994.

Tommasi, Mariano, and Andres Velasco. "Where Are We in the Political Economy of Reform?" *Policy Reform* 1, (1996).

Townsend, James, and Brantly Womack, *Politics in China* (Reading: Addison-Wesley, 1986).

Tucker, Robert W., and David C. Hendrickson. "America and Bosnia." *The National Interest*, Fall 1993.

Tutino, John. *De la insurrección a la rebelión. Las bases sociales de la violencia agraria, 1750–1940*. México: Ediciones Era, 1990.

Tyson, James, and Ann Tyson. *Chinese Awakenings: Life Stories from Unofficial China*. Boulder, Colo.: Westview, 1995.

Ungar, Jonathon, and Anita Chan. "Corporatism in China: A Developmental State in an East Asian Context." In *China after Socialism: In the Footsteps of Eastern Europe or East Asia?* edited by J. Unger and Barrett McCormick. Armonk, New York: M. E. Sharpe, 1996.

Urrutia, Miguel. "Colombia." In *The Political Economy of Policy Reform*, edited by John Williamson. Washington, D.C.: Institute for International Economics, January 1994.

Valle, Eduardo. *El segundo disparo. La narcodemocracia mexicana*. México: Editorial Océano, 1995.

Van Gulik, Robert. *Celebrated Case of Judge Dee*. New York: Dover Publications, 1976.

Vasconcelos, Jose. *La raza cosmica*. Barcelona: Agencia Mundial de Libreria, 1925.

Veliz, Claudio. *The Centralist Tradition of Latin America*. Princeton: Princeton University Press, 1980.

Veliz, Claudio. *The New World of the Gothic Fox: Culture and Economy in English and Spanish America*. Berkeley: University of California Press, 1994.

Vincent, R. J. *Human Rights and International Relations*. Cambridge: Cambridge University Press, 1986.

Vogel, Ezra. *One Step Ahead in Guangdong*. Cambridge: Harvard University Press, 1990.

Wakeman, Frederick Jr. "The Civil Society and Public Sphere Debate: Western Reflections on Chinese Political Culture." *Modern China* 19, no. 2 (April 1993).

Walder, Andrew G. *Communist Neo-Traditionalism: Work and Authority in Chinese Industry*. Berkeley: University of California Press, 1986.

Walder, Andrew G. "Corporate Organization and Local Government Property Rights in China." In *Changing Political Economies: Privatization in Post-communist and Reforming Communist States*, edited by Vedat Milor. Boulder, Colo.: Lynne Rienner Publishers, 1994.

Walzer, Michael. *Just and Unjust Wars: A Moral Argument with Historical Illustrations*. New York: Basic Books, 1977.

Wang, Guiguo. *Business Law of China: Cases, Texts and Commentary*. Hong Kong: Butterworth's, 1993.

Wang, Suiqu, Liu Zhongya, Li Wangin, Li Fengqin, Li Baoyue, and Ziao Shengxi, eds. *Shiyong anli shouse*. Beijing: China Youth Press, 1990.

Wang Yan, and Vinod Thomas. "Market Supplanting Versus Market Fostering Interventions: China, East Asia and Other Developing Countries." *China Economic Review* 4, no. 2 (1993).

Wasserstrom, Jeffrey, and Elizabeth J. Perry, eds. *Popular Protest and Political Culture in China: Learning from 1989*. Boulder, Colo.: Westview Press, 1994.

Watson, Andrew, ed. *Economic Reform and Social Change in China*. London: Routledge, 1992.

White, Stephen. *After Gorbachev*. 4th ed. New York: Cambridge University Press, 1993.

Whyte, Martin K. "Urban China: A Civil Society in the Making?" In *State and Society in China: The Consequences of Reform*, edited by Arthur Lewis Rosenbaum. Boulder, Colo.: Westview Press, 1992.

Williams, James H. "The Expanding Universe of Fang Lizhi." *The China Quarterly* 123, (1991).

Williams, James H. "Reforms and the Future of China's Environment." University of California–Berkeley Manuscript, 1993.

Williamson, John. *The Political Economy of Policy Reform*. Washington, D.C.: Institute for International Economics, January 1994.

Woo, Jung-en. *Race to the Swift: State and Finance in Korean Industrialization*. New York: Columbia University Press, 1991.

Woodside, Alexander. "The Two Latecomers: Politics and Economic Development Time in the Chinese and Vietnamese Reforms." Paper presented at the Transforming Asian Socialism Workshop at the Australian National University, August 1995.

World Bank. *The East Asian Miracle: Economic Growth and Public Policy.* New York: Oxford University Press, 1993.

Yan, Huai. "The Organization System." In *Decision-Making in Deng's China Perspectives from Insiders,* edited by Carol Lee Hamrin and Suisheng Zhao. Armonk, New York: M. E. Sharpe, 1995.

Yang, Mayfair Mei-hui. "Between State and Society: The Construction of Corporations in a Chinese Socialist Factory." *The Australian Journal of Chinese Affairs,* no. 22 (July 1989).

Yang, Mayfair Mei-hui. *Gifts, Favors, and Banquets: The Art of Social Relations in China.* Ithaca: Cornell University Press, 1994.

Yang Shangkun, 1942 speech in Dai Qing in *Wang Shiwei and Wild Lilies Rectification and Purges in the CCP.* New York: M. E. Sharpe. 1994.

Yergin, Daniel, and Gustafson, Thane. *Russia 2010 and What It Means for the World.* New York: Random House, 1993.

Ying, Songnian, and Hu Jiansen, eds. "Mou xian shuini chang su mou diqu wujiaju an" (A Case Involving a Suit by a Certain County Cement Factory Against a Certain District Price Bureau). In *Zhong wai xingzheng anli xuanping.* Beijing: Politics and Law University Press, 1989.

Yotopoulos, Pan A. "The (Rip) Tide of Privatization: Lessons from Chile." *World Development* 17, no. 5 (1989).

You, Dan, ed. "Shourangfang jieshou jishu fuzhu shishi, bu dei chaoyue ziji jing Gong Shang Xingzheng Guanli Bumen hezhun denji de shengchan jingying fanwei" (The Transferee Receives Technical Input and Should Not Overstep Its Own Registered Scope of Production Management Received Through Examination and Ratification By the Industrial and Commercial Administration Departments). In *Jingji fa anli xuan xi* (Compilation and Analysis of Economic Law Cases). Beijing: Law Publishers, 1990.

Young, Susan. "Wealth But Not Security: Attitudes Towards Private Business in the 1980s." In *Economic Reform and Social Change in China,* edited by Andrew Watson. London: Routledge, 1992.

Yu, Xingzhong. "Legal Pragmatism in the People's Republic of China." *Journal of Chinese Law* 3 (1989).

Zhang, Shouqiang, ed. "Zui gao renmin fayuan guanyu guanche 'Jingji hetong fa' ruogan wenti de yijian." In *Hetong fagui yu hetong shiyang huibian.* Harbin: Heilongjiang Science and Technology Press, 1988.

Zhang, Shouqiang, ed. "Zuigao renmin fayuan guanyu shenli jingji jiufen anjian juti shiyoun 'Minshi susong fa (shixing)' de ruogan wenti de jieda" (Responses to Questions by the Supreme People's Court Concerning Several Issues in the Specific Use of the '[Draft] Civil Procedure Law' in Handling Economic Disputes) (July 21, 1987). In *Hetong fagui yu hetong shiyang huibian.* Harbin: Heilongjiang Science and Technology Press, 1988.

Zheng, Henry R. *China's Civil and Commercial Law.* Singapore: Butterworth's Asia, 1988.

Zimmerman, William. "Synoptic Thinking and Political Culture in Post-Soviet Russia." *Slavic Review* 54, no. 3, (Fall 1995).

Zínser, Adolfo Aguilar. *Vamos a ganar. La pugna de Cuauhtémoc Cárdenas por el poder*. México: Editorial Océano, 1995.

Index

329

About the Editors
and Contributors

Timothy Cheek, associate professor, Department of History, The Colorado College, conducts research on modern Chinese history and politics.

Gaye Christoffersen, assistant professor, Department of International Relations, Eastern Mediterranean University, Turkish Republic of Cyprus, works on modern Chinese politics and international relations.

Jorge I. Domínguez, Clarence Dillon Professor of International Affairs, Harvard University, conducts research on Latin American politics and international relations.

David D. Finley, professor, Department of Political Science, The Colorado College, works on Russian and east European politics.

David Hendrickson, professor, Department of Political Science, The Colorado College, conducts research on U.S. foreign policy and international relations.

Juan D. Lindau, associate professor, Department of Political Science, The Colorado College, conducts research on Latin American politics and international relations.

Lorenzo Meyer, professor, Centro de Estudios Internacionales, El Colegio de México, conducts research on Mexican politics and U.S.-Mexico relations.

Robert A. Packenham, professor, Department of Political Science, Stanford University, conducts research on Latin American politics and international relations.

Pitman B. Potter, Faculty of Law, University of British Columbia, works on law and legal culture in China and the Pacific Basin.